Elena Kostioukovitch is an essayist and literary translator and the recipient of numerous prizes, including Best Translation of the Year (1988), Zoil (1999), Grinzane Cavour Moscow (2004) and the Welcome Prize (2005) given by the Russian National Association of Restaurateurs. She has translated a number of Italian works into Russian, and in 1988 her translation of Umberto Eco's *The Name of the Rose* made her famous overnight; the Russian translation became a literary sensation in its own right and since its first publication has never been out of print (with more than ten subsequent editions of the translation since published). She has gone on to translate other novels of Eco (*Foucault's Pendulum, The Island of the Day Before, Baudolino* etc), and is today the translator par excellence of the works of one of Italy's most famous writers into Russian.

Elena is married with two children and lives in Milan.

ALSO BY ELENA KOSTIOUKOVITCH

TRANSLATIONS

Foucault's Pendulum, by Umberto Eco

The Name of the Rose, by Umberto Eco

The Island of the Day Before, by Umberto Eco

Through the Lens of Aristotle, by Emanuele Tesauro

WHY ITALIANS LOVE TO TALK ABOUT FOOD

Elena Kostioukovitch

Forewords by
Umberto Eco and Carol Field

Translated by Anne Milano Appel

Duckworth Overlook

This edition first published in the UK in 2010 by
Duckworth Overlook
90-93 Cowcross Street
London EC1M 6BF
info@duckworth-publishers.co.uk
www.ducknet.co.uk

First published 2009 in the US by Farrar, Straus and Giroux

This work was translated from the Italian version.
Emanuela Guercetti first translated the work into Italian from the original Russian language.

Grateful acknowledgment is made for permission to reprint excerpts from the following:
"Bodalsya Turin's Kokakoloi" by Elena Babaytseva courtesy of Nezavisimaya Gazeta. *Italian Journey,
1786-1788* by Johann Wolfgang von Goethe, translated by W. H. Auden and Elizabeth Mayer,
copyright © 1962 by W. H. Auden and Elizabeth Mayer reprinted by permission of Curtis Brown,
Ltd. Sonetti by Giuseppe Giaocchino Belli, edited by Giorgio Vigolo with the collaboration of
Pietro Gibellini, Mondadori, Milan, 1984. *Le meraviglie d'Italia* by Carlo Emilio Gadda,
Einaudi, Turin, 1964. *Il pentolino magico* by Massimo Montanari, © Gius. Laterza &
Figli S.p.A., Roma-Bari, 1995. *Maccheronata. Sonetti in difesa dei maccheroni* by
Gennaro Quaranta, Arti Grafiche La Nuovissima, Naples, 1943. *A Roman
Journal* by Stendhal, edited and translated by Haakon Chevalier,
Orion Press, New York, 1957.

Image credits appear on page 449.

A catalogue record for this book is available
from the British Library

ISBN 978 0 7156 3988 7

Printed in the UK by
CPI William Clowes Beccles NR34 7TL

For Carla Tanzi

Contents

Foreword by Umberto Eco

Why should I be writing the foreword to a book about food? I asked myself the same question when the author asked me. I agreed, at first, because Elena Kostioukovitch is my translator in Russian, and I admire her not only for the care and patience she has shown toward my books, but also for her intelligence and vast culture. But is this reason enough, I wondered, given that I am not a gourmet?

To be clear, a gourmet is not merely someone who is content with an excellent duck *à l'orange* or a generous portion of Volga caviar with blini. This person is just a normal individual whose tastes haven't been perverted by McDonald's. A gourmet, an epicure, a true enthusiast of cuisine, is someone capable of traveling hundreds of kilometers to go to that special restaurant where they make the best duck *à l'orange* in the world. And I am not that sort of person. Generally speaking, given a choice between eating a pizza a few doors down the street and taking a taxi to go discover a new trattoria (especially one two hundred kilometers away), I choose the pizza.

But is that really true? I realized that I had traveled kilometers and kilometers in the Langhe (near where I was born, and which Elena speaks of in the chapter on Piedmont) to take a French friend (who, indeed, is a grand gourmet) to discover the legendary white truffles, and additional kilometers to take part in a *bagna cauda* dinner in Nizza Monferrato, where the meal began at noon and ended at five in the afternoon and everything, except the coffee, was based on garlic. And I once went to the most remote outskirts of Brussels to sample that Belgian beer called *gueuze* that is only served locally, since it will not stand up to transport (by the way, don't go; a good British ale is better).

So does cuisine interest me or not? Let's return for a moment to the examples I cited. In one instance it was to discover what type of beer the Belgians like, another time to introduce Piedmontese culture to a foreigner, and the third time to rediscover the zest of a ritual like the *bagna cauda* that brought back magical moments of my childhood. In all these cases I went looking for food not simply to satisfy my palate, but to experience a certain kind of culture; not only to savor a taste, but to experience enlightenment, or a flash of recollection, or to understand a tradition and make it known to others.

And I realized that if I am alone, I'll certainly go and have a pizza in a small trattoria down the street rather than venturing out on a culinary exploration. Yet as soon as I arrive in another country, even before visiting the museums or churches, I do two things: to begin with, I wander through the streets, trying to lose my way in order to observe the people, the shop windows, the colors of the houses, and to savor the aromas; and then I seek out the local food, because without the experience of food I would not understand the place I'm in and its unique way of thinking.

I also realized that with the exception of *Foucault's Pendulum*, where the heroes travel outside of Italy and come to understand Brazil by starting with a taste of Brazilian food, in the other novels (*Baudolino*, *The Island of the Day Before*, and my latest, *The Mysterious Flame of Queen Loana*, I make the protagonists eat a number of diverse Italian foods, just as I make the monks in *The Name of the Rose* eat at least once, and roam around the kitchen a great deal. If you venture out to the islands of the South Seas or to the Byzantine Orient, or to a universe that vanished hundreds or dozens of years ago, you have to let the reader eat in order to make him understand how the characters think.

I therefore have an excellent reason to introduce Elena's book. Because Elena, who certainly shows herself to be a prodigious connoisseur of Italian cuisine in all its nuances and mysteries, leads us by the hand (and let's say also by the palate and the nose) on a culinary journey, not only to familiarize us with Italian foods, but also to acquaint us with Italy, the country she has spent her life discovering. The book that you are about to read is a book about cuisine, but it's also a book about a country and a culture—indeed, about many cultures.

It is always awkward to speak about "Italian culture," just as it is awkward to speak about "the Italian landscape." If you rent a car and drive across the United

States, you can travel for days and days across endless plains; if you travel in northern Europe you can drive at length across equally vast stretches of rye fields. And let's not forget the steppes of Central Asia, the Sahara and Gobi deserts, and the wide expanse of the Australian outback.

One does not come to Italy to find the dizzying verticality of the Gothic cathedrals, the immensity of the pyramids, the cascades of Niagara Falls. Once you have crossed the Alps (where you might certainly have sublime impressions, but ones you could find in France, Switzerland, Germany, or Austria as well), you begin having a different experience. In Italy, the horizon never expands to titanic dimensions, because it is always limited by a hill on the right, or by the modest relief of a mountain on the left, and the road is continuously interrupted by small villages, at least one every five kilometers. On every stretch of the route (except in a certain section of the Po Valley) there will be a curve, a change of course, so that from region to region, but also within the same region, you will continually discover a different country, with infinite gradations from mountains to sea, passing through endlessly varied hills. There is little similarity between the hills of Piedmont and those of the Marches or Tuscany; at times, all you have to do is cross the Apennines, which traverse the entire boot like a backbone, from east to west or vice versa to get the impression that you are entering another country. Even the seas are different: those on the Tyrrhenian coast offer panoramas, beaches of a sort, and coastlines different from those of the Adriatic seaboard, not to mention the islands.

This variety applies not just to Italy's landscape, but also to its inhabitants. Italian dialects vary from region to region. If a Sicilian hears a Piedmontese from the northwest speaking, he will often not understand a word he is hearing. But few foreigners imagine that the dialects also vary from city to city, within the same region, and at times, though only slightly, from village to village.

This is because living together in the boot are the descendants of the Celtic and Ligurian tribes who inhabited the north before the Roman penetration, as well as the Illyrians of the east, the Etruscans and the various Italic stocks of the central region, the Greeks of the south, and scores of ethnic groups that over the course of centuries invaded the autochthonous populations: the Goths, the Lombards, the Arabs, and the Normans (not to mention the French, the Spanish, and the Austrians). On the country's northwest borders something very similar to French is spoken, while German can be heard in the mountains of the northeast, and Albanian in some places in the south.

This same variety of landscapes, languages, and ethnic groups also characterizes

Italian cuisine. Not the Italian cuisine that one tastes abroad, which, as good as it may be, is like Chinese food sampled outside China, a kind of koine, a generic brand, that draws its inspiration from various regions and inevitably gives in to the expectations of the "typical" customer who is looking for a "typical" image of Italy.

To come to know Italian cuisine in all its variety is to discover the monumental differences, not only of language but of taste, mentality, creativity, sense of humor, attitude toward suffering and death, loquacity or taciturnity, that separate a Sicilian from a Piedmontese or a Venetian from a Sardinian. In Italy, perhaps more than anywhere else (though the rule applies to every country), discovering local cuisine means discovering the spirit of the local inhabitants. Try tasting Piedmontese *bagna cauda*, then the Lombard soup *cassoela*, then *tagliatelle* Bolognese-style, then lamb *alla romana*, and finally Sicilian *cassata*, and you will feel as though you might have moved from China to Peru, and from Peru to Timbuktu.

Do Italians still get to know the many cuisines of their fellow countrymen as a means of fostering national kinship? I don't know. I do know that when a foreigner, moved by a great love for this land yet still able to maintain the detached gaze of an outsider, begins to describe Italy to us through its food, then Italians themselves will discover a country that they had (perhaps) largely forgotten.

And for that we should be grateful to Elena Kostioukovitch.

Foreword by Carol Field

Of course Italians like to talk about food. Italy *is* food and the food is Italy, literally, emotionally, historically, culturally, and symbolically. In America, when we talk about food, we describe it or the restaurant where we ate it or the recipe we used.

Italians talk constantly about food even when food isn't the subject. Bring up almost anything—painting, trees, literature, landscape, history, people, religion, even taxes or politics—and the vocabulary of food somehow finds its way in. Painting is full of still lifes with fruit and vegetables. Different trees produce the appropriate wood for grilling specific foods. The oil being discussed is likely produced from olives. Since one out of every two or three days used to be a religious holiday or the eve of one, Italians ate a large preponderance of meatless meals. If there was a tax on public ovens, Italians simply knocked them down and rebuilt once the tax inspectors left. As for politics, even Mussolini brought food to the conversation. As part of the Fascist plan to create a new, stronger Italian race, Mussolini tried to convince people to reject pasta, the country's primal dish, by following the example of Filippo Tommaso Marinetti, the futurist who made his point dramatically by shooting a bullet into a dish of spaghetti carbonara (Mussolini didn't succeed).

Would anyone be surprised that when Italians talk about food, the language of erotic entanglement is not far away? In Naples, soups made only with vegetables are, in Elena Kostioukovitch's words, "penintential, God-fearing, guilt-free." Add meat and the virginal soup becomes *maritata*, "married." Perhaps only a Tuscan, she says, would describe a sandwich as a "panino sinning with a slice of prosciutto." Even something as normal as the act of eating spaghetti involves a frisson of danger. All those dangling strands must be sucked noisily as they slither toward the mouth. Just think about twirling the thin noodles around a fork when it is already awash in red sauce.

In this remarkable book, Elena Kostioukovitch uncovers many of the secrets of Italian life by looking at food and the role it plays in the national conscious and unconscious. Born in Russia, Ms. Kostioukovitch moved to Italy, where she has lived for twenty years, enthralled by the Italian passion for food and fascinated by how deeply it penetrates the country's sense of itself. She is the ideal guide: an outsider who can see what native Italians can't perceive as unusual or remarkable. Not quite an insider and no longer a true foreigner, she has become much more knowledgeable than most Italians.

As an American, I have had a similar experience of being an outsider in Italy, falling fiercely in love with the country and its endless wealth of food. I, too, have been astonished by what Italians don't notice and what they take for granted. A random selection:

Italians can't possibly sit down for a meal if bread isn't on the table. As a result, they often talk about many things in a vocabulary based on bread. A good, bighearted man is *buono, come il pane*. To call a spade a spade is *dire pane al pane, vino al vino*. To meet one's match is *trovar pane per i propri denti*.

Toasted bread crumbs substitute nicely for grated cheese.

People in Bologna and Palermo make breakfast or a midmorning snack of a brioche panino filled with ice cream.

Italians know which wild greens and herbs are edible and seem to have it in their DNA to cook them enticingly. When an American interviewer called such a diet "eating weeds," I thought of the women who told me they owed their survival during the war to knowing which roots, leaves, and flowers were safe to eat.

Food saturates every aspect of Italian life and imprints the identity of every Italian. It is first and foremost the fragrant taste of home, the plate of pasta shared with family. It is the aroma and flavor and ingredients of the village. Special local dishes are shorthand for differences—from village to village, from region to region, from city to country. Italians may have a penchant for fighting with their neighbors, but they close ranks where allegiance to local ingredients and dishes is concerned.

There is a story, probably apocryphal, of the jeweler Bulgari being kidnapped, blindfolded, and driven a great distance to wherever he was held for ransom. He never saw either his kidnappers or the landscape, but after the ransom was paid and he was safely home, he was able to tell the police where he'd been held. How? He recognized the flavor and shape of the bread and the sauce on the local pasta.

Tell that story in Italy and everyone knows the punch line without even hearing it. The distinctive foods of each village confer a sense of identity to its citizens, who would never confuse them with something from another town. Like Elena Kostioukovitch, I have often eaten specialties made in a single town and remember the two together. I've had a salame made of sun-dried white figs, *sapa*, grape juices reduced to a syrup, and Mistrà, an anise-flavored liqueur, in a small town in Le Marche; sampled a tangy spread based on very aged Parmigiano-Reggiano and a mystery ingredient in a village in Emilia Romagna notable also for the bakery that makes twenty-eight kinds of bread just to go with savory salamis of the region; and snacked on the creamy zucchini tart called *scarpaccia* that is made in the Tuscan coastal town of Camaiore. Go to Viareggio, a few kilometers away, and *scarpaccia* unaccountably becomes a *dolce* sweetened with sugar.

When I first read this book, I was electrified. Finally someone had put together food and Italy and all the pieces that make the conversation whole. Ms. Kostioukovitch doesn't just look at regional or local specialties, or connect the food and practices of ancient Rome with today, or know the history of all the conquerors who have left their culinary imprint. Other books have done that. She looks at Italy's people and history, its institutions and attitudes about food and life, and the curious ways in which those attitudes are expressed.

What may be my favorite parts of the book are the interstitial chapters that deal with subjects as diverse as pilgrims, the liturgical and popular calendar, democracy, slow food, Jews, primary materials, eros, and restaurants. In one of my favorites, an illuminating collection of cooking instructions, Ms. Kostioukovitch quite rightly observes that women learned to cook not from books (most people own perhaps one, or a notebook from a bygone relative written in a spidery hand) but from mothers, grandmothers, and aunts. She intuits that outsiders might need some help knowing how to proceed once the ingredients are enumerated. Her list is illuminating, illustrative of the inventiveness of Italian cooks, and, incidentally, very useful. It includes: "Wall up a bass in a sarcophagus of salt; cut soft cheese with a wire; drown fish in a small amount of strongly flavored liquid; and put mineral water in a meatball mixture to make them softer."

As I read those essays, I felt I was reading about the Italy I know, the culinarily rich and fascinating country that sees food as a primary part of the enjoyment of daily life. They celebrate the tastes of home and express the author's fascination with their differences. They explain the generosity of Italians, for whom cooking is really an act of love.

In the face of change, Ms. Kostioukovitch sought out old practices. She found bakers in the south of Italy who still form breads shaped like body parts to be blessed and, hopefully, healed. Like her, I went to community celebrations of San Giuseppe in Sicily, held in the middle of Lent, in which symbolic altars were filled with magnificent symbolic breads and massive amounts of ritual food cooked by local families were served to an entire neighborhood. In the midst of this plenty, I found myself in one house with a small, cavelike kitchen in the basement with a single bare lightbulb where women were making exquisite *cassateddi*, ambrosial sweet ricotta-filled turnovers.

In this book you'll find the descriptions of religious feasts and their ritual dishes and *sagre*, country fairs exalting local food specialties. Both are celebrations tied to the calendar that take place in the communally shared moments of time out of time. They bring people together in a kind of actual or symbolic communion to eat food cooked in cauldrons as high as a man's shoulder, stirred with oarlike paddles and then dished out in vast quantities to feed a whole community.

In Elena Kostioukovitch's memorable descriptions, there are two final unforgettable rituals connecting food and culture. The first is at the festa of *L'Unità*, the Communist newspaper, where I remembered being surprised at how many people were eating beautiful steaks. From her I learned that a schism occurred in the Communist party in the 1990s: Massimo D'Alema, a Roman politician, disparaged the tortellini of Emilia Romagna, the homeland of the Left, where they were a symbol of democracy and revolutionary struggle. Further polemics followed, all using the tortellino as a symbol. D'Alema's government lasted less than a year and a half, and all the politicians who followed learned to praise the tortellino if they wanted to stay in office.

And finally: Cassata, the archetypal dessert of Palermo, carries the entire history of Sicily within its chocolate and sponge layers with ricotta and whipped vanilla mousse, decorated by candied fruit soaked in sugar syrup for exactly forty days. First made in monasteries centuries ago, it is the denouement of a Sicilian meal, and for the Mafia the dessert par excellence when served to a group of friends gathered around the unsuspecting victim who is choked with a noose as he swallows his last bite.

The last chapter of the book is called Joy.

Preface

I have been living in Italy for twenty years now, yet I can still recall very clearly the first months I lived in Milan. I understood and spoke Italian without any problem, but every so often my self-esteem suffered a harsh blow. I might be at dinner with friends, talking about a film we had just seen or about some item in the news, when suddenly I was no longer able to follow the conversation. What was it that had escaped me? In the blink of an eye, without any warning, everyone at the table had unexpectedly begun to discuss passionately the ways in which mushrooms could be cooked, or to describe a truly fantastic extra-virgin olive oil that an acquaintance had produced. It was exceedingly frustrating.

Talking with other foreigners, I later realized that they were all equally amazed by the fact that people in Italy talk about food a great deal, much more so than in other parts of the world. Whereas a British or Russian intellectual feels that an exaggerated attention to food may lower the caliber of the conversation and will primly skip over the subject, the Italian lingers over it with visible pleasure, dwelling at length on the details. Why? The expression *"Parla come mangi!"*—"Speak the language of your food"—embraces all-encompassing themes in Italy. What kinds of things do conversationalists evoke in memory or imagination when they recount past dinners, plan menus, or debate the quality of ingredients, in many cases not even mentioning their enjoyment of the meal?

I myself have often felt disoriented before this passion, so profound and pervasive as to extend to areas, such as the lexicon, that apparently have nothing to do with food.

Over time, I've become accustomed to it, partially by assimilating this lexicon, but I have not stopped badgering friends and acquaintances with a thousand questions: Why do all of you—your writers and journalists and politicians—love to talk about food so much? And why is it that you identify particular historic moments with references to food? What does chicory have to do with class struggle? Why did the Fascist regime try to abolish *pastasciutta* during the twenty-year period known as the Ventennio? What does the poet Tonino Guerra have in mind when he mentions *caffè sospeso*, a coffee held "in suspense," that is, paid for in advance by a customer who's feeling well-off and held for a future customer who may be down on his luck, in a radio interview? And if other peoples' bread tasted salty to Dante Alighieri, was it because of the tears he shed over it, as translators believe, or for some less romantic reason?

Little by little I, like all students of Italian culture, discovered hundreds of poetic and narrative works full of "culinary" references that disguised much more serious affirmations and ideas. This is because the abundance of metaphors linked to food is truly staggering: *andare a fagiolo*; *cacio sui maccheroni*; *buono come il pane*; *rendere pan per focaccia*; *troppa carne sul fuoco*; *mangiare il porro dalla coda*. These recall such English expressions as "icing on the cake"; "life is but a bowl of cherries"; "spill the beans"; "sour grapes"; "worth one's salt"; "cool as a cucumber"; "a piece of cake"; and many more. The collective imagination is expressed through numerous references to food.

This phenomenon is well-known, and the philosopher Andrea Tagliapietra, one of many experts who have studied it, summarized it quite well in his article "La gola del filosofo. Il mangiare come metafora del pensare" (The philosopher's temptation: eating as a metaphor for thinking): "We have an 'appetite' for knowledge, a 'thirst' to know, or a 'hunger' for information. We 'devour' a book, 'gorge' on data to the point of 'indigestion,' read or write 'ad nauseam,' never get our 'fill' of stories, 'chew over' some project, find it hard to 'digest' some concepts, and we 'absorb' some ideas better than others. We 'swallow' a story, particularly when it is told to us with 'sweet' words rather than a sprinkling of 'bitter' deliberations, 'acidic' or 'disgusting' witticisms, or worse yet, 'tasteless,' 'bland' allocutions. It is not by chance that the most 'appetizing' stories are those filled with 'peppery' anecdotes and 'spicy' descriptions, as well as 'savory' analogies, if you will."[1]

I think the answer to why Italians love to talk about food so much is this: in Italian culture, a person who shares a recipe is referring us to the region of his origins and, very often, proclaiming his own sense of belonging. Italian history evolved in such a way that every village or *borgo* was self-sufficient; no one city prevailed over another, and no provincial capital over the province nor the nation's capital over the surrounding cities. Foreigners from all over the world came to Italy on religious pilgrimages, or to get to know its artistic patrimony on a Grand Tour; thus even a village could feel that it was a central, important place. There could be no solitary backwaters in areas where there was such an uninterrupted flow of humanity! Nor could inferiority complexes toward large cities be manifested in villages and towns that boasted their own magnificent cathedrals, monastic schools, and libraries. "It's city and countryside all in one,"[2] Gogol wrote of Italy, choosing it as his adopted country and writing his best works there. And another Russian exile, Aleksandr Herzen, observed: "Every town has its own physiognomy."[3]

This book was born specifically to assemble in a single volume stories about the symbolic foods of each Italian region and their "ideological" meanings. Who serves Parmesan cheese with his pasta? Who prefers pecorino? Why should pizza be thin and not greasy, unlike the way it's made in fast-food places throughout the world? Why is *panettone* richer and more opulent than the Venetian *pandoro*? What are the disturbing poetic legends surrounding Sicilian *cassata*?

The more you know Italy, the more it becomes evident that each community has its "gastronomic emblem," namely, a dish or product that has been developed to perfection in that place: steak Florentine, risotto Milanese, radicchio Trevisano, Caprese salad. And the inhabitants are proud of this specialty.

The book is structured as an imaginary journey from region to region, north to south down the peninsula. For each region I attempt to identify which foods are immediately associated with which territory in the Italian collective imagination and why. Also included is a broad review of the lexicon along with its most prevalent expressions. I also allude briefly to typical dishes and products for each region, summarizing their characteristics without any pretext of being exhaustive (heaven forbid!); and, in an arbitrary, totally personal way, I cite the type of beverage that I ascribe to that zone through some free association of memory. In any case, I should point out that this is a book about food, and absolutely not about wine. How could it be, without at least doubling its size?

In writing this book I became fascinated with examining the culinary code that pervades all of Italy. This code is a language to be studied both by foreigners and by Italians themselves, a language that must be analyzed in depth in order to fully grasp all its nuances.

I say this with admiration: For Italians, more than for any other people in the world, talking about food does not mean simply naming an ingredient. It means celebrating a rite, uttering a magic formula, reciting like a litany the list of fish suitable for salting, or that of the spring herbs that make up the Ligurian *preboggiòn* bouquet. Pronouncing the names of the various dishes, the connoisseur of Italian cuisine mentally savors an entire restaurant menu, from the first entry to the last. And the menu is like a rosary, or like Don Giovanni's catalog of conquests. I have tried to create little personal catalogs of cooking methods, sauces and gravies for pasta, and pairings of pasta shapes and sauces. I have added them at the end of the book.

I touch upon completely different topics in "intermezzi": intervals randomly inserted between one region and another. Between one food and another, there will be occasion to speak about history, sociology, democracy, and totalitarianism. From one dish to another, Italian history and its various ties with the histories of other countries come to the forefront. I then emphasize how individual cultures that evolved within the peninsula had a great influence on the formation of the culinary code.

Exploring the culinary code is also a linguistic study. This is the secret behind Italians' joy in talking about food. It is a theme that allows them (and us) to discover the riches of memory, enjoy the curiosities of language, and share insights with friends. Since the culinary code is a kind of encyclopedia, we will enjoy exploring our gastronomic knowledge as in a catalog. The topic of cooking will also provide an occasion to talk about romantic essay writing and an explicit philosophy of living well and living soundly. Other digressions will focus on the self-esteem of those who like to display their knowledge of basic ingredients and their skill in navigating among saucepans and cooking stoves in conversation. We will discover how the culinary code represents, with the most compelling possible passion, a kind of glue, a unifying element of national identity, more so than other common values and ideals.

Examining the culture of food, we also come to understand its unique ability to inspire joy and create harmony. Whether at table with family, in a restaurant with friends, or at a scientific conference—wherever and however—food is talked about in a language that is accessible to all, exciting to everyone, democratic and positive. Those who chat about food may hail from all walks of life, yet whatever their origin and income level, they readily find a common language. Carlo Petrini, the founder of the Slow Food movement (which defends traditional, civilized cuisine), explains the unique, unifying language in these words: "There are some who describe it as a language: it has words (the products, the ingredients), which are organized according to rules of grammar (the recipes), syntax (the menu), and rhetoric (convivial behavior). Like language, cooking embraces and expresses the culture of those who practice it; it is a depository of the traditions and identity of a group. It self-portrays and communicates in a manner even stronger than language, because food is able to be directly assimilated by our organism: eating someone's food is easier and more immediate than speaking his language."[4]

In this way the language of a culture is born, resistant to consumerist infection. Consumerism and its vehicle, advertising, are obsessed with the here and now—the ephemeral. They are stubbornly aimed at devaluing what already exists and increasing the value of what is new. The language of culture, on the other hand, upholds history and dismisses trendy gimmicks as mere kitsch. The Italian culinary code is imbued with dignity, democratic feeling, and erudition.

By now you have gathered that the code is both the means and the end of this book. As a foreign student of Italian culture, I confess that discovering it and analyzing it have absorbed me completely, drawing me under its spell—just as I was drawn in so many years ago by the country that created this code, the Italy that I will never have my fill of discovering, and that each day increases my hunger for beauty and thirst for art. I know you will understand.

WHY ITALIANS LOVE TO TALK ABOUT FOOD

Friuli Venezia Giulia

The mark of the ancient Roman Julian clan is concealed twice in the name of this region. The word "Friuli" is derived from *forum Julii*. Proud of its distant conquest, ancient Rome aspired to affirm its supremacy in this province for eternity, through its constructions and laws, and through the imperial name. Nevertheless, the allure of this outlying area lies in its non-Roman character, its spotty Slavic nature resulting from its proximity to the Balkans. Notices written in Latin letters here often have a Slavic resonance. Bread (the principal food of all Slavic peoples) sometimes makes a fine showing in the center of the table and sometimes disappears entirely from daily use. At country fairs, sometimes wheat is sold, sometimes corn. In one village they eat *pagnotte*, round loaves; in a neighboring village, polenta.

In the Roman era and in the Middle Ages, Friuli Venezia Giulia was dominated by the opulent city of Aquileia, which abounded in mosaics and was rich with gold. Founded in A.D. 181, Aquileia was the center of all maritime trade between Italy, the East, and northern Europe. Consular roads leading to the Balkans passed through here, and via its port amber was imported into the Roman world. It was amber that allowed the already vast range of the local artisans' products to be expanded. In some towns in Friuli (for example, in Spilimbergo, which is known as "the City of the

Mosaic" and which still houses the Scuola Mosaicisti of Friuli, an instructional center of worldwide repute), the art of inlay and mosaics flourished, and has been handed down to our day. This art is even applied to small pieces of jewelry, but above all to the creation of street mosaic painting. The basic material for the mosaics was right under the ancients' feet: the yellow gravel of the Meduna River; the black, green, and red gravel of the Tagliamento; and the white gravel of the Cosa. Wonderful piazzas and terraces were made in Friuli Venezia Giulia with these stones, and with imported materials as well: blue cobblestones from Ireland, black ones from Belgium, and red ones from the Pyrenees. Friulian mosaicists acquired their reputation in the Roman era, but little has changed in the sixteen hundred years since the fourth-century pavements of Braida Murada, recently restored, were created. While stonecutters and laborers from the Spilimbergo area were summoned to work in many Italian and European cities toward the end of the seventeenth century, in the twentieth century they created famous mosaics throughout Europe (for example, in the Paris Opera House) and even overseas (St. Patrick's Cathedral in New York City).

Trieste, an open city and free port from time immemorial, is the capital of Friuli Venezia Giulia, but it has some difficulty fitting in with the rest of the region. Trieste has its own psychology and traditions, associated mainly with the memory of its role as an important center of Mitteleuropean culture in the period in which it was part of the Austro-Hungarian Empire.

The symbolic center of the actual place is represented, one might say, not by Trieste, but rather by the ghost of Aquileia. Though it no longer exists today, in the days of ancient Rome this city that arose on the muddy banks of the Grado Lagoon was the chief town of the province Venetiae et Histriae. Later on, after the fall of the Roman Empire, Aquileia was transformed into a bastion for the young Christian communities and the main transit point for pilgrims heading to Rome on foot. The lagoon offered protection from bandits and from religious persecutions. During the first raids of the Huns, the inhabitants of Aquileia hid on the islands in the surrounding marshes, where they were able to live on eels, crayfish, frogs, marsh birds, and monkfish. The marshes could offer shelter for months and years. The fugitives ate fish, used fish fat for lighting and heating, and covered their boats with fish skin, symbolically uniting in daily life the fish as the ideal symbol of Christianity and as a mainstay for survival in years of scarcity.

As a center of early European Christianity, Aquileia was comparable in importance to Ravenna or Milan. In 381 it was the site of the famous council in which

St. Ambrose, having come from Milan, denounced the Arian heresy. Thenceforth the diocese of Aquileia took the name "Veneziana," and in the fifth century escaped from Rome's dominion at almost the same time as the exarchate of Ravenna. The city was thus transformed into a territory of Byzantium. But in 590 Gregory the Great, now pope, decided to take remedial measures and sent a regular army against the separatist city. The region later became filled with schismatics, who played hide-and-seek among the small islands scattered throughout the lagoon. Later, when the period of pilgrimages and jubilees arrived (that is, from the eleventh to the fifteenth century) all of eastern Europe landed in Aquileia, continuing on to Rome on foot. The city was the first point of entry for the pilgrims, who organized themselves and coordinated the logistics of their journey. There were periods when the patriarch of Aquileia, head of the diocese of Venice, was no less influential than the pontiff of Rome.

In the eighteenth century Friuli Venezia Giulia was part of the Austro-Hungarian Empire, and it is natural to look for the bygone Mitteleuropean greatness of the Hapsburgs there. But much more discernible in the character of this area is the mark of that lengthy period from the fifteenth to the eighteenth century when the region was under the dominion of neighboring Venice.

Controlling the seas, constantly seizing new islands and founding new colonies, Venice was not too concerned about the well-being of those who had been easily and quickly subjugated in its own backyard. On the continent, in fact, it limited itself to constructing new military strongholds in areas with few prospects, such as Palmanova, a unique architectural complex built in 1593 by the best Venetian strategists, engineers, architects, and historians of fortification. Designed according to plans developed by city planners of the Renaissance, the city still preserves the form of a perfect nine-point star, surrounded by three orders of bastions: two rows of walls erected by the Venetians, and a third added in the Napoleonic era.

The Friulians were of interest to the Venetians mainly as manpower, to be employed in the construction of the capital and as potential recruits in Venice's war against the Ottomans. The consequences were devastating. Without a government and without organization, the Friulians soon experienced desolation and neglect, hunger and poverty, with uncultivated fields and a declining population that would perhaps have been extinguished entirely had it not been saved by corn in that period (see "The Early Gifts from the Americas"). Imported from the New World, easily cultivated and nutritious, corn spread throughout Friuli Venezia Giulia during the last quarter of the sixteenth century.

Polenta is still consumed daily in Gorizia, Udine, and Cortina d'Ampezzo, although there was a time when it had a very bad reputation. In the eighteenth century the population of northern Italy, which consumed polenta almost exclusively, fell ill with pellagra. Goethe, traveling in Italy between 1786 and 1788, diagnosed the cause of the peasants' poor health with a clinical eye:

> I believe that their unhealthy condition is due to their constant diet of maize and buckwheat, or, as they call them, yellow polenta and black polenta. These are ground fine, the flour is boiled in water to a thick mush and then eaten. In the German Tirol they separate the dough into small pieces and fry them in butter, but in the Italian Tirol the polenta is eaten just as it is or sometimes with a sprinkling of grated cheese. Meat they never see from one year's end to the other. Such a diet makes the bowels costive, especially in children and women, and their cachectic complexion is evidence of the damage they do themselves.[1]

Nowadays polenta is consumed more wisely, as if people were heeding Goethe's warnings: once cooked, it is toasted and served with salami, cheese, fish, and meat, thereby preventing the risk of vitamin deficiency and consequently of pellagra.

Frico (fresh Montasio cheese fried in butter, with potatoes or onions) is a regional specialty known throughout Italy. In the morning, before leading the cattle out to pasture, farm wives would leave potatoes and cheese rinds from the day before on a heated shelf above the stove: thus the leftovers of yesterday's supper were transformed into an excellent meal for today. Stoves in Friulian peasant homes are distinct: round, located in the center of the room, their perimeter surrounded by two copper shelves, one higher than the other. The shelves are heated by the central fire, but not intensely, just enough so that food on the lower shelf does not get cold and food on the upper shelf cooks very gradually, for many hours or sometimes for entire days.

Climatic peculiarities naturally influenced the local temperament. Friuli Venezia Giulia has the longest, snowiest winters in Italy, so the inhabitants distracted themselves by taking advantage of the most accessible raw materials and specializing in woodworking, primarily the production of chairs. Nearly all the chairs exported from Italy are manufactured in the areas of Mariano and Manzano, in Friuli. Artisans busy making a chair are portrayed on the sarcophagus of the eighth-century Lombard king Ratchis in the cathedral of Cividale del Friuli, while several documents preserved in the archives of the Doge's Palace in Venice attest to the fact that Friulian woodworkers were invited to the lagoon city from the fourteenth to the eighteenth centuries to produce chairs and seats for chambers in which audiences were held. Today there are approximately two hundred chair factories in the area and a monument ten meters tall, dedicated to the chair, stands at the entry to Manzano, near Udine, bearing the inscription: WELCOME TO THE CHAIR CAPITAL! Less important economically, but characteristic nevertheless, is another product of Friulian woodworking: the nutcracker.

In order to ensure the necessary supplement to their rather monotonous diet, Friulian peasant families in the poorest wooded areas (especially those in the hills, where oaks, chestnuts, and hazelnut trees grow) always raised a pig. The animal roamed freely, feeding on acorns and chestnuts. Friulian pigs, rightly considered quality specimens, are fed today with whey (a by-product of local dairy farming), marc (a by-product of the local wine industry), and also, of course, corncobs.

The butchering of the pig is still of fundamental importance in the daily life of the countryside. This is the most important event for both the family and the entire region: children stay home from school to attend it, and the adults take a day off. Family and neighbors await the great moment: the arrival of the *purcitar*, the itinerant swine butcher. First the pig's throat is surgically slit; then the animal is placed on a workbench to allow the blood to drain. Meanwhile the excitement grows all around. It is necessary to proceed quickly, since the intestines and blood must be processed within a day. The farmers roast tasty blood sausages and make a sweet bread with blood and cracklings (*pan de frizze dolce*).

In San Daniele del Friuli they age one of the two most famous *prosciutti crudi* (uncooked, cured prosciutto) in Italy, the San Daniele to be precise, which is eaten with figs or melon and is the subject of much romantic admiration. In Carnia, in the extreme north of Friuli, *speck* (smoked ham) and Montasio cheese are produced. This cow's milk cheese, aged from two to several years, was developed by Benedictine monks in the twelfth century for pilgrims who, traveling to Rome along the Aquileia road, needed provisions that were not perishable (see "Pilgrims").

Local wines considered particularly suited to accompany pork sausage—Collio, Grave del Friuli, and Colli Orientali—are among Italy's best white wines. In order to maintain their prestige, the state limits the area of the vineyards. Wine in Venezia Giulia and in Friuli is an indispensable accompaniment to human relationships, a cardinal element of the ritual of the *tajut* (little drink). The Friulian who has concluded his workday and wants to enjoy some well-earned relaxation sits in front of the entrance of a bar and invites acquaintances passing by to drink a little glass with him. This is a unique aspect of the richness and quality of social life: "The glasses are tiny, friendship is big." The wine is usually accompanied by *pinze* (focaccias) and *presnitz* (cakes of walnuts, raisins, and candied fruit).

It is common knowledge throughout the world that the Friulians distill exclusive grappas (in this area Friuli vies with Piedmont). The production of grappas in these parts is viewed as an aesthetic process. Elegant flasks and goblets in thin blown glass, intended for the bottling and sampling of grappas, are manufactured both in the region itself and in the workshops of Murano. A dazzling container with grappa, enclosed in a wooden case and displayed in the window of a fashionable bar in Rome or Milan, can cost as much as five hundred or a thousand euros—or as much as the vendor has the nerve to ask.

TYPICAL DISHES OF FRIULI VENEZIA GIULIA

First Courses *Bisna*, yellow polenta with beans and sauerkraut, seasoned with a *soffritto* of salt pork and onion. *Brodetto gradese*, Grado-style fish soup, with small fish from the local rivers. *Rane pescatrici* (angler fish), *acerine* (perch) in olive oil, garlic, and vinegar. Plum gnocchi. Friulian soup (*iota*), which contains beans, milk, white turnips, and cornmeal or, in another version, potatoes, sauerkraut, and smoked pork. A famous specialty is *pistum*, gnocchi made of bread crumbs, sugar, eggs, herbs, and raisins, cooked in pork stock.

Second Courses *Brovada*, pickled turnips (white turnips fermented in marc, grated, then stewed with salt pork in wine); *cevapcici* or *cevaps* (spicy pork and beef meatballs cooked on the grill); *smolz* (beans with olive oil, salt pork, and onion); Trieste-style *granseola* (spider crab meat sautéed in oil with garlic and parsley); *testina alla carnaiola* (sliced calf's head with a sauce of boiled brain and horseradish). Additionally, goulash and gypsy-style hare (*à la bohémienne*), in white vinegar, are also legitimately considered specialties of Friuli Venezia Giulia, along with other Mitteleuropean dishes inherited from the Austrian occupiers, who were dominant here in the first half of the nineteenth century.

Polenta. *Frico* (fresh Montasio cheese, cut into thin slices and fried in butter, often with potatoes or onions).

TYPICAL PRODUCTS OF FRIULI VENEZIA GIULIA

Cheeses Montasio and Tabor.

Resia garlic. Smoked sausage of meat finely minced in a *pestadora* (a hollowed-out wooden block), of various kinds: *pitina* (with wild rosemary), *petuccia* (with wild fennel), and *peta* (with juniper berries). San Daniele, Sauris, and Carsolino prosciutto.

Radic di mont or *radic dal glaz*, Alpine sow thistle, whose boiled shoots make a filling for savory pies.

Desserts *Gubana* (a cake roll filled with raisins and pine nuts), *presnitz* (cakes of walnuts, raisins, and candied fruit).

TYPICAL BEVERAGE

Grappa.

THE *SAGRA*

The word *sagra* (plural *sagre*) derives from the Latin *sacrum*: its early meaning refers to a popular festival dedicated to the patron saint of the village or town. But the *sagra* can also be a celebration of a certain dish or product, of a vegetable or fruit, of a wine, of a type of preparation, even of a specific part of the beef or lamb. In this way tribute is paid to the specialties (roast chestnuts, strawberries, frog's legs fried in batter) for which a particular village or city is renowned.

To mention a few at random: in the little Sicilian town of Ribera (Agrigento) in April, a lively orange *sagra* takes place (similar to the battle of the oranges at the Carnival of Ivrea): the participants cheerfully throw oranges at one another, race on oranges, slip and fall, and even get hurt. A *sagra* in honor of gnocchi is held in June at Castel del Rio, near Bologna. In July, in Tropea, there's the *sagra* of "blue fish" (oily fish) and red onion. In July, in Castelfiumanese, the *sagra* of the apricots. In August, in Norcia, the famous lentils of Castelluccio are honored, and in Eboli, the local mozzarellas. In the village of Albanella in the province of Salerno, the *sagra* of the pizza is organized in August. In August, Sardinia celebrates the *sagra* of the tomato (in Zeddiani, in the province of Oristano) and the *sagra* of Vernaccia wine (in Nurachi, also in the province of Oristano). Many arrive dressed in traditional costumes. These are rowdy festivals, with music and dancing. In San Damiano d'Asti, in September, there's the *sagra* of boiled meats. In the fall, in Marradi, near Florence, the chestnut *sagra*. *Torrone* (almond nougat) is the star of the November

sagra in Cremona and the December one in Faenza. The radicchio *sagra* is the main event of the month of December in Treviso. A national exhibit of "meditation wines" takes place in Mantua, in the Palazzo Ducale, on the last weekend of April, and on the second weekend of the same month the "Festival of Lost Flavors" is held in Zerbolò, near Pavia.

The Italian *sagra* is pagan in origin. Ancient Roman festivals celebrating food and eating practices were described both by Ovid and by the encyclopedist Ambrosius Teodosius Macrobius, who lived in the fifth century A.D. at the court of the emperor Honorius, and who characterizes them as "things of bygone days." Even after the triumph of the Christian religion, high spirits have continued to flourish on these days, and participants feast pleasurably under the banners of interceding saints and martyrs. Thus, in the village of Force, in the Marches, the *sagra* dedicated to the *cacciannanze*, typical focaccias of bread dough baked in a wood-burning oven, is also called the Feast of the Blessed Maria Assunta Pallotta. But these feasts have little to do with sanctity—so little that zealous

Catholics are often irritated by them and do not always participate. The *sagre* are for the most part organized by informal, nonreligious groups of individuals brought together by some interest, such as an association of fishermen, a committee for environmental protection, or a group of passionate local history buffs. Such feasts may even become an arena for ideological protest, and then the saints' statues on the tables are replaced by portraits of the founding fathers of political movements.

Even in these cases, though, the *sagre* are popular, open, lighthearted, and democratic feasts.

In every gorge, in every piazza, on every hill, Italians celebrate the fruits of their labor. To name a few more: the black bread *sagra* (Champorcher, Valle d'Aosta), the feast of Valpelline soup (Valle d'Aosta), the *sagra* of chestnuts (Châtillon, Valle d'Aosta), of *vin brûlé* (Étroubles, Valle d'Aosta), of peaches (Canale, Piedmont), of hazelnuts (Cortemilia, Piedmont), of the white truffle of Alba (Alba, Piedmont), of honey (Arese, Lombardy), of frogs (Bornasco, Lombardy), of rabbits (Brembio, Lombardy), of asparagus (Cantello, Lombardy), of risotto (Villimpenta, Lombardy), of cherries (Bareggio, Lombardy), of milk (Truccazzano, Lombardy), of goose (Mortara, Lombardy), of the porcini mushroom (Motta Visconti, Lombardy), of bilberries (Piazzatorre, Lombardy), of apples (Caldonazzo, Trentino), of olives (Pove del Grappa, Veneto), of asparagus (Bassano del Grappa, Veneto), of corn (Marano Vicentino, Veneto), of chicory (Crespadoro, Veneto), of strawberries (Faedis, Friuli), of crayfish (Remanzacco, Friuli), of olive oil (Moneglia, Liguria), of anchovies (Deiva Marina, Liguria), of focaccia (Recco, Liguria), of grilled meat (Terzorio, Liguria), of snails (Borgio Verezzi, Liguria), of rosemary focaccia (Lavagna, Liguria), of chickpea flour flatbread (Maissana, Liguria), of chestnut flour flatbread (Rossiglione, Liguria), of *porchetta* (roast suckling pig) and tortellini (Lavezzola, Emilia Romagna), of *cotechino* (pork sausage) (Val Tidone, Emilia Romagna), of bruschetta (Predappio Alta, Emilia Romagna), of roots (Soncino, Lombardy), and on and on.

Little by little, religious feasts (in the name of the local saint) and ideological feasts (in the name of the proletarian revolution) merged with the traditional pagan *sagre*, but a central place was always reserved for the local specialty or typical product. Today, in sports fields, parks, and recreational areas, under the tents of the feasts of *L'Unità*, a well-known Communist newspaper, families roast, prepare, eat, and clean up together, just as they once did in churchyards and piazzas.

There is nothing that brings people together like food. And if unity is ruptured at the level of higher politics, the fracture is also evident in gastronomic declarations. When in the nineties the Communist Party split into the Democratic Party of the Left (DS, or Democratici di Sinistra) and the Communist Refoundation Party, Massimo D'Alema, then secretary of the Democratic Party, summarized what had happened by resorting to the language of the culinary code. In fact, addressing those who intended to abandon the party in order to found another, he exclaimed: "With you . . . will go those who grilled the steaks at the feasts of *L'Unità*."[1]

But it did not end there. Political divergence found a place even within the DS itself, and in February 1998, concluding their meeting in Florence, D'Alema attacked the sacredness of that which no one had dared challenge until then: the tortellini of Emilia. Tortellini were the chief specialty of the *sagre* of "red Emilia Romagna"! They were an icon of the partisan movement, a symbol of democracy, the banner of the revolutionary struggle!

In attacking Emilian tortellini, D'Alema, a Roman, had probably not predicted the severity of the blow when he stated point-blank (just before being elected president of the Council of Ministers!) that he did not intend to cry over "a Left made up of liberal militants capable only of distributing flyers, putting up posters, and making tortellini."[2] Such skills, D'Alema declared, were not enough "to lead the nation."

As it turns out, in all probability he was the one this declaration prevented from leading the nation. The government of D'Alema lasted less time than expected (from October 27, 1998, to December 18, 1999), and one of the causes of its downfall was the lack of support on the part of the Emilian hard core, made up of former partisans and their supporters: voters from the central "tortellini" regions, who did not have much liking for D'Alema to begin with and who, after hearing speeches like this, definitively turned their backs on him. It would have been difficult to wound these voters more painfully. And in fact the former Communist mayor of Bologna, Guido Fanti, hurled a fierce reply back to D'Alema: "If we hadn't cooked our tortellini, you wouldn't be there."[3]

Indro Montanelli, immediately grasping the gaffe of the leader of the Left, indicated in an article that, by raising his hand against Emilian tortellini, D'Alema had attacked something sacred.[4] But the DS leader stubbornly did not give up: "There is a difference between a tortellino of government and a tortellino of the struggle."[5]

The Left was defeated a few months after these sacrilegious statements about Emilian tortellini, and Bologna, a red stronghold for forty years, was also swept up in the fall. The new anti-Communist mayor of Bologna (the first of the postwar period), Giorgio Guazzaloca, a butcher, sausage maker, and veal cutlet pounder, was advised by judicious individuals to publicly proclaim his devotion to tortellini.[6]

Tortellini forever, as long as Italy reigns! When at the end of 2000 the anti-globalists organized pickets in front of McDonald's (see "The Later Gifts from America") to coincide with the conference of the Organization for Economic Cooperation and Development in Bologna, tortellini were distributed gratis in front of the American fast-food outlets.[7] It was an expression of class struggle, of revolutionary ardor, of popular pride. The trumpet of battle sounded and the "tortellino of the struggle," rejected by D'Alema, resumed its rightful place.

Like the many cultural activities that inevitably conclude with refreshments, local *sagre* in honor of a city's patron saints, like Communist rallies, project a clear symbol of social reconciliation. Psychologists, sociologists, philosophers, and writers (such as Elias Canetti) describe how these events dissolve and extinguish conflict, creating a mollified public. The common celebration of religious rites and, on a secondary level, the convivial banquet can have this effect on the population. The crowd rejoices, forming an immense Rabelaisian collective body. It reconciles, eating an enormous communal meal: a roasted wild boar, a colossal fried fish, a gigantic frittata, a gargantuan polenta, a cyclopean mountain of pasta. In many cases the *sagra* represents a collective religious celebration (in honor of the local saint), in others the common exaltation of political ideas (the feasts of *L'Unità*, the anti-globalist tortellini), but in all cases it culminates in the consumption of a ton of good food. As a result, *sagre* are a very strong ennobling and reconciling force.

What's more, *sagre* and political picnics disseminate culinary culture. Thousands of people sample rare dishes, like donkey meat or frogs, only on the occasion of these feasts. In 1991, seventy tons of frog's legs were eaten at the festival of the Communist Party of Bologna.[8]

Veneto and the City of Venice

Just as Friulians celebrate the ritual of the *tajut* toward four or five in the afternoon (that is, they sit sipping wine, in the company of friends, in some bar or at a small sidewalk table), Venetians practice the particular habit *l'andar per ombre*, or "moving into the shade," starting at eleven in the morning. This "moving" means slowly ambling from one bar to another, drinking a small glass of chilled Prosecco at each. Legend has it that the expression originated with itinerant wine vendors who moved untiringly with their stands in search of shelter from the blistering sun, following the cool shadow cast over the piazza by the bell tower of San Marco.

Indolence, elegance, and gloom: these legendary traits of Venetian life, celebrated in British, American, and Russian poetry, are reflected in the city's characteristic cuisine. It was here that the hideous *risotto al nero di sepia*, black risotto with cuttlefish ink, was invented, drowned in the very ink with which the cuttlefish, like squid,[1] tried to intimidate the fishermen who threatened their freedom. When the central bones of the cuttlefish are extracted during cleaning, care must be taken not to damage the ink sacs, which are set aside. The mollusks are then cut into strips, which are marinated in the usual mixture of garlic, olive oil, lemon, and white wine, while the risotto is prepared by pouring the inklike fluid from the sacs into it.

The Venetians often cook dried cod, which in this city is called *baccalà*. They call

it that as a matter of principle, out of love for its melodious sound, consciously committing a terminological error. In all of Italy, apart from Venice, salted soaked cod (properly called *baccalà*) is distinguished from salted dried cod, called *stoccafisso* (stockfish). Consequently, the dried cod preferred by Venetian cuisine should be called *stoccafisso*. But the Venetians are obstinate: if they've decided on *baccalà*, *baccalà* it is.

The name for dried cod is one of those apparently trifling questions that is linked by an invisible thread to the Italian consciousness, linguistic and ethnographic-culinary. It was first in language, and later in cuisine, that the complicated process of constructing a national identity was determined at the time of the unification of Italy. One of the principal architects of this important effort was Pellegrino Artusi (1820–1911), a banker, amateur man of letters, and lover of fine food. Born in Forlimpopoli, Romagna, but an ardent champion of Italian unity, in 1891 he assembled a book of 790 recipes from the most diverse regions of the northern part of the country. At a time when the dialect of Tuscany had been affirmed as the literary language of the recently unified nation, the *romagnolo* Artusi wrote his collection in authentic Tuscan. Indeed, he had moved to Tuscany in 1851 in order to learn the language better, just as the Lombard Alessandro Manzoni had done in 1827, setting out for Florence to spend some time there to "rinse his clothes in the Arno" before publishing the revised edition of *I promessi sposi* (1840). The unitary language of the country was evolving; consequently, a survey of the common national cuisine was called for. Piero Camporesi writes in the introduction to Pellegrino Artusi's collection:

> *Science in the Kitchen*, besides being that delicious recipe book that everyone knows, at least by name—a fixed reference point for the Italian culinary tradition, the perfect handbook for a flavorful and, at the same time, balanced, diet—also performed, in a discreet, covert, intangible way, the exceedingly civil task of joining and fusing—first in the kitchen and then at the level of the collective unconscious, in the unplumbed recesses of popular consciousness—that heterogenous, motley group of people that only formally declared themselves Italians.*[2]

Thus, in his scholarly disquisition on dried cod, the great Artusi insists on the distinction between *baccalà* (soaked cod) and *stoccafisso* (dried fish): "The genus *Gadus morrhua* is the cod from the Arctic and Antarctic regions which, depending upon how it is prepared, is called either 'baccalà' (salt cod) or 'stoccafisso' (stockfish)." Among the *baccalari*, the erudite Artusi indicates two varieties of cod, Gaspé and Labrador: "The former comes from the Gaspé Peninsula, that is, the Banks of Newfoundland," namely from America.[3] Naturally this species of cod was unknown in Europe before the discovery of the New World, whereas the Labrador variety is exported by Europe, from Iceland, where it is found in the Labrador Sea. The taste of this fish is more familiar to Italians. It was this specific product that authors of ancient recipe books were alluding to when they wrote of ways to cook *baccalà*. And it is this cod, caught along the coasts of Labrador, that the specialized, periodic publications of the Ligurian Accademia dello Stoccafisso e del Baccalà (Academy of Stockfish and Baccalà) refer to.[4]

Whatever it's called, cod is in any case imported to Venice already sun-dried. It

---

*English translations not otherwise credited are mine. —A.M.A.

then undergoes complex processing. Before being cooked, it must be properly pounded ("*El bacalà xe come la dona, più la se bastona più la diventa bona*"—*baccalà* is like a woman, the more you beat her, the better she gets), and then soaked in water for two or three days, during which the entire surrounding area becomes saturated by a powerful odor. According to laws in medieval cities, you were not allowed to change the water of the soaking cod and throw it out more than once a day, since otherwise an uninterrupted deluge and stench would come from all the houses. City authorities in the Middle Ages allowed this water to be thrown into the drainage canal only at nighttime, in order to avoid traumatic consequences to the sense of smell and psyche of the more sensitive passersby.

Venice is quite different from the rest of the Veneto. In the lagoon city the eye is enchanted by the flaking walls of houses dating from the fifteenth and sixteenth centuries, by the aristocratic air of decadence, by princely salons whose Palladian floors are warped by time. In the Veneto, on the other hand, neat, tidy towns are set amid green hills, and the green of the countryside is dotted by the white of regal neoclassical villas, built by Palladio in the sixteenth century. It's an idyllic landscape that Goethe exalted:

> The magnificence of the new landscape which comes into view as one descends is indescribable. For miles in every direction, there stretches a level, well-ordered garden surrounded by high mountains and precipices.
>   . . . We drove on a wide, straight and well-kept road through fertile fields. There trees are planted in long rows upon which the vines are trained to their tops. Their gently swaying tendrils hung down under the weight of the grapes . . . The soil between the vine rows is used for the cultivation of all kinds of grain, especially maize and millet.[5]

The atmosphere in the bucolic Veneto is harmonious, industrious, cheerful, and folksy, and the cuisine is primarily that of the mainland, while in Venice, as one can easily intuit, it is entirely fish-based. In Venetian kitchens, and nowadays particularly in trattorias, little-known local fish and shellfish are generally served, such as sardines, sea snails (*caragoi*), clams (*caparossoli*), razor clams (*cape longhe* and *cape de deo*),[6] and mussels (*peoci*). They also serve clams known as *pevarasse*, mantis shrimp (*canoce*), and crabs (*granseole*), including those without a shell during the molting period (soft-shelled crabs, or *moléche*), which are eaten after being dipped in egg, floured, and fried. In the *bàcari* (taverns) scattered throughout the city, on the other hand, everyone consumes a *cichéto* (a little snack) from time to time, to soothe their hunger pangs: a little anchovy wrapped around an olive; half a hard-boiled egg with oil and pepper; creamed *baccalà* on toast; a little marinated fish; a roasted, seasoned scallion; a slice of artichoke heart with garlic and parsley or fried in batter; a little meatball; Spanish white beans boiled and seasoned with oil, onion, vinegar, and parsley; *nervéti* (pieces of gristle boiled and seasoned the same way). To eat them, you spear them with a toothpick. After which, an *ombra* (equivalent to an eighth of a liter) of white wine is called for to cleanse the palate.

Few spectacles are as picturesque as the daily fish market in the city of Chioggia or in the center of Venice, a couple of steps from the Rialto bridge. Here prized fish and crustaceans, even imported ones—grouper, monkfish, lobster—make a fine display, along with poor man's fish, such as *sarde* (sardines) cooked *in saòr*, or in a sour sauce (that is, *in carpione*, fried and marinated with onions and vinegar). *Sarde in saòr* is one of the oldest Venetian dishes, a very important source of nourishment for sailors and fishermen, who carried it with them, on board the boats, packed in precious barrels: the salt, vinegar, and oil served to preserve the fish, while the vitamin C in the onions helped to prevent scurvy.

By contrast, fresh fish is not eaten in the rest of the Veneto, between Padua and Verona, in the cities formerly under the powerful duchy of the Sforzas. Instead, dried fish is generally consumed, such as *baccalà* Vicenza-style, a great classic. Here vegetable gardens dominate, with their unforgettable local varieties. In the markets one glimpses bunches of wild herbs from the lands around the lagoon, such as *bruscandoli* (hop sprouts) and *carletti* (hop flowers), and numerous artichokes in all stages of growth.

Artichokes have a truly eventful "life journey" and can appear for sale in five distinct forms. In their youthful period they are known by the name *canarini* (the first cutting); these are very small, and are dipped in *pinzimonio*, olive oil with pepper and salt, or breaded and fried. Then come the *castraure* (literally "castrations"), fruit of the second cutting of the buds of the main stem; farmers do this to stimulate the growth of the remaining artichokes. The *castraure* are small, vernal artichokes to be cooked with garlic and oil or fried in batter. Finally, true artichokes (resulting from the third cutting) appear, to be prepared in a variety of ways. But that's not the end of it, because there are also artichoke bottoms (from the fourth cutting), delicious morsels to be sampled boiled, grilled, or fried, while the fifth cutting of the plant yields the flowers that have bloomed, to be gathered in bouquets and admired in all their purple glory.

The artichoke of the Veneto (from Sant'Erasmo, an island in the Venetian Lagoon) is so famous that its cultivators are interviewed as if they were movie stars, revealing Shakespearian passions behind the relaxed image of the produce gardener:

> When he speaks about *castraure* his eyes shine, as if he were in love. Giovanni Vignotto, a Sant'Erasmo native born in 1935, has an uncontrollable passion for the cultivation of the purple artichoke of Sant'Erasmo:
>
> "Is it true that there are false *castraure* of Sant'Erasmo?"
>
> "Unfortunately some scoundrels sell small Tuscan artichokes as *castraure* from Sant'Erasmo. Generally the authentic *castraure* are found at the Rialto market and in some of the best restaurants in Venice, which reserve them in advance. The crates that contain them have carried down the brand of the Consortium of the Purple Artichoke of S. Erasmo. Those who want to make the little Tuscan artichokes pass as Sant'Erasmo *castraure* are swindlers who should be exposed. They should be considered *castraure* thieves."[7]

In the Veneto there is an extensive peasant culture, similar to that found in Holland, which is unrelated to Mediterranean alimentary rituals. Indeed, the southern part of the region, the Polesine, is sometimes referred to as "Italian Holland" in the tourist guides. This area is situated below sea level and, like Holland, is the result of the reclaiming of marshes and swamps. The Veneto outside of Venice is a region without a center; there are neither inhabitants of the capital nor provincials here, but only numerous towns of modest dimensions, all with equal rights (Verona, Vicenza, Treviso, Padua, Bassano), none of which try to overshadow or surpass the others. They have only one thing in common: they seem committed to doing the opposite of what is done in Venice, or at least to doing the same things in a different way. Therefore, while legumes are an important ingredient in the cuisines both of Venice and of the rest of the Veneto, the capital and the region handle them differently. For the mainland part of the Veneto, dishes such as *risi e bisi* (rice with tender fresh peas) are characteristic. In Venice, this rice dish is almost exclusively made on April 25, for the spring festival of San Marco. On that day the doges would once solemnly and publicly sample the *risi e bisi* and the *castraure*. During the other months of the year, Venice prefers risotto, especially with shellfish.

In the rest of the Veneto, risotto is made with *zucca* (pumpkin), with asparagus, with Treviso radicchio, or with frog's legs (see "Risotto"). The swamps and the immense semiflooded zones close to the Venetian Lagoon abound with eels, which the local inhabitants call *bisati*. And only a simpleton confuses *risi e bisi*, rice with peas, with *risi e bisati*, rice with eels. Along the coast, lagoon and marsh birds, ducks especially, are hunted and roasted.

The Veneto was often used as a testing ground by aristocratic gastronomes and advocates of a culinary science who, when visiting their estates and dispensing advice to the farmers, experimented with new techniques of cultivation and selection on their lands, sometimes achieving truly remarkable results. In the fourteenth century, the physician and astronomer Marquis Giacomo Dondi Dall'Orologio imported hens never before seen from Poland and introduced them in the Veneto. Particularly esteemed for their beauty, they were meant to stroll around the marquis's garden. This species is today called the Paduan hen, *pita padovana*. It has long feathers, large wattles, and plumage that displays a remarkable variety of colors, from black and white to silver and gold. Paduan hens, according to the age-old recipe, are prepared with an herb stuffing and placed in an ox or pig bladder, which is then boiled in a pot of water. The air is let out of the ox bladder through a narrow tube, to prevent it from bursting. This type of cooking method is called *alla canevera*, or *canevera*-style (the *canevera* is simply the tube or hollow cane that acts as a vent).

We cannot overlook a Venetian specialty esteemed throughout the world: carpaccio. Carpaccio is thinly sliced beef, served raw like the Alba-style veal salad so loved by the Piedmontese (raw slices dressed with oil and lemon) or Alba-style raw beef (another Piedmont specialty, essentially a typical steak tartare). And yet, among all the different types of raw meat dishes that exist, it is the Venetian version that has managed to stand out. Today it is found on menus throughout the world. Its name transformed from that of a Venetian-born painter into the name of a dish, carpaccio can plainly be considered a local specialty. It was prepared for the first time around fifty years ago in Harry's Bar in the center of Venice. The most famous haunt in Venice, Harry's Bar was opened in 1931 by Giuseppe Cipriani, a virtuoso of appetizers and cocktails. Located not far from Piazza San Marco in a fairly inconspicuous alleyway, Calle Vallaresso, it was intended for informed, select customers. Frequent visitors to the bar included Ernest Hemingway, Somerset Maugham, various members of the Rothschild family, Arturo Toscanini, Orson Welles, Aristotle Onassis, Maria Callas, Truman Capote, Peggy Guggenheim, Charlie Chaplin, and so on, down to Princess Diana and many other contemporary VIPs.

A number of interesting gastronomic innovations were created in this bar, all christened with names of artists: the Tiziano cocktail, the Bellini. Carpaccio is part of this same tradition. The story goes that this famous dish was born in the second half of the fifties, when a doctor prescribed that an illustrious Venetian lady, Amalia Nani Mocenigo, eat raw meat in order to combat anemia. And so Giuseppe Cipriani made her a fillet of beef cut into very thin slices (the fillet is first wrapped in wax paper and placed in the freezer for a quarter of an hour; at that point, transformed into a solid block, it can be cut into slices half a millimeter thick).

This thinly sliced, seasoned meat with arugula and the sauce later called carpaccio (Worcestershire, fresh mayonnaise, a few drops of Tabasco) took its name from Vittore Carpaccio (c. 1455–c. 1526), the painter to whom numerous rooms of the Gallerie dell'Accademia, in Venice, are dedicated. The name was chosen because an exhibit of Carpaccio was having enormous success just when Giuseppe Cipriani tried out his dish of sliced raw meat. Carpaccio's fame is now so boundless that "carpaccio" is synonymous with thinly sliced raw meat, and in recent times also with sliced raw fish and sliced raw mushrooms. The term no longer indicates a specialty, but a type of preparation.

Between 1949 and 1979, the photographer Fulvio Roiter portrayed the Carnival of Venice in celebrated images that were repeatedly displayed and published. In these photos, color is the undisputed protagonist: round sad masks, stark white faces that stand in contrast to the aggressive vividness of the costumes, with dark, glittering water as background. Roiter's tragic, distinct photographs, immediately recognizable, are often reproduced on postcards and calendars. Anyone who has seen them does not forget them: nocturnal landscapes, sickly hues, and, among hundreds of wretched Pierrots, not a single Harlequin.

In 1841 the historian Pietro Gaspare Morolin lamented: "The worst vice of the Venetians is gluttony," alluding to the excessive gormandizing of the *buongustai* and the passion for rare and expensive foods. But in our era of mass tourism, when the majority of people who flock to the Carnival bring sandwiches from home and munch them as they walk the streets, leaving Venice with greasy wrappings rather than tourist dollars, the Venetian catering collective, though bitterly mourning the once elegant banquets in exclusive, semiclandestine restaurants, has nevertheless developed a broad range of more than fairly good sandwiches, from *panini* (on hard rolls) to *tramezzini* (on soft sliced bread).

The typical sweets of the Carnival are intended to be consumed on the go: *galani* (dough strips), *fritole* (sweet fritters), and *crapfen* (filled doughnuts), variations on the theme of sweet dough deep-fried in oil. In Italy every city has its own variety, and in Venice the shape and name of the Carnival treats even change from one district to another. On the island of Murano they are called *zaleti*, but if you move to another island in the lagoon, Burano, you'll find another name: *buranelli*. In Milan these sweet fritters fried in oil are eloquently called *chiacchiere* (gossip, idle talk). The name recalls the Florentine term for the last Thursday of Carnival, *berlingaccio*, that is, the day for *chiacchiere*.

A Florentine gloss from the eighteenth century helps clarify how closely these two sweet joys of the mouth—the pleasures of language and of eating—are associated:

ERCOLANI: But what does *berlingare* mean?

VARCHI: This is a word that applies more to women than to men, and it means to chatter, prattle, jabber, particularly when others have their gut full and their belly (for that is what vulgar people call the body, or the stomach) heated by wine: and from this verb the Florentines derive the names *berlingaiuoli* and *berlingatori*, which they call those who take delight in filling their mouths, gobbling, and lapping; and they call the Thursday that comes before Carnival day *berlingaccio*, which the Lombards call *giobbia grassa*, Fat Thursday, on which day, by a common custom so prescribed, it seems that everyone is permitted to enjoy themselves, feasting and brawling, with gluttonous delights and delicacies.[8]

TYPICAL DISHES OF VENICE AND THE VENETO

Antipasti *Baccalà mantecato* (creamed *baccalà*). It is often served with polenta.

Other antipasti: several fish (normally sardines and *sfogi*, sole) in a marinade of onion and vinegar. The fish already undergoes a first salting on the fishing boat and is sold that way, lightly salted, at the port; then it is fried and finally marinated. A rather laborious procedure, actually.

First courses Bean soup *al magasso* (with wild duck), *sopa coada* (pigeons in broth), *risi e bisi* (rice with peas), *risi e bisati* (rice with eel), *risi in cavroman* (rice with lamb), *risotto alla chioggiotta* (risotto with goby), *risotto alla trevigiana* (risotto with Treviso radicchio). Spaghetti or black risotto with cuttlefish.

Second courses Venetian-style liver, with a lot of onion, sautéed in a pan with olive oil. Capon *canevera*-style. Soft-shelled crabs, or *moléche*, caught in April and May, or October and November, the molting period (they are kept alive for twenty-four hours in egg beaten with herbs, and when they have gorged themselves on egg, they are fried in a frying pan and eaten whole). Female crabs (*masanete*). Sea snails (*caragoi*), murex (*garusoli*). Horsemeat stew (*pastissada*). Paduan hen (*pite*). Alpago lamb with herbs. Donkey stew. Duck *in vasetto* (confit), cooked and preserved in its own fat (a typical way in which many peasant cultures preserve meats). Snails (Sant'Andrea di Badia Calavena is called "the City of Snails").

Pearà. Though in Venice this term refers to meatballs of ox brain or veal with cheese, in the rest of the Veneto, especially in Verona, *pearà* is something quite different: a sauce that is added to boiled meats, prepared with ox bone marrow, bread crumbs, broth, black pepper, and grated Parmesan cheese. *Pearà* should not be confused with another Venetian specialty, *peverada*, a sauce served not with boiled meat, but exclusively with roast meat, especially poultry, that consists of chicken livers, anchovies, parsley, lemon, *soppressa* (a Veneto sausage), oil, vinegar, and garlic.

Polenta with birds (*polenta e osei*): little birds with sage and salt pork, skewered on thin spits, roasted whole and served with polenta. Turkey hen with pomegranate. *Toresani* (pigeons) on a spit, a typical dish of Vicenza. Purple Sant'Erasmo artichokes with lagoon prawns. *Bruscandoli*: hop sprouts boiled and seasoned with oil; *carletti* (hop flowers). With regard to polenta, it should be specified that in some provinces of the Veneto, particularly Venice, Padua, and Treviso, the more refined, delicate, and expensive white polenta—made of fine grain, obtained from a different, paler variety of corn—is eaten nearly exclusively instead of the classic yellow polenta.

Desserts *Fugazza* (focaccia with iris root and orange rind). *Pandoro*, the typical leavened cake that is made in Verona, elegantly ascetic, without any filling whatsoever. Although both are Christmas cakes (see "Calendar"), *pandoro* differs quite a bit from Milanese *panettone*, which is full of candied fruit, raisins, and even chocolate. Indeed, the two Christmas cakes are as different as the atmosphere of the two Carnivals: that of Venice and the Veneto and that of Milan. The Milanese Carnival is dedicated entirely to food and feasting; it also lasts four days longer than the period established by the Roman Church, because it ends not on Shrove Tuesday, but on the first Saturday of Lent. The Venetian Carnival, by contrast, is an elegant, refined spectacle of masks.

TYPICAL PRODUCTS OF VENICE AND THE VENETO

Cheeses Asiago. Monte Veronese. Grappa Morlacco cheese, made from the milk of a breed of cows on its way to extinction, the Burlina. Not long ago only 270 of them could be counted, but local proponents of Slow Food have taken the cows under their protection and today the number of Burlinas is growing (see "Slow Food"). Treviso Casatella, Soligo, and Schiz cheeses. Ubriaco del Piave, or "drunken cheese" (*formaio embriago*), steeped in fresh marc.

Cured Meats Prosciutto from the Colli Euganei and Vicenza *soppressa*. Treviso *luganega* (judging by its name, the recipe for this sausage would have been originally imported from Lucania, the ancient name for Basilicata; but in our day *luganega* is the pride and joy of Trevisan cuisine).

Fruit The colossal cherries of Marostica and the Veronese hills. Strawberries, apples, melons, and peaches of Verona. Kiwis and lemons from Lake Garda. Pears from the Adige. Chestnuts from the Trevisan mountains and honey from the Dolomites of Belluno.

Vegetables Beans from Lamon, red radicchio from Treviso, white asparagus from Bassano, garlic from the middle Adige valley. Purple Sant'Erasmo artichokes, whose buds, called *castraure*, are particularly esteemed.

Riso Vialone Nano Veronese (Veronese dwarf rice), a variety of rice with small grains, bred in the fifteenth century by the Benedictine monks of the abbey of Grumolo. The monks drained the marshes around Verona, put an end to its mephitic miasmas, dug channels throughout the region, and created rice paddies that still produce good harvests.

Extra-virgin olive oil from Lake Garda and the Veronese hills (see "Olive Oil").

TYPICAL BEVERAGE

Prosecco.

OLIVE OIL

ike other Mediterranean countries, Italy has based its economy and culture on the olive. The copious literature analyzing the relationship between this Mediterranean crop and the psychology, history, and religion of the peninsula is enriched each year by new materials on the subject issued on the occasion of important national conventions and acclaimed exhibitions. Every November the Expo dei Sapori and the Salone dell'Olio are held in Milan, the latter organized by the Associazione Nazionale Città dell'Olio (National Association of Olive Oil Cities) for olive oil samplers from all over the world. The exposition, financed by the Ministry for Agricultural and Forestry Policies, dedicates specific space to the production of oils bearing the Denomination of Protected Origin (DOP: Denominazione d'Origine Protetta), the preeminent Italian oils. On the last Sunday of November the Pane e Olio in Frantoio (Bread and Oil at the Oil Press) is held, an event that spans hundreds of Italian piazzas, offering samples of the new oil, homemade bread, and regional specialties, as well as visits to the oil presses. Particularly tempting is the display Olioliva holds at the same time in Imperia. In February, National Oil Week takes place simultaneously in Siena, Puglia, Milan, and Rome. Verona welcomes the International Olive Oil Salon each year. In June, Archeolio opens in Sicily: a world of taste in a sea of oil, with professional development courses for specialists and numerous stands for lovers of Mediterranean cuisine, based on olives and olive oil. Also in June, the exposition Bimboil is held in Rome. The list of venues and expos is endless.

As we know from art and from classical literature, Italy inherited the cult of olive oil from ancient Rome, which had in turn borrowed it from Greece, where the olive had a prominent presence in mythology. This cult had always been linked to agriculture, to the cultivation and ennoblement of land by man.

The Romans, like the Greeks, did not view virgin nature in a positive light. In their system of values, nature in its primitive aspect was the negative antithesis of civilization (*civitas*) and of the city (*urbs*)—that is, of the order created by man, who should aspire to distinguish himself from nature. The plowed field (*ager*) and the garden (*hortus*) thus stood in positive contrast to virgin nature (the *saltus*). This is confirmed, for example, in Cicero's speech in defense of Sextus Roscius, where the orator speaks explicitly about two contrasting attitudes toward rural life: "But I have myself known many men (and so, unless I am deceived, has every one of you) who are inflamed of their own accord with a fondness for what relates to the cultivation of land, and who think this rural life, which you think ought to be a disgrace to a charge against a man, the most honorable and the most delightful." Such a system of values had been affirmed since the times "when men were sent for from the plough to be made consuls," that is, recruited from their agricultural labors.[1] Virgil describes it this way in the *Georgics*:

> The farmer has been ploughing the soil with curving blade:
> it's his year's work, it's sustenance for his little grandsons,
> and his country, his herds of cattle and his faithful oxen.[2]

Classical texts tell us that grain, the vine, and the olive were the three pillars for Greeks symbolizing religious worship and the wealth of material culture. The Romans inherited this wealth and these values from Greece both on a metaphysical level and on a practical culinary level, transmitting the tradition of olive oil to their Italian descendants.

Oil unifies Italy like a national flag. Since 1994 the National Association of Olive Oil Cities, with headquarters in Monteriggioni, has appointed certifiers and tasters in an attempt to uphold the unblemished honor of this "gastronomic emblem" of Italy. Operating in the chambers of commerce of the main cities of the Association (Genoa, Savona, Imperia, Spoleto) are committees of tasters (called panels, American-style, for some reason) that ensure the quality of the olive oil. During the period of olive harvesting these experts, who train all year to be in their best form at the beginning of the season, taste every producer's oil once a week. The tasters, who do not drink or smoke and never use spicy condiments, are called upon to react mainly to three possible defects of the newly pressed oil: mold, acidity, and overheating. Mold needs no explanation. An acidic odor is passed on to the oil if the cask has been rinsed with alcohol or vinegar and has not been properly dried before pouring in the oil. Overheating occurs when the olives, left in heaps after picking, remain stationary for a long time without being stirred. If kept improperly for a long time, the olives spoil and begin to produce heat, and the oil becomes rancid.

Specialists tell us that current criteria of appraisal are different from those used in ancient times. Experts today have perfected their faculties to such a point and reached such a degree of sensitivity that they can recognize the flaws in the oil produced by their parents and grandparents. At the time when these generations were involved in production, they were more concerned with quantity than with quality. People were worried about making a living and could live with a lower overall quality.

The excessive preoccupation with quality and authenticity in olive oil production is a sign of our own times. Each and every consumer aspires to have Italian olive oil from

Liguria, Tuscany, or the lake region on the table. A very rich literature on the subject tells us that Italian olive oil is not 0.5 percent but a good 1 percent polyphenols, substances that protect against cancer and heart attack. High-quality Italian oil prevents gallstones. It protects against atherosclerosis (with unsaturated fats). It helps prevent rickets, since it contains olein, palmitin, and myristostearin, as well as vitamins A and E (antioxidants).

Many objections could be raised, however, regarding the *italianità* (Italianness) of the oil consumed by the masses. There is only enough Ligurian oil for the elite: to procure some, you must be a friend of a farmer. There is only enough Tuscan oil for the elite: to get some, you must be a friend of a count.

Veronese oil from Lake Garda is not even plentiful enough for the locals. Sometimes it is sold in shops, but its authenticity depends exclusively on the reliability of the merchant.

In Umbria, local oil can be bought in small towns.

In Puglia it is easier to buy unblended local oil (nearly 40 percent of all Italian oil is produced here!). Authentic Pugliese oil, probably by virtue of its modest quality, is also sold outside of Puglia.

Italians eagerly discuss the terminological nuances that designate the various types and subtypes of olive oil. The classifications, as one might duly expect, change both geographically and historically. Distinctions used in the last century, for example, are generally inapplicable to today's reality, which imposes different expressions and categories due to changes in ingredients and production methods.

But what do we find today on the labels of olive oil in the supermarkets?

There are a few principal categories:

Virgin olive oil, obtained mechanically without preheating. It has several subspecies: extra-virgin olive oil (acidity no higher than 1 percent); virgin olive oil (acidity no higher than 2 percent), ordinary olive oil (acidity no higher than 3.3 percent), lamp-grade virgin olive oil (acidity higher than 3.3 percent).

In addition there are refined olive oil (acidity no higher than 0.5 percent) and olive oil that is a blend of refined oil and other virgin olive oil, except lamp grade (acidity no higher than 1.5 percent).

The poorer qualities include oil obtained from olive residues with the aid of a solvent (crude olive pomace oil) and oil obtained from olive residues using a refining method and a solvent (refined olive pomace oil; acidity no higher than 0.5 percent).

Legislation prescribes the norms, and regulatory bodies pursue those who violate them. But rather than considering adulterations and spurious substances, let's talk about crystalline purity.

Italian recipes and cookbooks always demand extra-virgin olive oil. It is understood that this oil goes back to the sacred Roman culinary tradition, bestows longevity and health, and protects against disasters.

Some bottles contain the written inscription "This oil may be assumed to diminish the probability of vascular pathologies." This increases the bottle's fascination to buyers. And there is some truth in it: from many scientific studies we learn that extra-virgin olive oil falls into the category of functional food, that is, food that lowers the risk of illness, and "nutriceutical" food, or medicinal food.

One can of course suggest to those who sing the praises of "extra-virgin oil obtained directly from the olives and only through mechanical processes" and of the "oil of the first cold pressing" that for fifty years now only one pressing has been used, since current olive presses are powerful enough to immediately press everything there is to be pressed out of the olives; a second pressing simply does not exist. "Cold pressing" merely indicates that the oil is heated to a maximum of 27 degrees C. The most inferior ingredients are heated to 60 degrees C now, as oil once was.

Though we search for the words "Produced in Italy" on labels, what we find most of the time is, alas, "Bottled in Italy." That means that the oil, coming from Morocco, from Tunisia, from Turkey, and, more and more often now, Spain, is unloaded from enormous tankers in the ports of Genoa, Imperia, and Bari, great centers of olive oil processing and bottling. Poor-quality oils also arrive in abundance in these ports: lamp-grade, pomace oil, and sometimes even the pressing obtained from discarded olive residues: the product obtained from the "dregs of the dregs" goes into air conditioner filters. The imported oil is ennobled, diluted, cut, sometimes refined. And bottled with the label "Bottled in Italy."

Where then is the oil sung about in myths, so exalted and celebrated: the ideal, authentic, precious oil?

It lies in the collective imagination. Throughout our considerations of the typical products of sixteen out of the twenty Italian regions, we celebrate a higher reality, which also reigns in the consciousness of those who consume the "nectar of olives": the idea of a genuine, life-giving oil, a natural lymph that has nourished a people, tied to the spiritual foundation of life. The ritual use of oil is closely bound to the religious sacraments, and olive oil and holy oil are one and the same. At dinnertime on every table in Italy, leaving aside the label that appears on the bottle, there is a bit of ceremonial liquid, a source of immortality.

Trentino Alto Adige

Goethe, arriving in these outlying regions of Italy, exulted: "From Bolzano to Trento one travels for nine miles through a country which grows ever more fertile. Everything which, higher up in the mountains, must struggle to grow, flourishes here in vigour and health, the sun is bright and hot, and one can believe again in a God."[1]

Nevertheless, a traveler coming to these parts from the south or west may feel more as though he is in Austria-Hungary than in Italy. Although it can be unbearably hot in Trento and Bolzano in July and August, the Trentino has the reputation of being almost polar. It is here that inhabitants of the coastal zones (Liguria, Tuscany) escape to refresh themselves on the hills and mountains in the summer, when sultriness reigns throughout the Apennine Peninsula. The cuisine of Trento and of the Alto Adige (or South Tyrol) is characterized by the slogan "Withstand the rigors of winter!" The popular culture is permeated by the dramatic struggle against cold. Here the most joyous festival is the one that marks the end of winter, when a monstrous puppet is solemnly set ablaze.

The Trentino and the South Tyrol are more distinct than alike. While the first has a more typically Italian appearance, the South Tyrol is more akin to Austria. In the Trentino, white and yellow bread are eaten; in the South Tyrol, black bread.

These two halves of the same region even differ in terms of law. While land property in the Trentino is divided among legitimate heirs with no complications, the Alto Adige adheres to the medieval norm of *maggiorascato*, the right of primogeniture, here referred to as *maso chiuso* (literally, closed holding): plots of land cannot be subdivided, so property holdings remain vast. The government of half the region encourages the priorities of traditional agriculture and preserves this institution, a legacy of Venetian dominion. Goethe, who had attended the trial of a civil case in Venice, at the Doge's Palace, wrote on October 3, 1786:

> Fideicommissums enjoy a high legal status in the Republic. Once an estate is stamped with this character, it keeps it permanently, even though, for some special reason or other, it may have been sold several centuries ago and passed through many hands. If the question of ownership is ever raised, the descendants of the original family can claim their rights and the estate must be restored to them.[2]

Indeed, Goethe was astonished by the vitality of that ancient law, which strangely continues to be in practice even in the twenty-first century, though with a fundamental innovation: since 2002, firstborn daughters may also inherit.

The principal foods of the Trentino and South Tyrol are mostly Austrian: cabbage and potatoes; head cabbage fermented with salt, saffron, cumin, and other spices (sauerkraut); shredded pancakes in broth (*Frittatensuppe*); flour dumplings (*canederli* or *Knödeln*); sausage (*Würstel*); ham (*speck*); polenta; and the most exquisite apples of the Mediterranean area, not to mention the strudel made from these apples. In addition to the Austrians, to whom the local inhabitants are linked not only by geography but also by history (for five and a half centuries, from 1363 to 1918, the Trentino and South Tyrol were under Hapsburg dominion), the region was once dominated by another elite, which controlled the local population in a somewhat different, though no less active, way than the foreign conquerors. This was the Catholic clergy: Trento was a stronghold of the Catholic Counter-Reformation, site of the sixteenth-century Council of Trent.

One of the reasons the Holy See settled upon Trento for its conference to halt the spread of Lutheranism was the population's familiarity with receiving numerous foreign guests and its ability to offer hospitality and guarantee provisions for the visitors. Trento stands at the crossroads of important trade routes. The only mountain pass leading from Italy to Austria, the Brenner Pass, is accessible from here. The city is the perfect place for planning large commercial fairs. Even today there are markets each year dedicated to the exquisite salt pork, to seedlings, and obviously to its apples.

The Council of Trent had been announced in 1545, five years before the start of the sessions. These five years were devoted to preparations for the event. Little by little lodging and accommodations in the city were found for hundreds of functionaries from the Holy See, the Jesuit Order, the congregations and monastic orders, and for the ambassadors of all the episcopates and the nuncios of all the dioceses and Christian churches on the planet, not to mention the numerous individuals employed in "security" at that time. Small wonder that the city experienced a tumultuous economic and gastronomic renaissance during these years.

Rich folklore and literature show us that prelates and monks appreciated a good table and were able to skillfully evade the precepts of fasting and abstinence (see "Calendar"). Parish priests as well as pontiffs were targets of irony. Memorable in this regard is the sonnet "La cucina der papa" (the Pope's kitchen) by Giuseppe Gioacchino Belli:

It so happened that the cook appeared
this morning and invited me to visit
the most Holy Kitchen. Kitchen?
Some kitchen! I'd call it a seaport.

Vats, basins, pots and pans,
Sides of veal and slabs of beef,
chickens, eggs, milk, fish, herbs, pork,
plump game and all kinds of special dishes.

Say I: Well, cheers, Holy Father!
Says he: And you haven't seen the pantry yet,
where there's just as much of God's grace.

Say I: Oh well, excuse me, poor man!
Does he have some Eminence dining with him?
No, no—says the cook—the Pope always dines alone.

Not just the intellectuals, but the ladies of fine society also made witty remarks about the subject, as we know from Goethe:

Throughout the meal, the mischievous lady on my left did not leave the clergy in peace for a moment. During Lent, the fish is served in forms which make it look like meat, and this gave her inexhaustible opportunities for making irreverent and unseemly comments. She made great play with the expressions "a liking for flesh" and "a fleshly liking," saying that one ought at least to enjoy the form, even though the substance was forbidden.[3]

What with an obsession for the rules of fasting and an obvious attraction to the sins of gluttony, an opulent and substantial meatless cuisine was developed in Trento that outshone the local game-based traditions.

On days when meat was permitted, prelates were also served capercaillies (large grouse), fallow deer, chamois (antelope), and roe deer. The papal cook Bartolomeo Scappi, the "secret" (personal) chef who served the high-ranking hierarchies of the Council for its entire period, wrote about it. But since days of abstinence, according to the Catholic rules, make up nearly half the year, and since the clergy, willingly or not, was forced to respect the rules of the Church during the conference, dishes based on flour, milk, and vegetables still prevail today in the daily life of the Trentino. In these areas meat very rarely ends up in a casserole. Fish is hardly ever included in the meatless diet of the Trentino, or, if fish is used, it is freshwater fish (since the sea is far away). The cod purposely imported for Lent (stockfish and *baccalà*) is an exception.

Meat is therefore scarce in the typical dishes of the Trentino and South Tyrol, replaced by a variety of interesting flour-based specialties. The best oven-baked products were invented in the monasteries, where breads were made for daily distribution to the poor (a practice prescribed by the Church). The varieties and types of bread, a ritual element of domestic life, symbolically recounted the health, prosperity, and composition of the family. In the Trentino (more precisely in the Benedictine abbey of Monte Maria in Burgusio, in Val Venosta) a kind of family loaf was invented, baked as a "couple" in a single pan: the traditional Ur-Paarl rye bread, shaped as a figure eight. Each spouse had to eat half of it. For widows and widowers, a ring loaf was made instead. Similar double loaves are known in other national cuisines as well, for example, the Jewish challah. The best and most well-known types of South Tyrolean bread are called *Vorslag* and *Schüttelbrot*.

The grainy magnificence of the cuisine of the Trentino comes not only from oven-baked products, but also from pastas and, above all, from the renowned *canederli* (dumplings). Sometimes dishes are given names that involve some teasing of the clergy (e.g., the dumplings called *strangolapreti*, or priest-chokers). The dough of the *canederli* may also include potatoes, as in the case of sweet *canederli*. In preference to the five different varieties of potato that grow in Italy (the Avezzana of Abruzzi, the Agata of Emilia Romagna, the Tuscan and Ligurian Pastagialla, and the Viterbese of Lazio), the Trentinese clearly favor the Austrian variety that bears the name Sieglinde.

The main vegetables in this region, which is considered Nordic, are the same as those in Russia: potatoes and cabbage. Moreover, the Trentinese even prepare cabbage and cucumbers for the winter in *salamoia* (pickling brine), without vinegar! It is a practice that is quite widespread in Russia but absolutely inconceivable in other parts of Italy.

The Trentino is famous for its excellent red wines (Südtiroler Lagrein, Teroldego, Marzemino, Trentino Cabernet), and the most famous enological school in Italy, founded in 1874, is located in this region, in San Michele all'Adige. Besides wine, beer is also often present on tables in the Trentino, another indication of the Austrian influence on the local population's customs.

TYPICAL DISHES OF TRENTINO ALTO ADIGE

First Courses of the Trentino Gnocchi, *canederli* (dumplings), *strango-lapreti* (priest-chokers, a kind of gnocchi made of stale bread and spinach), ravioli of all kinds, macaroni pie, potato polenta (an ancient peasant food made with yellow flour mixed with an onion *soffritto* and boiled potatoes).

Second Courses of the Trentino Beans with salted meat, Trentino-style hare in sweet-and-sour sauce, Trentino-style chicken (stuffed with walnuts, pine nuts, bread soaked in milk, marrow, liver, and egg). *Probusti*, veal-and-pork sausages, smoked with birchwood.

Desserts of the Trentino Trentino *pinza* (a dessert of bread soaked in milk, with sugar and figs); *rosada* (almond cream).

First Courses of the South Tyrol *Frittatensuppe*, shredded "pancakes" in meat broth; the word is a curious mixture of Italian (*frittata*, omelet) and German (*Suppe*, soup). *Canederli* or *Knödeln*, dumplings.

Second Courses of the South Tyrol Marinated chamois (antelope), Merano-style snails. Sauerkraut, sausages.

Desserts of the South Tyrol Strudel and *Zelten* (*pandolce*, sweet bread, with dried candied fruits).

TYPICAL PRODUCTS OF TRENTINO ALTO ADIGE

Cheeses Trentino Grana, Grauchese, Puzzone di Moena, Spressa, Vezzena, goat cheese.

Alto Adige *speck* (ham), *Hauswurst* (homemade salami).

Trout from the mountain streams.

Renette apples from the Val di Non.

Olive oil from Lake Garda.

Black bread from Val Pusteria, Val Venosta, and Val d'Ultimo made according to the recipe of the Benedictine monks, and in particular the

Ur-Paarl (double bread) made of rye flour, spelt, and herbs, among them dill, fenugreek, and cumin.

Honey from Bolzano.

TYPICAL BEVERAGES

Noble red wines.

PILGRIMS

The concept of Italy as a locus of continual movement, a place of transit and at the same time a point of arrival, has a fifteen-hundred-year history.

The major communication routes of the Mediterranean passed through Italy. But the most important thing is that from the eighth to the twelfth century the road leading to the Holy Land ran through its territory. Then, starting in the thirteenth century, Italy became not simply a country for all the world's Christians to pass through on the way to Jerusalem, but a destination for religious pilgrimages in and of itself. In 1240 Pope Gregory IX proclaimed an indulgence for anyone who had prayed a determined number of times in the basilicas of St. Peter and St. Paul. And starting in the fourteenth century, after the fall of the last bastion of Christianity in the East, St. John of Acre, in May 1291, urgings to come to Rome completely replaced prior recommendations to visit the Holy Sepulchre. And though for Dante the theme of the pilgrim remains linked to Palestine, Rome nevertheless wasted no time in transforming itself into the "New Jerusalem" for the faithful. Sacred relics, both from the Holy Land and from Constantinople, were transferred to Rome. Every Christian was expected to go to Rome at least once, preferably on foot, along special pilgrimage routes, to visit the *mirabilia urbis*, the venerable relics housed in the seven famous churches: San Pietro in Vaticano (St. Peter's), San Giovanni in Laterano (St. John Lateran), Santa Maria Maggiore (St. Mary Major), San Paolo fuori le Mura (St. Paul Outside the Walls), Santa Croce in Gerusalemme (Holy Cross in

Jerusalem), San Lorenzo fuori le Mura (St. Lawrence Outside the Walls), and San Sebastiano (St. Sebastian).

The first Christian jubilee was proclaimed in 1300, at a time that was quite propitious for establishing a ritual that would unify all Christians. The end of the thirteenth century had generated widespread calamity in Europe, more or less like the turmoil that had occurred in the year 1000. Struck by famine and poverty, people were anticipating the apocalypse and an ascetic mood prevailed everywhere. Among the monastic congregations was the Franciscan Order, which assigned the most prestigious place in the social hierarchy to the poor and disenfranchised. These circumstances gave rise to a new concept of the absolution of sins. Those who could not pay the contribution for future beatitude while still alive could walk to Rome in the year 1300, to participate in the solemn processions and celebrations. A papal bull issued on February 22 promised the complete remission of sins to those who would pray each day, for four weeks that year, in the Roman basilicas of St. Peter and St. Paul.

As a result, countless pilgrims flocked to the holy places of the city. In the Middle Ages, a particular name was attributed to those who made a vow to go to Rome: *romeo*. (It is not by chance that the enamored Romeo appears to Shakespeare's Juliet for the first time as an unknown wayfarer [*pellegrino*] whom she calls "good pilgrim.") Originally *romeo* was a Greek term for someone who made a pilgrimage to Palestine, but soon enough, based on a false etymology, it began to be applied to travelers going to Rome.

The journey of the *romeo* was anything but easy. Before setting off, the pilgrim made a will and testament, agreed with his wife upon the duration and forms of possible widowhood, paid his debts, made peace with everyone, received the blessing of the clergyman, and saw to his clothing: the ritual cloak, sandals, staff, and knapsack. The pilgrims who went to Spain, to Santiago de Compostela, glued a conch shell on their caps. Those who went to Jerusalem applied a palm branch, while the majority, on the way to Rome, affixed a badge to their hats portraying the acheropite image of Christ.

From every part of Europe, from North Africa and from Asia, the routes of the *romei* converged on Rome. The Amber Road ran from the Baltic Sea through the Tyrol; the Norman Road from Byzantium and Asia Minor through Puglia, in southeast Italy, a region of castles and Norman cathedrals. Inhabitants from the coasts of the Black Sea and from northern Europe (the Varangians) also came by way of the Norman Road, passing through Byzantium. The Via Emilia (or Via Romea) led to Rome from the Balkans and eastern Europe through Aquileia and Friuli, then through the Veneto and Romagna. The Via Francigena set out from Britain, passed through France, and crossed the Alpine pass of St. Bernard to reach Aosta, Piedmont, Liguria, and the Tuscan coast before finally reaching Rome.

The Via Francigena could be described as humanity's main pilgrimage route. It was traveled by pilgrims on their way to Palestine and by those headed for the sanctuary of Santiago de Compostela. The latter embarked on ships of the Republic of Genoa in the port of Santa Margherita Ligure, where the cathedral of San Giacomo still stands today and where propitiatory ceremonies are held for those who sail. And of course the Via Francigena was also used to transport goods by land to France, England, and Holland. It is only natural, then, that the wealthiest culinary areas should be situated along this road: the most civilized, most cultured, and most refined cuisines of medieval, Renaissance, and Baroque Europe.

The position of host country meant Italy had to furnish foreign travelers with washstands and clean plates. The cuisine, too, evolved in relation to the demand presented by the enormous number of wayfarers and travelers passing through Italy. Italians invented various forms of nonperishable products "packed to go" for the pilgrims, and made focaccias and breads capable of being kept a long time in a knapsack. Even today, innkeepers and restaurant owners give free rein to their imagination on such occasions, though their excessive zeal may sometimes lead them to surpass the limits of good taste. For example, tourist menus for the last jubilee, Jubilee 2000, included the following specialties for the enjoyment of pilgrims and guests: *abbacchio del camerlengo* (papal chamberlain's lamb), *medaglioni del cardinale* (cardinal's medallions), *porcini alla sistina* (Sistine-style porcini mushrooms), *insalata cupolona* (cupola salad), and *cicoria del fraticello* (young friar's chicory).

Medieval monasteries, outposts of Catholicism, were the principal beneficiaries and agents of this economy centered on religious tourism. Between the seventh and tenth centuries the Mediterranean Sea became a dangerous communication route, due to Arabic expansion and the weakening of the Byzantine Empire, as well as an increase in brigands and pirates. As a result, the economy of Europe experienced a tragic stagnation that eased only in the eleventh century, due to the Crusades. In the eighth century, the Arabs controlled the Mediterranean and prevented Europeans from traveling and trading. This led to the economic decline of the old European cities that had flourished in the Roman era, and had acquired importance in the fifth to eighth centuries as transit points for goods delivered to Mediterranean ports and distributed throughout the continent as far as the Rhine Valley.

The entire European merchant class experienced a crisis. The importation of fine goods was reduced to practically zero. Both papyrus (for writing) and herbs (for medicine and for cooking) became unobtainable. During this difficult period, only Italy managed to maintain an important network of cultural and trade relations. These relations existed among both the castles of the nobility and the episcopal palaces, but above all among the monasteries. Regardless of the economic and political conditions, men, goods, and information circulated from monastery to monastery, along the Via Francigena and the other pilgrim routes, under the protection of Catholic guards.

It is common knowledge that in the so-called dark period of the Middle Ages the monasteries preserved existing and ancient book culture, chronicled history, recorded languages, and created libraries. But the monasteries also saved the economy, along with agronomy, zootechnics, tourism, and gastronomic culture. And, it should be said, the geopolitical structure of Italy as well.

The energy and creativity of the monasteries influenced the territory's cuisine. A healthy vegetarian regimen was observed in the convents, and the Mediterranean diet was refined and improved. At the same time, the expert monastery cooks with the tall white hats (this head covering of the anchorites later became an attribute of cooks' uniforms in all restaurants) did not fail to incorporate elements of the pilgrims' cuisine.

Ancient texts, including those on agriculture, were studied in the monasteries, and collections of recipes were compiled. Popular cuisine was thus perfected and refined. The libraries of the monasteries were fonts of culinary philosophy and practical knowledge. The kitchens and vegetable gardens of the monasteries functioned as experimental laboratories. Olive oil (*olio santo,* holy oil) is used, as we know, in the administration of several sacraments of the Catholic liturgy. Therefore the task of cultivating olives scientifically and selecting the best varieties fell to the monasteries. Many types of oven products were also invented in the monasteries, where breads were prepared for daily distribution to the poor, as well as for sale, of course.

The Benedictine monks invented the Sicilian macaroni pie described by Giuseppe Tomasi di Lampedusa in *Il Gattopardo* (*The Leopard*), the Roman and Neapolitan rice croquettes (*arancini*), Ascoli-style olives (*olive ascolane*) with their complicated filling, the Sicilian dessert *cassata,* and miniature almond-paste figures. Friulian smoked *speck* and Montasio cheese were expressly created by the Benedictine monks for pilgrims along the Aquileia route, in the thirteenth century.

Moreover the abbeys and their cooks fostered the intermingling of cultural traditions. In the monasteries, in fact, monks from various countries encountered one another. The monk Domenico Cantucci, having gone to Spain to take part in the Inquisition, imported saffron (*Crocus sativus*) to the Dominican monastery of Gran Sasso, and as a result magnificent saffron plantations were developed in Abruzzi.

Lombardy

The cuisine of this region is more varied than any other, since it was influenced by all its neighbors, not to mention the rather perceptible contributions of foreign conquerors. The Spanish, who dominated the region in the sixteenth and seventeenth centuries, left saffron risotto, now a symbol of Lombard cuisine, as a memento of their stay. And the Austrians, who governed Lombardy in the eighteenth and nineteenth centuries, introduced the typical Wiener schnitzel, here renamed *cotoletta alla milanese* (Milanese-style veal cutlet). The Lombard gastronomical repertory combines the products of the Alps (protein-heavy, as in any mountain cuisine) and those of the Po Valley (largely made up of carbohydrates, as in any lowlands menu).

The only influences that are impossible to trace to Lombardy are those of seafood cuisine. Nevertheless, Milan boasts the best wholesale fish market in Italy, which supplies Milanese restaurants specializing in seafood dishes. The latter are very pleasant to dine in, even if they have no relation to Milanese traditions and authentic Lombard cuisine.

Bergamo and Brescia, at one time under the rule of La Serenissima (Venice), still have a Venetian-inspired cuisine. In Mantua and Crema, Emilian dishes predominate. And the mark of Swiss cuisine is felt in northern Lombardy, particularly in the lake region of Como, a border city.

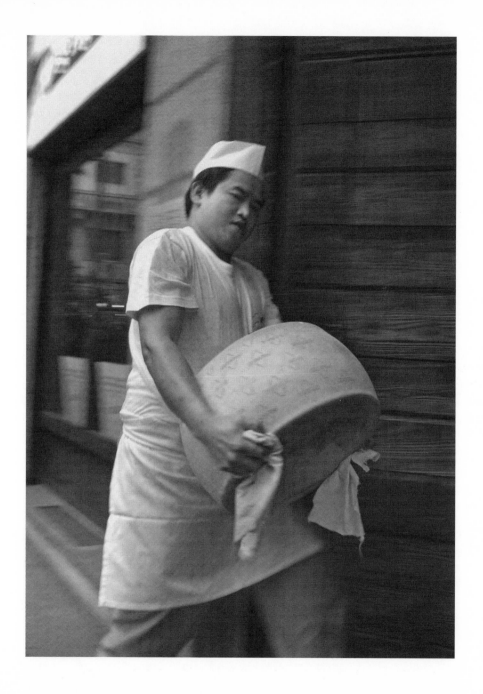

Como has been a cradle of culinary talent since very ancient times. It is not by chance that this city was the birthplace of the celebrated master Martino Rossi, author of one of the most important Italian books on the art of cooking, the *Liber de arte coquinaria* (1450). Martino, who worked for many years as the personal chef of the patriarch of Aquileia, also lived at the Venetian court, and later in Milan, with Condottiere Gian Giacomo Trivulzio. Trivulzio, formerly in the service of the Aragons of Naples and then of the king of France, who named him marshal and commander of the French troops in Italy, later entered the service of the dukes of Milan, where the court had become the political and cultural center for relations between Italy and Switzerland. From Martino we know that by the fifteenth century the fundamental component of Como's cuisine was freshwater fish, just as it is today: trout, perch, tench, shad, and small dried fish, soaked in vinegar and fried (*missoltini* or *misultit*). Risotto with perch spread from Como to all of northern Lombardy.

The Napoleonic invasion and rampant Francomania in the eighteenth century left behind a very particular dish: the *cassoela*, or casserole, analogous to the *pot-au-feu* of southern France. Composed of meat and vegetables, it is a substantial one-dish meal, generally served on Sundays and accompanied by polenta; elaborate and difficult to digest, it is certainly not to be eaten on one's lunch break. But other, more convenient one-dish meals allow the hardworking, rushed, methodical Lombard to sit down hastily at the table, fill up swiftly, and plunge back into his everyday work routine.

"The alimentary habits of the Milanese people are heavily influenced by their frenetic life: always in a hurry and assailed by the need to appear efficient, they resign themselves to considering food as simply a matter of loading up on nourishing substances necessary to accrue energy so they can produce and work with joy and diligence," writes Enrico Bertolino in a little book that is part of the genial series Le Guide Xenofobe. Un Ritratto Irriverente dei Migliori Difetti dei Popoli d'Italia (The xenophobic guides. An irreverent look at the best faults of the people of Italy). "Some eat only because the majority of antistress drugs must be taken with a full stomach."[1]

In any case it would be somewhat reductive to equate Lombard alimentary habits with the label "Milanese."

In the early and late Middle Ages, following the Lombard invasion of the sixth century, the primary city of this region was not Milan (which has dominated Lombardy only since the fifteenth century), but Pavia, capital of the Lombard realm. Pavia is a regal city, though its name at first deceives us, alluding not to imperial authority, but to papal power (in Latin, *Papia*). In the Middle Ages, Pavia enjoyed unparalleled prosperity by virtue of its favorable position on the only water route that allowed Venetian trading vessels to sail from the Adriatic to Piedmont. At the beginning of the eleventh century, while goods were in short supply in most of the beleaguered continent, in Pavia one could buy anything. Over time, merchants from France, Spain, England, Germany, or the East stopped in Pavia more and more frequently to buy goods from the Venetians and bring them back to their countries. Therefore, as northern trade developed, the importance of the route to the north grew.

Pavia entered a difficult period beginning in 1176, when the city (along with Frederick Barbarossa, who governed it) was defeated by the Lombard League (Milan, Bergamo, Lecco, Cremona, Mantua, and Brescia) in the Battle of Legnano. With the opening later on of a new trade route through the St. Gotthard Pass, leading to the Rhine Valley and passing through Basel and Lucerne, Milan's ascendancy began. The city was able to wrest regional supremacy from Pavia specifically after Archbishop Ottone Visconti was proclaimed its ruler in 1278, gaining not only religious power but also civil authority over the city. Thanks to this dual government, the city was strengthened even more. With the growth of Milanese power, Pavia and Milan exchanged roles, and Pavia became a political appendage of Milan. When a tunnel was dug under St. Gotthard in 1882, Milan no longer had any reason to fear possible competition for its role as Europe's main communications node.

The Duke of Milan, Gian Galeazzo Visconti (1351–1402), spent his summer holidays in the outskirts of Pavia and built a sumptuous castle there, where he loved to surround himself with literary figures. A taste for erudite pastimes, poetry, and refined society had been passed down to the duke from his uncle, Giovanni Visconti, ruler of Milan, who had hosted the exiled Petrarch at his court from 1353 to 1361. And so his residence in Pavia was expressly intended to pass time in a dazzling way, and the most sumptuous Renaissance banquets and feasts (whose main dishes were fresh meats and game) were given there. Leonardo da Vinci, arriving at the court of Ludovico il Moro (the second ruler of the Sforza family, which had supplanted the Visconti dynasty) in Milan in 1483, designed hydraulic systems and canals, among other things, that are still used today to irrigate the rice paddies that surround Pavia and extend almost to the gates of Milan.

It is clear from both the tourist guides and the toponymy (Via Laghetto and Vicolo Laghetto, the street and lane in the historic center) that from Leonardo da Vinci's time until Mussolini's, Milan could boast an efficient system of canals (*navigli*) connected to the Ticino and Po rivers. Milan was therefore a port serving five seas. Blocks of Candoglia rose-colored marble and Ossola granite were transported along the shipping routes through Lake Maggiore directly to the Duomo, whose construction took more than six centuries. Mussolini later ordered a large part of these channels to be filled in and covered with cobblestones, to combat the excessive mosquitoes and traffic congestion.

Stendhal was enthusiastic about the intelligent planning of the city's traffic (only a memory today) and about the elegant, expert paving (whose beautiful remains are still visible in the center of present-day Milan), and he described the drainage outlets, canals, and sewers both in the city itself and in its suburbs in a detailed report, accompanied by sketches and recorded in his diary.[2]

Milan's supremacy over the surrounding territory was possible thanks to the city's excellent water supply, which had a colossal reserve: the glaciers of the Alps! Flowing down from the alpine summits into subterranean caves, the meltwater from the mountain snows fills vast basins found in Milan's subsoil. You can guess this from the city's boulevards and piazzas, where, in spite of everything, the scrubby plants in the flower beds do not wither even in summer.

In the countryside, present-day irrigation systems have been perfected since Leonardo's time, and include a system of small fountains that spray a fine, dewy mist over the pastures and fields. The temperature of this mist is maintained at a constant 8 degrees C, which protects the fields and pastures from heat waves and drought, as well as from frost, making it possible for growers and breeders to yield several harvests of fodder a year. Hence the flourishing cattle-breeding industry, one of the areas in which Lombardy's agriculture has specialized. Although the economy in Lombardy is mostly industrial, the region holds second place in agriculture in Italy (after Emilia Romagna).

"The city of Bologna nestles against a ridge of hills which look towards the north, much as Bergamo reclines against a similar range of hills which face the south. Between the two there stretches the proud Vale of Lombardy, the most extensive cultivated valley in all the civilised world," Stendhal wrote on December 28, 1816.[3]

It was in this man-made paradise that Lombardy developed its economic power. In his *Notizie sulla Lombardia* (Notes about Lombardy), Carlo Cattaneo describes a land "nine-tenths of which is not the work of nature; it is the work of our own hands; it is an artificial country."[4]

Traveling from Milan to Pavia, Stendhal recorded on December 16, 1816:

From Milan to where I am at present, the highway cuts through some of the richest farming-land in Europe. At every turning, the traveller beholds dykes of running water, spreading fertility on either hand; his road hugs the banks of the deep-water canal which forms the shipping-link between Milan and Venice and gives access by sea to the Americas; on the other hand, however, he may as likely as not find himself set upon by highwaymen under the very glare of noon.[5]

With so much water available, Lombardy's two main crops are rice, grown in the Lomellina Valley (that is, between Pavia and Piedmont) and southwest of Mantua, and the grain harvested in all accessible valleys, to feed the flourishing swine and cattle industry. Indeed, in the thirteenth century, Bonvesin de la Riva, who initiated the study of grammar and was a tertiary in the Order of the Humiliati, wrote in his work *De magnalibus urbis Mediolani*: "Our lands, fertile with fruitful yield, produce a very great and very admirable abundance of every kind of grain." According to Bonvesin, thirty thousand bulls plowed the Milanese fields, and thanks to him we have impressive descriptions of the abundance of meats in the city markets.

Earlier, in the eighth century, folkloristic works were written that exalted the fabulous wealth of this region's meat, wheat, and wines. Here the food is caloric and substantial: perhaps precisely because people work hard and zealously, with an almost Calvinistic perseverance, from early morning until late in the evening. With no time to sit down at the table, Lombards find a way to transform traditional food into nourishing fast food. For example, the slab of beef, half a kilogram per portion, that in Tuscany is grilled over coals and known as steak Florentine in Milan is served in slices: all you have to do is exactly that, slice it width-wise, cook it two minutes, and you don't even have to chew it—swallow it and off you go. You can fill up even on eighty grams. Duty first, pleasure second.

In spite of their great prosperity, Lombards value parsimony, and their cuisine makes excellent use of leftovers. If it's still good, why throw it out? In fact the Milanese are proud of their characteristic *riso al salto*, or rice sauté (risotto from the day before sautéed in a pan) and of their *mondeghili*, meatballs made with chopped leftover stewed meat. This dish is sometimes served in Milanese homes with olives and little balls of rice, to accompany an aperitif.

Giovanni Raiberti referred to Milan as "the meatball capital," which does not appear to be a flattering judgment. In *I promessi sposi*, Renzo, Tonio, and Gervaso go to an inn shortly before the "surprise wedding," and Manzoni has them eat a large plate of meatballs. When the writer's mother, Giulia Beccaria, asked him the reason for such a choice, "don Lisander" (Alessandro) replied: "Dear mama, you made me eat so many *polpette* from the time I was a child that I thought it only fair to make the characters in my novel taste them too."[6]

Among the typical products of Lombardy, one stands out as a political statement, so to speak. It is the cheese Bel Paese, created in 1906 by the entrepreneur Egidio Galbani from Melzo, a town situated between Milan and Bergamo. Galbani, inspired by the success of French cheeses, decided to offer the international market a product that would have a less pronounced taste and a less insistent odor than traditional Italian cheeses. The name of the new cheese was invented in one of the earliest marketing campaigns in the history of the Italian food industry, with Galbani appropriating the title of a book by the abbot Antonio Stoppani for his "patented" product. Published in 1875, *Il bel paese* (The beautiful country) had enjoyed great success among the Milanese bourgeoisie. In its time Stoppani's book was one of the first attempts at a geographic and geopolitical description of the unified nation's effort to openly pursue a common sense of self. The expression *il bel paese*, common parlance in Italy by now, was used for the first time by Dante in the *Inferno: "del bel paese là dove 'l sì suona"* (of that fair land where *sì* is heard).[7] Here *bel paese* refers to the region where the Italian language is spoken, that is, the land of the "language of *sì*." Petrarch applied the expression *bel paese* to Italy as a geographic area defined by the Apennines, the Alps, and the sea: *"il bel paese / ch'Appennin parte e 'l mar circonda et l'Alpe"* (that fair country / that the Apennines divide and the sea and Alps surround).[8] In Antonio Stoppani's book the descriptive expression appeared for the first time as a publicity slogan, and it was a universally accepted formula by the twentieth century. Bel Paese cheese was one of the first attempts to promote a brand through an ideal image.

The list of Lombard cheeses is infinite. The northern half of the region is made up of Alpine pastures (Valtellina, Valchiavenna, and so on), where cheeses are produced mainly from cow's milk, while in many other regions of Italy, where the mountains are barer and the grass less succulent, goat or sheep cheeses prevail. In order not to have to depend on its neighbor Emilia Romagna—the other main producer of cow's milk cheese—for Parmesan, Lombardy created an aged, dry cheese of its own, irreplaceable in the kitchen. It's called Grana. Grana may be *padano* (from the Po Valley), the most familiar and most widespread, or *lodigiano* (from Lodi). The latter, produced in small quantities in the area around Lodi for specialists and connoisseurs, is aged for at least four years, and even after that length of time, the cheese is still said to "shed a tear," that is, it oozes drops of whey when it is cut. Two fundamental varieties of Grana *lodigiano* are known; their taste depends on the time of the milking. The first is the *maggengo*, or *maggiolino* (May), Grana *lodigiano* made from summer milk; it is produced with milk obtained from Saint George's Day to Saint Michael's Day (from April 23 to September 29). The second is the Grana *lodigiano vernengo* (winter), made with winter milk, which has a different flavor and a different vitamin content.

Gorgonzola cheese, produced in the provinces of Bergamo, Biella, Brescia, Como, Cremona, Cuneo, Lecco, Lodi, Milan, Novara, Pavia, Varese, Verbania, and Vercelli, and in the territory of Casale Monferrato, needs no introduction. It is distributed in food stores and restaurants throughout the world. A brother to Roquefort, green-veined, sticky, and viscous, with a delicately pungent flavor, it is delicious and unparalleled at the end of a meal. Accompanied by pears, it can create a uniquely surprising dish. Drizzled with honey, it makes an elegant dessert. Italians would probably agree to give up many things, but never Gorgonzola. The partisan diary of Giorgio Amendola, well-known exponent of the Italian Communist Party and head of the Resistance during World War II, attests to this. The clandestine hero describes his secret journey from Milan to Bologna in 1942 this way:

> After Lodi it was necessary to make a detour to take a ferry that went to an island in the Po. The column stayed on the island a long time because daylight had come. The journey became a rustic excursion. A trattoria supplied us with rabbit cacciatore, a wonderful salad, and above all a delicious Gorgonzola, tastier than I have ever eaten since, with plump, shiny worms that crawled out onto the plate.[9]

The sight of Gorgonzola did not always provoke such feelings of gratitude in everyone, however. The historian Massimo Caprara tells of the Mantuan socialist Andrea Bertazzoni, who fled to the Soviet Union after being sentenced to twenty years' imprisonment in Italy. Before getting into difficulties, Bertazzoni had worked as secretary of an agricultural cooperative in San Benedetto Po, and had specialized in zootechnics and the breeding of milch cows. Once in Russia, he decided to set up a dairy concern in the region of Rostov and managed the production of this cheese factory with success and satisfaction, dedicating all his free time to socialist edification. The factory produced Gorgonzola. In 1936, even before the outbreak of Stalinist terror, the cheese came to the attention of one of the heads of the local GPU (Gosudarstvennoe Pravovoe Upravlenie, the Communist Secret Police, a forerunner of the KGB), Viktor Garm, and based on the external appearance of the product, the Italian specialist was immediately arrested for sabotage. Newspaper headlines read: SOCIALIST-FASCIST SABOTAGE. TROTSKYIST AGENTS POISON THE CHEESE. The intervention of the people's commissioner to the food industry, Anastas Mikoyan, was indispensable; though the word "Gorgonzola" meant nothing to him, he had some idea of French Roquefort. An expert in dairy technology from the commissariat of the people, a Professor Slepkov, was sent to Rostov, and confirmed the conscientiousness of the manufacturers. Nevertheless, during the war he had to change professions, suffered unimaginable hunger, became a shoemaker, and, pickax in hand, contributed to the construction of the Fergana Canal and slept in the caravansaries, on the hard earth of the Sunni Muslims.[10]

The northern part of Lombardy is completely occupied by high mountains and the south by plains cultivated as rice paddies. It was in these same lowlands that the fascinating heroine of Giuseppe De Santis's *Riso amaro* (*Bitter Rice*) worked. In the film, the unforgettable actress Silvana Mangano played the part of a *mondina* (rice picker), one of the women who worked as seasonal laborers, day and night for two months, in water up to their knees, pulling up the plants in order to earn a few sacks of rice for themselves and their families. The job of *pilota* (husker) is also related to rice growing. It had nothing to do with aviation: *piloti* were the laborers assigned to husk the rice, separating the grains from the glume. The word *pilota* derives from *pilare*, to husk or hull. Still today in Villimpenta, near Mantua, the *sagra* of *risotto alla pilota* (*pilota*-style risotto) is celebrated on the second Sunday of May. On that day, a gigantic cauldron full of risotto with pork, spices, and herbs is carried into the piazza.

Risotto, as is by now known throughout the world, is the center and fulcrum of Milanese cuisine. The original risotto was made with ox marrow, golden in color and known for its medicinal taste, because the saffron used to flavor it was at the time a popular folk remedy for various ailments. Legend has it that the originator of the recipe was a master glassmaker from the studio of the famous Valerio di Fiandra (creator of the stained-glass windows of the Duomo of Milan) who in 1574 dropped a paintbrush dipped in saffron yellow into the rice. Is it true that every dish, in that century of opulence, the Baroque era, contained real gold? In our days this myth is upheld by the distinguished restaurateur Gualtiero Marchesi, on whose plates of risotto a small lozenge of the thinnest edible gold leaf actually floats. And is it true that the saffron added to Milanese risotto has the magical properties of a love potion?

In the sixteenth century Bartolomeo Scappi provided this recipe for Lombard risotto:

> To make a dish of Lombard-style rice *sottestata* [browned] with boneless chicken, *cervellate* [a kind of pork blood sausage with brains], and egg yolks.
>
> Take the rice cleaned as described above and cook it in a broth in which capons, geese, and blood sausages have been cooked; and when it is cooked so that it is firm, take part of this rice and place it in a large earthenware plate or one of silver, or rather tin, and sprinkle it with cheese, sugar, and cinnamon; then place over this rice some tiny dabs of fresh butter and boneless capon breast and goose with blood sausage cut into pieces, and again sprinkle with cheese, sugar, and cinnamon. In this way three layers are created, the last drizzled with melted fresh butter and sprinkled with the same mixture; it is then placed in an oven which is not too hot, and left to bake for half an hour until it takes on a little color; sprinkle with rosewater and serve hot. This rice can also be prepared another way: that is, once cooked, place butter on a plate, along with slices of fresh, unsalted *provatura* [mozzarella made from buffalo milk], and sprinkle with sugar and cinnamon and grated cheese; over that place the rice, and on the rice put fresh raw egg yolks, depending on the amount of rice, having however made depressions in the rice where the egg yolks will be placed; then over the egg yolks add more slices of *provatura* sprinkled with sugar, cheese, and cinnamon, and then cover it all with some more rice. In this way two or three layers can be made, with a little butter on top; let it bake over hot coals, or in the oven as above, and serve hot.

As we see, the addition of saffron to Milanese risotto was not yet in practice. And this is not surprising: saffron came to Lombardy with the Spanish, and became established in Milanese cuisine not in the sixteenth century, but in the seventeenth.

While this one gastronomic emblem of Milan comes from Spain, the other, the veal cutlet, is of Austrian origin. This, the aforementioned Wiener schnitzel, reigns on a par with risotto on the Milanese menu, though it is called *cotoletta alla milanese* (veal cutlet dipped in beaten egg and bread crumbs). The Milanese, of course, assert that it was not the Viennese schnitzel that inspired the Milanese *cotoletta*, but vice versa. Supposedly the proof is in a certain letter from Marshal Radetzky to Count

Attems, aide-de-camp to Emperor Franz Josef, that refers to the Milanese cutlet as an amazing innovation. What reason would Marshal Radetzky have had to be amazed if the Viennese cutlet had already been discovered by culinary science? (Actually, contrary to Italians' wishes, the marshal might very well have been amazed. The Milanese cutlet, whose name comes specifically from *costola*, rib, includes the bone, while the Wiener schnitzel is boneless. The Milanese cutlet is not dredged in flour and then breaded like the Viennese one, but dipped into the egg and directly into the bread crumbs, which adhere firmly to the meat's surface. By contrast, the slice of meat that is hidden inside the Viennese schnitzel slips easily and readily out of its coating. On the whole, the Milanese *cotoletta* and Wiener schnitzel are two different dishes, though inspired by similar philosophies.)

Another typical product of Lombardy, absolutely inimitable and esteemed the world over, is *mostarda* from Cremona. It is produced starting with cooked, concentrated grape must, to which crushed mustard grains are added. Fruit—cherries, plums, pears, figs—is then left to steep in it. This sweet, spicy preparation with a divine taste is served with boiled meat.

Lombardy is hardworking, generous, solid, stubborn, and independent. Milan, by contrast, seems to have decided that having fun is laudable and that worrying is counterproductive. So it extended Carnival season to the maximum ("maximum" meaning four additional days, though even only four days subtracted from the Lenten period is worth something). The festival's desserts are particularly opulent. The cake prepared for Christmas, *panettone*, is baked and served in paper. The traditional dough of these breads contains candied fruit and raisins; in recent times, almonds, custard cream, and bits of chocolate have also been added. Then—to hell with the expense!—the cake is served warm at the table, dusted with confectioner's sugar, covered with frosting, and spread with mascarpone. The Easter cake is called the *colomba* (dove), and it is filled with caloric ingredients that reflect the same enthusiasm that characterizes *panettone*.

The cuisine of the opulent city of Mantua deserves separate attention. During the Renaissance, the architect Leon Battista Alberti and the painters Andrea Mantegna, Giulio Romano, Rubens, and van Dyck worked at the court of the Gonzagas. Europe's first operas, composed by Monteverdi and Guarini, were performed in the salons of Mantuan palazzos (without need of any scenography). At the court of Marchesa Isabella d'Este (1474–1539) banquets were given whose memory lives on today, thanks primarily to one of the leading Renaissance poets, Teofilo Folengo

(1491–1544). Folengo signed himself with the pseudonym Merlin Cocai in his famous poem *Baldus*, where the hero Cingar, describing Jove's cuisine, provides us with the twenty best recipes of the ducal table.

Queen Christina of Sweden (portrayed in a famous film of the early thirties by the inimitable Greta Garbo) went to Rome to visit the Pope in 1655 and converted to Catholicism (in Rome she is said to have founded, among other things, a society of sciences and letters, the Royal Academy, a forerunner of the Academy of Arcadia). In the course of her travels in Italy, the queen stayed at the sumptuous courts of the gentry and on November 27 was a guest of the Gonzaga princes in Mantua. The cook engaged for the occasion was one of the most illustrious and highly paid in Italy, as well as a celebrated writer: Bartolomeo Stefani, author of the book *L'arte di ben cucinare* (The art of cooking well), 1662. In his treatise Stefani transcribed from an old notebook the menu of the reception in honor of the queen, at which he had served strawberries and spinach in winter (as if both he and the queen were living in the twenty-first century). The main purpose of such cuisine, in keeping with Baroque tastes, was to inspire the awe and admiration of the guests.

Such lavish banquets were risky, however: the overfed guests might suddenly lose their taste for new dishes. To combat satiety, Mantuans began chewing slivers of Parmesan cheese between the sixteenth and seventeenth courses and between the twentieth and twenty-first courses. Even today it is thought that the taste of Parmesan "cleanses" the mouth and helps reduce strong impressions, preventing tastes and sensations from overlapping.

TYPICAL DISHES OF LOMBARDY

Antipasti A wine broth (*bev'r in vin*), invented in the city of Mantua, is sometimes served as an aperitif (as a rule the wine added is Lambrusco, imported from adjacent Emilia). In accordance with the ritual, this wine broth was drunk before supper, standing in front of the fireplace. Another characteristic appetizer of the traditional cuisine is *nervitt* (veal cartilage), calf's-foot tendons and meat boiled, cubed, and served with a spicy sauce. The above-mentioned *mondeghili*, a dish of old Milan, are meatballs made with leftover stewed meat, eggs, and Grana cheese.

First Courses Different varieties of *agnolotti* (half-moon pasta) and ravioli; the *marubini* of Cremona; *agnoli* or *agnolini* (in Mantua in particular), ravioli filled with capon and marrow with cinnamon, cloves, and cheese; the *casonsei* of Bergamo and Brescia, filled with sausage or spinach and egg, raisins, cheese, and bread crumbs; the *tortelli* filled with pumpkin in Mantua. And in addition the *cappelloni* of Lomellina and the *pizzoccheri* of Valtellina.

Characteristic first courses also include soups, in Pavia the famous *zuppa pavese* (Pavian soup), made with eggs and hard bread. Typical of Lombardy is the soup of fava beans with *guanciale* (pork cheek fat) and gnocchi. It is made each year on November 1, All Saints' Day, since in many cultures the fava bean, which grows underground, is considered a symbol of the link with the afterlife; the dead are remembered on November 2, All Souls' Day.

Other typical dishes of Lombardy are the *gnocchetti alla lariana* (Larianstyle gnocchi) of Lake Como; broth with *mariconde* (little dough balls made with egg, cheese, butter, and bread) in Brescia and Mantua; Milanese soup with rice; Milanese risotto; risotto with snails; risotto with pork cutlet and with *trigoli* (water chestnuts); risotto according to the recipe of the Cistercian monks of the Charterhouse of Pavia, with freshwater shrimp, mushrooms, and peas, strictly without butter (the good monks' diet is always lean).

Bergamo is the land of *polenta taragna* (stirred polenta), for which buckwheat flour is mixed with cornmeal and seasoned with cheese: Bitto or Scimùd (both classic cheeses of the region); the polenta must be continuously stirred (*tarare*) with a long stick, the *tarài* (stirrer), to prevent it from sticking to the bottom of the pot; hence its name.

In past centuries in Bergamo, before the advent of ecological principles, *polenta e osei* (polenta with birds) was prepared by

> catching blackbirds *al rocolo* [alive, using nets]. This is one of the most popular pastimes in Lombardy. The women have a passion for *uzei colla polenta*. Towards the end of autumn, huge numbers of small birds (*uzei*) are caught in nets, then roasted and served up on a dish of freshly-made *polenta*—a yellow dough compounded of maize-flour and boiling water. This *polenta* is the staple food, winter and summer alike, of the Lombard peasant.[11]

Today the dessert version is more popular, where the polenta is replaced by *pan di Spagna* (Italian sponge cake) and yellow marzipan, while the little birds are made of chocolate.

Second Courses *Cassoela* (hearty soup): savoy cabbage expressly picked only after the first frost to be more tender when cooked, stewed with the less noble parts of the pig, such as rind, feet, ribs, and head; wild duck baked in a clay mold, in the style of Valcuvia (after baking, the terra-cotta shell is cracked with a hammer and discarded along with the duck's feathers, which remain stuck to the clay). Various types of stews and braised meats, to be enjoyed with Cremona *mostarda*. Milanese *cotoletta* (veal cutlet). Hare pie. Osso bucco: veal shanks sliced crosswise, with a portion of marrow in the center: this is considered to be the best part of the dish. *Polenta alla lodigiana* (Lodi-style), which in some way recalls *mozzarella in carrozza* (the "carriage" being the bread): two slices of polenta forming a sandwich with a slice of cheese in the middle, dipped in egg, breaded, and fried).

Stewed frogs; pigeons in a timbale or crust; *busecca*, stewed beef tripe. Also, in all the towns adjacent to the Lombard lakes, the typical freshwater fish, such as shad, char, lake salmon, trout, eel, grayling, perch, carp, burbot, pike, tench, whitefish, and chub.

Desserts Crumb cake (*torta sbrisolona*) of Mantua. Paradise cake (*torta paradiso*) of Pavia. All Souls' Day bread (*pan dei morti*): macaroons, raisins, dried figs, almonds, egg whites, cocoa to taste. This is eaten during the first days of November to commemorate the day of the dead, along with "bones of the dead" (*ossa dei morti*), made of sugar, an Italian tradition similar to that of American Halloween candies. On these days the dead, like the Lares of the ancient Romans, return to inhabit the ancestral home. They must be mellowed with sweets so that they will not do any harm. Therefore these sweet breads are placed around the house for the spirits. At one time, the bread for the dead would be completely devoured or reduced to crumbs by the following morning. Who could say whether it had been eaten by the dead or by mice?

Pan de mei, or bread made of sweet millet (today made with cornmeal), was also originally a ritual food. Millet, like lentils, has a special role in magical beliefs. But unlike lentils, which are associated with themes of death and hell, millet is a symbol of resurrection and immortality. Millet bread is eaten on St. George's Day (April 24) to augur a prosperous growing season.

TYPICAL PRODUCTS OF LOMBARDY

Cheeses Bitto from the valleys of the Bitto (Valtellina), Gorgonzola, Grana *padano*, Grana *lodigiano* (Lodi), provolone from the Valpadana, Lombard Quartirolo, Taleggio, Tombea, Valtellina Casera. The cheese Bagoss from Bagolino. Soft cheeses: Casolet dell'Adamello, Crescenza, Formaggelle del Monte, mascarpone. Pannerone of Lodi, a cheese that is one of the rarest in the entire worldwide dairy scene, is made without any salt. Lauded in the gastronomic guides are Silter and Casolin, peasant cheeses from around Mantua.

Cured Meats Salamis of Brianza, Varzi, and Milan, *bresaola* (a sausage made with salted meat, flavored with natural spices and wine, and subsequently aged), and *cotechino bianco* (white pork sausage). The inimitable *prosciutto di capra* (goat prosciutto) referred to as "violin" (or Stradivarius), which has a most unusual shape, and which is sliced by holding it between the shoulder and the chin, just as a violin is held: this mini-prosciutto weighs only a kilogram and is the gastronomic emblem of the Valchiavenna.

Grains Buckwheat from Valtellina; rice from Lomellina and the province of Mantua.

Fruit Apples from Valtellina, melons from Viadana, Mantuan pears.

Vegetables Asparagus from Cilavegna, onions from Sermide.

Olive oil from Lake Garda. Cremona *mostarda*.

TYPICAL BEVERAGES

Campari aperitif. Campari was created in Milan, at Caffé Zucca, in 1867. Before the unification of Italy, the Milanese drank *barbajada*: chocolate mixed with coffee and whipped cream (named after the man who created it at the beginning of the nineteenth century, the celebrated opera impresario and discoverer of Rossini, Domenico Barbaja). They also enjoyed *agher*, made of lemon and tamarind; *orzata*, familiar to readers of French detective fiction as *orchade* (at that time *orzata* was a drink made from a syrup of barley sprouts that was diluted in water, while today it is made from a syrup of sweet ground almonds); Marsala and various liqueurs; black cherry syrup . . . but Campari had not yet been invented. After Italy was formed in 1860–62, the Galleria Vittorio

Emanuele was constructed to celebrate national unity and the new aperitif was created.

Caffé Zucca, where Campari was first created, has survived until today, and from the Galleria looks out toward the Duomo of Milan. For the sake of historical accuracy, it should be noted that the Zucca was originally situated a few steps away from its current location, and bore the name of its owner, Gaspare Campari, the inventor of the famous aperitif. Later the café moved to the site it occupies today and was renamed Camparino. It subsequently changed names a number of times, until it got its current name, Zucca.

In any event, Campari was made for the first time right here, and only later on did anyone think to distribute it throughout the world.

SLOW FOOD

Founded in 1989, the Slow Food Association, as is evident from its name, is committed to counteracting the rise of fast food in daily life. As the rhythm of life accelerates in every way, many people no longer pay attention to the little things in life—the nuances of taste, color, and shape. Flavor constitutes a rich national heritage, and unique flavor should be preserved and protected, duly classified on the scroll of history. The message of Slow Food is simple and straightforward: we possess an invaluable food heritage that is worthy of preservation from a cultural standpoint. Let museums preserve these rarities, and people will propagate them and begin to use them. Otherwise human haste produces absurd results: we work uninterruptedly, and we become poorer. Let us therefore save those precious things that, once lost, can never be re-created.

The keyword of the Slow Food movement is "biodiversity." It is clear even to a child that if a genetic combination disappears from the globe, it will be impossible to restore.

The association has built structures where people gladly gather to get to know one another and spend their free time (or work time) rescuing genes on their way to extinction. And it is not just a matter of saving genes, but also books, words, and technologies. It is a noble, prestigious, and joyous occupation, and it all takes place against a backdrop of exquisite food, amid wonderful aromas given off by casseroles.

One of the first alarm signals was sounded by Slow Food in the nineties, when people became aware that the Burlina breed of cow was close to extinction. The cheese Mor-

lacco del Grappa, a typical product of the Veneto, is produced from the Burlina's milk. Breeders, oriented toward larger-scale production, had practically ceased breeding these cows, so that only a few specimens still existed in the provinces of Treviso, Vicenza, and Verona. Since the early nineties, the Slow Food Association has been committed to the effort of saving the Burlina. Half the movement's members took to wearing very noticeable T-shirts adorned with a picture of the cow. Now the Burlinas are protected like pandas, and their number is beginning to grow.

Slow Food achieved remarkable results in safeguarding some breeds of pig as well. In 2000, only several hundred specimens of the famous Tuscan pigs, black as Satan, remained in the world. This breed is known as Cinta Senese (Belted Sienese) because the body of the pig is encircled by a rosy-white band. Like the Mora Romagnola and the

Nero Siciliano, black pigs from Romagna and Sicily, respectively, the Cinta Senese had been practically supplanted by the Yorkshire, prized for its quick growth, and by the rosy, prolific Large White. Yet the Belted Sienese, muscular and independent, as it is described in an encyclopedia, "with a strong maternal attitude," had been grazing in the oak groves of Tuscany as early as the thirteenth century. A black pig with a white belt makes a fine showing in an early Renaissance fresco, Ambrogio Lorenzetti's *Il buon governo* (Good government) in the Palazzo Pubblica of Siena (1338). It is totally unique. The breed is immune from many contemporary diseases. And yet it is nearly extinct! Why? Simply put, it seemed to some people that breeding this strain was not so expedient. Ten years ago there were twenty thousand head, and today only four hundred remain. Will humanity allow this creature to disappear from the planet? Slow Food initiatives protect the Belted Sienese as well as the Black Romagna and the Black Sicilian.

The breeding of the Black Romagna, practiced in the provinces of Ravenna and Forli, was already considered unprofitable in 1949, when approximately 22,000 head remained. By the beginning of the nineties, only eighteen of these pigs had survived. Slow Food activists set to work, but their actions were not sufficient, and the Italian section of the World Wildlife Fund and the University of Turin intervened. Directing the effort was the devotee and agronomist M. A. Lazzari, who was able to save the last eighteen pigs of Romagna. Today these swine are bred on forty-six farms, not only in Romagna, but also in Piedmont and the Marches, and it actually seems that in this particular case man will be able to lend nature a hand.

Slow Food also protects an agreeable crustacean, the Crapolla shrimp, found along the Sorrento coast. This shrimp is marked by its long, narrow head and by the pale yellow stripes that encircle its body. Moreover, some farmers from Leonforte in Sicily are saving the black lentils of Enna, starting with eight hundred grams of seed that they were able to recover throughout Sicily.

In the student activist years of the youth protest movements at the end of the eighties, Carlo Petrini, a sociologist at the University of Trento, established the first Slow Food group in the most practical, rationalist region of Italy, Piedmont. The movement's idealism, rebellion, and humor, combined with Piedmontese pragmatism, produced an excellent result. Today the organization numbers 83,000 members and has spread well beyond Italian borders. Following Italy's lead, Germany, Switzerland, the United States, France, and Japan joined the movement. In Italy each section is called a *condotta* (district) or *presidio* (garrison), in the rest of the world a *convivium*. Slow Food is represented in 107 different countries of the world.

The organization's efforts are directed at opposing the standardization of tastes, informing consumers, maintaining traditions, and safeguarding biodiversity. In addition, it aims to preserve traditional structures and places where food has been successfully prepared in the past, for many decades or perhaps centuries. Slow Food encourages the restoration of historic restaurants and organizes courses, tastings, and trips. Locally there are over eight hundred chapters in sixty-five foreign countries and four hundred subchapters in Italy. The publisher Slow Food Editore has put out more than sixty original volumes in ten years. The movement also issues the periodicals *Slow* and *Slowfood*.

At a subconscious level, the word "slow" evokes the image of leisurely epicurean banquets, where diners voluptuously savor every microgram of precious food. Having been present at Slow Food luncheons and dinners, I can assure you that the tasting of the food in and of itself is not accompanied by any theatrics or exaggerated self-gratification whatsoever. Slow does not refer to the tasting, but to the sweeping of the crumbs from the tablecloth, say, or the wait for the dishes to finally be served. The essential thing in these encounters is not the goal of satisfying one's stomach, what in ancient times was called "the sin of gluttony," but something completely different: the act of getting together, the conversations had around the table. In Slow Food trattorias and restaurants, as in literary cafés, the most diverse aspects of the culture are discussed, and there are book presentations. The food is combined with public talks and interventions, and the result is a slowing down of the experience of time. But everyone eats at a normal pace. And when it comes to work, the Slow organization is very fast indeed.

Sometimes in other countries people have a rather vague idea about the specifics of this organization, as in this description from a Russian website:

Slow Food is a very influential organization and is anything but poor. Its means and reputation derive from the wealth and social position of its voluntary members: modern-day sybarites, impassioned by the idea of the slow, contemplative consumption of the gifts of nature and agriculture. These individuals detest the hamburger chains just as the militant "anti-globalists" do. But unlike the latter, they don't go around breaking windows, preferring to expend money, rather than adrenalin . . . The idea of taking part in Slow Food may seem boring to many. Indeed, how enjoyable can it be to attend an hour-long lesson on the subtleties of the taste and technology of goat cheese produced by farmers in northeast Italy?

In fact, Slow Food is not at all supported by rich sybarites, but depends instead on energetic enthusiasts. Its significance lies in a lofty moral conviction that responds to man's deepest needs: a sense of shame over the impoverishment of the planet. And, not least of all, it lies in the joy that that famous goat cheese of the northeast brings to the palate. As for the fact that "farmers" produce it, we'll say it again: the Italian gastronomic code is democratic. Academics, as well as pig breeders, are masters at it.

The organization's quarterly publications in the major languages of the world are expressly intended to inform this rather broad and diverse public. These bulletins are distributed in the United States, Holland, Austria, Great Britain, Ireland, Poland, France, and Canada, while Switzerland and Germany publish a newsletter independently. Slow Food has conducted educational work in the schools since 1993. Several "slowfoodian" innovations have even been successfully introduced by the Ministry of Education, and now in school cafeterias throughout Italy (including the one in the school attended by the author's children) menus are composed according to a territorial theme ("Abruzzi Week," "Sicilian Week") or a regional-landscape theme ("Seafood Cuisine," "Cooking of the Apennines").

The organization has managed to initiate several degree programs in culinary arts and enology, at twenty well-established scientific institutions. The Salone del Gusto, an exhibition and conference, has been held biennially in Turin since 1996. In the years in which the Salone is not held, there is the so-called Cheese Fair, dedicated to quality cheeses. It fills the streets and piazzas in the Piedmontese town of Bra, where the Slow Food Association has its headquarters. The cheese festival in Bra is a grand event, similar to a mega-*sagra* (see "The *Sagra*").

Slow Food's organizational efforts produced a truly splendid and visible result in 2004. For the first time, the University of Gastronomic Sciences was opened in Italy under the aegis of the association, offering master's degrees in gastronomic sciences and quality products and in "Food Culture: Communicating Quality Products" (conducted in English). The university has two locations—one in Pollenzo, Piedmont, and one in Colorno, Emilia—and consequently obtained funding from both the Piedmont and the Emilia Romagna regions.

In October 2004, in Turin, at the same time as the Salone del Gusto, an unprecedented conference took place, unique for both its conception and the type of participant. The significance of the event, entitled Terra Madre (Mother Earth), consisted in actually bringing together a worldwide community of individuals engaged in food production, the solution of hunger problems, and safeguarding the environment and the planet's ecological equilibrium—individuals concerned with quality and culture, who take either an active, practical stance toward the primary sphere of human existence or a theoretical, contemplative one, striving to study historical and anthropological aspects.

Five thousand delegates from 1,200 "food communities" of 131 countries of the globe participated in the Terra Madre conference. They included farmers, fishermen, and craftsmen who nourish the world in a sustainable way on a daily basis by protecting the environment and shaping the landscape. Participants were accommodated in private homes in Piedmont, Liguria, Lombardy, and Valle d'Aosta. Organizational support was offered by 1,250 Italian groups and myriad voluntary organizations throughout the world. There were seminars on local trademarks, environmental and gastronomic education, alcoholic beverage traditions, and certification for organic products.

The certification of products in zones and countries where commerce is not developed, and where cunning intermediaries are quick to sell uncertified goods, is a socially relevant issue. It is not surprising that the president of Slow Food, Carlo Petrini, was named European Man of the Year by *Time* magazine in 2004, specifically for the new prospects his activity offers farmers for the social advancement of their products.

Slow Food fights for the restoration of the past, but it conducts its battle under modern banners. The Latin, and therefore archaic, name for the chapters of the organization (*convivium*, a word that recalls Dante's treatise and Plato's dialogue) goes hand in hand with the innovative English name of the movement as a whole. Starting with the name itself, Slow Food is governed by irony and by a spirit of wholesome enjoyment. The association's modern website toys with symbols and images. The editors of the publishing house are clearly intoxicated by pearls from a Rabelaisian lexicon, offering curious slogans: "We are all fighting for the protection of the Piedmontese Blond Hen," "for the Mondovì melic biscuits" from Monregale, "in the name of Carmagnola's 'ox horn' capsicum."

What have the activists of the movement been able to accomplish so far? Quite a lot. They have managed to protect production of the exceptional wine Sciacchetrà in the nature preserve of the Cinque Terre, in Liguria. They have been able to restore life to Morozzo capons in Piedmont, to Valtellina buckwheat in Lombardy, to the Caprauna turnip in Piedmont, to the green winter melon *purceddu* in Sicily, and to the small plum-shaped Corbara tomato in Campania.

And what are their current crusades? Numerous rescue operations. To save Lodi's Granone cheese, which Casanova and Dumas Père went into raptures over; San Benedetto salami, cooked under ashes; the cardoon of Nizza Monferrato known as *cardo gobbo* (hunchback cardoon), without which it is impossible to make the famous Piedmontese *bagna cauda*; Sauris prosciutto, smoked for a month with beech wood; mullet *bottarga* (roe) from Cabras, dried in the briny wind of Sardinia; the violin goat prosciutto of the Valchiavenna. The black celery of Umbria needs saving, along with the violet asparagus of Albenga, the *zolfino* bean from the Val d'Arno, the copper-colored onion of

Montoro, the red garlic of Nubia, salted ricotta from Norcia, *mortadelline* (little salamis) of Campotosto known as "mule's testicles," the *biricoccolo* (a cross between a plum and an apricot) of Romagna, and the lentils of Ustica.

The movement is also concerned with rescuing Fatulì, a Lombard cheese made only from the milk of the "Blonde Goat" of Adamello. No more than five hundred kilograms per year are produced. The man once famous for this cheese, Bernardo Bonomelli, died in 2005, leaving two of his apprentices to safeguard his gastronomic patrimony from extinction.

Slow Food's work is widely publicized by the mass media. Its widespread appeal is largely due to its efforts to reawaken moral consciousness in people and foster social reconciliation. In a world that has seen the collapse of the ideologies of right and left, such culinary democracy is a continuation of politics by other means. It involves standing up to the industrial lobbies and multinational corporations. A visionary of its politics was Luigi Veronelli, one of the creators of the Italian "gastronomic code," an eccentric and dogged supporter of the ideals of good food. Veronelli died in November 2004, but a few weeks before his death, on his seventy-eighth birthday, he led one of his usual protest actions: a sit-in in the Pugliese port of Monopoli to protest against the importing of poor-quality olive oil (see "Olive Oil"). A philosopher by education, and publisher of newspapers and journals dedicated to material culture in Italy, Veronelli described himself as an "anarcho-enologue."

He was prepared to resort to any means necessary to defend the Italian culinary tradition (and not only that). In the fifties Veronelli spent six months in prison for inciting a revolt: he had urged the winemakers of Piedmont to protest against the excessive power of the monopolies and the lowering of standards in the wine industry. Later on he was imprisoned for another three months for publishing the books of the Marquis de Sade.

Veronelli was also the author of a few bizarre and scandalous works, such as *Vietato vietare* (It is forbidden to forbid), 2007; *Tredici ricette per vari disgusti* (Thirteen recipes for various aversions), 1991; *Le parole della terra. Manuale per enodissidenti e gastroribelli* (Words of the earth: A handbook for eno-dissidents and gastro-rebels), 2003, written with Pablo Echaurren; and *Alla ricerca dei cibi perduti: guida di gusto e di lettere all'arte del saper mangiare* (In search of lost foods: a guide to taste and literature on the art of knowing how to eat well), 2004. In addition he edited books that are very important for our topic, such as *La grande cucina* (Great Italian cooking), 1960, and *Mangiare e bere all' italiana* (Eating and drinking Italian-style), 1967, by Luigi Carnacina, and authored a series of guides to restaurants, wines, hotels, and olive oils. Within the Slow Food movement Veronelli worked on legislative initiatives that would have given mayors the power to certify the typical products of their territory, attesting to their authenticity. His appeals to a tempest in a glass of wine—to a sumptuous revolution that promoted the spirit of general peacemaking via food (see "The *Sagra*")—recalled somewhat the revolutionary plans of the Florentine Corrado Tedeschi. In 1953, Tedeschi founded the Partito Nazionale della Bistecca Fiorentina (National Florentine Steak Party), whose only principle was "the struggle for a social plan by which every citizen would be guaranteed a 450-gram steak per day." (We'll talk about this in greater detail in the section dedicated to Tuscan cuisine.)

Valle d'Aosta

Referring to this region, one of the representatives of the reigning Savoy dynasty at the time (the sixteenth century), Emanuele Filiberto, known as Testa di Ferro (Iron Head), said: "The Valle d'Aosta does not depend on us, like the others. It has separate laws and customs."[1] And yet Aosta was the only feudal territory of the Savoys and had been their personal possession since the dawn of time. The other regions of Italy had submitted to the Savoys of their own accord, though without oaths of vassalage.

The degree to which Italy is still far from uniform can be seen in its peripheral regions. In Valle d'Aosta the language and cuisine are not at all Italian. Aosta is spoken of mainly in books about French history: it is as Frenchified as the Trentino and the Alto Adige (South Tyrol) are Germanized.

This small (population: one million) but indomitable mountain region was inhabited in ancient times by a bellicose people, the Salassi, who opposed the Romans with fierce resistance. In the second half of the second century B.C., they defeated the army of the consul Appius Claudius Pulcher, and only in 25 B.C. did Aulus Terentius Varro Murena manage to defeat them by means of a ruse, taking 36,000 prisoners—including women, children, and the elderly—and later selling them as slaves.

The vindictive Romans called the devastated region Augusta Praetoria, from

which the present-day name Aosta derives. In 25 B.C. the region's capital, Augusta (Aosta), was constructed, with arches and aqueducts. Somewhat Spartan customs have prevailed in the city since antiquity. The chief annual fair, for example, that of Sant'-Orso, takes place during the *giorni della merla* (blackbird days), January 30 and 31, the coldest days of the year. At a time when the inhabitants of all the other Italian regions would rather not set foot outdoors, Aosta's streets are transformed into an open-air market for those who have enough backbone to tolerate the atrocious cold.

In this area, strong-willed, taciturn temperaments were formed. The famous missionary St. Bernard of Mentone (early 1000s–1081) is originally from here, not to be confused with St. Bernard of Clairveaux (1091–1153), ideologist of the Crusades. Also originally from here is St. Anselm of Canterbury (b. Aosta, 1033; d. Canterbury, 1109), missionary and founder of the famous abbey in far-off England. Besides Anselm, many other Valdostani ventured to England, far from their native land. In fact, the Via Francigena, which crossed the Alps at the St. Bernard pass and then continued on through Europe to England, passed through Aosta. This is the pilgrim route that serves as background to Chaucer's *Canterbury Tales* (see "Pilgrims"), and which Erasmus of Rotterdam also traveled in 1509, pondering his missive to Thomas More:

> As I was coming a while since out of Italy for England, that I might not waste all that time I was to sit on Horsback in foolish and illiterate Fables, I chose rather one while to revolve with my self something of our common Studies, and other while to enjoy the remembrance of my Friends, of whom I left here some no lesse learned than pleasant. Amongst these you, my More, came first in my mind, whose memory, though absent your self, gives me such delight in my absence, as when present with you I ever found in your company; than which, let me perish if in all my life I ever met with any thing more delectable. And therefore, being satisfy'd that something was to be done, and that that time was no wise proper for any serious matter, I resolv'd to make some sport with The Praise of Folly.[2]

The folklore of Aosta is full of dark tales about demons, which the local heroes, in truth, always get the better of. The most popular of these hero-interceders is St. Martin, who was able to hoodwink the devil by palming off on him a mill made of ice: though it functioned in winter, it melted in summer.

This small corner of paradise, with its few remaining inhabitants, was conquered in the early Middle Ages by the Burgundians and in the eleventh century by the Counts of Savoy, who managed to maintain good relations with the population thanks to a statute, the Charte des Franchises, which granted numerous privileges to the local communities. The charter was issued in the twelfth century by the *amico dei comuni* (friend of the communes) Count Tommaso I of Savoy, and subsequently expanded by Tommaso II and Amedeo V. For this reason, no one disturbed the Waldensian communities that since the thirteenth century have been established in the mountain gorges, where they survive today. Nevertheless, the Valle d'Aosta rebelled repeatedly: it convened the States-General several times, and in the end, during the drafting of the actual Italian constitution in 1948, it demanded for itself the legal status of autonomous region.

The cuisine here is not as varied as in other parts of Italy. The reason for the monotony lies in the lack of level terrain. Mountains, and still more mountains. This verticality is commercially exploited by the inhabitants, who have transformed it into a paradise for tourists. From castle to castle, ski lift to ski lift, the Valle d'Aosta is ever active: those who come in winter go downhill on skis; those who come in summer go climbing with their backpacks.

The valleys of the region are traversed by important commercial routes leading to France and northern Europe. Local customs differ according to distance from the border (at each kilometer the road changes its colors and aromas). But it is different altitudes that determine the greatest variety of customs and landscapes.

At an altitude of 1,700 meters above sea level, the most famous Alpine botanical garden in the world, Paradisia, can be visited in the heart of Gran Paradiso National Park, with headquarters in Valnontey, a small district of Cogne. And it is in the area of the Valle d'Aosta with the greatest altitude, the so-called roof of Europe, that the highest peaks of the Alps are found: Gran Paradiso, Monte Rosa, Cervino, and Monte Bianco (Mont Blanc). These summits can be reached after leaving behind valleys entirely cultivated with fruit trees (the meltwaters of the glaciers are sufficient even in the hottest summers). Higher up, along slopes exposed to the sun, grapevines take root. Then, according to the typical stratification zones of Alpine vegetation, there are chestnut woods scattered with beehives. Here the best chestnut honey in Europe is produced. Above the chestnuts, conifers grow, and above the level of the conifers stretch alpine meadows where milch cows graze.

Openings to mountain caves are found nearby the pastures, and are ideal places for aging exclusive cheeses. For this reason cheese and dairy production is particularly developed in the mountains of the Valle d'Aosta. In the dry climate, subject to abrupt decreases in temperature within a twenty-four-hour span, the action of molds and parasites is spontaneously neutralized in a kind of natural disinfecting. Cheese is produced and aged here, and dishes made of cheese are invented, such as fondue, the most typical of all. Fondue, like other Valle d'Aosta culinary traditions, was created to bring people together, just like coffee sipped in friendship from the same *grolla*, a local wooden goblet, or the horn from which everyone takes turns drinking wine. In the case of fondue, table companions dip crusts of bread into a common pot, kept warm over an alcohol burner. In the pot, the local melted cheese, or more often a blend of local cheeses, bubbles gently.

Other basic specialties of the Valle d'Aosta include bread soups with cheese.

The cuisine of these places is not very imaginative. Fresh fruit, bread, and, among the specialties, only the small Martin Sec pears, with a color ranging between rust and pale yellow, are worthy of note aside from the melted cheese. Unusually sweet, they are baked in the oven, in red wine with cloves, for not less than an hour, then served topped with whipped cream and accompanied by a glass of grappa.

TYPICAL DISHES OF THE VALLE D'AOSTA

First Courses Melted Fontina with butter and egg yolks (fondue, or *fonduta*). The warmish mass is scooped up with crusty bread or poured over polenta.

Second Courses Chamois or roe deer *valdostana*-style (*mocetta*, pieces of thigh or tenderloin, marinated, then braised, then cooked again on the grill), and also carbonade of beef, salted and cubed, with onion, salt, and pepper, left to simmer in wine for many hours. Cutlet *valdostana*-style: a slice of veal topped with Fontina, wrapped in slices of *prosciutto cotto*, dipped in egg, sprinkled with grated bread, then browned. Mountain trout *in carpione*: fried in large pieces, then marinated in vinegar.

Typical Beverages Special, and absolutely original, is *valdostana* coffee. It is mixed with grappa, lemon rind, and sugar; then the alcohol is set on fire in a large wooden goblet with numerous spouts. The goblet is called the *grolla dell'amicizia* (friendship cup), and friends take turns drinking from it, each from his own spout.

Another drink is the exceedingly strong *vin brûlé alla gressonara*, that is, Gressoney-style: wine boiled with black bread, sugar, butter, cinnamon, cloves, and nutmeg and passed through a strainer. In general the Valdostani love to drink. Perhaps this is the only place where you can find what we thought was typical only of the Caucasus: a goat's horn mounted in silver that simply must be emptied . . . as everyone knows, the laws of physics make it impossible to set a horn that is still full down on the table!

TYPICAL PRODUCTS OF THE VALLE D'AOSTA

Cheeses Fontina. Toma di Gressoney Saint-Jean, a cheese that is produced with fresh milk at an altitude of 2,200 meters (therefore only in summer) and aged for at least a year; it has an aftertaste of pepper and vanilla and the scent of moss and mushrooms. *Mocetta*: beef (formerly wild goat) salted and seasoned with garlic and sage, and thinly sliced as an appetizer. Renette apples from the Valle d'Aosta; Martin Sec pears.

Chestnut honey.

In the Valle d'Aosta a highly prized lard is produced: Lardo di Arnad DOP, which does not mature in evocative marble tubs like the Tuscan *lardo* of Colonnata (see "Tuscany"), but in chestnut wood casks (*dols*), on a bed of aromatic mountain herbs, in accordance with a process that dates back at least to the eighteenth century.

The salamis *teteun* and *boudin*. The first is made from the udders of the red or black pied breed of Valdostani cows. The second is a sausage of salt pork, spices, potatoes, and beets.

TYPICAL BEVERAGE

Génépy liqueur, a distillate of several varieties of artemisia (*A. spiccata* or *genipi*, *A. glacialis*, *A. mutellina* . . .), a very aromatic composite that grows above an altitude of two thousand meters.

JEWS

The first Jews settled in Rome in 161 B.C., when Judas Maccabeus sent ambassadors there to form an alliance against the united Greek and Syrian armies. The envoys were numerous and remained in Rome for quite some time. Then, after the destruction of the temple of Jerusalem by the Romans in A.D. 70, the first big wave of refugees arrived in the empire's capital, along with an even greater number of Jewish slaves, taken prisoner by the Romans during battle. Their sad procession in the triumphal cortege, under an enormous menorah (taken from the Jews as a trophy, evidently), is portrayed in a bas-relief on the Arch of Titus in Rome (first century A.D.).

Together, prisoners of war and refugees made up the Jewish community of Rome. For this reason, Italian Jews do not belong to either of the two great branches of the Jewish global diaspora: neither to the Sephardics, who passed through Spain, nor to the Ashkenazim, who passed through Germany. Italian Jews are a separate circumstance, and it was they who were the initial vehicles of Christian doctrine in Italy in the early centuries.

In the fourth century, the Jewish community in Rome numbered forty thousand people who inhabited Trastevere, the area across the Tiber. Roman Jews at that time enjoyed the same rights as other citizens, without any form of segregation. As is the case with other national communities, cohabitation occurred for cultural and practical reasons. And so it continued until 1492. That year, as Christopher Columbus (the scion of a Jewish

family, according to some) discovered America while sailing caravels flying the Spanish flag, the Catholic King Ferdinand and Queen Isabella drove the Jews out of Spain. Many of them fled to Rome, where their brethren summoned them, still well-off but concerned about the growing hostility of their Catholic neighbors.

With the unexpected arrival of a number of Spanish Jews, the Roman community became populous and visible. Meanwhile, the ideological mood toward the mid-sixteenth century, the period of the Counter-Reformation, became so intolerant that no one was surprised when the best friend of the Inquisition, Pope Paul IV (the same pontiff who wanted to destroy Greek and Roman statues deemed guilty of promoting paganism), ordered all Jews to be isolated from the rest of the city's population, in an outburst of religious fundamentalism. He had them confined in an enclosure in front of Capitoline Hill, at the Portico of Octavian, near the piazza where Rome's enormous fish market teemed with people every morning. From that moment on, Jews were permitted to go out only during the day, while at night the three gates of the ghetto were shut with imposing bolts and guarded by city sentinels.

For Jews, the brief but incisive rule of this pope (1555–59) marked the collapse of an entire way of life that was centuries old. In his papal bull *Cum nimis absurdum*, Paul IV defined as "absurd" the fact that for some reason Jews considered themselves on a par with Christians:

> Since it is absurd and improper in the highest degree that the Jews, who by their own fault have been condemned by God to eternal slavery, can, with the excuse of being protected by Christian charity and tolerated while living amongst us, show such ingratitude toward Christians as to abuse their mercy and claim superiority instead of submission: and since we have learned that, in Rome and in other territories subject to the holy Roman Church, their effrontery has reached the extent where they not only venture to live among Christians, but even near their churches, without wearing any identifying garments . . .

These four years set a precedent that would confine the Jews of Rome to the ghetto for the next three centuries. Their houses and goods were taken from them, and they were deprived of wealth and living space (or *Lebensraum*, to use the famous term). Only in 1870, after the Papal State was defeated by force and finally became part of the unified kingdom of Italy, were Jews permitted to move freely throughout the peninsula, no longer confined to their respective zones of residence.

In the sixteenth century, members of Rome's Jewish community had to change their customs and their entire lifestyle. Yet this new and highly restricted existence full of deprivations gave Roman Jews the opportunity and the chance to invent an imaginative cuisine, which brilliantly assimilated and enhanced earlier Roman traditions, giving them back to the city in a new, innovative incarnation. Today only experts can tell the difference between Piperno, the principal Roman restaurant specializing in Jewish cooking, and the adjacent restaurant, Gigetto, serving typical Roman fare. The two premises, situated a few meters apart, offer nearly the same choices: on the Roman menu we find more stewed meats; on the Jewish one, more vegetables cooked in an original way. As far as the unique pleasure that comes from dining there is concerned, the two places are perfectly comparable.

Not all of Italy, however, was prepared to take in the Jews driven out of Spain by Christian monarchs. Sicily, for example, was under Spanish dominion in 1492; the viceroys, submitting to the mother country's injunction, drove all Sicilian Jews out of the island, ordering them to abandon their homes within three months. After leaving Sicily, Jewish elders assembled four kilometers from the island, in Reggio Calabria, after which the community decided to follow the counsel of a wise rabbi and move as a body to Rome. As a result, Roman culinary splendors, already indescribable before, were enriched with elements of Sicilian cooking, in particular with a great variety of eggplant-based dishes. Before getting to know them better, the Romans considered eggplants indigestible and, on the basis of a false etymology, thought the name *melanzana* derived from *mela insana*, or unsound apple.

Eggplants were disparaged by the gastronomy theorist Piero Andrea Mattioli (1557): "A vulgar plant; it is eaten crudely fried in oil with salt and pepper like mushrooms,"[1] as well as by Antonio Frugoli (1631), according to whom "eggplants should be eaten only by people of lowly station or by Jews."[2] A somewhat different attitude toward the experience of national minorities is displayed by the agronomist Vincenzo Tanara (1644), who thinks that certain products (for example, eggplants) deserve attention just because they are appreciated by the Jews, who are so difficult regarding food: "[Eggplants are] for the consumption of people from the countryside and especially for families, since they are a customary food of the Jews."[3]

Thus eggplants found a home in the Roman ghetto, where they were fried, marinated, and stuffed. And these vegetables cost almost nothing in the markets of Tuscany, since "they were considered to be vile because they were foods eaten by Jews," writes Pellegrino Artusi in his cookbook.[4] Artusi used the Tuscan name *petronciani*; Bartolomeo Scappi called them *molignane*, Cristoforo da Messisbugo *mollegnane*; and in Rome the term *mari-*

gnani was used. In *Il novellino* Master Taddeo, "as he was instructing his medical scholars, propounded that whosoever should continue for nine days to eat eggplant would go mad."[5] Boccaccio in the *Ameto* called them *petronciani violati*, purple eggplants.[6]

Zucchini, on the other hand, was highly prized, much too expensive to be used by the Jews in ghetto cuisine. Only discards from the market reached the ghetto: the futile male flowers that sprouted uselessly at the ends of the zucchini. But Jewish cuisine treated them in such an exciting way that even today they constitute a grace note and a source of pride for Italian cooking. The flowers of zucchini or pumpkin, known more commonly as squash blossoms, are eaten with a cheese filling, stuffed with bread crumbs and anchovies and with egg and parsley, or fried in a light batter.

Artichokes also entered Roman cuisine from Sicily, probably introduced by exiled Sephardics at the beginning of the sixteenth century. Artichokes *alla giudea* or *alla giudìa* (Jewish-style) are made with round Roman artichokes, also known as *mammole* (literally, "violets"). Flattened with a heavy meat pounder or a stone, the artichokes are submerged in boiling olive oil until the leaves spread out in a fan; they are then left to dry on absorbent paper until they turn crisp. *Mammole* are also good blanched and dressed with olive oil. For artichokes *alla giudea*, smaller fruits, called *figlioli*, or baby artichokes, are selected. In addition to the *figlioli* (sons), there are also the *nipoti* (grandsons): these are truly minuscule and are cooked *alla romana*, Roman-style, with vinegar.

A preparation method such as frying immediately and clearly betrays its place of birth. There was not enough room in the crowded ghetto for large, well-equipped kitchens, but for frying all you needed was a deep pan and a fire. Except for olive oil, of course, though in Rome in those times it did not cost too much.

There is a version of *fritto misto* in batter *alla giudea*. This dish of mixed fried items does not in any way resemble the Piedmontese dish that bears the same name and uses the most unimaginable cuts of meat. According to Roman Jewish tradition, *fritto misto* is made of sliced vegetables in batter which are fried in hot oil.

Frying and selling to the public was one of the few occupations available to the Jews, who were permitted to sell their fried foods in the streets, and were allowed to open trattorias even for practicing Catholics. Other activities officially acceptable were those of junk dealer and moneylender. By law, Catholics did not have the right to lend money with interest (in part because the Church considered usury a sin), so this kind of activity was delegated to the Jews. As for fried food, it could furthermore be prepared in advance for the Sabbath and enjoyed cold, unlike soups and other dishes.

The history and daily life of the Jewish ghetto toward the beginning of the sixteenth century created the conditions for the birth of a masterpiece of Roman-Jewish cuisine, *caponata alla giudea*, in which eggplants fried in advance are combined in a single saucepan with sweet peppers and tomatoes, all cooked in a sweet-and-sour sauce over a slow flame and eaten cold. This dish, like the fried vegetables and some other fried foods, was prepared on Friday and served on Saturday. Caponata is even better after spending the night on the hearth than when it has just been made.

The rules of Jewish dietary hygiene (the *kashrut*) coincide in many respects with those of the Catholic fast.

These rules are based on the precepts of the Old Testament:

These are the animals you may eat: the ox, the sheep, the goat, the deer, the gazelle, the roe deer, the wild goat, the ibex, the antelope and the mountain sheep.

You may eat any animal that has a split hoof divided in two and that chews the cud.

However, of those that chew the cud or that have a split hoof completely divided you may not eat the camel, the rabbit or the coney. Although they chew the cud, they do not have a split hoof; they are ceremonially unclean for you. The pig is also unclean; although it has a split hoof, it does not chew the cud. You are not to eat their meat or touch their carcasses. Of all the creatures living in the water, you may eat any that has fins and scales. But anything that does not have fins and scales you may not eat; for you it is unclean. You may eat any clean bird. But these you may not eat: the eagle, the vulture, the black vulture, the red kite, the black kite, any kind of falcon, any kind of raven, the horned owl, the screech owl, the gull, any kind of hawk, the little owl, the great owl, the white owl, the desert owl, the osprey, the cormorant, the stork, any kind of heron, the hoopoe and the bat. All flying insects that swarm are unclean to you; do not eat them. But any winged creature that is clean you may eat. Do not eat anything you find already dead. You may give it to an alien living in any of your towns, and he may eat it, or you may sell it to a foreigner. But you are a people holy to the Lord your God.

Do not cook a young goat in its mother's milk. Be sure to set aside a tenth of all that your fields produce each year. Eat the tithe of your grain, new wine and oil, and the firstborn of your herds and flocks in the presence of the Lord your God at the place he will choose as a dwelling for his Name, so that you may learn to revere the Lord your God always.[7]

Summarizing the main kosher precepts based on this biblical passage:

1. Distinguish permitted animals (*tahor*: large and small cattle, poultry, and fish, but only those with fins and scales) from those prohibited (*tami*: of the quadrupeds, those that do not have a split hoof and at the same time do not graze, as well as the predators, reptiles, and insects; crustaceans and mollusks are also prohibited).
2. Permitted animals must be slaughtered in a ritual way.
3. The consumption of blood is prohibited: this is the primary and fundamental prohibition. Blood, repository and mystery of life, belongs to the Lord.
4. The consumption of certain types of animal fat is prohibited: these parts are consecrated to the cult of the temple of Jerusalem.
5. The consumption of the sciatic nerve is prohibited, in memory of Jacob's struggle with God (Genesis 32:26, New International Version: "When the man saw that he could not overpower him, he touched the socket of Jacob's hip so that his hip was wrenched as he wrestled with the man").
6. The consumption of parts removed from live animals is prohibited.
7. The consumption of the meat of diseased or mutilated animals is prohibited.
8. The mixing of meat and milk at the same meal is prohibited (Exodus 23:19: "Bring the best of the first fruits of your soil to the house of the Lord your God. Do not cook a young goat in its mother's milk": this prohibition has been interpreted in a variety of ways by rabbis and commentators).
9. The consumption of substances that threaten life and health is prohibited (in keeping with one of the main precepts: "Always choose life, not death").

So it was that the vast Jewish ghetto of Rome created and provided the entire Roman population with dishes that could also be eaten by Catholics during fast days. The kosher laws that prescribed not mixing vegetables with lard or butter corresponded to the precepts of Catholicism not to consume animal food on days of abstinence, or to at least limit it. Even the prohibition against consuming blood is similar to the Italian culinary tradition, in which meat destined to be smoked and salted is required to go through a process of desanguination. The word "prosciutto" in fact literally means that the leg is *prosciugata*, drained.

The exquisite, vitamin-rich Jewish herb pizza has been one of the favorite dishes of Roman Catholics and itinerant pilgrims during the entire Lenten period for centuries.

Piedmont

Piedmont, as its name tells us, lies *a pie' dei monti*, at the foot of the mountains that form the entire territory of the adjacent Valle d'Aosta, between the Alps to the north and west and the Apennines to the south.

The character of this region recalls the Valle d'Aosta, and Piedmont, too, was once under the rule of the Savoy dynasty, though with some interruptions. The Savoys fought against France repeatedly from the sixteenth century on. In the early eighteenth century the French took Piedmont from them, later gave it back, and afterward began to reconquer it. But even in periods when France's predominance was less discernible, the French spirit continued to be felt. Through its association with France, some characteristic features of Piedmont were formed: gallantry, refinement, perfectionism. It is not paradoxical therefore that typical peasant dishes—not unlike those of the Valle d'Aosta—are brought to perfection in Piedmont and prepared as true works of art.

Piedmont is a jigsaw puzzle of 1,209 towns and villages, each in its own unique setting, whether among fields, on hills or mountain slopes, beside lakes, or on the banks of rivers. Here, as in Valle d'Aosta, there are Waldensian towns (with their own cuisine and rituals). Franco-Provençal towns are found in the province of Cuneo, and Occitans who once came from Provence live in the extreme west.

Like the majority of cities in the north and in particular like nearby Aosta, Turin, founded by the Romans, was originally named after ancient families, in this case the Julian and Augustan clan: Julia Augusta Taurinorum. But the nickname *taurino*, alluding to an obstinate bull (*taurus*), prevailed, and in the annals of history the city was left with simply the name Turin.

Turin was the capital of two kingdoms: the kingdom of Sardinia from 1713, and later the kingdom of Italy from 1849 to 1861. No other city besides Naples has played this role in Italy's history—it was capital of the kingdom of Naples from 1282 to 1815 and capital of the Kingdom of the Two Sicilies from 1816 to 1860. Other cities might be capitals of counties, duchies, marquisates, or independent republics, but there have been no other capitals in Italy with such mythic and symbolic associations. These cities are famously home to objects venerated in Christianity, namely, the Shroud of Turin and the blood of San Gennaro in Naples.

The Shroud figures quite frequently in literary texts. A fictionalized version of its apparition is presented in the novel *Baudolino* by Umberto Eco. What is known about it for certain is that in 1349, in France, the knight Geoffroi de Charny claimed to possess a sheet of unknown provenance on which the features of a human figure (presumably Christ) were stamped. Louis I of Savoy acquired the Shroud in 1453. Since that time the relic has been preserved in the city of Turin.

It was from Turin, capital of the only state in the Apennine Peninsula free of foreign rulers, that the impetus for the unification of Italy came, beginning in 1848 (with the first war of independence). It was here that the national intelligentsia was forged in the nineteenth and early twentieth centuries that was able to define Italy's cultural and political visage. Camillo Benso, Count of Cavour, organizer of the struggle for national unity and an astute diplomat, was 100 percent Turinese—confirming the current designation (abrupt and simplistic to be sure): *torinesi falsi e cortesi* (Turinese: deceitful and polite). Not only that, he was irreversibly Piedmontese, to such an extent that he wrote his political works in French.

The Francophone Cavour was a living illustration of another Italian saying, which could serve as a slogan for this book: *Parla come mangi!* (Speak the language of your food). Cavour expressed himself in French both in his daily life and in politics, and as a gastronomic Francophile. The menu of his dinners is still offered today at the Ristorante del Cambio, a historical restaurant where a customer arrives and is seated on a crimson settee at a Baroque table adorned with a small tricolor flag, in a private alcove. There he is served just as they used to serve Cavour, and with the same dishes. The menus reflect the Continental, rather than Mediterranean, coloring of Cavour's culinary preferences, and even an anti-Mediterranean note. Dishes "with a French accent" are widespread in Piedmontese cuisine (and have been since antiquity, as we know from an eighteenth-century treatise on cooking, *Il cuoco piemontese perfezionato a Parigi*, The Piedmontese chef trained in Paris, 1766).

An example of this is the *finanziera*, a dish well-loved by Cavour. It is made of beef entrails and genitals, boiled in a mixture of vinegar and Marsala wine and flavored with the local Barolo wine. The canonical recipe also calls for kidney, calf's brain, chicken livers, sweetbreads, cock's combs, and mushrooms, all served in flaky pastry shells (vol-au-vents) or accompanied by plain risotto.

As in Lombardy, the spinal marrow of cattle is readily included in recipes in Piedmont, though here it is called *filone*, not *midollo* as in the rest of Italy. The substance of the marrow is incredibly fatty and is used for browning roasts, pork shanks, and porcini mushrooms. Bone marrow is also included in the recipe for *frisse*, meatballs of chopped lung, heart, and liver. An exclusive meat is obtained in Piedmont from the so-called fat ox (*bue grasso*); the meat can be recognized at a glance since it is *marezzata*, or veined with fat (what other countries call "marbled meat" for assonance and because of its external appearance).

The fat ox is bred in Carrù (Cuneo) and in Fassone, not far from Asti. It is a special Piedmontese white breed, fed with bran, whey, wheat, sugar beets, and often even zabaglione to increase muscle mass. These oxen can weigh as much as 1,250 kilograms and are not able to walk on their own. The Fat Ox Festival has been held in the village of Carrù since 1910, two Thursdays before Christmas (see "The *Sagra*"). A marble monument, entitled *Il Belvedere di Carrù* (the Apollo di Belvedere of Carrù), the work of sculptor Raffaele Mondazzi, has been erected to these titans in Carrù; on its base, six bas-reliefs immortalize the ox's brief journey from cowshed to slaughterhouse to celebratory table.

The *gran bollito* (boiled meats platter), a favorite dish of Vittorio Emanuele II, is accounted for by "the rule of seven": seven cuts of meat, seven "ornaments," seven dipping sauces, and seven vegetable side dishes. The seven cuts are *tenerone*, or chuck; shank; ribs; butt end; rump; rump tip; and rolled breast (boneless breast rolled up and tied around a filling of salt pork or prosciutto, cooked salami, two eggs, a whole carrot, herbs, and pepper, which is then cut into slices). The seven "ornaments," which are also meat, are cooked in separate pots. These constitute the true essence of the typical *bollito*: calf's head (complete with snout), veal's tongue, calf's foot, calf's tail, a chicken, a *cotechino* sausage, and a loin sausage (the plump boneless breast rolled around herbs and roasted at a high temperature is the only roasted piece that is part of the *bollito*). And that's still not all! To this marvel, seven side dishes must be added: boiled potatoes, spinach, red onions boiled in vinegar, turnips, carrots, celery, and leeks. Finally, this culinary madness is brought to the table with seven sauces: first a green sauce, then a red one, then a honey sauce, as well as a sauce of *cougna* (grape must jam) with raisins, a horseradish sauce, Cremona *mostarda*, and mustard.

Sometimes the meat is actually seasoned with fish, as in the case of *vitello tonnato* (veal in tuna sauce), a surprising combination of boiled veal with preserved tuna. The slices of veal are arranged on a plate and topped with the tuna sauce (fresh mayonnaise mixed with flaked tuna, hard-boiled eggs, capers, and anchovies).

Autumn is Piedmont's characteristic season. At that time, while a dense low fog spreads throughout the region, the first young wine is uncorked. Umberto Eco, who is originally from Alessandria, has given his readers incomparable descriptions of Piedmont's landscapes. The best-loved places in Eco's novels (such as the monastery in *The Name of the Rose*) and their best-loved characters (Jacopo Belbo, Roberto de la Grive, Baudolino) belong to Piedmont. Here is how these places familiar to the writer are described through the words of his medieval hero Baudolino:

"Halfway between these two cities there are two rivers, the Tanaro and the Bormida, and between the two there is a plain that, when it isn't hot enough to cook eggs on a stone, there is fog, when there isn't fog, there's snow, when there isn't snow, there's ice, and when there isn't ice, it's cold all the same. That's where I was born, in a place called the Frascheta Marincana, which is also a swamp between the two rivers. It's not exactly like the banks of the Propontis."

"I can imagine."

"But I liked it. The air keeps you company. I have done much traveling, Master Niketas, maybe even as far as Greater India . . ."

"Are you sure?"

"No, I don't really know where I got to. It was the place where I saw some men with horns and others with their mouth on their belly. I spent weeks in endless deserts, on plains that stretched as far as the eye could see, and I always felt like a prisoner of something that surpassed the powers of my imagination. In my parts, when you walk through the woods in the fog, you feel like you're still inside your mother's belly, you're not afraid of anything, and you feel free. Even when there's no fog, when you're walking along and you're thirsty, you break off an icicle from a tree, and you blow on your fingers because they're covered with chilblains."[1]

And it is in autumn that the hunt for the first truffles begins. The white truffle of Alba (*Tuber magnatum pico*) is the badge of Piedmont's gastronomical opulence. According to legend, Alba, the truffle capital, also took its name from it (*alba* is Latin for "white"). A black truffle is also found in Italy (*Tuber melanosporum*, the Perigord black truffle), but is much less prized.

In his *Physiologie du gout* (*Physiology of Taste*), 1825, the celebrated gastronome Jean Anthelme Brillat-Savarin (1755–1826) described the white truffle (despite its monstrous appearance) as the "diamond of the kitchen."[2] Savarin assigned a very precise meaning to his words: according to him, the truffle "is a positive aphrodisiac, and under certain circumstances makes women kinder, and men more amiable."[3] The comparison to the diamond is fully justified by both the truffle's quality and its market price. The white truffle of Città di Castello costs between ten and fifteen thousand euros per kilogram; the black truffle of Norcia five thousand euros. In 1954 the largest white truffle in the world (540 grams) was presented by the city of Alba to President Truman. It was a precious gift, the best Italy could offer to the American president in gratitude for humanitarian aid at the time of the Marshall Plan.

There is also a "summer" truffle, less esteemed, that costs only eighty to a hundred euros per kilogram. It is called *scorzone* and is used for industrial preparations and to flavor sauces. Inexperienced buyers—the culinary nouveaux riches—often jump at this second-choice luxury item and buy it up, mistaking it for a truffle of higher quality. The main problems that truffle buyers must be wary of are cheaters and swindlers. Some purveyors have been known to store ten Acqualagna truffles (of inferior quality) with one from Alba (diamondlike) together; the cheaper truffles become permeated with the aroma of the more expensive one, to a point where distinguishing them is almost impossible. Only later on, when they're eaten, will the less prized truffles give off a completely different scent. Does a truffle really come from Alba, or has it simply been stored with one that does? It's a good question, and the only safeguard against it is a personal relationship with the vendor and the good reputation of that particular truffle broker.

A romantic legend has it that truffles grow as a result of moonlight on frosty nights, when light filters through the cold, damp earth to the roots of the trees. Another legend says that they are formed from drops of stag sperm. Or according to an ancient belief, they grow in places where, in autumn, a lightning bolt strikes the ground near a tree root.

Truffles are sought using dogs, who can sniff them out better at night. The cost of a trained dog can be as high as twenty thousand euros. Pigs are famously known for truffle hunting, too. In Italy, however, it is not customary to entrust the job to swine, which are quite capable of not only finding the truffle but eating it, thereby consuming ten to fifteen thousand euros in one gulp. The French, on the other hand, do use pigs: for some reason French pigs behave more responsibly and do not devour the exquisite find.

In order to be displayed in all of its magnificence, the white truffle requires the most intense heat during cooking. Those few readers who may find themselves in possession of such a rarity and wonder what to do with it will probably be grateful for the following advice: Truffles must be heated in a frying pan of 999.6 silver, the purest, with a titanium handle (such frying pans have the highest thermal conductivity of all types of cooking utensils). In *Directions to Servants*, Jonathan Swift offered some judicious observations on the cleaning and care of silver frying pans for truffles. The best way to eat a truffle is to savor it heated, after slicing it, on simple, toasted homemade bread, and drizzling several milliliters of extra-virgin olive oil over it, provided that the oil is Umbrian: the latter has a taste that is not too pronounced, while Tuscan oil has a fruity scent that is too strong and Sicilian olive oil is too aromatic. Over the sliced truffle drizzled with oil, we suggest sprinkling several crystals of coarse sea salt (fine salt has no place in the distinguished recipes of Italian cuisine).

Truffle lovers should also keep in mind a sad rule. A given season is never propitious to truffles and wine simultaneously: truffles are good in autumn after a rainy summer; wine, on the other hand, after a dry, hot summer.

Alba does not hold an absolute monopoly over white truffles. Excellent ones are also found in the Marches, in the village of Sant'Agata Feltria, and in Tuscany, in the vicinity of San Miniato. Sometimes you come across a fortunate specimen in the most remote corners of the Molise. Successful truffle hunting also occurs farther south: it is difficult to imagine, but apparently white truffles sometimes grow even in Calabria.

The "war of the truffle" between Alba and Asti has been going on for years. Asti wants to begin selling as early as August 15 and sometimes manages to do so, while Alba is inclined to move the date toward autumn, because the later it is, the better the quality of the product. The calendar is established by the Order of the Knights of the Truffle and Wines of Alba (the same group that organized the museum of ancient farming tools at the Castello di Grinzane Cavour and reprinted *De Tuberibus*, a work by the sixteenth-century physician Alfonso Ciccarelli).[4] The Truffle Fair in Alba takes place the first Sunday in October. In a procession that recalls a Roman triumphal march, participants carry the best examples of the white truffle of Alba, renowned throughout the world. A wagon parade, a donkey race, and the selection of a beauty queen—the Bela Trifolera (the beautiful truffle-seeker)—follow. The clergymen of this cult are no strangers to beneficent impulses. Each year the Trifolau Association of Alba assigns the proceeds from the ten best specimens to some worthy cause.

There is one dish in the whole world that is eaten only in Piedmont. It is the Piedmontese dish par excellence: *bagna cauda* or *bagna caòda* (hot dip), a hot, fragrant mixture of oil and garlic, in which anchovies are blended along with melted butter.

Rules of preparation are complex. I cite the 1989 edition of the *Grande bagna caòda annuale degli Acciugai e dei Buongustai del Piemonte* (Great bagna caòda annual of Anchovy Vendors and Epicures of Piedmont):

1. The anchovies must be fine red anchovies from Spain, cured at least a year, fresh and fragrant, that is, just salted, cleaned, washed in water and wine, well dried, and boned; at least 2 or 3 anchovies per person (5 or 6 equal 100 grams).

2. The garlic may be reduced but never eliminated, since it is the "soul" of the *bagna caòda*! While "purists" prescribe a "head" of garlic, about 10–15 cloves, 2 or 3 cloves per person are sufficient, not boiled in water or milk, but simply removed from the bulb, sliced thinly, and left an hour or two, if desired, in a tureen of cold water, or better yet in running water.

3. The oil must be olive oil of good quality, preferably extra-virgin, though even normal oil is fine, excluding however all the seed oils; not less than half a (wine) glass per person is needed.

4. The vegetables, well cleaned and quartered, must be all those typical of Piedmont's gardens, with the exclusion of several that are unsuitable because they are too aromatic (for example: celery, fennel, radishes): "hunchback" cardoons from Nice, or, lacking those, *spadoni* (broadsword) cardoons from Chieri, raw peppers, roasted and peeled peppers, pickled peppers, turnips, Jerusalem artichokes, green, white and red cabbage, white hearts of escarole and endive, fresh leeks, chives, etc.

5. The cooking time must be brief and kept always at low heat; this is the decisive point for a good, healthy, and digestible *bagna caòda* . . .

It is a complete one-dish meal, consumed with lots of bread. Therefore, the wise Piedmontese limit themselves to serving tasty raw *cacciatorini* (salami) of pure good pork before the *bagna caòda*, just to prepare the taste buds for the first glass of young Barbera.

To make a truly grandiose *bagna caòda* meal, smoked herring canapés, little cubes of hot fried cod, and warm wedges of leek and spinach frittatas can be added to the sliced salami (in short, appetizers to have while standing up with an aperitif).

And after the *bagna caòda*?

Not the Piedmontese *grande bollito misto*, which, even if scaled down, would still be overdoing it. Instead, a large cup of hot concentrated beef consommé always goes well (see "Le ricette di Giovanni Goria," the recipes of Giovanni Goria, at www.saporidelpiemonte.it).

Bagna cauda is a "poor man's" dish that stands in sharp contrast to the Piedmontese extravagance represented by the truffles, the beef fillet, the fine chocolate, and so on. In the overwhelming majority of cases, in fact, Piedmont's food is expensive. Pasta is unknown in this region: pasta was used in areas where it was necessary to alleviate hunger by being frugal with ingredients and money. Piedmont is a land of plenty.

One might wonder why anchovies appear in Piedmontese cuisine. Strange as it may seem, salted anchovies were a sign of prosperity in the Middle Ages. Salt meant wealth. Anchovies are a most convenient way of combining savoriness with proteins and vitamins. And they were therefore used to season food as far back as the time of ancient Rome.

So it is not by chance that salted anchovies occupy a place of honor in the emblematic dishes of Piedmontese cuisine. Anchovies (*acciughe* or *alici*) abound in the fish-poor Ligurian waters that bathe that part of the coast along which Europe's most ancient salt route passed, from Liguria through Piedmont toward northern Europe. The convoys that transported salt (openly or contraband) salted the anchovies on the spot and carried them to far-off northern Europe and along the way to Aosta and to Turin and the other main cities of Piedmont.

The Ligurian anchovy met with great success in Turin, competing with salted sardines from Spain. Although the Spanish sardines cost less than the Italian anchovies, the Ligurian *alici*, slightly salted and immersed in delicate Ligurian olive oil, far surpassed any competitor in tenderness and richness of taste. Ligurian olive oil is considered the best for preserving fish. Tuscan oil, distinguished by its aroma and taste, is categorically contraindicated for anchovies.

The classic *bagna cauda*, as is evident from its name (a variation of *calda*, hot), should be heated, but never allowed to come to a boil. It is then placed in the center of the table, in a pan set over an alcohol burner, the same type used to serve fondue. Naturally, the hot dish is not suited to summertime meals: it is a treat to enjoy in autumn and winter. All the vegetables that accompany it are winter produce: cabbages, carrots, and, above all, Jerusalem artichokes. In spite of the name, these "artichokes" are not from Jerusalem and are not really artichokes: the name is a distortion of the Italian *girasole*, or sunflower, the family to which they technically belong.

In Piedmont, as in other regions situated between 44 and 48 degrees latitude (Lombardy and the Veneto), rice-based dishes are at the forefront of the cuisine. It was Camillo Benso, the untiring benefactor of Italy, who in his day brought the abundant waters of the Alps to the arid Piedmontese plains. In 1866 the count made plans for a regional irrigation system. A wide canal more than eighty kilometers long, with branches and tributaries, allowed the Alpine water to flow down into Vercelli, Novara, and Lomellina and irrigate the rice paddies. The canal still exists, functions as it should, and appropriately bears the name of Canal Cavour.

Thus *risotto alla piemontese* was born, with hard cheese and nutmeg, in meat broth. It is prepared with Barolo and mushrooms. Risotto is also a typical dish of the province of Vercelli. (Vercelli is the chief town of an agricultural zone where rice is practically a single-crop production. The Rice Exchange and the Rice Research Institute are found in Vercelli, and the most modern technology is invented and perfected there, to replace human labor in the rice paddies with that of well-designed machines.) But the classic risotto in Vercelli is made with frogs, which are as numerous in the rice paddies as mosquitoes. And so, the *sagra* of the frogs has been celebrated in Vercelli during the first week of September each year since the Middle Ages.

Typical dishes of Vercelli's *sagra* are risotto, broth, and frittata with frogs. Frogs were the fundamental ingredient of a caloric and supremely beneficial broth, which local physicians thought was equal in curative powers to the mythical chicken soup of the Jews of central Europe. And the physicians of Vercelli had great need of healthful remedies, since the Via Francigena passed right through Vercelli, and pilgrims on their way from the north to Rome (see "Pilgrims") generally stopped in this city to recover their strength and treat the ailments they had contracted along the way. Vercelli was left with more than a few unique buildings and institutions from that period, such as the Ospedale degli Scoti (Hospital of the Scots). A vast assortment of travel food was developed in Vercelli, intended for wayfarers: for example, the *salam d'la duja*, a large salami, not smoked, placed in a terra-cotta jar (*duja*) under a layer of lard.

The lard was produced by rendering salt pork. Nevertheless, even salt pork in its pure form cured in Vercelli and in Tuscany (in cities found along the pilgrim routes) became so renowned over time that it began to be viewed not as a poor man's food, but as a super-prestigious and beneficial product. In the twentieth century some types of salt pork occupied a place in the Olympian circle of elite dishes. This is particularly true of the Tuscan *lardo* of Colonnata, cured in marble basins, which we will describe in more detail in the chapter on Tuscany.

Polenta, a peasant food par excellence, is widely found throughout the north of Italy—and consequently in Piedmont. Polenta is celebrated at a special *sagra* in Ponti (in the province of Alessandria) each year on the last Sunday in April. Legend has it that as early as the fifteenth century the aristocratic Del Carretto family, whose members lived in the village, was in the habit of offering the community an enormous polenta seasoned with dried cod. To show their gratitude, the citizens decided to cast a tin cauldron of unimaginable dimensions for the count's oversized polenta in 1650. Since that time, polenta for the entire town is cooked in that cauldron during the annual *sagra*; a local denizen dressed as the count comes down on horseback from the hilltop castle, to give the signal that marks the start of the banquet.

The creation of both rustic, heavy dishes (e.g., the *finanziera*), as well as lighter, refined fare intended for the aristocracy, is part of the Piedmont experience. *Grissini torinesi*, Turinese breadsticks, were made for the first time for the delicate stomachs of the dukes. The word *grissino* derives from an old type of Piedmontese bread, the *gherse*, with a diminutive suffix: in short, a small bread. Legend also has it that in 1668 the Turinese baker Antonio Brunero produced the first *grissini* for the table of Vittorio Amedeo II, future Duke of Savoy, who suffered from digestive problems, and had been advised to eat bread crusts, discarding the soft, inner part. Later on, Turinese *grissini* were a favorite of Napoleon, who had them sent to the imperial table from Turin. This typical product of Turin is a cult object in Italy for all who want to lose weight.

The famous Piedmontese zabaglione, on the other hand, is accompanied by marrons glacés, sweets guaranteed to bestow appealing fullness of form (even if nowadays one very rarely encounters individuals with such desires). Chestnuts and marrons are a typical Piedmont product. The former, which are smaller, are the fruit of the wild chestnut tree, and every husk contains three of them. Marrons, on the other hand, come from prized cultivated varieties derived from graftings, and every husk contains a single fruit, generally larger and sweeter than that of the chestnut.

The protocols of Renaissance court cuisine still seem to be operative in Piedmont. Even chocolate (unknown, of course, in the Renaissance) is presented here in a very elaborate form: "cooked," or culturally transformed, according to Claude Lévi-Strauss and Roland Barthes. It was actually here—not in Switzerland, as is mistakenly thought—that a certain master Suchard, founder of the well-known industry, created the first sweet chocolate bars in European history. Turin's famous *gianduia*, or hazelnut chocolate, was also invented here. This product took its name from a typically Turinese figure, one of the principal stock characters of the commedia dell'arte, Gioan *d'la douja*, that is, "Giovanni of the Jug," a character known for being a heavy drinker. A Piedmontese pastry chef invented this particular Turinese chocolate specialty with milk and hazelnuts at the time of the French occupation, in 1807, when it was not possible for Piedmont to order cocoa powder because of the embargo and they had to make do with existing provisions. They began to manufacture chocolate that was half cocoa and half hazelnuts.

At the opening ceremony of the 2006 winter Olympic Games in Turin, the individually wrapped *gianduiotti* were a real leitmotif, sampled charmingly by fantastic giantesses of past times in crinolines and wigs. In the lavish Olympic show, these chocolates were presented as a symbol not only of Savoyard Piedmont, but of all of Italy, the host country, just like Botticelli's Venus.

Piedmontese pastry chefs also created another notable typical product made of cocoa: *bunet*: a rich chocolate mousse with rum and amaretti.

In the period of the "Italian miracle," in 1964, concurrent to the Beatles' rising star, the world was enlightened by the splendor of a new product, which the Italians dared hold up to American peanut butter. Giovanni and Pietro Ferrero, owners of the chocolate factory of the same name, introduced a new variation of *gianduia* cream to the Italian and later the world market: a spread developed purposely for school lunches and snacks. For the name of the spread, the Piedmontese added the sweet Italian suffix *-ella* to the American root "nut." Sweet sound, sweet taste. The delicious spread was light, heartening, and absolutely Italian, that is, versatile and unbeatable. Nutella kept American peanut butter off the plates of Italian teenagers and children. Nutella, loved by children (naturally) and adults, was also prized by nonconformists and leftists. As Italy's answer to America, it is winning, uplifting, and youthful, a sign of democracy and leftist ideals. "Nutella is left-wing, Swiss chocolate is right-wing," sang the popular singer-songwriter Giorgio Gaber. At the end of the twentieth century it won over the most avant-garde computer geniuses and cyber-anarchists, who invented the best decentralized system for file exchanges, impossible to control; they christened it "Gnutella" (www.gnutella.com) in honor of their favorite chocolate hazelnut spread.

Over the years, Nutella has been packaged in hundreds of different containers, among them jars, pots, jugs, and glasses. This has fueled a passion for collecting among food fetishists. In Italy, eight hundred grams per capita per year are consumed, and in Luxembourg, for some reason, a kilo per person. Ten thousand Web surfers united by a common passion—nutellomania—have gathered together on the site www.mynutella.it. Musical, film, theater, and literary works have been dedicated to Nutella, and a comic opera even exists: *Nutellam Cantata* (2001), by the composer Antonello Lerda.

Turin became Italy's industrial capital in the twentieth century, thanks to Fiat, and its publishing capital, thanks to Einaudi and UTET. It was the city most focused on the future and most inclined to experimentation. This spirit of intellectual creativity often seeped into the realm of food as well, and just as provocatively. On the evening of March 8, 1931, at the height of the Fascist era, the Taverna del Santopalato (literally, Tavern of the Sacred Palate) opened in Turin. Owned by the restaurateur Angelo Gioachino, its "precise purpose [was] to go from theory to practice in the Futurist controversy" through a program that would renew the taste and alimentary habits of the Italians; an objective that was to be realized through the invention of new dishes, created by notable Futurists.

Descriptions of these paradoxical dishes have been preserved:

Solar Broth (recipe of chef Ernesto Piccinelli). Bring the broth to a boil. Beat three eggs in a bowl and, continuing to whisk, add three glasses of Marsala, a tablespoon of oil, lemon rind, Parmesan, salt, and pepper. Slowly add the boiling broth while continuing to stir. Top the broth with ingredients that are the color of the sun: carrots, lemons . . .

Plastic-meat (Fillia's recipe). Plastic-meat (*carneplastico*, a synthetic interpretation of the vegetable gardens, flower gardens, and pastures of Italy) is a large cylindrical loaf of roast veal stuffed with eleven different kinds of cooked vegetables. This cylinder, arranged vertically in the middle of the plate, is crowned with a layer of honey and supported at the base by a sausage ring, which rests on three spheres of golden-brown chicken.

Sea of Italy (Fillia's recipe). On a rectangular plate arrange a base formed of geometric stripes of fresh tomato sauce and creamed spinach so as to create a precise green and red pattern. On this green and red sea, place groupings formed of small cutlets of boiled fish, slices of banana, a cherry, and a piece of dried fig. Each of these groupings is held together by a toothpick that keeps the various elements upright.

Steel Chicken or Chicken-Fiat (Diulgheroff's recipe). Roast a chicken . . . As soon as it cools, make an opening in its back and fill the inside with red zabaglione on which two hundred grams of spherical silvery confetti are sprinkled. Arrange cock's combs all around the opening of the back.[5]

When sampling the dishes, diners had to hold the fork in their right hand and let their left hand slide repeatedly over special panels that supplied tactile complements to the taste of the foods. One dish was paired with a silk swatch, another with a piece of emery board, a third with a lacquered plate. Spices were crushed in the dining room to stimulate olfactory perception. Not surprisingly, the Futurist restaurant had a short life—not because of prohibition by the authorities, but because of customer dissatisfaction.

TYPICAL DISHES OF PIEDMONT

Antipasti Veal in tuna sauce (*vitello tonnato*): boiled veal round cut into thin slices and topped with tuna sauce (fresh mayonnaise mixed with flaked tuna, hard-boiled eggs, capers, and anchovies).

First Courses *Agnolotti*, close relatives of Ligurian ravioli; in Piedmont, however, their filling consists of meat, eggs, and cheese. *Agnolotti* are boiled and served in meat broth, or else with melted butter and fresh sage. In the Langhe, however, and in the city of Alba and its surrounding area, ravioli in broth are not popular. When brought to the table, they are poured into a plate lined with a linen napkin, whose purpose is to absorb every last drop of superfluous liquid.

Various risottos, always with butter and minced onion *soffritto*. The *tajarin*, a speciality of the Langhe, are the only fresh, hand-shaped, long Piedmontese pasta made with egg. They are served with roast drippings.

One-Dish Meal *Bagna cauda*.

Second Courses Braised beef with Barolo; roasted Carmagnola Grey rabbit, whose meat is particularly tender. Onions stuffed with cheese, egg, and butter. *Finanziera*: boiled entrails, gizzards, cock's combs, and chicken livers with mushrooms, served in a bowl or in flaky pastry shells (vol-au-vents). White pullets of Saluzzo *alla cacciatora*, that is, hunter's style, with onion and tomato. Hare ragout or salmis, stewed in red wine with celery, onion, carrots, bay, parsley, sage, rosemary, and pepper. Stuffed Morozzo capons. Stuffed peppers; snails; donkey stew (*tapulon*); breaded Sambuco lamb with Jerusalem artichokes; pâté of Sambuco lamb liver with chestnuts. Golden tench of Pianalto di Poirino, marinated.

Desserts *Bunet* (chocolate mousse). Stuffed peaches and *bicerin*, coffee with milk and chocolate, described by Alexandre Dumas in 1852 as an "unforgettable drink." It was first introduced in the Turinese café of the same name, in Piazza della Consolata. A *bicerin* is a small glass with an iron holder.

TYPICAL PRODUCTS OF PIEDMONT

Grissini torinesi.

Cheeses Bra, the most famous of Piedmont's cheeses. It is no accident that every other year since 1997 a gathering of cheese producers from all over the world, called simply Cheese, has been held in the city of Bra. Also famous are the Piedmontese cheeses Castelmagno (containing penicillin mold, famous since 1277; a notarial document has been preserved that confirms the right of the producers to graze their cows on specific pastures in order to obtain the milk used for this particular cheese), Bruss, Grana Padano, Robiola di Roccaverano, Robiola d'Alba, Taleggio, Toma, and Ossolano. The cheeses Macagn and Montebore are produced high in the mountains and are wrapped in chestnut leaves. The cheese Bettelmatt of the Val Formazza has a particular flavor thanks to a very fragrant grass, the *mattolina* (Alpine lovage), which the cows in the area's mountain pastures graze on. Also well-known are the cheeses Soera, Spress, and Raschera.

Filetto baciato (literally "kissed fillet") of Ponzone: a slice of pork fillet wrapped in a sausage mixture. Coggiola *paletta* (aged pork shoulder). *Testa in cassetta* from Gavi (pig's head stuffed with boiled tongue, heart, and kidney and cooked in rum with pine nuts).

"Hunchback" cardoon (*cardo gobbo*) from Nizza Monferrato. During cultivation, it is skillfully bent so that the stalk loses elasticity and chlorophyll, turns pale, and becomes extremely tender. It is the only cardoon in the world capable of being consumed raw; for this reason it is indispensable for the classic *bagna cauda*. Turnips of Caprauna, succulent and mild, which do not tolerate being preserved in cellars; therefore they are left in the ground until the time they are cooked.

The cherries known as Bella di Garbagna; they do not do well when transported and preserved, so they are hardly ever cultivated today. Traditionally, these cherries are soaked in alcohol with cinnamon and cloves, to accompany the *bollito*.

The strawberries of Tortona, which can be tasted only in this city, and only for ten days a year in the second half of June, with Barbera wine. Piedmontese apples, a rare and protected species: the gray apple of Torriana, and the varieties Buras, Runsè, Gambafina, Magnana, Dominici, Carla, and Calvilla.

Piedmont hazelnuts, chestnuts from the Val di Susa, essential oil of mint from Pancalieri, extracted from a variety of *Mentha piperita luds* (peppermint) and used in the liqueur, confectionery, and pharmaceutical industries. Asti *torrone* and cornmeal biscuits from Monregalese. *Gianduia* hazelnut chocolate.

TYPICAL BEVERAGES

Piedmont produces some of the most noble wines, such as Nebbiolo, with its subvarieties Barolo and Barbaresco.

Vermouth was distilled for the first time in Piedmont, in 1786, from a mixture of herbs that also included absinthe or wormwood, virtually illegal today. We even know the name of the man who first thought of this refinement: Benedetto Carpano. From vermouth combined with gin some very celebrated cocktails were later born, such as the dry martini and the Negroni (Campari, vermouth, and gin).

RISOTTO

In contrast to the precision of making pizza or pasta, the gastronomic code with regard to risotto preparation is relaxed, resulting in a lot less stress. Rice is more forgiving of inexactitude and mishaps. It can be left on the stove for approximately half an hour: a minute more, a minute less is never fatal. If you make too much, it's not a tragedy, since it can be sautéed in a pan the following day. Risotto is a one-pot dish. And finally, the cook isn't consumed by trying to guess the best combination of shapes and flavors. Unlike pasta, with its thousands of shapes, rice is reduced to a few fundamental varieties. All you have to do is not mistakenly choose a long-grain variety (like basmati). And the seasonings are practically infinite.

Risotto is discursive. Making it inevitably involves talking. Risotto is always finished after the famished guests have already arrived, and they may even be crowded around the stove, chatting with the chef as it cooks. The person cooking wouldn't have it any other way, since standing in front of a pot of rice, stirring continually, and pouring ladles of broth in every three minutes is truly boring. But making risotto also entails some lively conversation. It has inspired many works of Italian literature. Like many Italian intellectuals, the great writer Carlo Emilio Gadda, author of *Quer pasticciaccio brutto de via Merulana* (That Awful Mess on Via Merulana), 1957, was able to cook quite well. What's more, he wrote recipes in the same unique, flamboyant style with which he usually wrote prose. The recipe drawn from the book *Le meraviglie d'Italia* is famous:

The preparation of a good risotto Milanese requires a quality rice, such as the Vialone type, with a large, relatively more compact grain than the Carolina type of grain, which has an elongated, almost spindle-shaped form. A rice that is not entirely "hulled," that is, whose pericarp is not entirely removed, meets with favor from those in the know in Piedmont and Lombardy: the growers, who use it for their personal cooking. To be specific, the grain here and there appears covered by the residual strips of a film, the pericarp, that has the appearance of a tattered walnut- or leather-colored covering, but very thin: cooked strictly by the rule, it produces excellent, nourishing risottos, rich in those vitamins that distinguish tender grains, seeds, and their outer husks. *Risotto alla paesana*, or country-style, from these rices turns out particularly exquisite, but so does risotto Milanese: a little darker, it's true, after, and despite, the golden baptism of saffron.

The classic vessel for cooking risotto Milanese is a round casserole, or even an oval one, of tin-plated copper, with an iron handle: the old, heavy casserole which from a certain moment on was never heard of again; a precious fixture of the old, vast kitchen. It was an essential part of the kitchen's "copper" or "coppers," and an erstwhile poet, Bassano, did not neglect to include it in his poetic "interiors," where gleaming copper more than once figures on the brickwork, capturing and reflecting a ray of sunlight that, once dinner is digested by the diners, *concocto prandio*, begins to fade. Since the old copper has been snatched from us, all that remains is to trust in its replacement: aluminum.

Holding the casserole over the heat by the handle, using the left hand and a felt pot holder, add slices or small pieces of tender onion and a quarter ladle of broth, preferably hot beef broth, along with first-rate Lodigiano butter. Butter, *quantum prodest* (just enough), depending on the number of diners. After first lightly browning this modest buttery onion mixture, toss in the rice, little by little, in small, repeated amounts until reaching a total of two or three handfuls per person, according to the anticipated appetite of those at the table: nor should the little bit of broth initiate the process of boiling the rice: the ladle (of wood, now) will therefore be busy, turning and turning. The grains will then become browned and will soon settle against the tin-plated, red-hot bottom, each one maintaining its own "personality" in this phase of the ritual: not sticking together or clotting.

Butter, *quantum sufficit* (just as much as needed), no more, I beg you; it must not bathe, or form a nasty sauce: it must anoint each grain, not drown it. The rice has to settle, as I've said, on the tin-plated bottom. Then, little by little, it will plump up and cook, as a result of adding the broth bit by bit; here you will want to be careful and painstaking: add the broth a little at a time, beginning with two half ladlefuls of it taken from a "side" bowl that you have ready. In it will be some brightly colored dissolved ground saffron, an incomparable gastric stimulant that comes to us from the dried pistils, their flower then duly crushed.

Risotto Milanese should never be overcooked—heavens, no!—but should be only slightly more than al dente on the plate, with each grain soaked and swollen with the aforesaid juices, yet an individual grain, not stuck to its companions, not mushed into a glop, in a soggy mass that would be disagreeable. Some grated Parmesan is just barely allowed by good risotto makers; it's a means of rendering Milanese sobriety and elegance more cordial. With the first rains of September, fresh mushrooms may be found in the casserole; or, after St. Martin's Day, at the time the risotto is served, dry slivers of truffles from a special truffle-slicer tool may be sprinkled over the dish by a solicitous waiter, duly remunerated when the feast is over. Neither the mushroom addition nor the truffle addition manages to pervert the profound, vital, noble significance of the risotto Milanese.

Whether or not onion has a right to be part of *risotto alla milanese* is the subject of many disputes. Elena Spagnol, an irrefutable authority in culinary matters, to whom many recipe books are credited, has convinced the author of the present volume that there is no place for onion in a good risotto. Nevertheless, reading Gadda, we find that the brilliant novelist sautéed minced onion in the pan before adding the rice to brown. Preaching in the same choir is the voice of the gentle poet of Romagna, Giovanni Pascoli, who in turn offers the rigorously Milanese recipe in his lyrical poem "Il risotto" (the cook he describes is from Milan):

> Friend, I've read your *Risotto in . . . Ai!*
> It's very good, but a little futuristic
> with all those "you'll do this, you'll do that."
>
> This, from my area, is more sure
> because it's in the present tense. She minces a little
> scallion in a simple pan.
>
> In it she adds butter the color of crocus
> and saffron (she's from Milan!); then
> she leaves her dish on the fire.
>
> You'll say: Butter and onions? I should add
> that there are also bits of chicken liver,
> tripe, and mushrooms.
>
> What a fine aroma comes from the fireplace!
> I already feel a little restored
> after my Greek and Latin!
>
> Then she crushes some tomato over it,
> and leaves it to simmer nice and quiet
> until it takes on a pale golden color.
>
> Only then does she cook in it
> the raw rice, as you say.

It's already striking noon . . . Here comes the risotto
alla romagna that Mariù makes me.

It's curious that this poem was written as an imaginary response to a poem described
by him as "Il risotto in ai" (*ai* being a form of the future tense) by another literary figure,
Augusto Guido Bianchi, editor of the *Corriere della Sera* and a Milanese friend of Pascoli
(their letters are now preserved in the Biblioteca Braidense of Milan).

. . . The casserole requires a hot coal fire;
one hundred grams of good butter and a few onions.

When the butter browns, you will then add
the raw rice, as much as you want,
and while it toasts, you will stir and toss it.
Broth is needed then, but very hot;

put in a little at a time, since it must boil
continuously, and never be allowed to dry out.
In the end, you will dissolve
a little saffron in it, you will do this
so that the yellow will color it.

You will let the broth be absorbed,
so that the rice will be dense, once it is cooked.
It needs a lot of grated cheese.
Thus you'll have the risotto of Milan.

Liguria

With an area of 2,124 square miles, Liguria has 217 miles of coastline. This small region nevertheless has as many mountains as Valle d'Aosta, Trentino, or Abruzzo. Therefore, what the Ligurians have been able to depend on during the course of their history is obvious: fishing, mountain goats, and the strength of their own enterprise.

Farming is hard work in this mountainous coastal strip of stubborn soil. It's conducted on terraces contained by low drystone walls constructed in irregular grids of shale or slate (cement and stucco are forbidden, in theory, by a special law to protect the environment, observed by almost everyone) and continuously patched by hand. Modern methods of cultivation have not yet caught on here: it is difficult to adapt large farming equipment to a plot of land that is merely a few spans wide. Thus, from an agricultural standpoint, Liguria remains an oasis of so-called bioproducts, a paradise for agritourists, a bastion of ecological and ethnogastronomic "food defenders" (see "Slow Food"). A relationship with simple things is so developed here that humble products—herbs, seasonal vegetables, and eggs—that are little appreciated elsewhere enjoy the highest consideration.

Liguria's cuisine is first and foremost the seaman's, and second a "cuisine of return"—that is, a cuisine of the land, that long-dreamed-of land that the sailor, once

back in home port, treads with unsteady gait. Throughout the entire voyage, the seaman has eaten hardtack and focaccia (the same ship's biscuits and flatbread that even today constitute an important component of the Genovese and Ligurian diet). Focaccias drizzled with olive oil, often topped with dried fish, such as *mosciame*— traditionally dried dolphin fillet, which today, following a national ban on dolphin fishing, is replaced by tuna fillet. Hot dishes were scarce: hot food was distributed only once a day on the ships, before noon, when the second watch was about to begin and the first had just ended. A pesto of basil and olive oil, plus other caloric ingredients (pine nuts and pecorino cheese) and a vitamin component (crushed garlic), was also spread on the focaccias.

Ligurians have a skeptical, even hostile, attitude toward their sea: "Anything good would never be called *mar*" (in the sense of *male*, evil), they say. Nevertheless, they are ready and willing to go to sea, and they do it with tenacity. Glorious navigators aside—among them the most illustrious, Christopher Columbus—the ablest, hardiest old sea dogs are found in crews from Liguria, and nothing is impossible for them. Genoa was dubbed "Genoa the Proud" in distant times, since by the eleventh century it dominated commercial traffic in the Mediterranean and was one of four Italian maritime republics (the others were Venice, Amalfi, and Pisa) that controlled trade with Asia and Africa, in competition with the Arabs and with Byzantium. Genoa eventually ruled over not only the Mediterranean but also the Black Sea, establishing colonies in Greece, Asia Minor, Spain, Africa, and Crimea.

Once back on land, the sailor has no desire whatsoever to gaze back at the sea. Instead, Ligurians turn their faces upward and blissfully contemplate the mountains. It is telling that the majority of the nation's alpine troops were recruited here, and that the local cuisine consists primarily of foods from the land. Once back from their voyages, sailors and fishermen couldn't stand any more cod and shellfish. They dreamed of savory pies with vegetables, spinach, mushrooms, fresh cheese, and ricotta. The seaman's wife prepared the pie dough the night before, baked it in the morning, and then went to welcome her husband at the port; with dinner ready and waiting, it was easier to enjoy the day.

The simplest version of such pie is the celebrated Ligurian focaccia. Sometimes it's made with onion, sometimes with cheese, but the fundamental ingredient is the local oil.

At the time when the tradition of preparing focaccia as a provision for seamen's voyages was developing in the wood-burning ovens of Genoa, olives were pressed locally and oil was abundant. Oil was the chief cargo transported, oozing out of the cracks of barrels stored at the port; though it may seem paradoxical, it cost less than flour. It was Genoa's main export, particularly to the neighboring regions of Italy, such as Piedmont or Lombardy, which produced other varieties of oil. Thus there was no reason for Ligurians to skimp on olive oil as they did on wheat flour, which was not a local product. Foccacias were made thin and flat, with little hollows so that the oil poured on top would collect in the depressions.

———

Aside from flour and oil, the third essential element of the Genovese focaccia is the large crystals of salt sprinkled on top. Salt was always readily available in Liguria; indeed, it was one of the chief commodities in the city's ports. In the old Italian world, a passion for salty, savory foods was stronger than the passion for sweets. Salt was a sign of power. An intelligent man is said to have *sale in zucca* (common sense). Four-month-old babies who are beginning to be weaned are first given a savory gruel made of Parmesan cheese, spinach, and olive oil as a supplement; with this pap the babies grow like leavened dough (this has been personally verified). The *salario* (salary) in ancient Roman times was a quantity of salt given as compensation to soldiers and functionaries on the road (along with grain, oil, and wine); only subsequently was it replaced by monetary payment (which nonetheless has kept the name "salary" until this day). Via Salaria was the name of one of the main Roman roads. Even the terms *salsa* (sauce) and *salumi* (cured meats) are derived from *sale*. Salt is an indispensable ingredient of many typical national dishes: *baccalà* (dried salted cod), anchovies, herrings salted in barrels, and spicy pickled peppers.

The demand for salt in the Italian diet has always been high. For travelers, salt was useful both in its pure form and for preserving other products. Only thanks to pure salt, found in nature and used to season vegetables, were sailors, soldiers, and the conquerors of new lands able to contend with long distances. Those who lived along pilgrim routes tried to sell salt to the wayfarers: without it, it would not have been possible for them to continue their journey. And everyone needed salt and spices to preserve perishables.

Obviously, it is not only in Italy that salt is indispensable; it has always been so for everyone, everywhere. Nevertheless, people who consume greater quantities of meat absorb salt directly from it. The Mediterranean diet, based primarily on vegetable foods that are low in sodium, requires greater supplements of salt than the protein-rich cuisine of the north.

The history of the Mediterranean is filled with conflicts over salt. Venice, Genoa, and Pisa fought among themselves for monopoly over the exploitation of the salt marshes in Sardinia, Sicily, the Balearic Islands, and North Africa. In the first decade of the sixteenth century an armed conflict erupted between Pope Julius II and the Duke of Ferrara, Alfonso d'Este. The pope, who owned the salt marshes of Comacchio near Ravenna, was outraged when the duke, who possessed the salt marshes in neighboring Cervia, began selling salt in Lombardy and Piedmont at lower cost than the monopoly prices the pope had established. During the Middle Ages, the European "salt route" passed right through Genoa, winding from Sicily (where the salt arrived by sea) toward France, Germany, and the interior of the continent, where it was transported overland, crossing the Apennines and the Alps. For the Genovese, therefore, salt was generally accessible, though they consumed it with relative frugality since they had to import it. But focaccia, in any case, was generously sprinkled with it.

Genovese focaccia has been made the same way since the Middle Ages. The dough is left to rise in the evening and at daybreak the focaccia comes out of the oven, ready for the fisherman about to set sail. Medieval "disciplines," or provisions dictating rules and regulations for the preparation of authentic Genovese focaccias, have survived and are valid even today. The complete production cycle must not take less than eight hours. The focaccia must be composed of not less than 6 percent Ligurian extra-virgin olive oil; it must be soft on the inside but crisp on the outside, and must have a golden color that acquires a whitish hue in each depression.

Focaccias, along with chickpea flour flatbreads; *ciappe*, flatbreads made of fava bean flour; and *testaieu*, breads made of chestnut flour, are poor man's foods, but they accompany the most succulent gifts of the garden and vegetable plot and are transformed into a daily feast. The various types of focaccias are served with fresh greens, crisp vegetables, and cheese. They are eaten with artichokes, pumpkin, leeks, and cardoons.

Herbs and vegetables prevail. Renowned among vegetable garden specialties are artichokes, some downright *pinzuti*, stinging, others more easygoing (the famous purple one that grows in Albenga). Green salads, the main source of vitamins in spring, autumn, and summer, are unparalleled; their variations assume a new name at every turn, in every new village of Liguria, since everywhere you go there are different dialects. From antiquity to our day, each spring Ligurians have collected bunches of herbs with whimsical names. The bouquet includes taraxacum (dandelion, *dent de lion*, or piss-a-bed), nettle, poppy, early savoy cabbage, borage, chard, wild radicchio, chervil, burnet, sowthistle (*Sonchus oleraceu*, or *sciscerbuas* in the local dialect), common brighteyes (*Reichardia picroides*), and goldenfleece (*Urospermum dalechampii*, or *bell'ommo*, in dialect). At the beginning of spring, or even in late winter, it is customary to walk the fields of Liguria and gather all these herbs to flavor fritters (*frisceu*), to use in savory pies, and to make the filling for ravioli.

All the land that is not cultivated as vegetable gardens is covered with olive trees, some three hundred years old. The olive groves themselves are three thousand years old, and it is clear that they will remain where they are for many centuries to come.

Olive trees do not permit easy access: it is difficult, if not impossible, to use farm machinery for this work. Therefore the olives are picked by hand, and from them comes an olive oil that is among the most prized in Italy.

During olive harvesting season, the Ligurian hills are wrapped in orange or green nets that run from one tree to another to form an uninterrupted, endless hammock, on which the olives fall when shaken down. These nets are a modern invention that appeared only after World War II. In distant times the olives were knocked down and gathered from the ground by hand or picked directly from the tree. During the harvest months, everyone worked in the olive groves, with no exceptions. And the most skillful were the agile adolescents. The figure of one of these child harvesters (though of almonds, not olives) is portrayed in Simonetta Agnello Hornby's beautiful novel *La mennulara* (*The Almond Picker*), 2003. Today the nets make the job easier.

Olive oil is excellent for frying. In Genoa in particular *friggitorie*, or fried-food shops, are widespread: prawns and sliced octopus are cooked in boiling oil there, right in front of the customer. These premises have nothing in common with anonymous fast food. They are an epitome of exquisite pleasure available to those who are in a hurry and want a bite to eat along the way. In the market stalls under the arcades of the narrow *carruggi* (alleyways) there is a triumph of exclusive delicacies: fish and shellfish, zucchini, artichokes, spinach, and lettuce, all fried in batter. Sometimes (rarely) the ancient traditional ingredients can also be found among the assortment of ingredients for frying: tripe cut into little strips and *baccalà* (dried salted cod). On the first Sunday of September in all the streets of the town of Portovenere, in the province of La Spezia, octopus is fried in oil, amid music and various attractions.

The excellent Ligurian oil is also an essential ingredient for Genovese pesto, known throughout the world. Pesto was invented in order to preserve the basil that abounds on the Ligurian coast through summer, even into winter. Besides a great quantity of basil, pine nuts must also be crushed in a marble mortar, using a wooden pestle, or *pestello* (from which the sauce gets its name). The pine nuts can be extracted from pinecones that have fallen from trees growing along the side of the road close to home, or, more unconventionally, they may be purchased.

The other two ingredients for pesto are garlic and Sardinian pecorino cheese. Some would-be experts dare to assert that this cheese can be replaced with Parmesan. But it is clear to every ethnogastronomist that, historically, the cheese in Liguria could by no means have come from Parma, situated beyond impassable mountains, but only from Sardinia, a sister-region located on the same sea and excellently connected to Genoa by ship transport. Sardinian pecorino is the accurate, authentic ingredient of true Ligurian pesto.

There is not much room for orchards in Liguria, but fruit-growing is practiced so intensively that fruit constitutes no less than 30 percent of the inhabitants' dietary allowance. The late-sixteenth-century physician Bartolomeo Paschetti, who moved from Verona to Genoa, complained: "My dear Genovese . . . Those who consume more fruit than other foods eat too great a quantity of it. Which condition many in your country and elsewhere incur by basing dinner and supper on fruits more than on other foods."[1]

TYPICAL DISHES OF LIGURIA

Antipasti *Gianchetti* (or whitebait): young anchovies, sardines, and mackerel known as fry or *novellame*. Fishing for *novellame* is rigidly regulated, so anyone who is not a local must know his way around in order to taste them. The local inhabitants naturally know where and when to find them, where and in which trattoria to order them. Whitebait is eaten fried or steamed.

Ligurian trout, fried and then marinated for twenty-four to thirty-six hours. *Boghe* (small fish) *in scabecio*, which is the Ligurian version of *in carpione*, in a sauce or marinade (it is prepared by frying the flour-dredged fish and placing them in a marinade of vinegar mixed with a *soffritto* of onion, garlic, bay, sage, and rosemary). Salted anchovies of Monterosso (a specialty on its way to extinction: earlier, this little fish was caught at night by the light of fishing lamps and was salted at dawn on the riverbank). Lean capon (*cappon magro*, a name that is obviously ironic), a typical Genovese dish made of numerous vegetables, fish, crustaceans, and other shellfish (lobsters, shrimp, oysters) in a garlic sauce. Fritters with beer batter (*frisceu*). Mussels. Stuffed mussels. *Condiggion*: ship's biscuits, garlic, and sliced vegetables of various kinds served with *mosciame* (fillet of dried dolphin, tuna, or other large fish).

Many Ligurian specialties have one characteristic in common: they do not require plates. In this region, few people dine at table. The sailor, the fisherman, and the farmer who has clambered up mountain terraces prefer to go without cutlery. If there's some cabbage, a parboiled cabbage leaf is used; if there's focaccia, the prepared food is arranged on that. A "food pocket," the so-called *cima ripiena*, a stuffed "bag" of breast of veal, is also popular, stuffed with sliced boneless veal, sweetbreads, brains, marrow, dried mushrooms soaked in lukewarm water and wrung out, peas, cheese, eggs, and fresh marjoram. After the stuffing is added, the "pocket" is sewn with a needle and thread, cooked, and left to cool.

Farinata (a flatbread of chickpea flour, often, in Liguria, flavored with onion, rosemary, and black pepper). Little cheese focaccias, pumpkin focaccia, focaccia with onions. Polenta of chickpea flour (*panissa*).

The Ligurian art of savory pies reaches its apex in the Easter pie, made of flaky puff pastry with boiled chard and spinach, skimmed milk, and three types of cheese (in honor of the Trinity): fresh ricotta, aged Parmesan, and grated aged pecorino. This pie also contains four whole hard-boiled eggs, to commemorate the four evangelists. And the puff pastry should, ideally, have thirty-three layers: thirty-three for the number of years Jesus lived. The herbs of the classic Ligurian *preboggion* (bouquet garni) are part of the Easter pie.

First Courses *Corzetti* (minuscule pasta disks), sold flat or rolled up in the shape of a figure eight, in a sauce of marjoram with minced pine nuts or fresh salmon, onion, and walnuts. Borage *cappellacci* pasta, in a walnut sauce. Vegetable *minestrone alla genovese*. *Trenette* (the name comes from the Genovese word *trene*, meaning laces or strings, but it also goes back to the pasta's ancient Roman name, *tria*, still preserved today in Sicily and Puglia, where they cook "*tria* with chickpeas"). *Trenette*, like other pasta shapes, in particular the *trofie*, is eaten with pesto. *Piccagge*: fettuccini served with pesto or artichoke sauce.

Pasties, savory pies, molds filled with *preboggion*. *Prescinseua*, a slightly acidulous fresh curd obtained from cow's milk, is also often used as a filling in pies.

Second Courses *Asado*, breast of veal cooked in the oven for no less than seven hours. *Cima ripiena* (stuffed breast of veal). Lamb fricassee with artichokes. Stewed stockfish (*accomodato*), a typical dish of San Remo. In other localities this same dish is called *buridda*; it is in any case a winter dish, generally of fish, with many regional variations. The one composed of stockfish with mushrooms, pine nuts, and tomatoes is famous. Genovese *cacciucco* (fish soup), imported from neighboring Tuscany: olives, pine nuts, and potatoes are added to a *soffritto* of oil, anchovies, and herbs; then the stockfish is cut into pieces. *Cacciucco* is eaten obligatorily at the beginning of the olive pressing season, when the first murky oil, greenish and somewhat bitter, is obtained from the olives: the oil is used to flavor the *buridda*.

Bel or *belu* or *trippette* (little tripe): stockfish entrails, requiring adequate soaking and prolonged cooking. Zucchini, eggplant, onions, and any other vegetable that can be prepared stuffed. The pulp of the vegetable is mixed with egg, soft bread, minced garlic, parsley, and herbs. In some localities the addition of boiled potatoes and dried mushrooms is called for. *Mesciua*, a characteristic dish of the area of La Spezia, is composed of chickpeas, beans, and wheat cooked in boiling water and seasoned with salt, pepper, and olive oil.

Desserts *Latte dolce*, or sweet milk (in Genovese dialect: *laete doce frito*); cookies fried in oil with grated lemon rind.

TYPICAL PRODUCTS OF LIGURIA

The chief local product is the extra-virgin olive oil from the Ligurian Riviera, among Italy's best (see "Olive Oil").

Less famous (in part simply because they cannot be more or equally famous) are the cheese of Santo Stefano d'Aveto, aged two months, and the mussels, or *mitili*, of La Spezia. The local basil, the most aromatic on earth, is renowned: it comes from farms situated in the area of Genoa Pra'. The *taggiasca* olive, small in size but very flavorful; ancient traditional techniques are used to process it, and it is ideal for preserving, and indispensable for preparing Ligurian-style rabbit. Purple asparagus of Albenga (in Albenga, to force the maturation of the early produce, asparagus is cultivated on cotton scraps, since the fermentation of the cotton fibers diffuses a warmth that makes the young asparagus grow more quickly, in about ten days).

Chestnuts. Ligurian (or Genovese) pesto. Walnut sauce, *marò* (seaman's) sauce, of fava beans, garlic, mint, and cheese: a specialty of San Remo. Salted anchovies or sardines.

Chinotti (bitter oranges), a rare variety of citrus (*Citrus myrtifolia*), cultivated only along the Riviera di Ponente, in the zone of Albenga, from which candied fruit, liqueurs, and the famous soft drink Chinotto are produced. Anise cookies of Lagaccio.

Rose syrup with lemon juice (a recipe born in Genoa).

TYPICAL BEVERAGE

Chilled white wine, drunk from a *pirone*, a cone-shaped glass carafe with a long, tall spout. The wine inside a *pirone* is slowly saturated with oxygen. Then it is poured from above, spurting directly into the mouth like a fountain, in a dramatic, picturesque way.[2]

THE EARLY GIFTS FROM THE AMERICAS

At the beginning of the modern era (from the seventeenth to the eighteenth century), both northern and southern Italy, typically so distinct from each other, suffered an identical, agonizing poverty. In all of Western Europe, a substantial part of the population lived in destitution during these two hundred years. In Italy malnutrition, if not starvation, reigned in rural areas. Poverty in the south meant filling stomachs with plants, fortunately rich in vitamins. In the north, on the other hand, where the population was hard-pressed to find nourishment in spelt soups, diseases raged and mortality was extremely high.

Things began to change in the eighteenth century, when the majority of territories in northern Italy were governed by the Hapsburgs: with the enterprise and the soundness typical of this dynasty, the Hapsburgs took energetic measures to fight poverty, promoting effective, constructive fiscal policies and introducing scientifically based reforms to agriculture. Hunger in the north was conquered thanks to the introduction of new crops in the rural areas of this vast region—crops that had been imported from the New World a century and a half earlier. The Austrian government supported and disseminated corn, and in some areas the potato, making them part of the Italian diet. The tomato did not need to be promoted: it was already widespread in the south and by unanimous, blissful acclaim was happily part of southerners' daily rations.

And so corn, a novelty that had reached Europe from America at the end of the six-

teenth century, became widely known in Italy thanks to the Hapsburgs, who at the time ruled Austria, Hungary, the Netherlands, northern Italy, and the Balkans. Up until the end of the seventeenth century, they had also exercised authority in Spain, to whom the discovery of the New World was owed. It is true that popular tradition, scientifically unfounded, attributed a different origin to this plant. The Tuscans called it (and still call it) *granoturco*, the Venetians *sorgo turco* (Turkish grain and Turkish sorghum). The Turks, however, call the same grain Egyptian wheat, while the Egyptians refer to it as Syrian wheat. The French who live in the Pyrenees call corn Spanish grain, which is in fact closer to the truth. Surprisingly, no one has ever given it the name that is most appropriate, namely, Mexican grain.

From Columbus's letter reporting to the Catholic sovereigns, it is clear that after having seen corn in the newly discovered lands, he and his crew were quite impressed by it:

> They then had bread and various fruits brought, and red and white wine, but not made from grapes, rather they must have been made of fruit, the red from one kind and the white from another, and similarly some other wine made of maize, which is a seed contained in a spikelet like a panicle that I brought to Castile, where there is already much of it; and it appears that the best maize is considered to be of great excellence and has great value.[1]

Among the many testimonies, the comments of other travelers of Columbus's time—Gerolamo Benzoni (1572),[2] Pietro Andrea Mattioli (1568)[3]—are curious, and also those of later observers: José de Acosta (1589),[4] Juan de Cardenas (1591),[5] and on the Inca, Garcilaso de la Vega (1609).[6] In Pietro Martire of Anghiera we read:

> They also make bread, with little difference, from a type of grain, *panìco*, which is found in great abundance among the Lombards and the Spanish of Granada. Its panicle is longer than a hand's span and ends in a point, almost the size of an arm; the kernels are arranged by nature in admirable order, according to shape and size, and they resemble a pea: when they are unripe, they are white, once matured they become very dark; when broken their candor exceeds that of snow; they call this species of grain maize.[7]

In the charming children's book *Il pentolino magico* (The magic pot), Massimo Montanari, a famous historian of Europe and of food, popularized an eighteenth-century text from the pen of the writer Giovanni Battarra. The latter recounted a curious dialogue (set in 1780), typical of a family of small tenant farmers in Romagna:

> "The custom of planting corn," the father says in response to a question from his son Ceccone, "goes back about forty years ago [that is, to around 1740]. In the beginning we planted it in small quantities, just enough to make polenta eight or ten times; then, seeing that the harvests were successful, we allotted it more space. And if you, my sons, had been here in 1715, the year of the famine, you would have seen the families of poor peasants like us searching for grass and roots to eat plain, without any condiments, or making bread from acorns or vine shoots. Now that we have this new food instead, we are able to get by even in the worst years. What's more, they are introducing certain foreign roots now, similar to truffles, that they call potatoes."

"What are they used for?" Ceccone asks.

"They are an excellent food for men no less than for animals," the father explains, "and if we, too, are able to plant them, we will no longer suffer from scarcity."

"Are you joking?" Mingone, the other son, interrupts.

"I'm serious," the father admonishes him. "This morning the landowner gave me two haversacks of those tubers, which are eaten cooked in several ways: boiled, roasted under the coals, flavored with milk or butter . . . and bread is also made from them."

"Bread? But the bread that is made from these roots will taste different than that made with wheat flour."

"A bread with good taste and color, that does not harden for a month, and does not get moldy . . ."

"That would be a great advantage," Mingone comments. "Those of us who consume eleven or twelve sacks of wheat per year could save by half. But tell me, can bread be made using only potato flour?"

"It can be," the father replies, "though they say that such bread is somewhat difficult to digest."

"Well!" Mingone exclaims. "Indigestion doesn't bother peasants. On the contrary, they think they are more full that way."[8]

Educated gentlemen subsequently introduced corn to the people, teaching them to make polenta from it. The trouble was that corn had been brought to Europe without any notion of its correct dietary use.[9] The absence of vitamin B_3 (niacin) in corn caused pellagra, sometimes called "sickness of the rose," to begin spreading among the Italian population, afflicting them with a disease that throughout the world assumed the name of Italian leprosy (*lepra italica*). Another disease of those who ate polenta exclusively was goiter (cretinism), caused by a deficiency of iodine in the water and in the food. A deficiency of iodine (and an excess of polenta) was typical of the diet of the mountain province of Bergamo; consequently the people of Bergamo became the favorite targets of long-standing jokes.

The Europeans did not know that the Mayas and Aztecs softened corn with lime water to make it more edible.[10] Only later on, once Italians realized the need to introduce a protein component into the diet, did they add cheese or butter to polenta, along with highly salted foods: anchovies, spicy salami, game (in Bergamo), hare (in Lodi). Only then was polenta freed of its reputation as a harmful, dangerous food for the poor.

The corn that was first imported had a particular flavor, and the panicles or cobs contained only eight rows of kernels. Present-day corn, a product of genetic selection, has cobs with kernels arranged in fifteen or as many as twenty-four rows. Unfortunately, however, genetic selection has diminished corn's flavor quite a bit. In recent times, the Slow Food Association has been engaged in rescuing the original variety of this plant, the eight-row corn of the Garfagnana region. Only a few cobs of this variety remained in Italy in the final years of the twentieth century. And although this species is grown in vast plots of land today, that is still not sufficient to avert the danger of extinction.

Besides corn, authorities in northern Italy also imposed "from above" the potato, the so-called American chestnut. The potato arrived, naturally, from America, though not through Spain, as corn did, but rather through France, where it had been introduced into daily life (with great success) by the gastronome of the court of Louis XVI, Augustin Parmentier. Parmentier had planted the first potato tubers experimentally at the royal riding academy. Given the Italians' strong aversion to and rivalry with France, they received the potato grudgingly. It was only when forced by circumstances, against the background of a new, tragic famine at the beginning of the nineteenth century (caused by several wars), that the potato was successfully introduced into the population's diet.

Unlike the other early gifts from America, the tomato (*tomatl*, "succulent fruit" in the Nahuatl language) took root spontaneously in the south. In the second half of the sixteenth century, Europeans attributed magical virtues and aphrodisiacal properties to the tomato. At first they called it *pomme d'amour* (love apple), but the Sienese botanist Pietro Andrea Mattioli successfully renamed it *pomme d'or* (golden apple). The French, British, and Germans instead followed the American phonetic pronunciation and began calling the new fruit tomatoes.

People of the sixteenth century could not help but be struck by the beauty of tomatoes when observing them. Costanzo Felici, a physician from Modena, wrote that they were "more beautiful than beneficial."[11] The first pictorial representation of tomatoes in Europe, like the first representation of corn, is found in a painting by Arcimboldo of 1592: in the portrait of Rudolph II as Vertumnus, cherry tomatoes (*Lycopersicon cerasiforme*) make up the lips.

The tomato's story is the complete opposite of the potato's. While the potato was imposed from above, introduced almost by force, tomatoes first caught on among the lower classes in the sixteenth century, and later aroused the interest of aristocrats. Toward the middle of the sixteenth century, common people in southern Italy were already eating tomatoes, frying them in oil with salt and pepper, like eggplants. The dominant classes, on the contrary, showed a certain resistance in accepting the crop.

Only toward the end of the eighteenth century did the great chefs and gastronomes, starting with Vincenzo Corrado, begin to take a serious interest in tomatoes. And only beginning in the mid-nineteenth century (only 150 years ago and not before) did the very dish that is considered an authentic gastronomic emblem of all Italy appear in Naples: *pasta al pomodoro* (or *vermicielli c'a pummarola*, as pasta with tomato sauce is called in the Neapolitan dialect).

Ippolito Cavalcanti, Duke of Buonvicino, describes these feasts in the book *Cucina casareccia* (Home cooking), written in the Neapolitan dialect, along with the *Cucina teorico-pratica* (Theory and practice of cooking) of 1850, describing how he happened to taste pasta with tomato sauce for the first time in 1839.

In Naples—where they had spontaneously invented fast food by selling steaming hot macaroni along the city's streets—pasta was still *bianca*, or *incaciata*, that is, sprinkled with cheese, in Goethe's time. Only toward the middle of the nineteenth century did Neapolitan *pastasciutta* acquire that very emblematic and patriotic look that we all know—white and red with a touch of green basil—which subsequently entered the bloodstream of every Italian and became famous throughout the world.[12]

It was at this time that the four-tined fork was invented in Naples, in consideration of these innovative macaronis bathed in scarlet sauce. Upon the explicit request of the Bourbon king Ferdinand II (1831–59), the royal majordomo Gennaro Spadaccini in the 1830s introduced into use a short fork with four tines, replacing the longer one with three. While it was practically impossible to wrap the spaghetti around a three-tined fork without losing the sauce, the task became fairly easy with a four-tined one. Thus, thanks to the importation of the tomato from America, humanity was forever enriched with this utensil.

Emilia Romagna

Both Emilia and Romagna take their names from great roads of
ancient Rome. Via Emilia, constructed in 187 B.C. by the
consul Marcus Emilius Lepidus and straight as an arrow, leads
from Rimini through Lombardy and Piedmont (Novara and Tor-
tona) to Aosta and the strategic St. Bernard Pass, which in ancient times was the only
opening in the chain of Alps leading to France. Via Emilia crosses Bologna, Modena,
Reggio Emilia, Parma, Piacenza, Imola, Faenza, Forlì, and Cesena, and in nearly all
these cities it constitutes the principal thoroughfare, or *decumanus*. The plan of many
Emilian cities today reflects the ancient chessboard design of the Roman military
encampment. It is the result of the so-called centurionization adopted in the *ars gro-
matica*, as surveying was called in Rome. Like the avenues and streets of New York,
the streets in the cities of the Roman Empire were perpendicular and parallel to one
another, and were called *cardones* (horizontal or cross streets) and *decumani* (longitudinal streets). In this way square sectors approximately 710 meters per side were
formed. These were the dimensions of the plot of land that a veteran of the Roman
army was usually given as retirement pay upon being discharged.

Via Emilia has not changed its name in over two thousand years, even though in
official nomenclature it is now State Route 9.

Via Romea, which gave its name to Romagna, is not as rectilinear: winding

gently through the hills, it leads from Rimini to Rome. The exact translation of the term "Romea" is "road of the pilgrims." The name "Romea" was often used generally as well, applied not only to this road, but to other routes of penitence. Via Francigena (French Road), Via dell'Ambra (Amber Road), Via dei Normanni (Norman Road), and Via Petrina (St. Peter's Road) are also referred to as "Romea" in various texts.

In the Roman era, when the tradition of pilgrimages did not yet exist, Via Romea had another name: Via Popilia, in honor of the consul Publius Popilius Lenatus, who had had it constructed in the second century A.D. Via Popilia acquired great importance when the emperor Honorius transferred the capital of the Western Roman Empire from Rome to Ravenna at the beginning of the fifth century.

When Rome later acquired spiritual authority in the Christian world, thereby becoming the destination of pilgrimages for all *romei* (pilgrims), the name changed to Via Romea. It went from the eastern extremity of Europe—Czestochowa, Poland—to

Italy; in Italy it broke off at Aquileia (an important stop for many pilgrimages) and took the sea route, touching land again at Ravenna; from there it moved into the interior of the territory, crossing Tolentino, Assisi, and Spoleto, and led the pilgrims to Rome's holy places.

From Aquileia some pilgrims pushed on to Padua for a lengthy stop, where there was a large, notable hospital. Here the pilgrims could catch their breath, get examined and treated, and then resume the long journey toward Rome. From Padua, the road ran through swampy areas (the marshes were drained only in the twenty-year Fascist period, the Ventennio) to the prosperous abbey of Pomposa (eleventh century), which rose on a dry islet. At this abbey, an important transit point for pilgrim routes, the Benedictine monks were intensely involved in accommodating the wayfarers. The monks offered both spiritual comfort and physical support (often at a high price) to the wealthy—the merchants and the powerful of the world—many of whom stayed at the abbey for months. The arts flourished in Pomposa, and a significant library was assembled. The abbey was one of the strongholds of the mystic Middle Ages, a cradle of liturgical chant. It was here, listening to the Hymn of Saint Giovanni in 1026, that Guido d'Arezzo invented the graphic marks to indicate musical notes that are still universally used by composers.

A region of intersecting roads, Emilia Romagna embodies the principle of relentless movement. Here it is easy to chart the mingling of ideas and images over time through architectural styles. At every kilometer, the traveler sees unfolding before him a new entry in the encyclopedia of figurative arts: the Romanesque cathedrals of Modena, the Gothic cathedral of Bologna, the Byzantine mosaics of Ravenna, the city of Ferrara (a Renaissance jewel), and the decadent Liberty-style buildings in seaside Rimini. In Romagna and Emilia the force of movement can be felt, the poetry of speed, the allure of open space. Every resident possesses either a motorbike or a bicycle. It was in Emilia that the engineer Lamborghini, the Maserati brothers, and the great Enzo Ferrari were able to realize their talents. Ferrari race cars are still designed, assembled, and tested in Maranello, near Modena.

Emilia Romagna presents two faces of Italy. Emilia was as rich and fertile as Romagna was poor and problematic. This dual identity developed after the dissolution of the Roman Empire and the Lombard conquest in 568. The Lombards took possession of the western half of the present-day region (Emilia), while the eastern part of the territory (Romagna) remained under the dominion of the Eastern Roman Empire. Soon enough, under Pope Adrian I, in the eighth century, with the aid of the "recalled" army of Franks led by Charlemagne, the Papal State took the entire territory of Emilia from the Lombards, turning it into its own colony. The feudal marquises, subject to the clerics, squeezed unpaid labor and taxes out of the population until the pressure became intolerable and a period of revolts followed. Free communes governed by elected magistrates, or *podestà*, sprang up all over Emilia beginning in the tenth century. The first of these to win autonomy were Bologna, Piacenza, Modena, Reggio, Parma, and Ferrara. The communes were perennially warring with one another, and the power of the stronger families was established as the cities struggled. This is how the aristocratic families of the Farnese in Parma, the Visconti in Piacenza, and the Estes in Ferrara distinguished themselves.

On the other hand, Romagna—which came under the dominion of the Papal State later on, after being under the control of the Eastern Roman Empire and Venice—could not rebel when the time came, because its cities had not learned to defend their independence. At the beginning of the sixteenth century, with the weakening of Venice and the defeat of its armies in the Battle of Agnadello (1508) at the hands of the League of Cambrai, which included the armies of the pope as well, Romagna became part of the Papal State and remained so until the unification of Italy.

The landscape of the region is defined by the valley of the Po River and by the mountainous ridge of the Apennines. To the right and to the left of the river is the the Pianura Padana, the Po Valley, with its characteristic rows of sparse poplars and plowed fields, among which are scattered ancient square farmsteads, solid as little fortresses. Inside each square parcel is a barnyard. All around it are cultivated plots, planted with corn and succulent grasses, and meadows where cattle graze. Pigs are fed by foraging. Some are even bred to root about freely; they are so well trained that they return to their ties by themselves at night, after having accumulated some fat in the vast chestnut and oak forests on the slopes of the Tuscan-Emilian Apennines. Indeed, the historian Polybius wrote in 180 B.C. that oak woods are so abundant there, the majority of Italian pigs feed on acorns that have fallen to the ground.

It is not surprising that Emilia and Romagna are home to the most famous cured pork meats of Italy—the prosciutto of Parma and *culatello* of Zibello—as well as the most renowned aged cheese on the planet: Parmigiano-Reggiano. When buying prosciutto in Emilia, you must be prepared to answer the deli clerk's questions: prosciutto from Parma or Modena? Aged a year or eighteen months? And do you want the upper end of the prosciutto (the *fiocco*) or the *didietro* (*culatello*, or behind), which is sliced once the enormous round bone has been removed from the prosciutto?

The vast, level plots of land in Emilia and Romagna are well suited to cultivation. Along with Puglia and Campania, Emilia Romagna is the greatest producer of tomatoes, sugar beets, peas, and beans in Italy. The Po, meanwhile, is rich in prized freshwater fish. One of the local specialties is sliced freshwater fish stewed in a cast iron pot: tench, goldfish, carp, pike, and sheatfish. These dishes are served with polenta. Abundantly displayed on the hillsides are vineyards of Lambrusco grapes and large fruit tree orchards, grown with the most modern methods.

All in all, Emilia, combined with Romagna, formerly a valley of poverty, is the belly of Italy today. Emilia, it should be said, has always been synonymous with gluttonous dishes: mortadella, prosciutto, Parmesan, homemade egg pasta of all shapes. To digest all this abundance, a good vinegar is needed as dressing. And not just any vinegar, but the balsamic vinegar of Modena, the world's most noble.

The history of aromatic vinegar, an extremely important component of the Italian culinary tradition and of the Mediterranean diet, is very colorful. In the Middle Ages, vinegar was considered a medicinal substance, capable of disinfecting the organism and preventing epidemics of gastroenteritis. In the eighteenth century, balsamic vinegar became a commonly used medicine. And not just any medicine: the Modenese historian Ludovico Antonio Muratori (1672–1750) considered it a powerful remedy for the plague.

It is not surprising, then, that the production of vinegars developed close to cities with great hospitals or universities. Modena is one such city, situated between the university centers of Pavia and Bologna. The balsamic vinegar of Modena is a classic, a gastronomic emblem not only of its city of origin, but of all of Italy.

Balsamic vinegar is mentioned for the first time in a text written by the Benedictine monk Donizone, who lived between the eleventh and twelfth centuries. Starting in the fifteenth century, recipes for the vinegar, which is made of grape must, are found in cookbooks: it has no substitutes either at the aristocratic banquet or in the poor man's modest kitchen. We find mention of it as well in the third satire written by Ludovico Ariosto, a native of the duchy of Ferrara, in 1518. The author of *Orlando Furioso* cites vinegar in his poem not as the apotheosis of fine cuisine, but as the basis of temperance. In Ariosto's satire, the well-read protagonist yearning for freedom does not need the rich morsels that have fallen from the lord's table, such as thrush, partridge, and wild boar. He is satisfied with a turnip boiled at home and seasoned with vinegar and *sapa*, or wine must (the *mostarda* mentioned many times in this book). This is the best of all foods:

> *At home, I much prefer a turnip*
> *that I cook myself, and once cooked I spear it on a stick*
> *and peel and sprinkle it with vinegar and cooked must,*
>
> *this I prefer to the thrush, partridge, and wild boar served at other people's tables,*
> *similarly under a modest blanket*
> *I sleep as well as under one of silk or gold.*

The technological cycle requires that the vinegar be aged in special cave-vaults where abrupt temperature changes are recorded each day. The aging process of the product lasts at least twelve years; particularly prized varieties are aged for twenty-five or thirty years, and even longer.

To make such a vinegar (a nectar more expensive than vintage cognac), you take the best wine, white or red, Lambrusco or Trebbiano, bring it to a boil, and then add the mother. This mother, composed of the bacteria responsible for the acidification (*Acetobacter aceti*) that is found in the gelatinous deposit that forms on the bottom of the casks where the mature product is stored, is a real treasure, and is jealously guarded to maintain its secrets and keep it far from the curiosity of "gastronomic spies." In the early phase, the decoction is kept in very large containers, called *botticelli*. Later, as new servings of the mother are added, the liquid is poured into smaller and smaller barrels. A special collar is put on each barrel, which acts as a barrier against unwanted bacteria. With decanting and adding, a complex alchemy is followed: a little liquid is poured from the larger barrel into a smaller one, according to canonical proportions; three weeks to a month are allowed to go by; then more adding, more pouring, and so on. The first barrels must be made of mulberry wood, the subsequent ones of chestnut and cherry, the last ones of oak and ash. Every now and then cloves, cinnamon, coriander, licorice, and nutmeg are added (this recipe is also secret). And so balsamic vinegar, at one time sold in pharmacies, has become an unparalleled ingredient in cooking.

Many Italian cities have earned nicknames over the centuries. Venice is called La Serenissima, the Most Serene; Genoa La Superba, the Arrogant; Brescia La Leonessa, the Lioness; and Rome La Città Eternal, the Eternal City.[1] Bologna has two nicknames: La Grassa, the Fat, and La Dotta, the Learned (it was in Bologna that the first law university in Europe was founded, in 1119). "One eats more in Bologna in a year than in Venice in two, in Rome in three, in Turin in five, and in Genoa in twenty," wrote Ippolito Nievo (1831–61) in *Le confessioni di un italiano* (The confessions of an Italian). Pavel Muratov's response to Nievo:

> In Bologna there is something light that cheers the eye, agreeably not too complicated. It is a city of contented, healthy people. The fattest granaries and vineyards of Italy surround it, producing a renowned wine. No other place can compare with Bologna for the abundance, variety, and good price of every possible and imaginable foodstuff, and it is no accident that the Italians call it "Bologna la Grassa."[2]

That the nickname was not bestowed in vain is evidenced in the description of a Bolognese feast of January 28, 1487, when Giovanni II Bentivoglio, ruler of Bologna, celebrated the arrival of his son, Annibale, and his wife, Lucrezia d'Este.

> To begin with, the crowd could admire *pignoccati*, pine nut biscotti, and *cialdoni*, cornets of sweet pastry, accompanied by sweet wines in silver vessels; then roasted pigeons, pig's liver, thrush, and partridge with olives and grapes, all arranged on 125 silver platters, one of which (in accordance with the custom of the time) would be served for every two guests. Then a gilded basket with bread passed by. Afterward a sugar castle was carried in, with merlons and towers: it was entirely filled with live birds that, once released, flew out to the great amusement of the guests. Next came a roe deer and an ostrich, followed by meat pies and calf's heads,[3] then stewed capons, veal breasts and loins, kid, sausages, pigeons, and, along with the meats, the *sapori* or relishes, that is, the sauces, in gilded silver vessels; puréed vegetables and various other gravies served as side dishes. After that came peacocks cooked and then re-dressed with their feathers in the shape of a fan; each gentleman received one, adorned with his family's crest. Meanwhile trays of mortadella, stewed hare, and venison were prepared— and displayed in the piazza—but all covered with their skin, to make them seem alive. And still more trays of doves and pheasants, accompanied by apples, oranges, and additional sauces. And sugar cakes with almond paste, *giuncate* [curds of freshly made cheese] with biscotti, kids' heads, roasted doves and partridges, and a castle—of sugar like the other one—full of live rabbits . . .
>
> Still another castle was brought in at this point; in it was a large wild boar who,

unable to get out, was grunting . . . As the boar snorted and bellowed, the stewards served the golden roast suckling pigs. At the end, cheeses and ice creams were presented, along with pears, pastries, sweets, marzipan, and other similar delights.[4]

Given such love of extravagance, it is not surprising that, in centuries which exalted plump women, the women of Bologna were considered the most irresistible, the most appetizing. "Ah! Bologna! how sweetly mixed are the elements in thy women!" wrote Boccaccio. The Marquis de Sade also spoke about the beauty of Bologna's women, with no small satisfaction, in the notes on his second Italian journey (1775). Reputation and anecdotes ascribe to the residents of Bologna, and especially to its female denizens, a lively sexuality, which evidently emerges in the blissful enjoyment of food, but which is probably also influenced by the atmosphere of this old university town: in bygone days 35 percent of the city's population was made up of young men who came there to study, but also to flirt and have a good time. Even today, judging from society news, it seems that the most beautiful women of Italy are found in Bologna and Parma.

If the cuisine of Liguria is a cuisine of return (to dry land) and that of Emilia is a cuisine of indulgence, then Romagna's is logically a cuisine for traveling. Its badge is the medieval "sandwich," namely, the *piada* or *piadina*, the most famous specialty of Romagna: a soft, round flatbread wrapped around a filling of vegetables or cheese. The *piada*, whose name is related to the word *piatto*, flat, is cooked on the grill or in the hearth, on a *testo*, or earthenware slab. It is also the subject of a poem that Giovanni Pascoli wrote about the preparation of *piadine*:

> *And you, Maria, with your gentle hands*
> *knead the dough, then stretch and flatten it*
> *and there it is, smooth as a sheet and big*
> *as the moon, and on outspread hands*
> *you bring it to me and settle it gently*
> *on the heated* testo, *and then go away.*
>
> *I turn it and, with the tongs, poke*
> *the fire beneath, until infused*

by the moderate heat, it crisps and bubbles up
and the aroma of bread fills the house.[5]

The *piada* was often a makeshift solution, a handy expedient when bread was in short supply in the cupboard. It took little time to prepare since the dough for the *piada* did not have to rise (starting in the early twentieth century, it became customary to add baking soda or brewer's yeast to the dough, along with milk, lard, or honey).

The cost of baking *piadine* was inexpensive, in part because just a few coals were sufficient and there was no need to consume firewood. Accompaniments to the *piada* also cost very little: wild herbs or vegetables, raw or cooked in a pan, or, more rarely, fresh cheeses. Ancient varieties of the classic *piada* were *piadotto* (water, cornmeal, and raisins: today it is found only in old recipe books) and *cassone* or *crescione*, whose shape recalls the Roman calzone: a *piada* folded in half and stuffed with the usual greens or (in the Forlivese mountains) with squash, potatoes, and ricotta.

Piadina is thus an example of poor man's fast food, suitable to serve as nourishment for wayfarers. But to say that Romagna's gastronomy is exclusively "travel cuisine" would be a cliché. No region of Italy can be described by means of a single stereotype. The truth is much more complicated, even in Romagna's case. Romagna's Comacchio Lagoon and its many swamps make up an unusual world, far removed from fast, easy roads and the carefree euphoria of travel: an unreal, romantic atmosphere.

The sweetness of the word "lagoon" tricks the imagination, generating associations with the caressing breezes of Polynesia, but Comacchio does not resemble Polynesia although the sunsets here, too, are fabulously beautiful: flocks of birds fly over the lagoon in the blood-red sky, and abandoned beacons and the ruins of medieval strongholds rise above the swamp. But furious currents here pierce both body and soul. The dampness goes right through you. The area of Comacchio at one time was saturated with water; the main profession of the inhabitants was digging channels for reclamation. Consistent with their profession, they were called *scariolanti*, pushers of *carriole*, wheelbarrows. The hard work in the cold must in some way have driven the local population to develop political ideas that were radically leftist and even anarchical. It is no accident that, in the twenties, it was in this corner of Romagna that many ideological conflicts, scandals, and fights flared up between anarchists and Fascists.[6]

After having dug a number of canals near the city, the local *scariolanti* went elsewhere in search of work. Their work was always in demand, of course, in Venice first of all, and second by the architects at the court of the Este family in Ferrara. For many centuries the swamps around Ferrara, which today have vanished, required the constant intervention of the reclaimers. Finally, in Mussolini's time, the Comacchio laborers were dispatched in an organized way to construct the great works of the regime: the reclamation of the Pontine Marshes near Rome and the draining of the terrible Sardinian marshes. Thanks to them, Fascist high-rise cities rose in place of the swamps: Latina, Sabaudia, Pontinia, Aprilia, and Pomezia in Lazio and Mussolinia (today Arborea) in Sardinia.

Two important occupations of the local people in these swamps are fishing and eel catching. The catadromous eels, born in the ocean, swim toward the delta of some great river after three years or so and spend the greater part of their lives in freshwater, until the age of eight to ten years: only then do they return to the ocean, thereby condemning themselves to death. Once sexual maturity is reached, the eels cross the cold, foggy marshes of the Po Delta, reach the open sea, and swim to the Atlantic Ocean; after swimming across it, they mate near its western shore, in the Gulf of Mexico, deposit their eggs, and die in the Sargasso Sea. While still in freshwater preparing for their suicidal migration, the eels, having reached approximately eight years of age, change color from yellow to silver and begin gobbling up food to accumulate fat before the long reproductive season in the Sargasso Sea, where they will then pay with their lives for a single moment of amorous exaltation.

The eels' migration begins in the coldest season, between the end of November and the end of December. Sometimes the eels also have a second migration, in the month of February. To prevent the fattened eels from slipping into the sea, fishermen install complex systems of traps called *lavorieri*, made of reeds. These are positioned at strategic points where seawater, warm and flowing, saturated with oxygen, pours into the lagoon. The reed traps are environmentally perfect. Eel fishermen, in fact, do not use plastic nets or enclosures even today, as a matter of principle. The *lavoriere* is devised in such a way that young eels three years of age (called blind eels), swimming in the opposite direction—from the ocean toward the historic birthplace of their forebears, in the marshes of Comacchio—can easily pass through it. Entering along with them are mullet, bass, and whitebait—a gift that allows the inhabitants of the area to vary their menus. The eels swimming from the river toward the ocean, on the other hand, remain trapped in the *lavorieri*'s weave. They are removed from the traps on frosty nights, in absolute silence, with a full moon providing a faint light that is sufficient to at least partially see what is thrashing around in the water (artificial illumination is not advisable).

The wonderful Museo Civico delle Valli, a museum that illustrates how the still fishing method used for many centuries was organized, is situated in the valleys of Comacchio. During the period of the eel migration, the fishermen settled down in huts built on rafts. A shipboard discipline reigned among the crews, with a rigid hierarchical scale from the lowest rank (cabin boy) to the highest (captain); and there had to be a scribe in every crew to keep accounts. Somberly committed to their monotonous work—pulling the slippery tapered fish out of the marsh—the workers, at the end of the season, could choose between two options. They could transport the catch to Venice on *marotte* (rafts with special eel cages attached to the bottom, submerged in the water), keeping the eels alive, only to let them meet an atrocious death in the frying pan after a morning at the market. Or they could process and marinate the caught eels there on the spot, in the "fish factories." In that case, the beheaded eels continued to thrash about on the slimy floor for at least an hour. Then, finally, they could be threaded on skewers and roasted over a fire while the fat drippings were collected in pans and preserved in cans.

Spit-roasted eels are a renowned typical product for export. It is known that during the Congress of Vienna four barrels of smoked, roasted eels were brought from Comacchio for Metternich personally. In that way the inhabitants of Romagna dreamed of ingratiating themselves with Metternich: the historically radical, freedom-loving region hoped to obtain longed-for independence from papal power when the time came for the definitive partition of Europe. To be fair, Metternich was not to be bought: he took the eels, but did not stoop to compromises.

Eels are also roasted on the grill split in half, giving them the shape of a violin (*anguilla a violino*). Or they are roasted directly on live coals (*a braciolette*). Particularly prized are the larger specimens, called *capitoni*. On Christmas Eve, in many regions of Italy, people go wild searching for this rare treat, to display it on the holiday table. The most prized specimens are intended for the festive table: the females, which reach a length of nearly a meter and a weight of almost five kilograms. The smaller eels are called *buratelle* and are less sought after.

The sliced eels were exported, and the local inhabitants were left with the scraps: the heads. These became traditional ingredients for an important regional dish, *brodetto* (fish soup), which besides being eaten as is could also be used as a base for the typical risotto. According to William Black, author of *Al Dente*,[7] even seagulls once ended up in this broth. Experts claim that in Comacchio's cuisine you can even find a stew of eel entrails and a salami made with pieces of eel left over from processing, stuffed into eel skin and left to dry.

In Salsomaggiore Terme, another village with a completely different character, salsobromoidic waters gush right out of the ground. There, among therapeutic waters and rejuvenating muds, Gemma salt, billed throughout Italy as a valid alternative to sea salt, is extracted and packaged for sale. From these parts, between the provinces of Piacenza and Parma, the Via Francigena of the penitents crossed the Apennines, connecting Pavia to Lucca (see "Pilgrims"). Upon reaching the thermal springs of Salsomaggiore, the Rome-bound pilgrims would rest and linger a bit in the salt waters. They washed their horses in Bagnacavallo and knelt before the image of the Madonna of Careno in Pellegrino Parmense. It is in Pellegrino Parmense that the celebrated Fair of Parmigiano-Reggiano takes place each year, at the beginning of July. Evidently Parmesan, a hard, highly caloric, and vitamin-rich cheese that does not spoil even in the warmest months, was also considered a food for the pilgrims' journey. Toward the south lies the ancient town of Bobbio, celebrated for the abbey founded by St. Columbanus in 614. The town of Bobbio is also famous for its snails, including those that are smoked (their *sagra* is celebrated each year, in December), and its highly sought-after white truffles.

The city of Ferrara has always been a fashionable, aristocratic place. One of the most opulent courts of the Renaissance, Ferrara was the principal showcase for the creations of Italian designers and perfumers in the fifteenth and sixteenth centuries. The ceremonious, solemn ducal life called for sumptuous banquets, for which ceramic tableware was expressly produced in the fifteenth century in the city of Faenza, not too far from Ferrara. Arabic plates were used as models, having been brought to Romagna by pilgrims and monks returning from the Spanish sanctuary of Santiago de Compostela. The plates were called majolica, after the island of Majorca. Thus the splendid majolica of Faenza was born, today part and parcel of the history of European applied art. Faenza was also the birthplace of desserts that were as gaily colored as the ceramics: candied fruit and fruit cup medleys.

Following the disorderly binges of the Middle Ages, decorous behavior became a norm for diners in Ferrara, in accordance with the elegantly laid tables. The introduction of etiquette demanded persistence on the part of the host, presence of mind on the part of the guests, and swift service from the household staff. Those invited to the banquet were made to understand that meat could no longer be torn apart with one's hands, but at the same time this held the hosts responsible for ensuring that it was sliced and served on time on individual plates. As a result, the success of the meal was determined by the swiftness of the steward, the servant assigned to carve and serve the meats. In Ferrara, this task was assigned to skilled virtuosos, who were intellectuals to boot. In 1533, Ferrarese majordomo Cristoforo da Messisbugo was so skillfully able to carve the meat on the plate of the most distinguished guest, Emperor Charles V, that the emperor bestowed on him the title of Count Palatine. At the time, Cristoforo was already the author of the first printed handbook on the art of serving at banquets,[8] a work that was later supplemented by a number of recipes and reprinted many times over with the title of *Libro novo nel qual s'insegna a far d'ogni sorte di vivanda secondo la diversità de i tempi così di carne come di pesce* (New book that teaches how to make every kind of dish depending on the different seasons for meat as well as fish).

The scholarly Cristoforo da Messisbugo was not the only one of his kind. Besides Cristoforo, Ferrara was home to the noted author of *Il trinciante* (The carver), Giovan Battista Rossetti. Working in a similar capacity in Parma was Vincenzo Cervio, author of a cookbook with the same title. Bartolomeo Stefani worked as a carver in Bologna, not in the sixteenth but in the seventeenth century.

Tradition is always combined with innovation in Emilia and Romagna. Intellectual activity is prized here, and ideas deified. Socialism was so well received here in the twentieth century that it generated Mussolini's *fasci*, or political groups, which were formed for the first time in Romagna. In the fifteenth century, Prince Alberto III of the Pio family, a refined humanist and man of letters, imagined an ideal city and sketched its plan on paper. The architect Baldassarre Peruzzi transformed the dream into reality, and the city of Carpi was born: intelligently laid out, with a circular plan, the city is industrious and still today opulent (Carpi is also the capital of a textile district). From the time of its origins, Carpi has vaunted its own culinary rarity. The recipe of the famous Carpi *mostarda*, unlike that of Cremona *mostarda*, does not call for sugar: the fruit, boiled in must with the mustard, is sweetened with orange syrup.

Among the gastronomic specialties of Ferrara, however, one has survived unchanged for six centuries and is still prepared according to an ancient, rigid ritual. It is the *salama da sugo*, which is not at all a salami. Before ending up at the table, this product requires lengthy boiling in water (either in a bain-marie or steamer), wrapped tightly in a cloth so that it does not split open (today there are excellent little plastic bags that can endure cooking) and hung in such a way that it does not touch the pot. To eat it, you uncover it and scoop out the soft, juicy mixture with a spoon: cutting it with a knife is forbidden. It is usually accompanied by mashed potatoes, though much more typical of Ferrara, with its customary sweet-savory contrast, is mashed pumpkin: potatoes, as we know, came later, from America. An entire epic was dedicated to it, the *Salameide* by Antonio Frizzi (1772), from which, in particular, it is clear that the *salama* is composed mainly of liver, and not of meat:

> *From pig liver mixed with a little meat,*
> *ground and chopped in a grinder,*
> *a succulent* salama *my Ferrara*
> *makes, which is not found elsewhere . . .*

According to the recipe that Riccardo Bacchelli (1891–1985) describes in his popular novel *Il mulino del Po* (*The Mill on the Po*), 1938–40, for the *salama* to age it must be kept in a cold place for five years (one year, according to Pellegrino Artusi). It must then be boiled for a long time, for eight to ten hours in keeping with one theory, ten to twelve hours according to another. Giuseppe Longhi—in his book *Le donne, i cavalier, l'armi, gli amori* (Of loves and ladies, knights and arms, I sing)[9]—says that the *salamina* was considered irreplaceable at wedding banquets in the lavish court of Ferrara for its hematopoietic virtues and because it gave a man who has tasted it virile potency and tender ardor. Domenico Vincenzo Chendi, parish priest of the Romagna village of Tresigallo (in the province of Ferrara), who lived in the eighteenth century, compiled a treatise on the upright agrarian life: when he reached the subject of cured meats and, in particular, the *salama da sugo*, he wrote that, among the divine punishments hurled down upon the Jews, the heaviest punishment was the "deprivation of this excellent and most beneficial food."

TYPICAL DISHES OF EMILIA ROMAGNA

First Courses Variations on the theme of ravioli. The traditional filling is made of roasted meat and Parmesan, or soft bread and egg, or greens (spinach, chard) with Parmesan. The pasta dough, unlike the dry kind, kneaded with water, is a blend of flour and eggs in which there should not be a single drop of water (see "Pasta"). Emilian stuffed pastas, such as tortellini (Bologna and Modena), *agnolini* (Piacenza and Parma), *cappelletti* (Reggio Emilia and Ferrara), and pumpkin-filled *tortelli* (Ferrara), are famous. Well-known in Romagna are *agnolotti, garganelli, passatelli, strozzapreti*, and *ravioli* with chestnut filling (Faenza). Fried gnocchi in Emilia. In addition to the filled pastas, the *panzerotti*, a specialty of Piacenza, deserve separate mention: these are a type of *crespella* (crepe or pancake) filled with ricotta and spinach (*panzerotti alla piacentina*, Piacenza-style). Lasagna, widespread throughout the region, should also be mentioned: composed, as everyone knows, of layers of pasta noodles alternating with *ragù* and drizzled with béchamel. Tagliatelle, fresh egg noodles in the shape of long, flat ribbons, are served and eaten with many sauces, but traditionally with meat *ragù*. A sauce of cubed prosciutto fried in butter is also used. Spinach is found in the dough of green tagliatelle.

Another basic item of the local cuisine is the *piadina*.

In Emilia focaccias called *chizze* are made, stuffed with slivers of Parmesan and then fried in lard, along with the so-called *crescente* (riser), the focaccia from Bologna (the raised part of Piazza Maggiore in Bologna bears the same name: Crescentone). Bits of lard are added to its dough, which is composed of flour and ice water.

Soups These are typically very thick, with ten varieties of fish at the same time (ironically they are called *brodetto*, light broth), sometimes made with eel. In the eel-based *brodetto* no oil is added: its own fat is sufficient. Also famous are marinated eels (factories for their production have existed in the Po Delta for more or less three hundred years). These eels are first roasted alive over oak wood coals, then immersed in the marinade.

Second Courses To be truthful, there are no particularly interesting second-course dishes in Emilia and in Romagna: for the most part they are traditional meat dishes that differ from city to city. Although the pig, with everything that can possibly be derived from its butchering, is foremost at the top of the gastronomical pyramid in Emilia, there is one place in the region (Piacenza) where horsemeat (*picula d'caval*, ground up like meatballs) and goat (cubed and cooked in white wine) are more prized than pork. Parma's specialty is pigeon roasted on a spit; Modena's is hare. In Sarsina, the town where Plautus lived and wrote his works, the typical dish is mutton from young sheep (the *castrato*), stuffed with juniper berries. In Reggio Emilia, it is turkey (turkey pie). In Guastalla, near Reggio Emilia, it's guinea hen. Throughout Romagna, it's lamb (*romagnola*-style), with peas and tomato sauce.

In Reggio Emilia boiled greens seasoned simply with oil and salt are often eaten. In Casola Valsenio, in the province of Ravenna, you can visit an incredible botanical garden, the Giardino delle Erbe (Herb Garden): four hundred species of edible herbs, grown on four hectares of land, a genuine living encyclopedia. In Reggio herbs are used to stuff the *piadine* and to make a savory pie aptly called the *erbazzone*.

The most famous of the herbs of Romagna is called *stridoli* or *strigoli* (*Silene vulgaris angustifolia*); it is used in a soup made with meat broth and homemade egg noodles called *maltagliati* (literally, "badly cut"). A *sagra* for *strigoli* (a kind of bladder campion) is also celebrated in the Romagna village of Galeata di Forlì.

TYPICAL PRODUCTS OF EMILIA ROMAGNA

Parmigiano-Reggiano. Naturally, it is produced in Parma and Reggio Emilia. As one of the wonders of the world, it relegates the other cheeses of the region to the shadows. Among them, however, the cheese known as

Fossa (for the underground pit in which it matures) deserves mention for its exoticism. Fossa cheese is a typical product of Sogliano al Rubicone and matures in deep pits, buried in tufa and eaten by worms. The history of this rarity goes back to 1486, when the army of Alfonso of Aragon, son of the king of Naples, was defeated by the French; at that time Alfonso requested "hospitality" from Gerolamo Riario, ruler of the city of Forlì. Asylum was offered to him, but there was the problem of feeding his army: formerly an enemy and now a friend, it was in any case ravenous. Therefore, as soon as the soldiers turned to pillaging, the peasants hid the food supplies, only to discover, months later, the prodigious taste of the cheeses that had been left to age underground in the stone pits. The buried cheeses did not dry out like those left in storehouses and cellars, but preserved their fluids, became imbued with aroma, and acquired an amber color. It is thought that a good pit must have been used for no less than ten years: only then do enough microorganisms accumulate to assure the quality of the cheese's ripening.

At the beginning of August, straw is burned in the empty pits to disinfect them, and then the walls are covered with fresh straw. The cheese is wrapped in a cloth and lowered to the bottom of the pit on Assumption Day (August 15), to be taken out about three months later, on St. Catherine's Day (November 25).

Emilian salamis are part of the repertory of the nation's glories. The classic Bolognese mortadella made of pork and beef is more noble than the common mortadella of Modena, composed only of pork. Wine, pepper, mace (the dried, ground layer between a nutmeg shell and its outer husk), coriander, and garlic are found in both. The filling of this salami is stuffed into a pig's bladder (a synthetic gut is prohibited). The sausages undergo a lengthy heat treatment at a temperature between 75 and 77 degrees C. Cristoforo da Messisbugo gives the earliest recipe for the preparation of

mortadella. First he describes in detail the process of cleaning and emptying the pig bladder; then he lists the ingredients of the filling mixture,
after which he explains how the casing is to be stuffed: stamp the mixture
with your fist in a certain way and add a glass of red wine. Chopped meat
is then added to the mixture, along with muscles of the sacrum, singed
ears, prepared tongues, and toasted feet.

Besides mortadella, another worldwide celebrity is the prosciutto of
Parma, which is obtained only from young pigs raised freely on the slopes
of the mountain. It represents a harmony of savory and sweet that is
unique among the prosciuttos. Establishments for smoking and salting
these prosciuttos are found in Langhirano, a town near Parma. Langhirano
is called the "university of prosciuttos": for some time salamis and prosciuttos, both cured (*crudo*) and cooked (*cotto*), have been transported here
from other Emilian provinces, so as to make them *rinsavire* (come to their
senses): they are hung in dry air for five months in long rows of huts and
then complete their aging in Langhirano's natural caves, each for the
period of time required by its processing method.

The king of Parma prosciuttos is the *culatello* of Zibello. It is obtained
from the center part of the prosciutto, and only from pigs fourteen months
old, fed with whey, bran, corncobs, and orzo. It takes a leg of fifteen kilograms for a *culatello* of four kilograms (weight is lost with the trimming,
dripping, and drying). *Culatello* must be aged for fourteen months. The
Consortium of the Culatello of Zibello, which safeguards and certifies the
quality of the product, has established that processing must occur solely
and exclusively in the period between October and February, when the
Bassa Padana (Po lowland) is enveloped in fog and cold. It is in that period
that the meat obtained from the leg of the adult pigs, raised according to
traditional methods, is skinned, trimmed of fat, deboned, separated from
the *fiocchetto* (the leaner, interior part of the leg) and carved by hand, so as

to give it the characteristic pear shape. These operations will then be followed, after approximately ten days, by the salting and so-called investiture, that is, stuffing the pig bladder with the sausage mixture and tying it with the string, which after maturation will form a wide, irregular mesh. Aging in cellars takes the *culatello* from winter fogs to summer heat, to arrive on our tables the following winter at the peak of its most original flavor qualities.

Each year no less than seven thousand authentic *culatelli*, home-produced and bearing the brand of the Consortium of the Culatello of Zibello, reach the market. An additional thirteen thousand are produced with the aid of machines. These sausages are labeled DOP (Denomination of Protected Origin). With the scraps of the *culatello*, that is, the parts removed from the prosciutto during the trimming, another typical regional salami is made: the *mariola*, to be eaten cooked or cured after a long aging process.

A specialty of Piacenza is the *coppa piacentina*. The Piacenza *coppa* (pork sausage) is obtained from the muscle located under the collar of the heavy pigs of the Po Valley. The processing begins with dry-salting and continues with a period in the refrigerator of at least seven days, after which the *coppa* is "massaged" and covered with a pig's parietal diaphragm. Finally the *coppa* is tied up with string and the covering is perforated. The final weight must not be less than 1.5 kilograms.

Zampone IGP (Protected Geographic Indication) is from Modena. Legend has it that this salami was invented in 1511 at Rocca della Mirandola, a village in the province of Modena. In that year, the city was besieged by the troops of Pope Julius II and the inhabitants of the city were forced to eat parts of the pig that earlier no one had considered edible. Out of necessity, they began processing the skin, the tendons, the offal, and the thymus. They very soon discovered that the products that resulted were in demand even in times of peace. After lengthy boiling with salt, pepper, cinnamon, nutmeg, and cloves, a glutinous, viscous, but not repellent—indeed, even inviting—mass is obtained from the pig's thymus, offal, sinew, throat, snout, and skin. A pig's trotter is stuffed with this mixture, which is then recooked with tendons and can be canned: before eating, it is cooked again for not less than four hours.

In other regions, an analogous stuffing is used to fill not the pig's trotter, but the bladder: the result is *cotechino* sausage, similar as to its filling, but completely different in terms of how it looks. Being "difficult" dishes, and historically significant, *zampone* and *cotechino* are a symbolic part of the New Year's Day menu and are eaten with lentils: the sausages represent abundance and the lentils money (the shape of each lentil being similar to a coin).

Also part of the repertory of typical regional products are *ciavarro*, a *salciccia matta* (crazy sausage) made with garlic wine, cracklings, and pig's head, which is mostly eaten in Romagna. And not to forget cooked shoulder, a specialty of San Secondo.

Gifts of the fruit orchards and vegetable gardens: white asparagus of exceptional flavor (their *sagra* takes place in Malalbergo, near Bologna, the third Sunday of May). The green asparagus of Altedo, the cherries of Vignola, the onions of Medicina, the potatoes of Budrio, scallions—excellent in all of Romagna. The white garlic of Piacenza, chestnuts from Castel del Rio.

Rock salt. Sea salt, in the area around Cervia. The saltworks in this locality were created in very ancient times, by the Etruscans or by the Greeks. The extraction of a particularly prized salt is still performed today, with practically manual methods. One of the principal saltworks is situated in the village of Camillone.

TYPICAL BEVERAGE

Dry, slightly sparkling Lambrusco wine.

CALENDAR

Giordano Bruno, burned at the stake by the Inquisition in February 1600 in Campo de' Fiori in Rome, is the author of a 1584 treatise, *La cena delle ceneri* (The Ash Wednesday supper), in which Copernican astronomy is extolled. To understand the meaning of the title, and the distinctiveness of the typically Italian way of conducting a philosophical dialogue, we must remember that Ash Wednesday—the first day of Lent for the Catholic Church—is so named because on that day the priest puts ashes (obtained from burning the palm fronds from the previous year's Palm Sunday) on the foreheads of the faithful, accompanying the gesture with the words: "Remember, man, that thou art dust and unto dust thou shalt return" (Genesis 3:19). The Catholic rite has distant biblical origins: covering the head with ashes as a sign of penitence, and practicing both fasting and abstinence on that day.

The opening of *La cena delle ceneri* recounts a supper held in an English home, during which Giordano Bruno and his hosts begin a philosophical discourse. Giordano Bruno was used to a certain tradition that in Italy, on Ash Wednesday, called for penitence at the table, true, but in serene conviviality, marked by gentle melancholy. The English custom, instead, contrasted greatly with all that. The essayist and poet Baron Dudley North (1581-1666) attests to the English rules of conduct on this first day of Lent in the book *Forest of Varieties* (1645), noting that in the English church the ancient ritual of hair shirt and ashes on Ash Wednesday was accompanied by the reading of public maledic-

tions against unrepentant sinners, with the faithful repeating "Amen" after each malediction. Baron North adds that many on this day tried to stay away from church, so as not to hear the maledictions mouthed by their neighbors, and children who did not wear a somber, dispirited look at school were taunted and beaten by their companions.

One might suppose that, finding himself in England, Giordano Bruno was aware of the conflict that underlay the English concept of Ash Wednesday and for this reason chose that very day for a work whose principal theme was disputation. Nevertheless, because he brought a typically Italian approach to the religious calendar, he knew that in Italy, on the day following the end of Carnival, banquets were held in any case, while still observing the requirement of abstinence, since everyone intended the supper to be an agape (love feast) with strong religious significance, even in its renunciation.

The tradition of the Lenten banquet is still maintained today in certain localities, for example in Lazio, in the village of Gradoli. A confraternity works all year to organize a *sagra* banquet, collecting "offerings for Purgatory." Part of the money collected is used to redeem the souls languishing in Purgatory (see "Pilgrims"), and part of it buys food for the "Purgatory Dinner." Only men can be members of the confraternity, while women have been allowed to take part in the banquet just since the 1950s. Generally speaking, the troupe at the Lenten supper preserves features of the ancient monastic confraternities. Within the group squads are formed: the first sees to the fish dishes, the second prepares the legume dishes (in the village a local specialty, the Gradoli lentil, is grown just for this purpose), and the third team handles egg-based dishes. All the dishes are meatless, in accordance with the precepts of the Catholic Church, but the expressions of the participants at the feast are not at all penitential.

Keeping in mind this Italian tradition of soothing conviviality, intended to lead the faithful pleasurably into the mood of the upcoming weeks of penance, it certainly seems as though Bruno's lexicon and all the symbology in his treatise were dictated by the Italian gastronomic code. Bruno begins by drawing upon terms of comparison from mythology and from history. He wants not only to place his interlocutors and readers in a convivial situation, but also to describe the particularity of the upcoming banquet against the background of other celebrated and memorable ones:

> This book is not a banquet of nectar for Jove the Thunderer, signifying majesty; not a protoplastic one for man's desolation; it is not the banquet of Ahasuerus for a mystery; not that of Lucullus for fortune, nor that of Lycaon for sacrilege; not that of Thyestes for tragedy; not that of Tantalus for torment; not that of Plato for philosophy; not that of Diogenes for

poverty; not that of leeches for a trifle; not that of the archpriest of Pogliano for Berni's satire; not that of Bonifacio Candelaio for comedy. But this is a banquet so great and small, so professorial and studentlike, so sacrilegious and religious, so joyous and choleric, so cruel and pleasant.[1]

And so Giordano Bruno, right in the opening phrases of the dialogue, draws from universal myths and historical testimonies all the possible occasions on which the protagonists of those myths dine. After which, almost as if to confirm our thoughts on the "gastronomic emblems" of Italian cities, he writes:

> ... so Florentine for its leanness and Bolognese for its fatness, so cynical and Sardanapalian, so trifling and serious, so grave and waggish, so tragic and comic that I surely believe there will be no few occasions for you to become heroic and humble; master and disciple; believer and unbeliever; cheerful and sad; saturnine and jovial; light and ponderous; miserly and liberal; simian and consular; sophist with Aristotle, philosopher with Pythagoras; laughter with Democritus and weeper with Heraclitus.[2]

And further on, the metaphor of the banquet extends to the teaching of philosophy:

> I mean that after you have sniffed with the Peripatetics, supped with the Pythagorians, drunk with the Stoics, there will still be something left over for you to suck with him who, showing his teeth, smiled so pleasantly that his mouth touched both ears. Indeed, by breaking the bone and extracting the marrow, you will find something that would make a dissolute of St. Colombino, Patriarch of the *Gesuati*, would petrify any market-place, make monkeys split their sides with laughter, and break the silence of any graveyard.[3]

Thus the typically Italian love for culinary metaphors leads the dissident and heretical Bruno to express himself in line with Catholic tradition, whose religious calendar prescribes not so much what you must *do* on a certain day as what you must *eat* on that day.

The southern mentality, more closely bound to religious tradition, involves a rapport with food as an ever-conscious element, at all times meaningful in everyday ritual. The heroes of history and mythology are remembered as one along with objects or situations in some way intrinsic to food:

> Why do you think that old Homer
> has been read and reread for so long?

Maybe so that by casting our thoughts
in the footsteps of that noble intellect,
they'll travel a thousand miles away,
from one marvel to another?

What an idea! not in the least!
You know why we like the bitter battle
of Troy, and why we like the *Odyssey*?
Because every so often the table is set;
because Ulysses and the others, at the proper
time and place, can be both heroes and cooks.

Socrates, who was so revered
and who so honors human reason,
if you were to read the Banquet
of Xenophon and that of Plato,
you would see that he taught his philosophy
among platters and feasting.

The Bible is full of tasty delights:
our father Adam for an apple
committed the first folly,
and infused a rose between man's teeth.
If he gambled the garden for an apple
what won't we do for a turkey?

The poem, entitled "Brindisi" (Toast), was written by Giuseppe Giusti in 1843. With his liberal revolutionary thinking mixing the sacred and the profane, Giusti went so far as to compose variations that were decidedly blasphemous:

Moving on then from the Old Testament
to review the stories of the New,
charges, offices, more than one sacrament,
parables, precepts, examples, I find
(if you ignore a miracle here and there)
that Christ performed them all at suppers.

It seems that that superhuman mind
preferred taste and appetite;
as was seen at the wedding of Cana:
when at the height the wine ran out,
he with his noble, divine power
changed water to wine on the spot.

And as a final proof, the place chosen
to serve God as a receptacle,
which by the Jews was called ark,
Holy of Holies and Tabernacle,
is called ciborium by the Christians,
a word taken from the refectory.

. . . Therefore it seems that we believers
in the Father, the one in the middle, and the Son
are destined to drink and eat heartily,
and keep a napkin on our knees;
and if this seems like heresy to you,
allow me to say it: So be it.

Extremes have much in common. The most impudent blasphemy here probably reveals a surprising steadfastness of principles affirmed by religion. What's more, seeing food everywhere, paying attention to every detail of the gastronomic code, means being a true Italian, an exemplary product of Catholic upbringing.

Italy is characterized by a rather suspicious attitude toward the jovial, full-blooded way of life of northern Europe, that Bruegelian lavishness which knows nothing of fasting. Not dogged about fasting, but moderate about eating (see "The Mediterranean Diet"), refined and exacting, Italy mistrusts abundance, seeing it as an imprecise approach whose intent is to compensate with quantity for a lack of quality. It is no accident that Mussolini's propaganda in the years of the Fascist Ventennio created an image of the enemy (the British) with the slogan "The people who eat five meals." The giant who sits at the table five times a day (breakfast, lunch, five o'clock tea, dinner, and supper) made the "sober" Italians shudder. People from the north, who ingest meat, milk, butter, beer,[4] and vodka, are still today perceived as different from the those of the south, brought up on wine and olive oil, nourished with wheat, vegetables, and fruits.

It bears repeating that the chief feature of the Italians' attitude toward food is an ongoing quest. What to eat (see "Ingredients")? Where to eat (see "Restaurants")? How to combine different foods (see "Pasta")? How to prepare them (see "Preparation Methods")?

And, finally, at what moment of life should a certain dish be eaten?

The answer to this last question has always come from the religious calendar, which formalizes and ritualizes the lives of Italians by dividing the days of the year into two categories: those on which certain foods are prohibited, and those on which other foods are prescribed.

Let's begin with the prohibitions, the requirements for abstinence and fasting. Undoubtedly a demographic policy was at the heart of all the fasts that excluded wine and meat from the population's daily life, in accordance with the teaching of Saint Paul: *Si vis perfectus esse, bonum est vinum non bibere et carnem non manducare* (If thou wilt be perfect, it is well not to drink wine or eat flesh)—namely, a desire, on the part of the Church, to limit liberal sexual behavior as much as possible.

In the chapter "Lazio and the City of Rome," we tell how in Italy laymen as well as members of the clergy contrived to get around such prohibitions, or more accurately, to observe them shrewdly, without depriving themselves of the joys of the table and other kinds of pleasures. There have never been extremely rigid fasts anywhere in Italy, or so it seems, except at times among the monks. Two orders distinguished themselves for their austerity among the other monastic communities: the Franciscans, whose order was formed at the beginning of the thirteenth century, and two centuries later, the followers of Francesco di Paola (1416–1507), a reclusive anchorite and ascetic, and spiritual guide to Louis XI, king of France. In truth, it should be observed that with respect to the total number of monks living and operating in Italy, those who practiced such fasting were few. Fasting was observed much more strictly in other European countries. The historian Fernand Braudel reports that in France, at the time of Louis XIV (seventeenth century), it was forbidden to sell meat, eggs, and poultry during Lent (except to the sick, upon presentation of two certificates: one from the priest and one from the doctor). In Italy, on the other hand, it was not state officials who safeguarded the order, but specially designated representatives of the guilds and municipal administrations (this aspect is analyzed in the chapter on food in Iris Origo's splendid study of medieval daily life, *The Merchant of Prato: Francesco di Marco Datini*). According to several communal statutes, the citizens could not eat meat on Friday and Saturday.

The ecclesiastical calendar was often put into rhyme by poets and versifiers, in order to facilitate its memorization. The Tuscan poet Folgore da San Gimignano (the pseudonym of Giacomo di Michele, or Jacopo di Michele, c. 1270–c. 1332) in his *Sonetti de la semana* (Sonnets of the week), 1310, left us a list of foods subdivided according to the days of the week ("Wednesday: hare, partridge, pheasant, and peafowl / and cooked beef and roasted capons"); and in the cycle of sonnets *Collana dei mesi* (Sequence of the months), c. 1323, provided recipes for a diet related to the months of the year, specifying that in February you must eat game and in March (during Lent) fish and eels ("trout, eel, lamprey, and salmon, / dentex, dolphin, and sturgeon, / every other fish along the entire coast").

The *Collana dei mesi* was so familiar to contemporaries that it became the object of a parodylike rehash in the work of a poet-minstrel from Arezzo, Cenne della Chitarra (thirteenth to fourteenth centuries), author of a cycle of sonnets entitled *Collana delle noie e di fastidi di vario genere* (Sequence of irritations and annoyances of various kinds), in which even everyday exasperations are distributed according to the months. The fourteenth-century poet Antonio Pucci (1309–88), who worked as a town crier for the communal administration of Florence, presented his material in a similar vein: he would proclaim edicts and laws in a loud voice and then, in his free time, rewrite them in farcical language for the public's amusement. Pucci is the author of a cycle of sonnets on temperance, deprivations, and diet during the days of Carnival, Lent, and Easter, whose title recalls that of Cenne della Chitarra's cycle: *Le noie* (Annoyances), c. 1350. In a little poem entitled *Le proprietà di Mercato Vecchio* (The goods of the Mercato Vecchio), Pucci also dedicates more than a few verses to the foods specifically prescribed for each month by the religious calendar:

> For Lent there are garlic and onions,
> and parsnips, and no more meat,
> since it pleased the Holy Church to so decree.

So, then, what was to be eaten on the various days, according to the requirements? On Easter, lamb, adopted for the festive Christian menu as a symbol of the crucified Christ, and borrowed from the gamut of ritual dishes of the Jewish Passover, where it symbolized the liberation of the Jews from the slavery of Egypt and their return to the Promised Land. Also conveyed from Jewish Passover tables to the Catholic Easter dinner were the bitter herbs that, for example, constitute the Ligurian Easter herb bouquets called *preboggion*, the filling for the Easter pie.

The dietary requirements of the Church have remained somewhat unchanged from the tenth century to our own time. Some aspects of the culinary tradition of the nineteenth century are easily reconstructible based on the sonnets of the Roman poet Giuseppe Gioacchino Belli (1791-1863), a master at representing the plebeian dialect. Food, obviously, occupies a central place in his unconventional and irreverent works. Here is a sonnet dedicated to an Easter banquet, "La Santa Pasqua" (Holy Easter):

> Here we are at Easter. Already you can see it, Nino:
> the table is wholesomely bedecked
> with Our Lady's herb, Roman mint,
> sage, sweet marjoram, violets, and rosemary.

> Already prepared since last week are
> ten flasks and a good barrel of wine,
> already by God's grace the fireplace is smoking
> to celebrate the feast in the Christian way.

> Christ is risen: joyously!
> On His day no one worries about the expense
> or gives a damn about their troubles.

> Soup, eggs, salami, English trifle,
> artichokes, grains, and the rest,
> all for the glory of Holy Church.

The herbs that "bedeck" the Easter table described by Belli are clear traces of the Jewish Passover ritual, assumed and restyled by Christianity. The Easter soup, *brodetto*, mentioned in passing, which in reality constitutes the the main dish of the festive banquet, also has a more specific name: *stracciatella alla romana* (a type of Roman-style egg-drop soup). *Brodetto* (as usual in Italy, the more substantial the soup is, the more ironic its name, for instance, *brodetto*, light soup, or *acquacotta*, cooked water, are anything but light or watery: both are thick, dense soups) is prepared only for the most solemn occasions, the most festive days of the year, like Easter. It requires beef, lamb, egg yolks, lemon, fresh marjoram leaves, bread, and pecorino cheese. Toasted crostini and fresh marjoram are placed in each bowl; the meat broth, flavored with egg, is poured in and sprinkled with grated hard cheese, nearly always pecorino. The egg yolks are beaten with lemon juice in a bowl, using a wooden spoon, and the highly concentrated *brodetto* is poured over the emulsion. It should absolutely not be boiling hot, to prevent the egg from setting and thereby turning this exceptional *stracciatella alla romana*—well blended, with a smooth, velvety texture—into an ordinary *stracciatella*: the kind in which filaments of boiled egg white float. This dish should not be confused with other *stracciatelle*, namely, with *stracciatella guarnita* (garnished with eggs), *stracciatella campagnola* (country-style, with tomatoes), or *stracciatella millefanti* (made with semolina). As for the English trifle, it is the well-known Italian sponge cake dessert (*pan di Spagna*) drenched with rum, custard cream, and chocolate.

The Catholic Easter is linked to two ancient Roman prototypes. First, the Days of Minerva, which were celebrated on the occasion of the spring equinox. Second, the feast bidding farewell to winter: the Lupercalia, which always fell in February. During the Lupercalia there was a day (called *dies Februus*, that is, day of purification, of propitiation) on which goats were sacrificed and ritualistic races were organized. Young goat or kid is still today an unfailing dish on the Easter table, along with lamb. And on the day after, Easter, the Monday of the Angel, popularly called Pasquetta (Little Easter), it is customary to take a walk, to simulate the race around the Palatine Hill or the race up and down the Via Sacra. This tradition of the Monday of the Angel is also connected to the day of Resurrection, when Jesus appeared to two disciples on the way to Emmaus, a few kilometers from Jerusalem. To commemorate the walk of the two disciples, the day of Pasquetta would therefore be spent taking a walk or going on an outing "outside the walls" or "outside the gates." On Pasquetta, Italian families usually leave the cities en masse to spend the entire day outdoors, in the mountains, in the hills or countryside, bringing the *cestino pasquale* (Easter basket) with them, for a leisurely picnic, maybe a barbecue, with family and friends.

The Easter cake is the *colomba* (dove), made with a dough similar to that of the Christmas *panettone*, but without raisins and shaped like a bird. Legend has it that the cake was prepared for the first time by cooks at the court of Alboin, founder of the Lombard realm in Italy: the same man who offered his wife, Rosmunda, wine in the skull of her father, Cunimond, king of the Gepidae, for which reason she later poisoned him. Determined to conquer Pavia, Alboin besieged it for three years and managed to capture it only by starvation. He then made the devastated city the capital of his realm and proclaimed that for the Easter feasts of 572, a new paschal delight would be introduced in the shape of a dove, the symbol of peace. So goes the account of the origin of this cake of northern Italy (an account that clashes considerably with the character of such a ruthless man as Alboin). Of course the representation of the dove, or of any other bird, both as a symbol of spring and as a symbol of the Holy Spirit, is much more ancient, an integral part of springtime celebrations in many cultures, including the Slavic cultures (the Slavs make little *panettoni* shaped like larks).

Eggs, too, are a symbol of Easter, and are often decorated. As in other countries and religions of the world, they symbolize the days of the spring equinox, because they allude to the sun, to resurrection. During the Easter festivities of 2006, 365 million eggs were consumed in Italy (according to data from the National Aviculture Union).

At a time when daily life was still regulated by tradition, on the Sunday after Easter, that is, on the Octave of Easter, or the eighth day after Easter, married women returned to their parental home, without their families, for a moving symbolic dinner. The menu of this traditional meal, if it can be found in its more ancient version, is almost childlike, and replicates a mood of a quotidian simplicity that has been forgotten: broth and tender boiled meat.

On St. Mark's Day (April 25), *risi e bisi*, rice and tender new peas, are eaten ceremoniously in Venice: the peas symbolize nature's early bounty. On St. Peter's Day (June 29), fish is eaten in all regions of Italy in honor of Peter the fisherman. For the Venetian feast of the Redeemer, celebrated on the third Saturday of July, sea slugs and fish *in saòr*, salted, fried, and marinated, are eaten. With the feast of the Madonna della Salute (Our Lady of Good Health), on November 21, a joyous historical event is commemorated in Venice: during the plague of 1630, when half the population of Europe died, the epidemic did not touch the lagoon city. On that day mutton from young sheep (*la castradina*), dried in the sun and smoked, is eaten in memory of the time when the Venetians ate this meat, preserved in storehouses for who knows how long, in order to avoid contact with the outside world and thus ward off contagion of the plague.

On November 1, All Saints' Day is celebrated throughout Italy, and on November 2, All Souls' Day. In the last decade of the twentieth century, Halloween was also added to these feasts, automatically imported from America and assimilated in an exclusively commercial way. On the days of All Saints and All Souls, it is obligatory to eat fava beans, symbolically associated with the world of the hereafter. Fava beans, in the mythologies of many people, are perceived as something supernatural: from the sprout of the fava grows a stalk that reaches the sky, and in the fable the magical beans fulfill the heroes' desires. Pythagoras was so fearful of fava beans that he sacrificed his life for them: he could have saved himself from death, but he refused to walk through fava bean fields. Horace recalls the episode:

> When will they set before me beans,
> Pythagoras' kin,
> And those little cabbages
> oiled with thick bacon-grease?[5]

It is probable that the Pythagoreans venerated the fava bean as a refuge for the souls of the dead. Pliny affirmed the same thing.[6] European popular mythology attributes to fava beans the significance of immortality or disdain for death: favas acquire their vitality from the soil, growing so vigorously that the second mythological significance of the fava is phallic potency, virility. At ceremonial times, Italians eat fava beans both mashed and in the form of cakes.

As far as Halloween pumpkins go, the windows of stationers and toy stores are filled with decorations that recall them (as fashion dictates!). From a gastronomic viewpoint, however, the pumpkin will probably never earn a place at the holiday table, just as Halloween will never become deeply rooted in Italian culture.

In any case, Halloween was born to celebrate the dead in the same period in which they are commemorated in Italy (the end of October and beginning of November). During these days people make or buy *panpepati*, spicy cakes that are called *pan dei morti*, bread of the dead (chocolate, pine nuts, raisins, jam, cream). Originally *pan de mei* or *pane di miglio* was also a ceremonial food for the dead: a sweet biscuit made from millet (today replaced with corn). Millet, like the fava bean, has a special role in magical beliefs. But unlike fava beans, symbolically associated with images of death and the underworld, millet is a symbol of reawakening, of hope in a joyful future. Millet bread must be eaten for the feast of St. George (April 24), to favor a rich harvest and prosperity.

Throughout Italy, especially in the countrysides, it was customary to organize banquets on November 11, St. Martin's Day, the day on which contracts with farmworkers and tenants were dissolved and annulled (in fact the farmers were evicted from their houses, so that *fare sanmartino*, observing St. Martin's Day, in the popular language of some regions, actually means to relocate), and the agreed-upon share of the harvest passed from one tenant to another. In Umbria, the Fossa cheese was unearthed from its pit on that day, and ancient peasant rituals were relived.

In accordance with tradition, the planning of the Christmas feast calls for dishes that rec-ollect poverty and ancient times: dishes that re-create the spirit of the manger of Bethle-hem in all its evangelical simplicity. Broths and soups of every kind and *bollito* are usually prepared for Christmas.

Christmas Eve is generally marked by going out to midnight Mass (in the more reli-gious families), or by sitting down at the table and waiting for midnight (in all other fami-lies, which by now form the majority in Italy). The emotional gathering of all the generations, of family and relations, from near and far, in anticipation of the event is the most heartfelt moment of the feast. The menu of this supper varies depending on the city. In Rome and Venice it is on the eve that one eats the most. You eat what God sends you, and God, on Christmas, sends every Italian household just what that family deserves. Christmas is in fact the prescribed occasion for sending edible gifts to friends, or to those who have done you a favor, and especially to those whom you want to or must ingratiate. Reading Giuseppe Gioacchino Belli's sonnet "La vigija de Natale" (Christmas Eve), we see what spectacles were offered to the observer who stood musing in front of certain extravagant entrances:

> Ustacchio, on Christmas eve
> go stand in front of the doorway
> of some monsignor or cardinal
> and you will see a procession enter.
>
> First comes the crate of *torrone*,
> then a big tub of caviar,
> now pork, next poultry, then capon,
> and now a flask of the owner's wine.
>
> Then come the chanterelles, then lamb,
> sweet-scented olives, fish from Foiano,
> oil, tuna, and eel from Comacchio.
>
> Well then, till late at night, little by little,
> you will see, Master Ustacchio,
> how devout the Roman people are.

On December 25 the table will be overflowing with all these foodstuffs, sent by various donors. But in addition to these unexpected dishes, the mandatory ones must be on the table: tortellini in broth, or another pasta with meat filling, and confections of raisin, honey, and walnuts, in particular the same *torrone* (nougat) mentioned in the sonnet.

In other Italian cities far removed from liberal Venetian and Roman customs—especially in the south—there is a tendency to observe fasting on Christmas Eve. In Puglia, for example, in the city of Gioia del Colle, tradition dictates that no one sit down at the table until nighttime on December 24. Family and friends visit one another and exchange gifts, racked by hunger, while awaiting midnight Mass.

Today, the Church has reduced the number of fasts considerably: the faithful limit themselves to eating meatlessly or fasting on the Fridays of Lent and to abstaining from food for one hour before receiving Communion. In the past, when Communion was a weekly obligation and fasting was defined as total abstinence from food from the moment you awakened in the morning (actually from midnight of the day before), the hardest day of the week was Saturday. No one was allowed to put anything edible in the mouth on Saturday until the "Sunday" Mass that evening (Sunday in the religious sense begins Saturday evening, just as the Jewish sabbath begins on Friday evening). Popular poetry abounds with descriptions of the torments of Saturday: the populace bear up, waiting for sunset and the evening Mass, after which they can at last dig into an enormous bowl of tripe in sauce and then indulge in all the other joys of life, spending time with women and smoking tobacco.

Tripe, though of animal rather than vegetable origin, was perceived as a kind of intermediary food, somewhere between eating meat and abstaining from it. The Roman recipe for the well-known Saturday tripe, which is recalled in this "sabbatical" sonnet by Belli ("La sabatina," Saturday evening vigil), like the Milanese recipe for *busecca de magher* (stewed beef tripe), comprises onion, celery, carrots, and, in Rome, wild mint as well. The tripe is cooked in this sauce for five hours, constantly skimmed.

The menu for the New Year's Eve dinner, or the Night of San Silvestro, resembles a propitiatory ritual or a love potion. Everything that is eaten on this night must favor the realization of desires. Thus lentils (similar to coins) are usually cooked as well as *zampone* (stuffed pig's trotter) or *cotechino* (pork sausage). Centuries ago, similar dishes of meat in gelatin saved the Italian population in times of scarcity during war years. Gelatin for abundance and lentils for wealth are the most important symbolic components on the table on feast days. Fresh fruit must be placed on the table on New Year's Day in order for it to last all year long, magically transporting those at the feast right into summer or fall. In the past, procuring fresh fruit for the table of the big dinner was not so easy. We know that grapes are jealously conserved for the New Year's dinner starting in autumn, when they are hung from the beams of the loft.

In Liguria there is a type of pasta in the shape of a coin intended for New Year's Day; every pasta disk is made by hand with a little wooden mold, though in the past a real Spanish doubloon was used. These edible "coins" are called *corzetti*. In northern countries, similar coins and medals made of chocolate, and wrapped in gold foil, are given as gifts on New Year's Day.

On January 17, the feast of St. Anthony Abbot is celebrated throughout Italy. Anthony, who lived in the third to fourth century, suffered from cancerous ergotism (a form of gangrene caused by the ergot fungus); now the saint's aid is invoked by those who suffer from the disease that takes his name, St. Anthony's fire. Surviving on only bread and salt, St. Anthony lived for 106 years in a hermitage in the desert. He lived as an anchorite, fought against demons, and protected swine. He had contracted ergotism as a result of being poisoned by ergot, a fungus present in the rye flour used to make bread. Suckling pig (*porcellino*) is made on January 17, wherever the tradition is still alive, and St. Anthony is also portrayed with a little pig peeking out from behind the hem of his habit. But—and this is an important detail—the *porcellino* of St. Anthony must not be eaten in solitude; rather, it is to be shared with the poor invited to the meal, or donated entirely, without even having been touched.

At the beginning of the grape harvest it is customary to ritually eat goat stew: the Dionysiac animal is thought to influence the good quality of the wine. At the beginning of the olive harvest, an unfailing dish is *stoccafisso accomodato* (stewed stockfish, or *buridda*). This is the typical dinner during the time of the first olive pressing in San Remo and other Ligurian localities where olive groves abound (Savona, Imperia, Riviera di Ponente, and Riviera di Levante). In each case the dish is in fact prepared with the first oil: murky, greenish, and a little bitter to the palate.

During Carnival, obviously, excess reigns everywhere; still, it does not consist of eating enormous portions, but rather in munching a little of this and a little of that. Therefore, salamis and deep-fried fritters are welcome: actually, the food must be quick to eat but also hypercaloric, in anticipation of the forty-day Lenten fast. In the Veneto and in Friuli,

Carnival treats are called *crostoli* (ribbons), in Venice *galani* (ribbons), in Tuscany *cenci* (knots), in Piedmont and in Liguria *bugie* (lies), in the northern regions *stracci* (scraps), and in those of the south *frappe* (fringes). In the Marches they are made with chestnut flour, while in Sicily the exquisite cannoli are filled with sweet ricotta. In Pesaro *arancini*, filled, fried rice croquettes, are made at Carnival time.

Tuscany

The beauties of Tuscany have always been extolled by those who have done the canonical Grand Tour of Italy (and those who still do it). Though the expression "Grand Tour" was used for the first time in the seventeenth-century travel notes of Richard Lassels,[1] the idea of it is found in embryonic form in the sixteenth-century travel observations of Michel de Montaigne. By the eighteenth and nineteenth centuries, the so-called Grand Tour constituted an obligatory stage of a classical education. In 1738 and 1748, excavations at Herculaneum and Pompeii were begun. In 1764, these ancient Roman cities were described by the art historian Johann Joachim Winckelmann in his *History of Ancient Art*. The main objective of the Grand Tour was to visit the excavations in Rome, Sicily, and the area of Naples, and to admire Renaissance art in Florence and Venice. Tuscany represented an intermediate leg of the journey, leading to these fascinating tourist destinations, but travelers passing through the region always remained enchanted with it.

As Dickens put it in the notes of his Italian tour: "Returning to Pisa, and hiring a good-tempered Vetturino and his four horses, to take us on to Rome, we travelled through pleasant Tuscan villages and cheerful scenery all day."[2]

Travelers to Tuscany arrived from Romagna, then a poor and depressed part of the Papal State. The population lived there in abject poverty throughout the year, and individuality was suffocated. Travelers entering Tuscany noticed by contrast how

effective the creative work of free men could be, a creativity that was even embodied in the landscape. Goethe writes:

> The most striking thing about Tuscany is that all the public works, the roads and the bridges, look beautiful and imposing. They are at one and the same time efficient and neat, combining usefulness with grace, and everywhere one observes the care with which things are looked after, a refreshing contrast to the Papal States, which seem to keep alive only because the earth refuses to swallow them.[3]

Descending into Tuscany from the Apennines, the traveler notices that even the sky assumes a magical Mediterranean color. Before him lie the landscapes painted by Duccio di Buoninsegna, Pietro Lorenzetti, Bartolo di Fredi, Sano di Pietro, and Giovanni di Paolo. Gentle hills geometrically divided into arable land and vineyards: nature ennobled by man's effort and intelligence, with fields, wineries, oil presses, mills, and coopers' and potters' shops. Well-to-do, cultured citizens decorated their country estates as if they were works of art.

The earliest articulated considerations on the cultural exchange between the countryside and the city are contained in Vincenzo Tanara's treatise *L'economia del cittadino in villa* (The economy of the city dweller in his country house), 1644, as well as in Marco Lastri's book *Regole per i padroni dei poderi verso i contadini, per proprio vantaggio e di loro* (Rules for estate owners toward farmers, for their own advantage and that of the farmers), 1763. Added to those is a collection of advice to farmers concerning their health. In Italy, especially in the eighteenth century, during the Enlightenment, knowledge of agriculture was rather widespread in aristocratic and upper-middle-class circles. In this regard, Stendhal describes an amusing episode that occurred in October 1816 in Milan:

> Only two nights ago, the owner of one of these proud mansions, finding himself unable to sleep, was strolling up and down beneath the porticos at five o'clock in the morning, while the dawn lay hidden in a steady fall of warm rain. All at once his eye was caught by a figure emerging from a side entrance on the ground floor, and he recognised one of his acquaintances, who was, as it chanced, an exceedingly handsome young man. Putting two and two together, he quickly concluded that the stranger had passed the night unbidden beneath his roof. Knowing that the young man had a genuine interest in agriculture, and using the rain as a pretext for conversation, the husband, without interrupting his sheltered stroll beneath the portico, kept his rival for two whole hours standing there in the downpour while he plied him with endless questions on farms and farming. Not until eight o'clock had struck, and the rain showing no signs of abating, did the husband most gallantly take leave of his acquaintance and return within the house.[4]

Conversations about agriculture took place even in less peculiar situations. Scholars dedicated their lives to formulating rules for farmers and agronomists. Marco Lastri (1731–1811), who lived into his eighties in perfect health, was one of these indefatigable researchers and published the extremely useful manuals *Calendario del seminatore* (The sower's calendar), *Calendario del vangatore* (The digger's calendar), and the aforementioned *Regole per i padroni . . .* , all in 1793, as well as the *Corso di agricoltura di un accademico georgofilo autore della Biblioteca georgica* (Agricultural course of a

Georgophile academic author of the Georgic Library), in five volumes, 1801–1803.

So that enthusiasts and researchers like Marco Lastri might have the opportunity to meet, trade experiences, and discuss and critique their scientific activities, the Accademia dei Georgofili (Georgophile Academy) was established in Florence in 1753 at the initiative of the Lateran canon, Ubaldo Montelatici. The goal of the Academy's members was to conduct experiments and make observations to perfect "the most beneficial Art of Tuscan cultivation." The Academy was the first organization in Europe to bring together the "great minds intent on the perfection of Agriculture." It proved how effective the results of theoretical agronomy could be when transferred from cities to rural localities and extended to tenant farmers and peasants quick to comprehend.

With regard to the Tuscans, the journalist and editor Giuseppe Prezzolini recounted:

> The most civilized people in the world, those Tuscans; with a breeding ingrained and secular, no mere veneer of rote. In a motto, a maxim, a rhyme, a nickname, a remark, you know them for what they are. In that tiny drop of popular sense you feel an experience filtered down through the ages. They have mind-reading manners. The peasant, save in rare cases, shows a depth and humanity uncommon and lofty.[5]

Stendhal agrees with him: "The Tuscan peasant is a singular creature; this race of uncultured husband-men forms what is perhaps the most agreeable society in Europe; and I find it infinitely more attractive than the urban population."[6]

Everything in Tuscany is simple, precise, robust, linear, and seasoned with wholesome irony. Just think about the names of the dishes: a soup so thick that a spoon will stand up straight in it is called *acquacotta* (cooked water). The people seem vigorous and hearty, uncontaminated, full of a lively sense of humor. Spirits and actions are plain.

In Tuscan cities, as we recall from late medieval history, half the population sympathized with the Guelphs, the other half with the Ghibellines. Within these individual political camps the same clear-cut polarization could be observed: the Guelphs were divided into Whites and Blacks, the Ghibellines into "major" (noblemen, landowners, bankers, etc.) and "minor" (mercants and artisans). Individualism and personal choice left their mark on the life of social groups, from the relatively large cities to quarters and villages.

The strong expression of individuality, naturally, led to harsh interpersonal antagonism. It is difficult to find anywhere else a *campanilismo*, or parochialism, as developed as it is in Tuscany. The Pisans hate the Livornese and also the Florentines. The Florentines detest the Sienese. Grosseto is hostile to Florence. Livorno lives on mockery directed against Pisa, rendered particularly amusing by the fact that the Tower of Pisa really does lean. One would be hard-pressed to find elsewhere a parochialism so mired in backbiting and cynicism, ideological contention, and even scuffling and brawling. It is also difficult to find another place where people are capable of swearing so furiously. Tuscan swearwords are considered among the most inimitable in the Italian array.

Tuscan cuisine, in its conciseness and essentiality, recalls the military life of ancient Rome. The Tuscan banquet dispenses with the ceremonial: perhaps because Tuscany's history never experienced absolutism, hierarchies based on favoritism, or the distribution of posts according to length of service and court etiquette. Tuscan dishes are easy to prepare, and allow the possibility of rushing out into the fray at the earliest necessity, without losing any time—chewing a chunk of bread along the way. "Beans, cold meat, turnips, stale bread, apples and pears, Marzolino cheese and a little home-grown wine to quench the itch of the cheese. The meal is frugal."[7]

Simple in its preparation and damned in its name is chicken *alla diavola*, devil-style, symbol and pride of the Tuscan city of Impruneta, couched among the Chianti hills. It is eaten on October 18, during the traditional feast of St. Luke, the local patron saint. In Pistoia, on market days, roasted thrush and chine of pork, studded with garlic, are prepared.

The cuisine of Tuscany is thus simple and rustic, but demanding and aristocratic as far as quality of ingredients and methods of preparation are concerned. Here, the rules that regulate the pairing of ingredients are exacting. Cooking is done primarily over a live, open fire: each type of food calls for different woods, with their distinctive aromas and ways of burning (high flame, low flame). Thin flour flatbreads are made using hazelnut branches, meat is smoked over beechwood or roasted over olive wood, while bread is baked using oak. Woods from cluster pine, acacia, and chestnut are not suitable for cooking, while arbutus wood is excellent for cooking any type of food. Second in popularity is grilling over coals. Tuscans cook everything on grills arranged over coals: from Florentine-style steak, *bistecca alla fiorentina*, to porcini mushroom caps; from fatback-stuffed game to eels fished from the Arno.

Indeed, eels are not at all a special prerogative of the marshy coast of Venice and Romagna. And although those from Comacchio are more well-known, their sisters from Tuscany inspired the Tuscan burlesque poet Francesco Berni (sixteenth century) to compose a true hymn to them: Berni ridiculed everything, including the noble epic of *Orlando innamorato*, but when it came to eels, he was quite serious:

> *Had I a thousand tongues or more*
> *and were I all mouth, lips, and teeth,*
> *I could not fully sing the praises of the eel,*
> *nor could all my relatives,*
> *who live, have lived, and will live,*
> *that is, future, past, and present.*

Tuscany loves all that is aromatic, that comes directly from the farm to the plate, still fresh and crisp. Pliny devoted several ample passages to the aromatic herbs of Tuscany in his *Natural History*. He recounts that the local fish welcome the curative qualities of herbs, and that minced parsley is sprinkled in stagnant pools to safeguard the health of the fish: "Fish, too, when found to be in an ailing state in the preserves, are greatly refreshed by giving them green parsley."[8]

In the Middle Ages and the Renaissance, the University of Pisa, which specializes in medicine, selected herbs both for physicians and for cooks. Cosimo de' Medici, ruler of Florence, did not want his city to be inferior, and he had the curator of Pisa's Botanical Garden, Luca Ghini, urgently summoned into his service. Thus the Giardino dei Semplici (Herb Garden) was created in 1545 by order of the ruler of Florence, and also through the efforts of the landscape engineer Niccolò Pericoli, nicknamed "Tribolo" (trouble). Later, in 1753, the garden was turned over to the care of the Accademia dei Georgofili.

The principal condiment for herb-based dishes is, of course, olive oil. Tuscan oil was already celebrated in antiquity, and has not lost its renown since that time. As rulers of the Tuscan region, the Medici required landowners to plant one, two, or three trees each year in every olive grove. Olive trees live for four hundred years or more, so today when we use Tuscan olive oil we are still enjoying the fruits of Medici foresight: the Frantoio, Leccino, Moraiolo, and Pendolino varieties of olives.

Celebrated throughout the world is *pinzimonio*, a combination of oil and vegetables much loved by Tuscans. *Pinzimonio* recalls the *bagna cauda* of Piedmont, the difference being that the oil here is not heated almost to the boiling point, as it is in Piedmont, but rather is mixed cold with vinegar, adding black pepper and salt. Raw vegetables cut into pieces—artichokes, tomatoes, celery, chives, raw asparagus, carrots, peppers, radishes, and Belgian endive—are dipped directly into this mixture at the table. A similar dish exists in the gastronomic tradition of Rome and Lazio, where it bears the name *cazzimperio*.

This type of cuisine is the exact opposite of neighboring Emilia Romagna's. While their neighbors prefer complex preparations, Tuscans prefer to eat products raw or barely cooked over the flame. No greasing or stuffing, no sauces or spices, just a pinch of black pepper from time to time. Often not even salt is added to the food. Tuscan bread does not contain salt; the *fiorentina* is flavored exclusively with olive oil. When the exiled Dante mourned from Ravenna: "You are to know the bitter taste / of others' bread, how salt it is, and know / how hard a path it is for one who goes / descending and ascending others' stairs,"[9] he was not alluding to the salt of poetic, nostalgic tears, but to common cooking salt. The meaning, in fact, is that at home Dante was used to eating insipid Florentine bread, while in Romagna, as we recall, there are great salt marshes; the bread of Ravenna would seem too salty to any Tuscan, not just to a very embittered poet. It is not surprising that Tuscan bread has no taste: but in recompense, it sets off marvelously the decisive tastiness of Tuscany's exquisite salamis, goat cheese, and prosciuttos.

Bread in Tuscany has always been the foundation of the meal and a state concern, as it was in Rome in ancient times. It was supplied to the city's population in a government-sponsored process. In the villages of Tuscany, not to mention the cities, the preparation of bread has always been assigned to specialists of the trade, not to ordinary housewives.

The Tuscan eats bread for breakfast, dunking it into his *caffellatte* (milk and coffee), and before lunch he satisfies his early hunger with a bruschetta, a piece of warm, toasted, crusty bread, drizzled with olive oil and spread with something tasty: tomatoes, liver, olive paste, diced chicken gizzards, entrails. If there is only aromatic oil and nothing else on the bruschetta, or on the bread, it is called not bruschetta, but *panunto* or *fettunta* (oiled bread or slice).

In Pistoia they make *necci*, focaccias of chestnut flour, and also *brigidini* and *berlingozzi*, biscuits that are crispy on the outside and soft inside. Even the typical Sienese cake is called bread: *panforte* (literally, "strong bread"), round, spicy, and full of raisins, honey, almonds, pumpkin, and candied citrus fruits. The recipe for *panforte* is attributed to a certain Ubaldino, whom Dante placed in the sixth circle of Purgatory: "I saw their teeth were biting emptiness / both Ubaldin da la Pila and Boniface."[10] This Ubaldino degli Ubaldini da Pila was the brother of Cardinal Ottaviano degli Ubaldini da Pila, who is also remembered in *The Divine Comedy*. According to the legend, his brother the cardinal transmitted to Ubaldino the recipe for the cake, which he had received from a nun called Berta at the convent of Montecelso: the nun, ashamed of her gluttonous confection (almonds, nuts, candied fruits, spices!), had renounced the treat she had created. The cardinal's brother Ubaldino, being a layman and not a monk, had no reason to feel ashamed. Thus in the eyes of history he became the creator of the *panforte*, that incredible Italian confectionery specialty.

In the beginning, *panforte* was a typically Sienese creation; later it became a national product. It is mentioned in Venetian chronicles as early as 1370 as a confection imported for the Venetian Carnival. Both *panforte* and other Tuscan sweets, such as *cantucci*, the biscuits from Prato, and *ghiottini*, should be dunked in the dessert wine *vin santo* (holy wine).

Bread is an essential ingredient of *cacciucco*, Livornese fish soup. Grated bread is sprinkled over macaroni, bean dishes, and cabbage. At the end of the meal, shavings of goat cheese, dried figs, walnuts, and grapes are arranged on a slice of bread. An afternoon snack is prepared with bread, butter, and sugar and a few drops of aged sweet wine.

Tuscany wisely maintains the image of rustic simplicity that it has earned for itself. Even in the most elegant restaurants, soup is served in ceramic bowls. Customarily brought to the table in ceramic bowls is *ribollita*: originally this was a soup made of meat from the day before, *"ribollita"* (reboiled) for the following day with fresh vegetables added. *Pappa al pomodoro*, a bread and tomato soup, is also served in earthenware bowls.

The chief pride of Tuscan cuisine is famous throughout the world: the enormous *bistecca alla fiorentina* (steak Florentine). It is obtained exclusively from the loin of the Chianina breed of cattle (from the Chianti Valley), and each portion weighs no less than 450 grams. The slice of meat is cooked directly over the coals with no spices and no salt.

In the book *Vita di Nicolò Machiavelli* by the quintessentially Tuscan Giuseppe Prezzolini, a true hymn to the triumphant Tuscan spirit, the *fiorentina* is elevated to the role of symbol and gastronomic emblem of the region:

With a dash of catmint, a pinch of sage, and a whiff of rosemary . . .

In the first years of the sixteenth century the Florentine table, emancipated from the Mastodonic and unenlightened medieval pabula, made for the belly and not for the palate, had attained to some of its immortal masterpieces, which we have since been able to repeat but not to improve upon. May I present then my compatriot, this grilled tenderloin, the pride of a calf's collop, still clinging, as you see, to the bone from which he was bred; observe his healthy complexion, which, saving his youth, might seem, I admit, apoplectic, like a slab of red marble, veined with white stains; on either side fired to meet you and spruced up with a drip-drip of oil and a dash of pepper, salt, and parsley; no blame to you, beef, though you do blush, yet blush not but outface the raw jowl of roast beef, Albion's bloody darling, and the crusty scowl of Milanese cutlets; for, believe me, you have nothing to fear by comparison.[11]

In 1953 a certain eccentric gentleman by the name of Corrado Tedeschi proclaimed the birth of the National Florentine Steak Party (mentioned in "Slow Food"). It was a regularly established political party, whose sole ideal principle was to fight for "450 grams of steak per capita assured to the people."[12] This is how Article 4 of its charter read: "It is time to end restrictions." "To be truly such, a beefsteak must weigh at least 450 grams. If it weighs a kilo, so much the better. But no less than 450 grams, because otherwise it becomes a cutlet and then my party would no longer be the Beefsteak Party."[13]

That year the party obtained 1,201 votes in the district of Milan, 347 votes in Florence, and several votes in Verona. As slogans, the party's founders selected the jingles "Better a steak today than an empire tomorrow" and "A pension and a cup of hot chocolate for all Italians indiscriminately." Tedeschi proposed reducing the electoral campaign to a ceremonial lottery with dinner and dancing. Once in government, he intended to establish the Institute of State Buffoons and abolish all taxes. A Miss Beefsteak would be selected under the aegis of the party.

Given these tastes, it is not surprising that Tuscany absolutely elevated ancient traditional methods of farming and cattle breeding. Formerly, in Goethe's time, this "archaeological" approach to farming seemed bizarre:

The peasants plough deep furrows but still in the old-fashioned manner. Their plough has no wheels and the share is not movable. Hunched behind his oxen, the peasant pushes his plough into the earth to break it up. They plough up to five times a year and use only a little light manure which they scatter with their hands. At sowing time, they heap up small, narrow ridges with deep furrows between them in which the rain water can run off. The wheat grows on the top of the ridges, so that they can walk up and down the furrows when they weed. In a region where there is a danger of too much rain, this method would be very sensible, but why they do it in this wonderful climate, I cannot understand. I saw them doing this near Arezzo. It would be difficult to find cleaner fields anywhere; one cannot see the smallest clod of earth; the soil is as clean as if it had been sifted. Wheat seems to find here all the conditions most favourable to its growth, and does very well.[14]

A vast body of scientific literature exists on the breeding of Maremma cattle. But even Zeri lamb is the result of a particular art of breeding: it is not easy to obtain lamb (or spring lamb) and mutton that responds to all the quality requirements demanded by Tuscans. It should be noted that pecorino (sheep's milk cheese) does not exist in the region of Zeri: all the milk in that area, in fact, serves to nourish the lambs. Milk lambs and rams are oven-roasted in an earthenware pan.

In the Mediterranean scrub of the Maremma, near Grosseto, where the Etruscans lived in ancient times, the inhabitants' favorite specialty (as we learn from recipe books) is stewed pheasant in *acquacotta*. Despite its name, there is no water to be found in the dish. The pot is full of tomatoes and roasted mushrooms, drizzled with eggs beaten with Parmesan, each strictly separated from the other by a layer of bread. This rare dish goes back directly to Etruscan times. Boned pigeons, covered with rosemary and served with a side of white beans "from Purgatory" (the same as beans in a flask, *fagioli nella fiasca*), have the same origin. The third Etruscan recipe that has survived until today is porcini mushroom caps wrapped in grape leaves and grilled over the coals.

Many kinds of mushrooms, not just porcini, are eaten here. In what were once Etruscan lands, chanterelles, morels, miter mushrooms, and honey mushrooms grow in the span of a year. In San Miniato, in November and December, expert searchers go on a hunt for white truffles, worthy of competing with those of Alba. A consortium has even been established to protect this typical product of the region.

Tuscany has a long coastline, part of it rocky and exposed to storms, part of it sheltered by the Argentario Peninsula, which forms a placid lagoon. On the exposed, rocky section of the coast stands the well-known port of Livorno, which was a kind of Italian New York between the sixteenth and nineteenth centuries. In the imagination of many travelers, this city was a symbol of terrestrial paradise. Evgeny Baratynsky, in the 1844 poem "The Ship," anticipated the approach to that astounding place with trepidation:

> *Tomorrow I will see Livorno's towers,*
> *tomorrow I will see Elysium on earth!*

When the city was governed by the Medici, they most likely intended to create an ideal city there, a free port, a forerunner of how many perceive the United States today. There is a manuscript, which it is possible to consult in Florence, called Legge Livornina (Livornine law), signed by the Grand Duke of Tuscany, Ferdinand de' Medici, on July 30, 1591. It invited "Levantines, Ponentines, Spaniards, Portuguese, Greeks, Germans, Italians, Turks, Moors, Armenians, Persians and those of other States . . . to reside and to frequent and to trade in our delightful city of Pisa, and the port and slipway of Livorno."[15]

The city became populated with energetic people. Adventurers, former criminals, and individuals with a past to hide were accepted into the community. Moreover, great tolerance was shown, both ethnic and religious. For example, Jews were allowed to hire maids (though not wet nurses) and workers of the Christian faith. Naturally, a large Jewish community was established and prospered in Livorno, as sizeable as Rome's and Venice's (see "Jews").

Livorno was the only city in Italy that had not formed a ghetto for Jews. The port on the Tyrrhenian Sea became a coveted destination, not only for Sephardics chased out of Spain in 1492, but also for Jews from other large Italian cities, where they had lived for more than a hundred years (a thousand, in the case of Rome).

The city of Livorno grew at a rapid pace. The sciences were developed there. From the jetty of Livorno, Galileo studied the celestial vault with the help of a telescope that he had invented. The arts and medicine flourished, and banks were born. Ships from hostile states and nations, which in other circumstances would have destroyed one another, rocked peacefully side by side in the port. Pirates, weary of their stressful occupation, conducted talks with city authorities to turn over their treasures and ships to the city's coffers, in exchange for the right to Livornese citizenship. The city also established a large mercantile center in Tunisia for the acquisition of wheat, coral, and ostrich feathers. Through this financial channel, among other things, money was recycled and ransoms paid to pirates for hostages they had captured.

Thriving communities were formed around the Dutch, Armenian, and Greek churches. The cuisine of Livorno, naturally, reflected the variety of this bubbling cauldron. Thanks to the Livornese Jewish community, or more exactly thanks to those members who after a temporary transfer were "repatriated" from Muslim Tunisia, Italian cooking was enriched by what was perceived as a new incarnation of the manna of the Old Testament: African couscous. Pellegrino Artusi wrote in his authoritative book (recipe 46):

> Couscous is a dish of Arab origin, which the descendants of Moses and Jacob, in their peregrinations, have carried around the world. But who knows how many and what kind of modifications it has undergone in its travels. Nowadays it is used as a first course by the Jews of Italy, two of whom were kind enough to let me taste it and see how it is done.[16]

Ariel Toaff, from a family of Roman rabbis and an authoritative historian of Italian Hebraism, confirms in his book *Mangiare alla giudia: la cucina ebraica in Italia dal Rinascimento all'età moderna* (Eating *alla giudia*: Jewish cooking in Italy from the Renaissance to the modern age) that this dish entered Italy through the Livornese Jewish community. From Toaff's monograph we also learn that couscous requires prayer during its preparation. Spiritual energy (for the Muslims, *baraka*) is contained in this food: while mixing it with the fingers and kneading the tiny balls of couscous, sacred formulas must be murmured.

The semolina is placed in the *mafaradda*, a large soup tureen with flared sides, and sprinkled with salted water. Microscopic balls are then formed from this mass, using a rotary motion of the fingers. The grains of couscous must be left on a cloth to dry for several hours. Then they are put in the *cuscusera*, a special colander or strainer, placed over a large pot (*marga*) of boiling water, covered with a cloth, and left to absorb the steam. The *cuscusera* must be left over the steam for not less than three quarters of an hour. Then, placed back in the *mafaradda*, the couscous is left to stand for ten to fifteen minutes.

This is how the couscous itself—that is, the semolina base—is prepared. But there is also a technique for preparing the sauces. These can be of mutton, lamb, chicken, or beef with *harissa* (a purée of hot red pepper). In addition, there are vegetables and spices: zucchini, carrots, favas, white beans, onions, tomatoes, turmeric; and, of course, olive oil is added. Cooks with a creative approach (God help us) add various other ingredients to the couscous and sauces depending on their imagination, for example, chocolate, pistachios, or cinnamon.

Between the nineteenth and twentieth centuries, Livorno was the land of social protest and rebellion, a stronghold of the Italian anarchist movement. *Cappuccino alla livornese*, Livorno-style cappuccino, is a classic recipe turned upside down: the milk foam is found not on top of the coffee, but underneath, at the bottom of the cup. In 1964, there was talk of pranks *alla livornese*, when three "authentic" sculptures of Amedeo Modigliani were found on the bottom of Livorno's Fosso Reale (a ditch of the Medici canals); they later turned out to be fakes, sculpted by three merry students following a drinking binge. The three stone heads made sparks fly among the world's art experts; it took a great deal of effort to convince elated connoisseurs, critics, art historians, and Paris art dealers that it was only a practical joke. Inspired by the caper, a Università degli Stupidi (University of Fools) was instituted in Livorno, where seventeen years after the memorable event the trio of brilliant student pranksters were presented with an honorary degree.

The one-of-a-kind, indescribable, and incomprehensible *cacciucco* was invented in Livorno. This is the name of a fish soup that is part of the same family as the French bouillabaisse, the Greek *kakavia*, the Spanish *zarzuela*, and the Portuguese *calderada*. The name comes from the Turkish *küçük*, which means "not much." It is a dish composed of leftovers and scraps of fish. Livorno's commerce has rested on the fish trade for centuries. And while the expensive seafoods—bass, lobster, and mullet—were destined for sale, the remains of their processing and the smaller fish went to the fishermen themselves, and ended up in the fish soup with slices of stale Tuscan bread. The bread's blandness sets off the marvelous flavor of the fish leftovers, as well as the taste of the pungent Tuscan sauces. Tradition requires that the soup contain at least as many varieties of fish as the number of c's found in the word *cacciucco*. *Cacciucco* cannot be prepared without scorpion fish, which is distinguished, according to William Black's expression, for its "Yeatsian terrible beauty."[17] As to its beauty, however, not all opinions agree, and in some regions the designation *scorfano* (scorpion fish) is conferred on people, both men and women, who are truly ugly.

This fish is covered with venomous dorsal spines and sports a big, lumpy head. Livornese fish soup is served in a deep soup plate over slices of Tuscan bread, and contains small fish, little pieces of giant squid, calamari, spotted dogfish, mullet, mantis shrimp, and large mussels. Also found in the soup are cuttlefish, octopus, conger, smooth dogfish, and gurnard, along with whole cloves of garlic. The entire mixture is topped with a tomato and onion sauce and cooked over a low flame, with the addition of hot red pepper.

Another specialty of Livorno is Livornese-style mullet. The mullet, for this recipe, must be large ones, and they are cooked with garlic and tomato sauce. Since ancient times, the city has exported its typical products (Leghorn hens from Livorno are known throughout the world) and imported ideas. As a result, the local cuisine assimilated couscous and extraordinary desserts from the Arabs and from the Jews. Traces of Spanish influence are present, too, as evidenced by the presence of paella, a yellow rice dish with saffron and prawns.

Sauces do not dominate Tuscan gastronomy, but if a sauce is made on the northern coast (north of Livorno) it will be composed of just olive oil and black pepper, while on the southern coast (around Livorno) tomatoes are also acceptable. Red pepper is characteristic of the Adriatic coast and is not used much on the Tyrrhenian coast. The tomatoless, northern part of the Tyrrhenian coast is Versilia: there "white" dishes are cooked (even the Viareggio-style *cacciucco* is called "white"). Around Livorno, however, tomatoes adorn any dish (Livorno did not take long to establish lasting, stable commercial contacts with the New World).

In the lagoonal region of the Tuscan coast, that is, in the area of Argentario and Orbetello, lagoon fish abound: eel, bass, gray mullet, and gilthead. Like everything else in Tuscany, they are roasted on the grill or over coals. Less often, these fish go into making spaghetti sauce *all'ammiraglia* (flagship-style). Pasta in Tuscany is not particularly adored, yet on the coast people eat *cappelletti* (pasta shaped like little hats) stuffed with bass. Truly unusual is the local custom of eating preserved fish as a snack, instead of sandwiches or fruit. Eel (*scavecciato* in dialect), for example, is fried, sprinkled with bread crumbs, seasoned with oil, vinegar, garlic, and mint, and eaten cold. Eels are also smoked and known as *sfumato* (smoked eel). Tuna is also eaten as an afternoon snack (the dorsal part, *tonnina*).

TYPICAL DISHES OF TUSCANY

Antipasti Bruschetta: slices of toasted bread topped with chopped veal spleen, onion, anchovies, capers, and pepper, but also with chopped entrails (heart or lung, etc.), liver, chicken giblets, and razor clams. The topping may also consist solely of pieces of tomato or abundant olive oil and salt (*fettunta*, oiled bread).

First Courses *Panzanella*, an excellent summer dish: bread soaked in water and vinegar, seasoned with anchovies, tomato, onion, olives, and basil. The typical pastas of Tuscany are *bavettine* (Livorno) and *pappardelle* (Arezzo) and they are accompanied by thin slices of fish. But in general Tuscans find it more natural to make country-style soups as first dishes, such as *ribollita* and *pappa al pomodoro* (bread and tomato soup) and, of course, the Livornese *cacciucco*.

Second Courses Florentine-style steak (*bistecca alla fiorentina*), of approximately half a kilo, cooked on the grill without seasoning or salt. Also typical is boiled meat with abundant black pepper; the character of this dish is obvious from the name itself: *peposo*, peppery. Florentine-style tripe is popular, cut into little strips and cooked with oil and aromatic herbs, tomatoes, and basil. Tripe is also prepared by cooking it with veal shank in an earthenware pan.

Among the most surprising meat dishes, the "tuna of Chianti" deserves description: it is made without tuna but with suckling pigs, victims of zootechnic selection, in June and July. During these hot months, in fact, pork is not eaten in the customary way because it is too heavy. Moreover, salting is also difficult in the heat of summer, since instead of being cured, the meat spoils. Therefore the suckling pig, instead of being salted, is boiled in wine production residues, the so-called *vin brusco*, or tart wine (from the first pressing of white grapes of the Trebbiano and Malvasia varieties). The cooked meat is then placed in oil. It is thought that at the end of this processing the suckling pig takes on the flavor of fish. The Tuscans, who in ancient times did not have access to prized fish such as tuna, gladly found a substitute for it in their homemade surrogate. At one time "fake tuna" had almost fallen into disuse. Today the dish has been recovered by "cuisine archeologists" and can be sampled in the town of Panzano in Chianti.

Also typical of Tuscany are the *cee alla pisana* (Pisan-style baby eels), newborn eels caught in Pisa at night along the banks of the Arno: attracted by the light of fishing lamps, they are later fried with oil, garlic, and sage and served sprinkled with Parmesan. In coastal Tuscany Livornese-style mullet (with tomatoes and herbs) is common.

White beans in a flask (*nella fiasca*), also called "Purgatory beans," are cooked in a glass flask from Chianti. After removing the woven straw covering from the flask, water and oil, in addition to the beans, are poured in; garlic, rosemary, and sage are added; and the bottle is buried in nearly extinguished coals (or suspended over the hearth for a number of hours). The dish can be viewed in the painting *Il mangiafagioli* (The bean eater) by Annibale Carracci (1560–1609), on display at the Galleria Colonna in Rome.

A typical Tuscan preserve for the winter is arbutus jam.

TYPICAL PRODUCTS OF TUSCANY

Sheep's cheeses: Tuscan pecorino and Tuscan Caciotta. The rinds of these cheeses appear to be tinted with the colors found in medieval Tuscan frescoes. Such coloring is obtained by lining the inside of the mold with a layer of tomato (which makes the cheese orange on the outside), walnut leaves (which make it brown), or charcoal (producing a black rind).

Biroldo from Garfagnana (a mountainous region in Tuscany), a spicy salami made with pig's head and entrails; *buristo* blood sausage; fennel salami. The renowned Colonnata lard, which truly has to do with columns, being a secondary result (and this is the paradox) of the extraction of Carrara marble from caves bearing the name Colonnata. The secret of this lard (salt pork) lies in the type of salting. The fatty parts of the pig, sprinkled with top-quality sea salt, are placed in marble tubs rubbed with garlic and herbs. And these tubs are none other than the hollows left after cutting the blocks of Colonnata marble. A first layer of lard is placed on the bottom of the basin, then a layer of sea salt, coarsely crushed black pepper, fresh garlic, rosemary, and sage, and then additional layers of lard are added. Once it is filled, the tub is sealed with a slab of marble and left intact for six months or more.

The marble of the caves of Colonnata is ideal for aging the lard because it is particularly porous. In the late nineteenth and early twentieth centuries this lard, today earmarked for gourmets, was considered the food of anarchists. According to the political literature and newspapers of that time, workers in the marble caves were distinguishable by their libertarian bent. It was among them that the cadres of the revolutionary movements were formed. Visitors to the caves still today are ceremoniously shown the ancient spikes and spatulas created to skewer and turn the lard couched in the cavity.

In Orbetello the tradition of smoking fish, a practice brought there in the sixteenth century by the Spaniards, is preserved. Not unexpectedly, it was in Orbetello, at the time of ancient Rome, that the fish sauce *garum* was prepared, an essential ingredient of Roman cuisine. Nowadays here eels from the lagoon, both marinated and smoked, and gray mullet *bottarga* (salted and dessicated roe) are jarred in this sauce.

Marrons from Mugello, chestnuts from Amiata. A typical Tuscan product for export is chestnut flour: the flour used in the focaccias of Garfagnana. Also famous is the spelt from Garfagnana, which comes from the same areas of northern Tuscany.

Tuscan bread is an excellent typical product; it is impossible to list all the varieties. We will mention the *pane pazzo* (crazy bread) with pepper;

the bread of Radicofani with honey, pepper, and raisins (a true *panpepato*); All Saints' bread with almonds and walnuts; and December bread with pumpkin. There is braided Lenten bread, the *carsenta* of Lunigiana, a large leavened bread that is baked wrapped in chestnut leaves, and represents a ritual element of the Good Friday meal. The yellow bread of Arezzo, by contrast, is served at the Easter Sunday table. And the bread of Sant'Antonio, patron saint of pigs, cattle, and cattle breeders, is made on January 17, the saint's feast day. *Ciaccia*, a bread made from maize flour, a specialty of the Maremma, has always been considered a poor man's food. *Donzelle* (round loaves), or *ficattole* or *sgabbei*, are fried in olive oil in a deep pan. *Fiandalone* is the bread of the woodcutters and charcoal makers of Monte Amiata. Added to it are chestnut flour and rosemary sprigs. Bread seasoned with rosemary is also called *di ramerino* (with sprigs). Strangely enough, there is no rosemary in it, though a certain quantity of rosemary oil is added to the dough. *Pan marocco* contains pine nuts, while the *marocca* of Casola is made with chestnut flour and mashed potato. There is herb bread with chamomile, wild mint, and red pepper added. *Panigaccio*, produced in Lunigiana, is baked on an earthenware slab (*testo*) and sprinkled with grated Parmesan. The Lucca variety, *buccellato*, is sweet and also includes sultanas and aniseed. *Castagnaccio* is made with chestnut flour, which is ground prevalently in Garfagnana, along with raisins, rosemary, and pine nuts. *Schiacciata* is made with pork cracklings, potatoes, herbs, and even tomatoes. The soft *ricciarelli* of Siena are almond cookies exported from Tuscany to all parts of the world.

Principal vegetable products: the purple and red onion of Certaldo, once praised by Boccaccio in the *Decameron*:

> Certaldo, as perchance you may have heard, is a town of Val d'Elsa within our country-side, which, small though it is, had in it aforetime people of rank and wealth. Thither, for that there he found good pasture, 'twas long the wont of one of the Friars of St. Antony to resort once every year, to col-

lect the alms that fools gave them. Fra Cipolla—so hight the friar—met with a hearty welcome, no less, perchance, by reason of his name than for other cause, the onions produced in that district being famous throughout Tuscany.[18]

Cannellini beans from Sorano, and also the *zolfino* bean that grows in the mountain zones.

From Tuscany, travelers also bring back dried figs, tied in pairs and alternating with aniseed.

TYPICAL BEVERAGES

The legendary red wines Chianti and Brunello di Montalcino.

PASTA

P asta is Italy's most economical and easily obtainable food. It is the ingredient most receptive to a creative approach and individual interpretation. It is the most nutritious, and most in keeping with the Mediterranean diet—a food that allows the unlimited addition of whatever complementary nutritious, vitamin-rich substances the cook desires. Perhaps most important, pasta readily lends itself to a multiplicity of preparations, all invariably delicious and a feast for the eye; preparations in which one often finds the most sunny and popular ingredient in Italian cuisine: the tomato.

To avoid terminological confusion, it is important to distinguish between *pasta secca* (dried pasta) and *pasta fresca* (fresh pasta). With fresh pasta, also called egg pasta, the binder is not water, but egg. Therefore it may be kept only for a few days and only in the refrigerator.

It is no accident that in many foreign languages the term "macaroni" is used as a blanket term instead of "pasta." It was the Italians themselves who set the example for this generalized use of the word *maccherone*. From the twelfth to the early nineteenth centuries, it was they, in fact, who applied the term "macaroni" to all types of pasta. Then, having encouraged this lexical habit around the world—that is, the custom of viewing "macaroni," like "spaghetti," as a synonym for "pasta"—the Italians abruptly shifted the ground rules and changed the use of the word. So for at least two hundred years now the word "pasta" has been used more generally, while the term *maccheroni* (and no longer "macaroni") has acquired a narrow, regional meaning.

For some reason—maybe because of their funny, elongated shape, or because of the sound of the word, or for some other reason—the fact is that spaghetti and macaroni are the favorite targets of various adages, proverbs, and caustic witticisms. For example: *"Guaje e maccarune / Se magnano caude"* (Troubles and macaroni are swallowed hot), according to the words of Giambattista Basile, who in the seventeenth century assembled and rewrote the popular heritage of fables and legends in the collection *Lo cunto de li cunti.*[1] Provoking, but on the other hand quite accurate, are the words formulated by Cardinal Giacomo Biffi in an address to students of Johns Hopkins University in Baltimore, when he stated that the Italians have but two universally accepted values: religion and spaghetti.

Spaghetti seems to be the ideal funny food for inspiring bold expressions and jokes. It is often encountered in humorous tales. A favorite story is one about the Neapolitan

Ferdinand I of Bourbon, a king with a prominent nose: during the years of his reign (1816–21), in order to capture popular sympathies, it is said that he would appear in the piazza in Naples in the act of gobbling down spaghetti, tangling and twisting himself up in the strands of pasta like a clown. Whether it's true or not, no one knows. In eighteenth-century England the term "macaroni" referred to a dandy, the vain fop who imitated Continental (Italian) fashions with affected mannerisms and a mincing gait purporting to be refined, with padded shoulders, a wasp waist, and a great many accessories. He makes a notable appearance in the popular American song "Yankee Doodle."

Literary history is familiar with the phenomenon of "macaronic" verse. The word "macaronic," used by literary historians and theorists since 1543, dates back to the poem *Macharonea* (1488) by Michele di Bartolomeo degli Odasi (Tifi Odasi or Typhis Odaxius, who died in 1492). The "macaronic" concept reflects the idea of a combination of right and wrong, just as different ingredients are mixed together in a dish of macaroni.

Above all it is a deformed Latin, an amalgam of languages *nostrana e forestiera* (our own and foreign). The founder of this artifice is considered to be Ausonius (fourth century A.D.), who introduced Greek words into Latin. Numerous macaronisms are found in Rabelais and Molière.

Amusingly enough, poems written in the macaronic style often discuss macaroni itself. In *Baldus* (1571), by the greatest macaronic poet, Teofilo or Theophilus Folengo (1491–1554), who wrote under the pseudonym "Merlin Cocai," the gods of Olympus are portrayed in the act of cooking. Jove, preparing the macaroni, hurls thunder and lightning around him, making an infernal racket with forks and skillets. In the role of Ganymede, a Master Prosciutto lives on Olympus, and illustrates the technique of preparing pasta. Subsequent to Folengo, the image of Jove casting storms over the world (that is, preparing pasta) was presented in the poem *Lo scherno degli dei* (The mockery of the gods), 1618, by a poet of the court of Pope Urban VIII, Francesco Bracciolini (late sixteenth to early seventeenth century). Octet XX, line 60, describes the process of making macaroni according to a technique that has remained unchanged and is still used today by housewives: wrap the pasta dough around a rolling pin, cut thin little slices (*fettuccine*), then follow the recipe:

> And then when that thin layer is wound
> a hundred turns around a clean rolling pin,
> with a sharp tool cut and loosen
> the floury burden from it;
> and the white strands, submerged,

at last brought to a high boil,

steam proudly, like thunder and lightning,

and so the macaroni cook, boiling away.

The leader of the Italian baroque school, Giovanbattista Marino (1569-1625), included in his collection *La Galleria* (The gallery), 1619, verses presumed to be those of Merlin Cocai (that is, Teofilo Folengo), in which he skillfully linked the term "macaronic," applied to burlesque poetry, to the idea of "macaroni" as a typical dish:

The great Macaroneid composed by me

is made exactly like macaroni.

For on top they have a crust of cheese,

and inside they are stuffed with capons.

Because so much erudition is concealed there

that it should not be swallowed in two gulps.

And if the covering is quite savory,

he who gets to the bottom licks his fingers.

A famous series of attacks arose between Giacomo Leopardi and the Neapolitans over macaroni. The gloomy poet of Recanati, who probably never ate macaroni in his life, derides the Neapolitans' love for this type of pasta in a few lines from *I nuovi credenti* (The new believers), composed in 1835:

. . . all to my detriment

Naples arms itself to vie in defense

of its macaroni; since putting death before macaroni

    weighs too heavily on her.

And she cannot understand, since they are so good,

    why villages, lands, provinces, and nations

are not happy by virtue of them.

But the Neapolitans responded in verse with the "maccheronata" in the form of a sonnet by Gennaro Quaranta:

And you were unhappy and sickly

Oh sublime poet of Recanati,

who, cursing Nature and the Fates,
searched inside yourself with horror.

Oh never did those parched lips of yours smile,
nor those feverish, sunken eyes,
since . . . you did not adore the *maltagliati*,
the egg frittatas and macaroni pie!

But had you loved Macaroni
More than books, which cause black bile,
you would not have suffered harsh illnesses . . .

And living among corpulent fun-lovers,
you would have lived, ruddy and jolly,
to perhaps ninety or one hundred years.

In 1860 macaroni (as a symbol of Naples) was utilized as part of an "alimentary code," in which culturally significant food communicates in place of words. During a party attended by Constantino Nigra, Piedmont's ambassador to Paris, the Empress Elisabeth's chamberlain, disguised as Cavour, sat down at the table and was brought various foods alluding to the historical situation of the moment: Stracchino and Gorgonzola cheeses (an allusion to the annexation of Lombardy), Parmesan (the duchy of Parma) and mortadella of Bologna (Emilia). After the *aleatico* (a sweet red wine) he was served Sicilian oranges, which he devoured with gusto. Last of all came a large plate of macaroni, the gastronomic emblem of Naples. The dish was rejected by the chamberlain (on the instructions of the empress) with the words "No, that's enough for today, save the rest for tomorrow." The event, so the story goes, was immediately reported by Nigra to the real Cavour, to communicate the empress's allusion that she was willing to cede Sicily, but not Naples.

Elevating pasta to the status of a national symbol, comparable to the portrait of Dante, is a custom that goes back a long way. Heinrich Heine, in his book *The Memoirs of Herr von Schnabelewopski,* refers to macaroni as "Beatrice":

Does not the yellow fat, passionately spiced and flavoured, humorously garnished and yet yearning ideal cookery of Italy, express to the life the whole character of Italian beauties? . . . All swims in oil, delicate and tender, and trills the sweet melodies of Rossini, and weeps from onion perfume and desire. But macaroni must thou eat with thy fingers, and then it is called—Beatrice! I often think of Italy, and oftenest by night . . . From the macaroni flowed sweet streams of golden butter, and at last a fair white rain of powdered Parmesan. But from the macaroni of which one dreams no one grows fat—Beatrice![2]

In more recent times (1954) Giuseppe Prezzolini, the illustrious historian of Italian literature and writer who lived most of his life abroad, in the United States, had this to say:

What is the glory of Dante compared to spaghetti? Spaghetti has entered many American homes where the name of Dante is never pronounced. Moreover Dante's work is the product of a single man of genius, while spaghetti is the expression of the collective genius of the Italian people, who have made it a national dish, but who, by contrast, have not shown that they have adopted the political ideals and behavior of the great poet. That Australian whom Moretti told about could not have understood the harmony, not to mention the meaning, of a verse of Dante, but a plate of *tagliatelle* must have convinced him that he was confronting a "culture."[3]

Cesare Marchi reflects:

Ennio Flaiano said that our nation is an assemblage, more so than a people. But when the dinner hour strikes, seated before a plate of spaghetti, the inhabitants of the Peninsula know that they are Italians just as those beyond the Channel, at teatime, know they are British. Not even military service, not even universal suffrage (not to mention taxes) exert the same unifying influence. The unity of Italy, which the fathers of the Risorgimento dreamed of, is today called *pastasciutta*; no blood was shed for its sake, but rather a great deal of *pummarola* [tomato sauce].[4]

The first dry pasta was created as a provision for sailors. Sicilian seamen took long, thick macaroni on board with them, while in Liguria they chose the shape of little curly vermicelli (worms).[5] Genoese merchants transported vermicelli all over Europe: there is evidence of their appearance in Provence and in England as early as the fourteenth century.[6]

Dry pasta was an invention of the coastal cities, an aid to medieval commerce and an expression of the vigorous, flourishing character of the Italian Renaissance. Stores of vermicelli on the *Niña*, the *Pinta*, and the *Santa Maria* made it possible for the Genoese Columbus to endure until he discovered America. On the coasts of the Tyrrhenian Sea, in Sicily, in Puglia, and in all those regions where life was subject to instability, brisk action, and swift preparations, dry pasta was the primary source of sustenance (as can be clearly seen by leafing through the catalog of the exhibit *Il rancio di bordo: storia dell'alimentazione sul mare dall'antichità ai giorni nostri* [Ship's rations: a history of food at sea from antiquity to our times], 1992), while in the valley of the great, peaceful Po River, amid the serene fields of northern Italy (Emilia, Lombardy, the Veneto), there was no demand for such a product. There they preferred *pasta fresca*, egg pasta made fresh each morning by housewives (and to this day characteristic of these regions).

The secret of making pasta lies in the proper method of drying. The surface of the pasta must attain a specific porosity that can generally be obtained only by rolling out the dough by hand rather than by machine. By so doing, two basic goals are addressed: first, the pasta, when boiled in a pot, must absorb as much water as possible; second, once served, it must absorb as much sauce as possible.

The production of dry pastas, moreover, was a delicate process, which in particular required excellent ventilation; only in specific climatic conditions could a product with the proper qualities be obtained. In Rome, for instance, where there is less wind and less sun, pasta does not dry as well as in Naples or Genoa, so an enriched pasta came into use there, made with egg (dry egg pasta).

As we know, two basic types of wheat exist: hard and soft grain. The first (*Triticum durum*) is also called semolina. Soft grain (*Triticum vulgare*, that is, "common") is used for egg pastas. The kernel of the hard grain is longer and transparent; that of the soft grain is rounder and opaque. The first grows only in dry, sunny climates, such as the south of Italy; the second tolerates humidity, so it is also grown in the north, in the Padana, the Po Valley. This is another of the many reasons why dry pasta is consumed in the south, and egg pasta in the north.

Besides, how could there be egg pasta in the south, where eggs have always been scarce? In the north, hens live in warmed cages and lay eggs the entire year. In the south, they stop laying eggs in November and only resume around Easter. Thus in the south eggs were a rare, precious product, used as commodities of exchange with purveyors in place of money, while in the well-to-do north they were eaten with a certain liberality. Some types of egg pasta require up to ten eggs for each kilogram of flour. Clearly such squandering was inconceivable in the economy of the south.

In the production of a proper dry pasta (the kind made without eggs), hard grain must be used exclusively, whereas soft-grain dry pasta is a fraud and an insult to the very essence of the macaroni standard: it sticks to the pot, it does not absorb the sauce, and it makes the consumer fat. *Triticum durum* began to be imported from the Chersonese back in the times of Vespasian, in ancient Rome; unlike *Triticum vulgare* it can be traced back to Afghanistan, where it had been brought at one time by Syria and Palestine. It was this wheat that was imported in Genoa and Naples during the period of the Renaissance to produce the famous dry pastas. The quality of dry pasta is regulated by law number 580 of 1976, "Rules and regulations for the processing and marketing of alimentary grains, flours, breads, and pastas." The most authoritative tasters live and work in the port cities: the same cities from which dry pasta has always been exported, and therefore controlled and certified. The best Italian professionals work in the vicinity of Naples. Historically, the most famous production of alimentary pasta in Italy was developed right in the province of Naples. The natural processes, developed over the centuries, demanded Neapolitan sunshine and a cheerful sea breeze. The strong sun of Campania fostered the rapid drying of the product, assisted also by the sea breeze that blows constantly over the hills of Gragnano: a breeze saturated with the aroma of the surrounding chestnut groves.

The Genoese were considered almost equal in reputation among purveyors of dry pasta, though they did not use local wheat, as in Sicily and in Campania, but imported wheat. They bought Sicilian or Russian grain, transported it to Genoa, and produced the pasta there, allowing it to dry in the Ligurian climate (similar to that of Naples, with a light breeze blowing morning and evening through the leaves of the chestnut trees on the hills).

At the National Pasta Museum, opened in Rome by the Agnesi Foundation in a splendid fifteenth-century building (Palazzo Scanderberg, number 117 in the piazza of the same name), objects and documents illustrating the history of pasta in Italy, from the time of the Etruscans till today, are displayed in fifteen galleries. In the museum one learns that the best pasta is produced with wheat of the Taganrog variety: it was distinguished for its unsurpassed color and wonderful consistency. Russian wheat, brought from Taganrog over many centuries, was an essential element of the economic equilibrium of southern Italy. Even under the Bourbons, despite the embargo due to local political factors, this wheat continued to be imported in the Kingdom of the Two Sicilies. The importation of wheat ended after the revolution of 1917, when all the seeds were eaten during the famine in the region of the Sea of Azov. Since that time, Italian pasta producers insist, macaroni no longer has the flavor it had in the past.

The mirage of Taganrog wheat continues to stir the imagination of Italian pasta makers even to this day.[7] The variety called Taganrog (though we were unable to determine whether its genetic code truly matches that of the Russian wheat esteemed in past centuries) is today grown only in Argentina.

It is important to realize that the production of pasta in the past did not involve the phase of reducing the grain into flour. Only today, when all the work is done by machines, is the wheat ground dry and mixed at a later time. Traditionally, instead, the process always started with the whole grain, which was mixed with water and ground during the mixing process.

From the time of Vitruvius to the end of the nineteenth century, that is until the appearance of hydraulic mechanisms, the best pasta in Italy was produced in Genoa and Naples. In Genoa they began by mixing the dough of semiground wheat by hand; the dough was then transferred to a special wooden tub containing a grinding-mill with stone querns, and covered with lukewarm water. Workers ran around the tub, turning the mill. The grain was crushed, lost almost all of its brittleness, and formed an elastic, sticky dough.

In Naples, by contrast, the tub into which the mixture was poured was made of stone and the grinders of wood, the water added was boiling, and the mill did not move in a circle, but up and down. Workers operated these plungers with their feet, like cyclists. In this way they were able to mix dough made of wheat that was not completely ground and the mixture retained its brittleness, from which the glittering character and superior quality of Neapolitan dry pasta derives.

Then it was time for the extrusion, usually through bronze disks. Modern materials, such as Teflon, do not produce a perfect result. The edges of the holes are too uniform, and make the surface of the pasta so smooth that in the end the particles of sauce have nothing to cling to. Whereas culinary perfection requires that the surface of all pasta shapes contain some irregularities, no matter how microscopic.

In 1917 Fereol Sandragné, taking a brick manufacturing machine as a model for his innovation, replaced the plungers with Archimedean screws. Later, in 1930, a real revolution occurred in the pasta industry: a continuous action press was introduced, which enabled the blending, kneading, and extrusion of dry pasta without interrupting the production cycle.

Earlier pasta was dried only on wooden posts and only in certain locations. As a result, a lot of pasta of excellent quality was produced in some parts of Italy, while elsewhere pasta was scarce and mediocre in quality. Even the vast choice of shapes only recently became available to all Italians, with the development of transport and commerce oriented toward a global market. This was facilitated after World War II by the introduction of artificial pasta-drying units: now its production no longer depends on the climate of individual localities. In the era of automated production, Italy began to put enough pasta on the market to nourish the whole country.

It was the very possibility of a global approach and the differentiation of shapes that made it possible for dry pasta to establish itself as the prince of foods and become a national symbol. In the eighteenth century, when Goethe was traveling through Italy and wrote his famous travel notes about Naples, no one spoke of pasta as a category. Each region built its culinary philosophy around several subspecies of pasta. What Goethe saw and tasted in Naples was a specific local subspecies, macaroni: long, fat hollow cylinders of pasta, a variety invented and eaten exclusively in the Kingdom of the Two Sicilies. For Gogol, too, macaroni was associated mainly with Naples: "And so, you are indeed in Naples . . . Before you picturesque *lazzaroni* can be seen [people of southern Italy were derogatively referred to as *lazzaroni*: idlers and scoundrels]; these *lazzaroni* eat macaroni; macaroni as long as the distance from Rome to Naples, that you covered so quickly."[8]

Only after the birth of a unified Italian state, and even more so with the emergence of the "Mediterranean diet" trend, did a new idea of pasta become rooted in the fantasy of Italians and foreign enthusiasts alike: the idea of pasta as a whole, of a pasta catalog, of pasta as an array of shapes, offering the possibility of almost infinite variety, like multicolored LEGO bricks.

In naming the shapes, metaphors and flights of fantasy are most welcome: spaghetti (little strings) existing side by side with *spaghettini*, even thinner *spaghi*, penne (feathers), *pennoni* (pennants), *bucatoni* (hollow straws), *fidelini* (similar to spaghetti), *trenette* (laces), and *tortiglioni* (spirals). Some names are borrowed from zoology: farfalle (butterflies), *conchiglie* (shells), *lumache* (snails), *creste di gallo* (cock's comb), *code di rondine* (swallowtail), *occhi di bove* (ox eyes), *occhi di elefante* (elephant eyes), *occhi di lupo rigati* (ribbed wolf eyes), *occhi di passero* (sparrow eyes), *girini* (tadpoles), vermicelli (worms), linguine (little tongues), *bavette* (bibs), and orecchiette (little ears). Or from the realm of botany: *fiori di sambuco* (elderberry flowers), *gramigna* (weeds), and *sedani* (celery stalks). From religious practice we have *capelli d'angelo* (angel hair), *maniche di monaca* (nun's sleeves), *avemarie* (Ave Marias), *cappelli del prete* (priest hats).

Any Italian cooking expert must know how to match the shapes to the various sauces. Generally speaking, you realize how charged with symbolic meaning the sacramental phases are: the selection of the condiment, the cooking, and the decision of when to drain the pasta. Don DeLillo revealed the significance of this symbology in his novel *Underworld*, where he talks about the Italian-American community:

> She heard the women talk about making gravy, speaking to a husband or child, and Rosemary understood the significance of this. It meant, Don't you dare come home late. It meant, This is serious so pay attention. It was a special summons, a call to family duty. The pleasure, yes, of familiar food, the whole history of food, the history of eating, the garlicky smack and tang. But there was also a duty, a requirement. The family requires the presence of every member tonight. Because the family was an art to these people and the dinner table was the place it found expression.
>
> They said, I'm making gravy . . .
>
> This food, this family meal, this meat sauce simmering in a big pot with sausage and spareribs and onions and garlic, this was their loyalty and bond and well-being.[9]

The most famous sauces are Genoese pesto and Neapolitan pesto; Bologna's *ragù*; *amatriciana*, the so-called dish of the five p's: pasta, pancetta (bacon), *pomodoro* (tomato), *peperoncino* (red pepper), and pecorino (sheep's milk cheese); *carbonara*, with bacon or pork cheek, pecorino cheese, egg, and sometimes lard; *arrabbiata*, with bacon, garlic, hot red pepper, black pepper, black olives, white wine, and grated pecorino; *puttanesca*, with tomatoes, anchovies, capers, olives, pepper, onion, garlic, and red pepper; and *aglio e olio*, with garlic, oil, and red pepper.

A catalog of condiments does not exist. For an approximate idea of their potential abundance, it is indicative that for spaghetti alone, that is, for that one single shape (the long, thin pasta of a certain diameter), 112 condiments can be counted at La Spaghetteria on Via Solferino in Milan. The menu of this restaurant lists 112 dishes: spaghetti with lemon, with orange, with strawberries, with watermelon, with pineapple, with lilies, with gardenias, with tulips, with violets, with fresh roses, with dried roses, with plums, with pumpkin, with bilberries, with red currants, with figs, with lobster, with frogs, with walnuts, with melon, with ricotta, with truffles, and with forget-me-nots (apparently, this last name has an ironic significance since the dish is actually mercilessly dosed with garlic and hot pepper).

Umbria

I n contrast to the immediacy of Tuscany, with its robust, active practicality, Umbria appears to travelers as bathed in an aura of romance:

> Umbria! The name seems to describe a countryside of faint shadows that populate valleys, and gather in the ancient hilltop cities, filling the air on deeply silent nights . . . Here the sun shines gently through a transparent veil, so tranquil and limpid are the waters that flow . . . The world will find a treasure of innocence and contentment here that will redeem its many sorrows and losses. And until that moment Blessed Umbria will appear as a hallowed refuge for all restless, troubled souls, an island of salvation for anyone who has raised the distress signal on his ship of life.[1]

Here the landscape presents no chasms or peaks, but gentle rolling hills. Authentic forests still grow on Umbria's hillsides, and its lakes are fairy-tale settings. Hermitages and monasteries, such as that of Assisi, founded by St. Francis, are still found today in Umbria, metaphysically correlated to the harmony of nature. In Jacopus de Varagine's *Legenda aurea* (Golden legend), it is said of Francis that he picked worms up from the ground so that passersby would not trample them. Francis brought honey and wine to the bees, to help them get through the winter; he rescued the lamb

led to slaughter, freed the rabbit from the leghold trap, and called all animals brother. The poetic world of his *Cantico delle creature* (Canticle of the creatures) is embodied by the hermitage of Assisi, a sanctuary to St. Francis's nature mysticism.

Overall, Umbria is a kind of preserve for saints. St. Benedict, founder of Western European monasticism, was born in Norcia in A.D. 480. Seven centuries after Benedict, St. Francis led part of this monastic movement (the Friars Minor) on the path to apostolic-missionary asceticism, in many ways similar to the path of his older contemporary Peter Waldo, who founded the Waldensian community in Valle d'Aosta. St. Clare, founder of the Order of Poor Clares, was also from Umbria. The population, infected by its saints' mystical ecstasy, built worthy temples for them. The Romanesque cathedrals of this region are indescribable, from Norcia to Orvieto, from Spoleto to Assisi and Gubbio, their interiors covered from top to bottom with frescoes by Giotto, Fra Filippo Lippi, and Luca Signorelli.

In May a medieval costume feast is held in Assisi. Wild boar is roasted on a spit in the piazza and spelt soup is distributed. And it is precisely from the wild boars, which graze freely in the dark forests, that the principal typical product of Umbria is obtained: wild boar prosciutto.

Umbria is sparsely populated, so breeding and farming here are not intensive. Food is traditionally derived from the meadows, lakes, and woods. Even the cooking untensils are provided ready-made by nature. The flatbread *al testo* (the local focaccia) is cooked on a *testo*, or disk, in the past made from river gravel (now mainly of cast iron).

The best Umbrian food is sometimes referred to as "black gold," a name that designates equally well the black wild boar prosciutto and the black truffles typical of this region. The white truffle is also present: in Val Tiberina, in Orvieto, and in Eugubino-Gualdese. The famous black truffle flourishes in Norcia and in Spoleto. Among the truffles, the winter and the so-called muscat varieties are recognized.

In general, there is such kindhearted spirit here that people would rather take milk and eggs from domestic animals than butcher them. It is no coincidence that this proverb was born in Umbria: "If a farmer eats a chicken, it means that one of the two was not well." This principle does not apply to pigs, since neither eggs nor milk is obtained from a pig. A pig can only be eaten, and the noble art of pork processing is so rooted in Umbria that throughout Italy those who specialize in pig butchering are called *norcini*, from the town of Norcia.

The prosciuttos of Norcia are the undisputed pride of this region. In Umbria (though in the rest of Italy as well) it is said that no part of the pig is wasted. Some parts are consumed fresh, others made into sausage and enjoyed a few days later, still others cured. The leg, the part from which prosciutto is obtained, is aged. The prosciutto, after a long, exacting process, is dry-salted and kept in salt for about a month. The salt, wisely administered, serves to dehydrate ("drain") the meat. After this first phase, the formerly fresh leg is washed, then reshaped, seasoned with pepper and garlic, and hung for the long drying period (along with many other future prosciuttos) in an environment with a constant temperature.

After seven to eight months, the prosciutto is ready for "puttying": the *norcino* butcher fills the cracks formed on the leg with *assogna* or "stucco," a product made from fatty substances. Afterward the two key factors in this art must do their work: salt and time.

This is how *capocollo* ham, salami, head cheese, sausage, loin sausage, "pocket" *prosciuttini*, and the famous "mule's testicles" are born.

Porchetta (roast pork), on the other hand, is a whole pig stuffed with entrails, fennel, and herbs. It is also eaten between meals (as a *porchetta* sandwich) and sold everywhere in markets, at concerts, at gatherings. I personally recall an unforgettable sight in Turin in May 2006: among the crammed book stands of the Salone del Libro, three men, panting, dragged an enormous *porchetta* dripping with fat over to the Umbrian booth, rendering the traditional party that Umbrian publishers open to everyone even more festive. The huge *porchetta* is made up of an entire pig or two, their skins sewn together to form a single body with one head. The entire thing is stuffed with smoked meat, pancetta. Although the party was taking place in an unusual setting of elite culture, it seemed identical to the *sagre* held in all Italian towns. The *porchetta*'s head had an amiable expression and seemed to be observing the newly printed titles stretching as far as the eye could see in the nearby stands. The neck and body of the *porchetta* appeared exaggeratedly long, as if in a previous life it had been a dragon rather than a pig. Could it have been stretching its neck out of curiosity?

Here in Umbria there is an inland sea, Lake Trasimeno, and a great abundance of streams. The Tiber also flows through Umbrian territory. Freshwater fish such as carp and trout are caught in the clear local waters (Umbria has almost no factories), often with a fishing line, along with several varieties of carp, trout, vairone, roach, chub, ray-finned carp, rudd, perch, grayling, barbel, bleak, tench, and even eels.

The great number of monasteries scattered along the medieval pilgrim routes lends the Umbrian landscape an aura of physical and spiritual welfare, of serenity. It is not surprising that even the political history of this region confirms its image of scant aggression.

The cities of Umbria have never been powerful. They had no access to the sea, they had no colonies or ports, they did not engage in manufacturing and trading. But though far from centers of power and from economic interests, free communes developed here from the eleventh to the fourteenth centuries: Perugia, Assisi, Foligno, Spoleto, Terni, Orvieto, Gubbio. And even in the years that followed, the region tried to maintain a certain peaceful neutrality amid Italian fighting.

TYPICAL DISHES OF UMBRIA

First Courses Handmade, country-style *spaghettoni* with various condiments and different names: *ciriole* in Terni, *bigoli* in Gubbio, *bringoli* in Lisciano Niccone, *umbricelli* in Perugia and Orvieto, *strozzapreti* in Todi, *manfricoli* in Baschi and Otricoli; if they are thinner, as in Spoletino and Ternano, they are called *strengozzi* or *strangozzi*, because they resemble shoelaces. *Impastoiata*: polenta with beans.

Second Courses Norcia-style woodcock, stuffed with giblets, sausage, thyme, marjoram, and olive oil. Cardoons with eggs. Snails (Foligno). Frittata with truffles. Hare stuffed with olives. Stuffed *palombacci* (wild pigeons). Wild boar prosciutto with fennel. Carp wrapped in *porchetta*. Clitunno River trout with black truffles.

Desserts *Torciglione* (twisted spiral) (Perugia): a *ciambella* or spiral-shaped cake made with sweet almonds, pine nuts, and sugar, in the shape of a snake coiled around itself, with an almond sticking out to represent its tongue.

Christmas Specialties *Maccheroni dolci* (sweet macaroni), tagliatelle or *bocconotti* (*pasta frolla* pastries) with chopped sweets, nut kernels, sugar, lemon, and cinnamon. *Pinocchiata* (pine-nut cake) made of melted sugar and pine nuts, with a typical rhomboid shape: there is a white version (sugar only) and a brown version (with cocoa).

TYPICAL PRODUCTS OF UMBRIA

Black truffle (*Tuber melanosporum*). The renowned *barbozzo* (*guanciale*, or pork cheek) prosciutto. Liver salami (*mazzafegati*). Red onions of Cannara, beans from Lake Trasimeno, black celery from Trevi, potatoes from Colfiorito and Campitello. The very delicate oil produced in clayey-calcareous lands (in Umbria the particular climactic conditions allow for the slow maturation of olives endowed with, among other things, a very low acidity rating). The DOP (Denomination of Protected Origin) specifications for Umbrian oil provides for six subzones: Assisi, Spoleto, the Monti Martani, the Colli Amerini, the banks of Lake Trasimeno, and the area around Orvieto.

Spelt, used in a soup with prosciutto bone (Monteleone di Spoleto). Lentils from Castelluccio, so tender that no soaking is required before cooking. Typical products of Colfiorito, on the other hand, are red potatoes, ideal for gnocchi, and the now rare *cicerchie* or *cecere* (chickling pea, a type of vetch, not the same as chickpea), a poor man's legume that at one time around Lake Trasimeno was cooked with pork rind.

PREPARATION METHODS

When we are getting ready to cook and open a book of recipes, we expect to find instructions that will explain which ingredients to combine with others and in what sequence. There is, however, another aspect to the matter, one we're assumed to have learned elsewhere: the preparation methods, which are not described in Italian cookbooks. Everyone learns these methods in the home. Thus disputes often arise among partisans of different culinary beliefs. For example, those surrounding Milanese-style risotto, a topic on which everything has been said and resaid, or so it would appear. Yet there is no unanimity of opinion as to these preparation methods. Should Milanese risotto be cooked in an aluminum pot or one of unglazed earthenware? Should it be stirred constantly, or given only one brisk stir at the beginning, never taking one's eyes off the rice as it cooks, until it is removed from the heat? Should the onion be browned in it or not? When should the cheese be added: while the risotto is still simmering or after the heat is turned off? Should the rice be sprinkled with wine to refine the flavor, before beginning to periodically ladle in the broth? Participation in these disputes necessitates a smattering of chemistry, history, and ethnography, and requires knowledge of classical literature, as well as aesthetic sensibility and intuition.

The Italian culinary tradition is so rich that cooking methods that have an exotic, fascinating effect on the eye—especially the eye of a foreigner—form a rather long list. Deliberately excluded from this list are techniques of agricultural and industrial food pro-

cessing; we will consider only those operations that must sooner or later be confronted when cooking at home:

> for artichokes *alla romana*, strip the tough outer leaves;
> for *giudia*-style artichokes, pry open the leaves and flatten the artichoke with a
>   stone;
> bind together the asparagus;
> toss the pasta in a pan over a vigorous flame;
> salt eggplants and let them sit, so they will lose their bitterness;
> bash live octopus;

let meat hang until it ages;

blanch and peel tomatoes, then prepare the julienne;

chop pine nuts;

soak prickly pears;

rinse dried cod, changing the water often;

dry salad greens in a special spin-dryer;

cut *puntarelle* (young, tender shoots of catalogna chickory) into thin strips, using the appropriate device;

stud onion with cloves;

bone fish and prepare *baffe*, or fillets (fish halves without head and bones);

"wall up" bass in a sarcophagus of salt;

remove seeds of cucumbers and tomatoes one by one;

peel citrus fruit thoroughly, removing even the thin skin covering each section;

crush basil in a mortar;

mince garlic with a double-handled, crescent-shaped chopping knife;

prepare "zests": little strips of lemon or orange rind (eliminating the white part, that is, the bitter part, of the rind), and scald them in hot water to bring out the strong flavor;

cut a sprig of parsley with scissors;

cut soft cheese with a wire;

extract the ink from cuttlefish;

lard meat to facilitate its cooking, inserting small strips of fatback using special needles;

remove eyes from octopus;

fillet sole;

prepare bouquet garni for stock, later discarding it;

boil garlic in milk to remove its strong odor;

be able to distinguish between "marbled" meat (where the fat is infiltrated in the connective muscle tissue), "mottled meat" (where the fat is infiltrated in the primary muscle tissue), and "veined meat" (where the fat is infiltrated in the smaller muscle tissue), and know how to cook each of these three types;

fry garlic in olive oil to prepare a condiment in which the scent of garlic will be present, but not the garlic itself;

prepare slivers of Parmesan;

grate nutmeg;

wrap melon in slices of prosciutto;

wrap prosciutto in slices of beef to make *saltimbocca*;

grind black pepper into grains in a wooden pepper mill;

reduce meat or fish stock to preserve it and later use it to flavor foods;

decant red wine from the bottle into a carafe to oxygenate it;

remove the tendons from chilled veal spleen;

soak salt cod in milk;

make curls of butter;

"barding": cover meat, fish, poultry, and game with layers of salt pork to protect them from excessive heat during cooking; for example, bard quail with bacon before cooking;

remove a squid's beak;

trim the sharp tips of an artichoke;

apply a "chimney," a rolled cardboard tube placed in the center of certain preparations (meat en croute or pâté), to allow the steam inside to escape while cooking in the oven;

stuff squash blossoms with meat and cheese;

cut truffles into thin slices using a truffle-slicer, a special utensil equipped with a micrometric screw to obtain slices of infinitesimal measure;

braise *in civet* (onion): a method that provides for the final binding with the animal's blood and chopped liver;

cook *in salmì*: a method suitable for hares, roe deer, and doves, similar to *in civet*, but without the addition of blood and liver;

peel peppers;

truss a bird: tie the legs and wings of a bird to its body with kitchen twine so that it does not get misshapen during cooking;

shape polenta in a cloth;

score meat and fish: make small cuts in them in order to facilitate cooking and the absorption of aromas and spices;

boil broth by placing it on only one part of the burner, so the foam will accumulate on one side of the surface and be easier to remove in one step;

cook in a bain-marie, that is, in a saucepan set in a larger pot containing water (the method appears to have been introduced by alchemists, whose science was widespread in the sixteenth century);

"drown" fish: soak it in a small amount of strongly flavored liquid (court bouillon or wine, or "crazy water" highly seasoned with hot pepper), which should be scalding but not boiling, never exceeding 80 degrees C;

collect the juice from a roast in a special dripping pan for future use in gravies;

prepare the *concassé* (coarsely chopped mix) of fresh tomato, by cutting an X in tomatoes that have been blanched for a few moments, then drained and peeled; the tomatoes are then divided into four sections and cut into regular cubes of half a centimeter per side;

marinate fish in salt, sugar, and spices for two days;

prepare a mirepoix, that is, the flavoring mix composed of diced celery, carrot, and onion;

prepare the *brunoise*: vegetable cubes approximately two centimeters per side (these can be frozen);

pour mineral water in the meatball mixture to make them softer;

cook risotto *all'onda*: the consistency is excellent, neither too liquid nor too firm, when the risotto forms a "wave" as the pot is moved;

prepare "foundations" or stocks, natural substitutes for the bouillon cubes that are now omnipresent even though they are not considered very nutritious;

crogiolare (bask or laze comfortably): cook a food over a slow fire, with a little liquid, for a long time;

clarify broth by adding a beaten egg white, or (according to ancient recipes) some caviar;

shape flour into a well; after forming a small volcano of flour, pour eggs, salt, and water into the crater;

nappare (from *nappa*, cloth): cover a preparation with a sauce;

prepare a roux, browning flour lightly in butter in a frying pan; it is used to thicken sauces;

prepare zucchini blossoms for frying: after picking the flowers in the morning when they are still open and firm, remove the pistil and the bitter center part and flatten them so that the tips of the flower are not creased and furrowed;

taste pasta to determine if it's cooked al dente;

"flush" or "purge" entrails or bones in cold running water, to remove impurities and various bloody adhesions;

boil lobsters and shellfish in seawater;

thicken sauces by adding potato flour, cornstarch, butter, cream, egg yolks, or puréed vegetables;

prepare seasonings for sauces ahead of time to obtain a homemade flavor addi-

tive without the monosodium glutamate that abounds in ready-made bouillon cubes; made from coarse salt, meat, carrot, onion, and celery, which are
first ground in a mixer, then scalded to let the water evaporate, then again
ground in a mixer, then warmed in a frying pan, and finally, when they are by
this time dried, ground up a third time and heated . . .

And on and on and on, dozens of other methods, the listing of which would require
too much space and energy in order to do justice.

All these methods, recommended by Italian gourmets and by the manuals, are con-
ceivable and morally acceptable, on the whole, and periodically implemented by the
author herself . . . with the obvious exception of bashing the octopus.

The Marches

The memory of the people who lived in the Marches in antiquity, the Piceni, has been preserved in a number of toponyms (Ascoli Piceno, Potenza Picena, Acquaviva Picena). The Piceni (from the Latin *picus*, woodpecker), like the other Italic peoples, were in their time subjugated and assimilated by the ancient Romans. In the early Middle Ages the Holy Roman Empire began (or ended) here. The name of the region derives from the fact that in the Middle Ages the Marches were known as border zones, governed by marquises (*marchesi*). The marquisates of Camerino, Fermo, and Ancona were part of the region of the Marches in the tenth century.

Since medieval times, the inhabitants of the Marches have had the reputation of being skilled artisans and craftsmen. Their style of work is not the reproduction of established models, not the diligent reconstruction of old métiers practiced by the trade guilds, but is aimed at perfection, development, progress. The Marches are Italy's Japan. From the shipyards of Ancona the world's largest cargo ships are launched. Household items, electrical appliances, footwear, clothing, mopeds, furniture, and musical instruments are manufactured in the cooperatives of the Marches, supplying all of Italy and half of the nation's export. Among the musical instruments are accordions: the best ones are made right in the Marches, in Castelfidardo. Assembly and finishing of the accordions may be done in other regions, but the internal mechanism must absolutely come from the factory in Castelfidardo.

Here, everyone is constantly studying. The university campus of Urbino practically coincides, as in Oxford, with the area of the city center. Forty colleges are located within the piazzas and Renaissance quads, while the very modern Casa dello Studente (student center) is carved into the side of the mountain. This combination of youth and antiquity gives the effect of an ideal city, in the spirit of that moral and artistic perfection found in the painting *La città ideale* (The ideal city) housed in Urbino's Ducal Palace, and attributed by some scholars to the architect Luciano Laurana, who with Gentile da Fabriano, Bramante, and Raphael created Urbino's beauty.

Complexity, creativity, and an unconditional love of effort also characterize the cuisine of this region. Tradition prescribes that the cooks of the Marches diligently process all food elements, sparing neither time nor energy. Here everything that can be stuffed is stuffed, from wild boars to tiny olives. Here large pasta cylinders, cannelloni, are filled with asparagus and prosciutto (typical of some other regions as well, however). Calamari is stuffed with ground veal. Food is cooked for a long time and in an elaborate way, with smoked pancetta found even in the murexes (*Murex brandaris*), the gastropods from which royal purple dye is extracted. *Olive ascolane* (Ascoli-style olives), produced here and sold throughout Italy, are stuffed with meat and prosciutto instead of a nut: the mixture is made with herbs, egg, Parmesan, nutmeg, and cinnamon. After the filling is inserted, the olive is dipped in flour, egg, and breadcrumbs, left to cool in the refrigerator, then fried in plenty of olive oil for a minute to a minute and a half.

Included among the region's typical dishes are many extremely laborious, complex delicacies: stuffed mutton head, stuffed pork rinds, cooked on the grill and then stewed, and *ciarimboli* (entrails seasoned with garlic, salt, pepper, and rosemary, dried by indirect heat from the fire, then cooked on the grill). There is a bizarre dish, Urbino-style snails (young ones) with chicken gizzards, whose invention is attributed to Beatrice d'Este, who lived in the fifteenth century and was the wife of the Duke of Milan, Ludovico il Moro. Beatrice acted as patroness to Bramante and Leonardo da Vinci, and encouraged Leonardo to design unique kitchen devices such as a mechanical roasting spit and a range hood to eliminate smoke from the fireplace.[1] As if this were not enough, if we are to believe the legend, Beatrice created many interesting culinary combinations, for example, morels and glazed carrots, hearts of artichoke and spring turnips.

One senses instinctively that the arts of cooking and music share similar creative mechanisms: in both arts, success depends on interpretation. Especially prized is the ingenious reinvention of what is prescribed, a judicious deviation from the norm. As a result, there are many books, many anecdotes real or invented, about the association of music and cooking. It is said that the most glorious son of the Marches, Gioacchino Rossini, was a legendary gourmand who wept only three times in his life: when they booed his first opera, when he heard Paganini play, and when, on a boat, he dropped a turkey with truffles into the lake. It is also said of Rossini that he brought several recipes to a cardinal so that he might bless them. After the premiere of *The Barber of Seville* (1816), he wrote a letter to the soprano Isabella Colbran, telling her not about the famous fiasco of the performance, but about a sauce for truffles. Evidently she was not stupefied; on the contrary, she was so enchanted that she married him.

Other than idling about, I do not know of a more delicious occupation for me than eating, eating as one should, mind you. Appetite is to the stomach what love is to the heart. The stomach is the orchestra conductor who governs and drives the great orchestra of our passions. An empty stomach is a bassoon or small flute, in which discontent rumbles or envy whines; by contrast, a full stomach is a triangle of pleasure or cymbals of joy.

The jovial Rossini, author of these lines, is also the author of interesting recipes. In 1842, on the occasion of the Bologna premiere of *Moses in Egypt*, he invented "pheasant in a pyramid of salt," stuffed with herbs (bay, juniper, rosemary, thyme) and wrapped in gauze rubbed with garlic. The resulting mummy, covered with coarse salt in the form of a pyramid, was baked in salt (as is often done with gilthead and monkfish) and served on a mountain of couscous, symbolizing golden desert sands.

The Marches is a region where cooking is studied seriously. At Porto Recanati, in the province of Macerata, the Accademia del Brodetto (Fish Soup Academy) flourishes. Poets and musicians of the Marches reach the heights of romantic absurdity in their flights of gastronomic fancy. Tonino Guerra, poet, writer, and friend of Fellini, lives in the Marches, in the *borgo* of Pennabilli; I have been his guest and can attest to his efforts to save several species of vine, planted near Andrey Tarkovsky's gravestone; together we visited his creation, "the garden of forgotten fruits," where he grows medlars, jujubes, and *biricoccoli* (natural hybrids of an apricot and a plum).

In Mondolfo (Pesaro), the most opulent *sagra* of gluttony is held right in the middle of Lent: the Spaghettata della Quaresima (Lenten Spaghetti Feast). Legend has it that the village-born musician Amedeo Tarini, locked in a fierce battle with the parish priest, managed to have the feast celebrated regularly by promising that the condiment for the many quintals of spaghetti would be made of anchovies, tuna, and olive oil, in full accordance with Lenten restrictions.

Antipasti *Olive ascolane*, stuffed with meat (chicken, veal, pork), prosciutto, mortadella, cheese, eggs, and bread, then dipped in egg and breadcrumbs and fried.

First Courses *Vincisgrassi*, lasagna noodles with a sauce of chicken giblets, chicken livers, veal sweetbreads, veal brains, prosciutto, and marrow to taste.

Second Courses Urbino-style fillet: a pocket is made in the fillet, which is then filled with frittata and prosciutto. Pesaro-style olives: they are not olives at all, but little veal steaks or roulades wrapped around a filling of prosciutto and basil.

Stuffed rabbit. The stuffing is prepared with veal, mortadella, grated cheese, and breadcrumbs mixed with the rabbit's liver and heart, with an accompaniment of salt pork, garlic, nutmeg, cloves, and other spices, all bound together with a beaten egg. This rabbit is cooked on the hearth.

Another typical dish of the Marches are eels cooked in wine. Dante portrays the torments of Pope Martin IV (pontiff from 1281 to 1285), who gorged himself on the eels from Lake Bolsena (a typical product of another region, Lazio), cooked however in Vernaccia, according to a recipe of the Marches:

> . . . *the one beyond him, even more*
> *emaciated than the rest, had clasped*
> *the Holy Church; he was from Tours; his fast*
> *purges Bolsena's eels, Vernaccia's wine.*[2]

Rabbit in *porchetta*. The boned rabbit is stuffed with *prosciutto cotto*, pancetta, and salami, garnished with wild fennel sauce, and cooked in the oven.

Crocette (sea snails) in *porchetta*. Cuttlefish stuffed with cheese, breadcrumbs, and egg. Mussels are also stuffed in the same way, but the filling includes *porchetta* with garlic, rosemary, wild fennel, peeled tomatoes, and parsley; arranged in a baking dish, the mussels are sprinkled with the soft center of bread and cooked on the grill or in the oven.

Desserts *Caciuni*, in the form of a crescent, filled with pecorino cheese, egg yolks, breadcrumbs, sugar, and grated lemon rind. Before being baked in the oven, the *caciuni* are scored on top so that a little bit of melted cheese will ooze out of the *raviolo*. Also popular is *bostrengo*, a rice pudding with chocolate and pine nuts.

TYPICAL PRODUCTS OF THE MARCHES

Fossa (pit) cheese. We have already encountered a similar cheese in Romagna, where it is produced on the banks of the Rubicon, in Sogliano, near Forlì. The processing method for the Fossa cheese of the Marches is identical. As in Romagna, it is placed in a cloth sack, covered with wheat and straw, then closed in a "coffin" and lowered into a "grave" of tufa. Each tomb is unique in terms of its temperature and humidity, and the cheese remains buried there from August 15 (Feast of the Assumption of the Virgin) to the beginning of November. Since the climate here is more southerly than in Romagna, the cheese ripens faster, and the pits are opened earlier: not on St. Catherine's Day (November 25), but at the beginning of the month, on All Saints' Day. Tonino Guerra invented the apt name of "Ambra di Talamello" for pit cheese (Talamello being the village in the Marches where it is produced), since it takes on a golden hue underground. The writer, a refined aesthete known for his advertising testimonials, here played a role similar to that of Gabriele d'Annunzio, the controversial Italian poet, journalist, and novelist, who was asked to invent a name for the large department stores in Milan and Rome known as La Rinascente. Today Ambra di Talamello, now a registered trademark, is considered the official commercial name of Fossa cheese.

Cagiolo cheese, similar to ricotta. *Ciauscolo*, a soft salami that can be spread on bread, whose recipe includes orange rind.

Truffles. A third of the national truffle harvest is sold at the famous truffle fair in Acqualagna each year. These are truffles of secondary quality, inferior to those found in Piedmont, in the area of Alba. Sly brokers often buy truffles in Acqualagna, leave them next to those of Alba for a while to let them soak up their divine aroma, then resell them at a high price.

Prosciutto of Fabriano. Horsemeat from Catria. Apricots of Sassoferrato and Macerata, Angelica pears of Serrungarina. Peaches of the Valle dell'Aso. Pink apples of Amandola. *Cucuccetta* pears of Sant'Emidio. Broccoli (from any province of the Marches). Ascoli artichokes. Early artichokes of Jesi.

Honey (from any province of the Marches).

TYPICAL BEVERAGE

Anise liqueur.

THE LATER GIFTS FROM AMERICA

Products of colonized America were introduced in Europe in the sixteenth century (see "The Early Gifts from the Americas"). Toward the middle of the twentieth century, America again brought its products to Europe. Half of the Old World viewed this as an indispensable, timely aid, the other half as intolerable expansionism. Italy, custodian of ancient alimentary traditions, was particularly offended by this "culinary colonization." Leo Longanesi (1905–57), a distinguished publisher, journalist, and master of wit, made a droll remark that many adopted as their own: "I will eat American canned meat, but I'll leave the ideologies that go with it on my plate."[1]

It should be noted that without this American canned meat, Italians would have been finished. In December 1944, in Rome, people were able to buy two hundred grams of bread and one hundred grams of pasta a day, plus a liter of olive oil per person each month, with food ration cards. According to sociologists' calculations, that means that an average citizen in Italy received only 900 of the 2,500 daily calories required to live. The rest had to be bought on the black market.

This black market is the backdrop and main theme of many popular books and films, among them Roberto Rossellini's *Rome, Open City*, 1945; Eduardo and Peppino De Filippo's *Naples Millionaire* (aka *Side Street Story*), 1945; and Curzio Malaparte's *The Skin*, 1949. From these books and films, we're able to know what took place during the months of the war in the markets of Rome and Naples. What happened in aristocratic circles is recounted, only in part, in Malaparte's novel.

SPECIALITÁ
GELATI
PRODUZIONE PROPRIA
TAVOLA FREDDA
Bevete
Coca-Cola

But not even the leaders of the fledgling Italian Republic who populated those circles ate their fill. King Vittorio Emanuele III had fled on September 9, 1943. The last king of the House of Savoy, Umberto II, went into exile on June 13, 1946. Their residence, the Palazzo Quirinale, had gone to the president of the new Italy, along with all its contents, which did not include anything edible. The inlaid Florentine credenzas were empty when the new tenants moved in. Faced with these difficulties, the first Republican government decided to dispatch an expedition to the presidential estates of San Rossore, to extract pine nuts from pinecones that had fallen to the ground in the royal park.[2] Undersecretary Pietro Baratono was given full authority to inventory the royal treasures that had been requisitioned. Appearing in the inventory is a bag of Santo Domingo coffee, bought on the black market back in 1943 for the personal use of King Vittorio Emanuele III. Although the bag had been in the pantry for two years, it gave off such an enchanting aroma that Baratono recounts having had a spell of dizziness, accustomed as he was, during the war years, to the disgusting surrogate *ciofeca* (a poor-quality wine or any repulsive beverage). The shortage of food was so severe that before leaving Italy on September 9, 1943, the queen mother, Elena of Savoia, nicknamed *la Pietosa* (the compassionate one), asked to bring with her into exile carrots and turnips planted by the court staff in the garden's flower beds.[3]

During the government of Ivanoe Bonomi (June 18, 1944, to December 10, 1944), when parties and receptions were held at the ministry, a liveried servant would lean over to whisper in the ear of every guest to whom he offered the tray of meatballs: "Two, Mr. Minister."[4] Giuseppe Saragat (1898–1988), future chairman of the constitutional assembly and president of the republic from 1964 to 1971, in 1944 found himself in prison in Rome: he had been arrested for anti-Fascist activities. His cellmates recall that he captivated their imagination by describing different types of food products (see "Ingredients") and ways to cook them (see "Preparation Methods").

When Luigi Einaudi became president of the Republic in 1948, he ordered food supplies brought from his personal estates in Piedmont for government receptions. This aroused conflicting reactions in the press. Believing that the food issue should not be resolved in that way, a caricature artist portrayed the president and his honor guard as bottles of exclusive Nebbiolo. The caricaturist was tried for contempt against the person of the president.

Despite such excesses, the food crisis was confronted with great vigor internationally. It was the United States that fed Italy and the entire part of Europe that remained free from Soviet occupation. In September 1947, the first American Victory ship arrived in Italy and the Italian government received alimentary assistance, gratis, in the form of

9,200 tons of wheat. The formal ceremony for the consignment was orchestrated by American ambassador James Clement Dunn. Embarrassed, and realizing to what extent national pride was wounded by these charitable acts, the Italian prime minister, Alcide De Gasperi, accepted the gift on behalf of Italy and delivered a speech.

Similar ceremonies (even notably more pompous) were repeated time and again. The first ship had been intended as emergency assistance. Soon afterward, however, the ERP (European Recovery Program), or Marshall Plan, took effect, having already been approved in June 1947 (the acronym ERP was much ridiculed by the Left, who called the beneficiaries of American aid "ERPivores" in contrast to herbivores). The U.S. program called for conveying to Italy (which it did) food commodities worth almost $1.5 million, among them flour or wheat, essential for the production of pasta, and milk, oil, jam, and chocolate. Ambassador Dunn skillfully played the extraordinary political cards that he'd been dealt. U.S. ships landed in Italy every day. And when they reached a round number, like a hundred, propagandistic initiatives quickly unfolded. These "hundredth" ships docked each time in a different Italian port, selected on purpose. The one-hundredth ship landed in Civitavecchia, the two-hundredth in Bari, the three-hundredth in Genoa, the four-hundredth in Naples, the five-hundredth in Taranto. The band would play, speeches would be given, and newsreels rolled.

In December 1947, the *Exiria*, the four-hundredth ship carrying U.S. humanitarian aid, tied up at the festively decorated dock of the port of Naples. The prow of the ship displayed the image of President Roosevelt where a figurehead had once stood.[5] Ambassador Dunn held three grains of wheat in his hand: the first was symbolically presented to De Gasperi, the second to the Archbishop of Naples, the third to a simple dockhand picked out of the crowd. Then the ambassador cradled a baby in his arms, a small Neapolitan *sciuscià* (orphan). The orphaned child was given not a symbolic grain, but a whole sack of flour and two crates of canned food.

The five-hundredth ship arrived in the port of Taranto two weeks before the momentous political elections scheduled for April 17, 1948, when the fate of Italy was to be decided in the heated contest between Christian Democrats and Communists. Each side's chances of winning were nearly identical. After the victory of the anti-Fascist Resistance, half of Italy was made up of former partisans and their relatives; entire regions (Romagna, Emilia) were preparing to vote for the Communist Party. On the day the five-hundredth ship arrived in Taranto, Ambassador Dunn gave a speech that delivered an onslaught that was even more decisive to Italian public opinion than the preceding ones. Dunn summarized the results of all the food commodities delivered by America over several months: 800,000 tons of wheat, more than half the total volume of the nation's consumption! 1,800 tons of pasta! 6,900 tons of fats, 1,150,000 tons of vegetables . . .[6]

All these food products corresponded to the Italians' traditional rations. If Italians felt uncomfortable, it was because national pride had been offended. Protests over aesthetics and taste arose later on, when Coca-Cola and McDonald's came into the picture.

On April 16 of the same year, 1948, posters were put up in all the piazzas in Italy declaring that if the Communist Party won a majority of votes in the following day's elections, American supplies of food to Italy would cease. The Communists had already raised the issue with their Communist Party comrades in the Soviet Union. But the Soviet Union itself had been brought to its knees. Still, the Soviet Communists had already offered their Western comrades whatever help they could: in February 1948, the Soviet ship *Baku* had delivered several hundred tons of wheat to the port of London. This cargo was meant for British Communists. "If the Soviet ship *Baku*," an anonymous commentator wrote, "on its course from east to west were followed by hundreds of other ships, laden with grain, minerals, petroleum, and materials for exchange, all controversy over the Marshall Plan would end. Neither Europe nor Italy would have any reason to prefer wheat from Minnesota to wheat from the Ukrainian *kolchoz* [collectives]."[7]

But the wheat in the Ukrainian *kolchoz* wasn't even enough for people there to live on, and the *Baku* remained an isolated case, as history shows.

At rallies, the Christian Democrats spoke in a simple, straightforward way: "Don't think . . . that with [Communist leader] Togliatti's speeches you'll be able to flavour your *pastasciutta*. All intelligent people will vote for De Gasperi because he's obtained free from America the flour for your spaghetti as well as the sauce to go on it."[8]

In the elections of April 1948, the Christian Democrats won a majority and defeated the Socialists and Communists, who had formed a coalition as the Popular Democratic Front. This victory left its mark on the history of Italy for the next fifty years. In those fifty years, ideological and political protest against U.S. interference in European internal affairs, typical of Socialist youth groups, often took the form of "anti-American food" propaganda[9] and rejection of "American gifts," namely, the new food products that came to Europe from the United States after the war, especially the most obvious: Coca-Cola, potato chips, and McDonald's.[10]

In fact, Coca-Cola was demonized in postwar Soviet propaganda. Though later, during the Moscow Olympics of 1980, a few symbols of the West (temporarily) entered the Soviet Union—including Pepsi-Cola, which even began to be produced in limited quantities—at the time it was actually forbidden to so much as name Coca-Cola. It is no accident that Gabriel García Márquez described Russia as a country of "22,400,000 square kilometers without a single Coca-Cola advertisement": such is the title of his travel notes written on the occasion of the International Youth and Student Festival of 1957. In Paris in the years 1948–52, demonstrators in the squares went so far as to overturn trucks carrying bottles of Coca-Cola. In Italy, both Communists and nostalgic Fascists came to suspect that human bone dust was part of the recipe for Coca-Cola. Having encountered consumers' instinctive resistance, the Coca-Cola Company conducted an offensive in Italy, sparing no means, bombarding viewers with television commercials even at Christmastime and attempting to bury *aranciate* (orangeades), *spume* (effervescent soft drinks), *gazzose* (fizzy drinks), and *chinotti* (bitter-orange drinks) in the landfill of history.

And what happened? In their attempt to stand up to Coca-Cola, the three major political forces—Communists, Fascists, and Christian Democrats—paradoxically formed a united front.

Catholic religious authorities had from the outset cast a suspicious eye on the little bottle from overseas, whose feminine curves appeared as seductive and dangerous as the boogie-woogie. Moreover, every country priest understood very well that Coca-Cola threatened not only local morality but also local wine production. So the Christian Democrats in government stubbornly worked to push the imposition of high excise duties through parliament, to hinder the advance of this product in the supermarket chains that were opening across Italy.

The Fascists, in turn, hated Coca-Cola because it had come to Italy on the bayonets of their victors, because (like its brother, chewing gum) it threatened national popular values, and because it sowed depravity, mendicancy, and prostitution all around.

As far as the Communists were concerned, they, too, made the most extreme statements in their battle against Coca-Cola. The verses of the ballad singer Franco Trincale say it all:

> For every Coca-Cola you drink
> You've paid for a bullet for America,
> And if the marine doesn't miss his mark
> A Vietnamese comrade is killed.

This hostile attitude has become even more unyielding lately, in a time of anti-globalists and the World Social Forum. The World Social Forum declared July 22, 2003, "International Coca-Cola Boycott Day." The proclamation boycotting the great multinational had been preceded a couple of years earlier by a more or less private media event, though significant for Italy: Silvio Berlusconi, leader of the Forza Italia Party, who at that time (2001) was preparing to become prime minister for the second time, had proclaimed Coca-Cola one of the pillars of his movement, publicly declaring that "Coca-Cola has been a great symbol of liberty." The newspapers reacted with intense agitation, publishing articles with eloquent titles such as "Coca-Cola from Vietnam to Silvio."[11]

Moreover, a group of daring individuals decided to declare war against the multinational corporation and ban the sale of Coca-Cola in one locale at least. War was declared against the American soft drink by twelve members of the Turin city council. Fully aware of their limited capabilities with respect to the powerful corporation, they merely proposed banning Coca-Cola from the menus of buffets and cafeterias of City Hall and other city offices. Most likely this limited, though resolute, action would have passed unobserved, had Coca-Cola not been one of eleven official sponsors of the Winter Olympics that were to be launched in Turin in two months' time. The American corporation's contribution to the Olympic Games amounted to more than 10 million euros. A small scandal resulted. Turin's mayor, Sergio Chiamparino, held urgent talks with Coca-Cola's spokesperson in Italy, Nicola Raffa, assuring him that the city as a whole did not share the irresponsible idea put forth by several representatives of City Hall. The Olympic Committee was forced to release an official statement, stating that the organizers of the games could not do without the funding support of the sponsors. The newspapers published the indignant reaction of Deputy Sports Minister Mario Pescante, who said that Italy had once again made itself the laughingstock of the world.[12]

The McDonald's chain has had a difficult time in Italy.[13] Some locations were boycotted and shut down: in September 2005, yet another McDonald's was forced to close in the Pergine Valley, in Trentino. Italian tourists considered it undignified to go there while vacationing in locations where the seductions of traditional cuisine abound, and foreigners alone were not sufficient to make it profitable. As if that weren't enough, the McDonald's restaurants are mistreated, forced to change the most sacred commodity, their logo. In the Galleria Vittorio Emanuele, the liveliest spot in Milan's historic center, a black and gold script was devised for McDonald's in the same style as the arcade's other shop windows. This was no doubt imposed by a city resolution obliging the shops in the Galleria to make the style of their signs "conform."

Inside, instead of hamburgers, there are counters with brioches and slices of panettone, and they serve an excellent espresso. In such a place, one wonders what's left of McDonald's.

Lazio and the City of Rome

R ome was already overpopulated in ancient times. The number of foreigners was equal to, if not greater than, that of the
residents. After the fall of the Empire and the triumph of
Christianity, Rome became the destination for all the pilgrims of
the Christian world, as well as for ordinary travelers. As the headquarters of the
Church, it was also the residence of clergymen and papal officials.

With this new physiognomy, the city, both sanctuary and teeming hostel,
adapted almost naturally to the rhythms and requirements of the religious calendar
(see "Calendar") imposed by the sacredness of the location. As Massimo Petrocchi
tells us in his collection of historical testimony about life in seventeenth-century
Rome, the observance of fasting imposed strict discipline on the inhabitants, which
also seeped into their dietary habits. To avoid committing the sin of gluttony,
Romans, with a charming sense of humor, managed to find loopholes to satisfy their
appetite on both feast days and days of abstinence. The high-ranking clergy, lacking
"supervisors" (at least in this world), seemed to be free of such concerns.

Indeed, despite all the talk about fasting, Roman pontiffs were certainly not distinguished for their asceticism. The Boniface VIII timbale, still known today, takes
its name from the pope who held office from 1294 to 1303: it was he who proclaimed
the first jubilee (see "Pilgrims"). This succulent dish includes macaroni, meatballs,

chicken gizzards, and whole slices of truffles, all contained in a pastry crust. The next Boniface, Boniface IX (1389–1404), adored liver meatballs, the so-called *tomaselli*, derived from his secular name, Tomacelli.

Beginning in the sixteenth century, papal passion for elaborate dishes grew. In his biography of pontiffs as viewed by their chefs, the illustrious humanist and papal gastronome Platina[1] writes of Paul II, who demanded a wide variety of dishes at his table and always praised the worst ones. He occasionally shouted when he did not find his favorite foods at dinner. He drank a lot, though only the most ordinary wines, and on top of that he watered them. He loved shrimp, timbales, fish, salt pork, and melons, so much so that he was killed by a stroke: the night before he died, he ate two huge melons without leaving a morsel on his plate.[2]

Leo X (pope between 1513 and 1521), a member of the Medici family, brought from Florence the lavish culinary customs of his city even before Catherine de' Medici conveyed them to the court of France. As understood by the lords of the Medici dynasty in the sixteenth century, "Florentine customs" signified a return to the traditions of crass imperial Rome, made up of endless, extravagant banquets, with long disquisitions about food. The Roman who wanted to be seen in a good light and admitted to the Curia shook the dust of the Lazio countryside off his shoes, and, renouncing the simple food of his ancestors, agreed to sit amid luxurious marbles and furnishings at Lucullan feasts in the Florentine style. He even agreed to laugh at the pope's jokes: Leo X, for example, who liked to amuse himself at the expense of his guests, had hemp ropes served instead of eels, so that the unfortunate dinner guest had to chew and choke on them for the entire evening.

Giuseppe Prezzolini was able to sketch a lapidary but incisive portrait of Rome and the customs of that time in his vivid, scathing style:

> Rome was *caput mundi*, the world's latrine, headquarters of the universal leprosy. It was a country of gang wars, imposing ruins, puddles, chronic malaria, general filth, luxury and beggary hugger-mugger neighbors. Witches were burned there and in the Vatican there were courtesans and astrologers. There Luther was excommunicated and Christ sold by the hour. A continual congress was held there of pimps, gluttons and rascals, innocents and saints. To the better contemporaries Rome was Sodom, Gomorrah and Babylon rolled into one . . . The Pope had his minions, his sons, his concubines. He would fatten his cardinals to slaughter them, when they were prime with coin: jingle-bell, jingle-bell, report in hell. The cardinals had sons and nephews . . . Certain Popes loved the table better than war.[3]

Toward the middle of the sixteenth century Julius III (pontiff between 1550 and 1555) ascended the papal throne. As we know from biographies of the time, this pope spent the final years of his pontificate in a sumptuous villa on the outskirts of Rome, giving himself over to worldly pleasures. It appears from the daily logs of the papal cooks that stuffed peacocks (a food of wealthy aristocrats, certainly not of penitents) and onions from Gaeta (their aphrodisiac virtues are legendary) were brought to the pope's private rooms daily. Paul IV, who became pope shortly thereafter (he was pontiff between 1555 and 1559), could remain seated at the table for as long as five hours, sampling twenty courses in a row.

Pius V (pope between 1566 and 1572), who was later canonized, led the Church back to austere simplicity. A Dominican and a fanatical persecutor of heretics, he had been an inquisitor before becoming pope. Once he donned the papal tiara, he banned secular feasts in Rome. Nobles who violated this injunction had to pay a fine. For all others, a first violation required a religious penance, the second a public thrashing, and the third a jail sentence. Disciplines and regulations introduced in the monasteries were so strict that not everyone was able to endure them. The Inquisition punished crimes committed twenty years earlier, and the pope never mitigated the sentences. On the contrary, if there were too few executions, he rebuked the judges for not showing enough zeal. Pius V was free of vices, nepotism, and spinelessness (he excommunicated Elizabeth I of England) and ate without witnesses. Nevertheless, his private chef—who as luck would have it was not only a gastronomic expert but also a literary talent—left us direct testimony of his appetite. This chef was none other than Bartolomeo Scappi, mentioned several times in this book, author of the first major Italian recipe book and reformer of Western European cuisine. In his volume of 1570, *Opera dell'arte del cucinare* (On the art of cookery), Scappi described several of the pope's favorite dishes, such as freshwater fish from Lake Garda, saltwater fish from the Ligurian Sea, and black caviar from Alexandria, Egypt. From the book, and from what we know in general about Chef Scappi's creative ways, it is clear that Pius V did not indulge in elaborate, dramatic foods. As a refined gourmet, he preferred sobriety. The pope insisted on absolute formal observance of religious laws concerning fasting, and the cook, on his part, could only rejoice at this, since he could not stand the extravagance of the Florentine popes and wanted to follow the principles of an authentically Renaissance cuisine, which involved harmony and equilibrium.

In 1549, Scappi was so good in the kitchen that he had to provide meals for the cardinals assembled in conclave to elect the man who the following year would be proclaimed Pope Julius III. It was thanks to his services that the excellently fed prelates managed to pleasantly get through their confinement of more than two months. This decreed his success: once elected, Julius took him on as his "secret," or personal, chef. Scappi remained in service throughout Julius's pontificate, and went on to serve another six popes.

The ecclesiastical calendar prescribed the observance of days of abstinence (160–200 days per year), and the Romans conformed, some out of devotion, others simply out of decorum. For this reason pasta seasoned with olive oil and all kinds of vegetarian dishes are found in the Roman diet. There is also a specific gastronomy for Lent: boiled pike or soup of pasta and broccoli in skate broth.

Aristocratic and wealthy bourgeois, meanwhile, complied with the usages and customs imposed by the clergy. Stendhal, an acute observer of Roman life at the end of the eighteenth century, wrote:

> Almost all the middle class of Rome was wearing the ecclesiastical habit.
>
> An apothecary with wife and children, who did not wear an abbot's dress, exposed himself to losing the practice of his neighbor the cardinal. This dress cost little and was highly respected, for it could cover an all-powerful man; that is the advantage of the absence of decorations. Only black habits were therefore to be seen.[4]

To survive and prosper, the high-ranking inhabitants of Rome had to be good at diplomacy. If they wanted to maintain good relations with influential prelates, they knew they must not violate the moral code. Specifically, they must strictly observe, at least in public, the rules for abstaining from meat (see "Calendar").

Everyone who flocked to Rome during the course of the last millennium, whether as a pilgrim or a worker, had to be lodged somewhere. Pilgrims, merchants, wholesalers, suppliers of the papal court, contractors, architects, artists and their students, adventurers of various kinds, workers from other towns, monks, lovers of the beauties of antiquity, and bored idlers: all had to find a place to stay and a place to eat. Hotels and inns were required. Stations to change horses, farriers to care for them, and forges where they could be shoed. Hospitals to treat the consequences of the pilgrimages and prevent epidemics. Tiberina Island in the middle of the Tiber, in the city center, became the area of quarantine. The part of Rome that today is the Vatican state also had clinics and hospitals.

Two hundred inns and two hundred hostels were recorded in eighteenth-century Rome, along with more than a hundred places where you could drink a bracing coffee; then, as now, these places were called *caffè* (cafés). Bars (with espressos, cappuccinos, brioches, sandwiches, and aperitifs) appeared only in the twentieth century. Since many people who came to the city did not know how to read or write, Roman signs (Hotel! Trattoria! Inn! Café! Tavern!) were eloquent and colorful, and the walls of the establishments were painted with images so clear that even simpletons could understand: here they let you sleep, here they give you a drink, and here you can eat as well. For the same reason, barrels were displayed on the doors of taverns to advertise their offerings, and vine shoots (*frasche*, boughs) were planted around the entrances. Wine bars or taverns in Rome are still called *frasche* or *fraschetterie*.

Thus it was that a dense network of trattorias was created in Rome. Cordial, though not very courteous, customs reigned (and reign) in these trattorias. The Roman *popolino*—as travelers and satirists in the past have described the populace, with a great deal of exaggeration—is wholly bent on squeezing money out of foreigners. A simple hospitality, rather brusque and basic in its style and cooking, can be found in every bar or café, on the ground floors of Roman buildings; this simplicity stands in contrast to the splendor and ceremony of the Vatican.

Rome is one of those rare cities where the number of foreigners has exceeded the local population for centuries, and where the number of single men (including the clergy) significantly exceeds that of women. For these reasons, there has always been a great demand in Rome for launderers and caterers.

The Romans, at least those described in literary works and travel diaries, seem to have an aversion to domestic frying and cooking and tend to take their meals in the trattoria *sotto casa* (downstairs). This habit was formed over time, and not just because trattorias in Rome are plentiful and excellent. The city has always been overpopulated and the buildings are many floors high; consequently, there has always been a real risk of fire. Rather than cook on the stove at home, it was more pleasurable and safer to go down to the tavern on the ground floor of one's own building.

The menus of ancient Rome were divided into two main categories. When prestigious events were organized—theatrical banquets such as those described in Petronius's *Satyricon*—the most elegant foods were brought from Greece, Syria, Carthage, and Egypt and sometimes even from India: "A platter followed, with a gigantic boar on it—a freedman's cap on its head, no less. From its teeth hung little baskets woven of palm leaves, the one full of Syrian dates, the other of Egyptian ones."[5] At times these foreign rarities were provisioned in advance, and kept in the cellar, farmyard, or stable, awaiting the opportunity to savor them:

> *The peacock, clad in Babylonian tapestry*
> *Of plumage, fattens in captivity*
> *To sate your appetite. Numidian hens*
> *And eunuch capons serve you. Even the stork,*
> *Sweet, welcome foreign guest.*[6]

The wealthier individuals cultivated and bred exclusive foreign plants and animals on their country estates, always with a view toward banquets:

Don't you think he buys stuff. Everything's homegrown: wool, cedar resin, pepper. Looking for chicken's milk? You'll find it. Anyway, he wasn't happy with the wool from his estates, so he brought rams from Tarentum and had them ball his herd. He wanted his own Attic honey, so he had bees imported from Athens. Some are gonna breed into his stock and make his own little boys a little better. Just a couple days ago he ordered mushroom spoor from India.[7]

All these are examples of extraordinary provisions, intended to be striking, to be a display of magnificence. But for the usual, everyday food of the masses, from the time of ancient Rome and through the Middle Ages and the years that followed, fresh products, supplied by farmers, were used. What does the character from Juvenal's satire offer his friend?

> *Now learn my bill of fare not furnished from the market.*
> *There will be a plump little kid from my farm at Tibur, of all the flock*
> *none tenderer than he, of grass he reeks not,*
> *and has never ventured yet to nibble*
> *the low-lying willow twigs,*
> *more milk than blood is in his body;*
> *there will be also mountain asparagus,*

the farmer's wife has left her spinning-wheel to cut it.
Big eggs, too,
I have nestling warmly on wisps of hay,
beside the hens that laid them;
and grapes that have been kept for half the year
as fresh as when they hung upon the vines.[8]

In 1817 Francesco Cancellieri, in his *Lettera . . . sopra il tarantismo, l'aria di Roma e della sua Campagna* (Letter concerning tarantism, the air of Rome and its countryside), invaluable for scholars of material culture, wrote: "Rome also abounds with all kinds of foods, and lacks nothing of that which lavishly serves to maintain life, being abundantly supplied by its most fertile surroundings." It was only thanks to the fertile lands surrounding it and the rare mildness of its climate that Rome was able to survive without difficulty, despite the exceptional number of foreigners living alongside the native population. Another example of a densely populated—indeed overpopulated—city of the south that nonetheless never suffered from hunger in peacetime is Naples, as we will see.

In Rome itself and around Rome, there are many bovines: bulls, large cows, all with white or straw-colored hide. There are also many large rams and ewes, which have long hair and inordinately long tails, and they are all white, there are no black ones. There are also numerous pigs, big and fat, and they are all black, there is no other color hide. There are also a number of large goats. And even a quantity of turkeys, which are brought to Rome in large flocks, five hundred and even a thousand heads . . . And at inns for foreigners they roast a number of pigeons, and more pigeons than hens are served in soups. In Rome, at the homes of Roman residents, in the houses of respectable people of every kind and at inns for foreigners, numerous foods are had: roasts, soups and pies, and all sorts of very exquisite foods.[9]

The ancient Romans, then, preferred preserved, imported foods for feasts and fresh products of the countryside for everyday life. The same can be said of the contemporary Roman table. For Christmas it's customary to place a plate of marinated Norwegian salmon at the center of the table and, if finances permit, a bowl of Iranian beluga caviar. But on weekdays, for lunch, Romans eat tripe, fresh lettuce, focaccia with oregano and marjoram, vegetable frittata, and zucchini flowers fried in batter.

According to tradition, most of the fresh produce is subject to only minimal processing, since the host is in a hurry to feed his many guests.

The food preferred by Romans throughout the ages is the egg: economical, simple, ever-present, readily available, and quickly and easily consumed.

The slaughterhouses in Rome have been in the same identical location for two and a half millennia: in the Testaccio district. Not surprisingly its inhabitants—undoubtedly beneficiaries of all possible imaginable by-products obtained for free (the so-called fifth quarter of the ox, discarded by butchers, though tasty)—have developed an unparalleled imagination. It is in Testaccio that rigatoni pasta *alla pajata* was invented. The *pajata*, or *pagliata*, is the tender intestine of the calf. It is prepared without emptying or washing it inside, since it contains nothing more than chyme. The reason it is so clean is that, sadly, the animal is made to suffer from hunger for a long time before being butchered.

In Testaccio and in Trastevere *padellotto* (from *padella*, frying pan) is also typical: a mixture of milk veal entrails, liver, and spleen, usually served with artichokes. Characteristic of Rome is *coda alla vaccinara*, oxtail stew, in hot sauce, while the pinnacle of perfection of Roman cuisine is *abbacchio*: roasted milk lamb three to four weeks old, a delicate and expensive product.

The gastronomic emblem of Rome, the vegetable that is most *romano*, is the artichoke. This vegetable requires scrupulous care, both when it is growing in the garden, and when it is being cooked. Artichokes are planted from August to October; then, according to the calendar, a complex weeding takes place, prior to the *dicioccatura* (stubbing) and *scarducciatura* (pruning) operations (the pinnacle of horticultural virtuosity). As a result, one single shoot, the best one, remains in each plant. The flower forms only in February or March, and the consumption season for artichokes is spring.

There is a strict hierarchy of artichoke varieties in Rome. The king of the artichoke garden is the purple *cimarolo* (from *cima*, top or best). Following it is the *romanesco* with its large, rounded petals, which grows in the Castelli Romani area, south of the city (here the soil contains a high percentage of volcanic lava, which gives the vegetables a special flavor). This variety of artichoke was also called *mam-*

mola. There is also a special Roman variety known as *catanese*, with an elongated shape and no thorns, which grows in the areas of Cerveteri, Sezze, and Albano.

The preparation of Roman-style artichokes requires only water and a very small amount of oil—ideal, therefore, for straightforward, large-scale cooking. In the more caloric variant of this dish, it is recommended that garlic, parsley, and wild mint be inserted between the petals, before drizzling with oil, meat broth, and wine. The recipe *all'agro* (with vinegar) is also much loved by the Romans: it consists in boiling the artichokes in water and vinegar, then adding parsley, oil, vinegar, wild mint, and salt.

Nevertheless, there is also a more exclusive, and much more laborious, preparation method. It is artichokes *alla giudia* (Jewish-style), with an incomparable flavor, like the majority of dishes created in the old Jewish ghetto nestled alongside the Vatican. These artichokes, after being flattened, are plunged into a deep pan filled with boiling olive oil (at a temperature of 120 degrees C, neither higher nor lower), where the heat causes them to expand and fan out; then they are dried skillfully and thoroughly, and spread out carefully for a beautiful presentation. Removing the boiling flowers from the oil, three drops of cold water must be sprinkled on them, so that the edges of the petals burst with crisp bubbles, which then tingle deliciously on the tongue.

Roman cuisine also includes an absolutely extraordinary dish, which falls into the category of archaeological treasures inherited from the Etruscans: *matticella*, from *matticelle*, the shoots left over after pruning the grapevines. Otherwise unusable, these dried shoots are burned in the fireplace, and the artichokes are cooked in the abundant residual ashes, after being carefully cleaned. A hollow grapevine is then inserted in the center of each artichoke, through which olive oil with mint, garlic, and salt is trickled very slowly into the flower.

The artichoke *sagra* is held in Ladispoli, not far from Rome, on the second weekend of April.[10]

Rome is a city of pilgrim and tourist processions, of demonstrations, political protests, and union rallies, of military parades, sports marathons, bike races, and scout meetings. It is therefore a city where one can sate both thirst and hunger on the go, without sitting down. There are ten times more bars here than in any other Italian city or village, all of them offering excellent coffee and cappuccino. Cappuccino is drunk in the morning, and only in the morning, after which Roman baristas happily refuse to make it. But the idea of asking for a cappuccino occurs to tourists at any time of day. Accustomed to everything by now, a Roman barista, hearing the absurd demands of these barbarians, will hurriedly serve them a cappuccino without so much as a smile.[11]

A traditional Lazio cuisine—one that differs from Rome's—is practically nonexistent. By the mid-nineteenth century the region around the capital was still a land of desolation, ruins, languid indolence, and *dolce far niente*. Aleksandr Herzen, a Russian exile, writes of the countryside around Rome:

> At first what strikes you is its deserted aspect, the lack of cultivated fields, the absence of wooded areas; everything is poor, bleak, as if we were not in central Italy at all . . . but little by little you come to know this eternal desert, this wilderness that frames Rome. Its silence, its opalescent distances, the bluish mountains on the horizon become more familiar . . . There a donkey slowly plods along, its harness bells jingling; a swarthy shepherd, with ram-skin overalls, sits dejectedly and watches—a woman carrying vegetables, wearing a brightly colored dress and white kerchief on her head, stops to rest, her hand gracefully supporting the bundle she balances on her head, and gazes off into the distance.[12]

To Goethe the outskirts of Rome appear so exotic that they remind him of Africa: "Very early next morning, we drove by rough and often muddy roads towards some beautifully shaped mountains. We crossed brooks and flooded places where we looked into the blood-red savage eyes of buffaloes. They looked like hippopotamuses."[13]

Between the Lepini Mountains and the Apennines stretches the area known as Ciociaria (the name is derived from *cioce*, shoes of ancient Greek design that the local inhabitants have worn for millennia). Until not long ago, the *ciociari* were considered a semiprimitive people like the gypsies (La Ciociara, the female protagonist in the novel of the same name by Alberto Moravia, is fascinating, proud though illiterate, and romantically impetuous).

> Sheepfolds . . . are watched over by tall young shepherds in traditional sheepskins worn wrapped around their hips and reversed, with the fur on the outside—the eternal costume of fauns. They watch indifferently as the carriages pass, bringing people from another world, but nothing stirs their enchanted somnolence . . . Looking out at us

from their round black eyes, deep as bottomless wells, is the cunning truth of beasts and demigods.[14]

Though it has little to offer in the way of riches, Ciociaria gladdens the eye and one's artistic sense. On its hills, near the villages of Alatri, Porciano, and Ferentino, there are beautiful lakes, as in the northern part of the region, where the largest ones were formed in volcanic craters: lakes Bolsena and Bracciano, Vico, Monterosi, and Martignano. In Ciociaria and in the nature preserves around Rome, in the small towns and rustic villages, the cuisine is still pastoral, almost Greek: greens, and focaccias with cheese. In the agricultural valleys, on the other hand, there are fertile orchards and abundant vegetable gardens. Among the gifts of the garden, perhaps the most famous are the green pea of Frosinone and a wide variety of beans: those from Lake Bracciano; the *scatoloni* (large white beans) of Accumoli, the cannellini of Atina; the *quarantini* ("forties") of Bolsena (so called because they take about forty days to ripen).

The typical dishes of the coast are prepared with various saltwater fish. One of the most interesting places on the Lazio coast, both from historical point of view and a gastronomic one, is Gaeta, a very ancient border city between the Papal State and the kingdom of Sicily. According to tradition, it was founded by Aeneas. On a geographical map, the city is unmistakable: from its center, a long, straight strip of land extends out into the sea. This miracle of nature has made the position of the port unique. With its naval bases, Gaeta still today retains the strategic and military importance it had formerly. The ancient stronghold, fortified by the Byzantines, was able to withstand attacks from the Saracens, Goths, Visigoths, and Lombards in the Middle Ages, and only once, in the eleventh century, was it forced to surrender to the enemy under pressure from the Normans. In the fifteenth century the Aragonese dynasty rebuilt and fortified the citadel, which is still today called the Angevin-Aragonese castle, despite the fact that its history is decidedly more ancient than the duration of that dynasty in Italy.

The dukes of Gaeta considered themselves vassals of the popes. In times of political turmoil in Rome and the Vatican, therefore, the popes often took refuge by fleeing to nearby Gaeta. This is where Gregory XII, deposed by his own cardinals in 1409 during the Great Western Schism, sought asylum. And Pope Pius IX fled to Gaeta, in November 1848, following the anticlerical revolution and the proclamation of the Roman Republic.

The chief specialty of Gaeta is its olives: neither black nor green, as olives should be, but the color of red wine, small and aromatic. They are only picked manually, and are left to soften in running water for a few weeks. Only afterward are they placed in brine. At that point, sweetness, savoriness, and bitterness combine to form a unique bouquet of flavor. These olives are added to octopus salad and put on pizza. Also famous in Gaeta are the *tielle*, focaccias that can be dressed with endive and pine nuts; squid; chopped octopus with olives; zucchini with cheese; tomatoes; fish; garlic; raisins; or capers. In addition, sea urchins are renowned in Gaeta: to be eaten raw, they are yellow on the inside, and rich in iodine.

Hot Antipasti Rice croquettes (*arancini*), rice balls (*supplì*) filled with meat, entrails, and mozzarella. The name *supplì* comes from the French word *surprise*. At times they are also called *supplì al telefono* (telephone-style) because of the strands of mozzarella that stretch out from the *supplì* when it is bitten.

First Courses Pasta with a sauce that is quick to prepare, such as *amatriciana*, the recipe of the five p's: pancetta (bacon), *pomodoro* (tomato), *peperoncino* (red pepper), pecorino cheese, and pasta. Though originally from the village of Amatrice, in the province of Rieti, this specialty is now regarded as a typical example of Roman cuisine. *Gnocchi alla romana*, eaten on Thursdays by all Romans since the dawn of time. For Romans, gnocchi are made exclusively with semolina, flattened and cut with special round molds. These gnocchi are served with butter and cheese. In other Italian regions far from Rome, on the other hand, gnocchi are made with boiled potatoes, egg, and flour, forming little balls to serve with *ragù* sauce.

Pasta *carbonara*-style, introduced into the Roman diet by Abruzzese cooks (see "Abruzzo and Molise"). *Sbroscia*, a soup of freshwater fish. *Pajata*, or *pagliata*: milk veal intestine with onion, parsley, celery, garlic, and tomato. Sea urchins as an antipasto, or as a base for pasta sauce.

Second Courses Lamb, artichokes, oxtail stew, beans with tripe, fried brains *alla romana*. *Saltimbocca alla romana*: sliced beef or veal wrapped around pieces of prosciutto with sage leaves and fastened with toothpicks. Lamb chops *a scottadito* (hot from the grill). In Ciociaria, calf tendons (*nervetti*) with green parsley sauce.

Quail with herbs. Bass with porcini mushrooms (in the finest restaurants, near seaside resorts along the coast). Another typical dish of Ciociaria is *cicoria pazza* (crazy chicory), which is eaten in Alatri with garlic, hot red pepper, olive oil, and salt.

Rome probably offers the widest choice of salad greens. Batavia lettuce, Lollo Rosso lettuce, white, gold, green, and even red leaf lettuce, with a slight walnut taste. Roman lettuce, exquisite when just picked, accompanies the most unforgettable kind of Roman salad green, *puntarelle*, the name for catalogna sprouts cut into thin slivers, then soaked in ice-cold water (in the Italian climate, ice and, in general, any cold dish were luxuries in ancient times) and seasoned with olive oil, vinegar, anchovies, salt, and garlic. The red radicchio is different from that found in Treviso and Verona, and has a different flavor. Then there are the dark green Roman salad and Belgian endive (a type of chicory grown in the dark in caves, in which chlorophyll is absent; hence the leaves have a completely pale color). A typical dish of Roman Jewish cuisine is endive with anchovies. Salad greens are bought in markets in the city's central piazzas: oak leaf, dandelion, escarole, and also *rughetta* (arugula), famous through-out the world, a variety of *rucola* (rocket). Incidentally, rocket in and of itself, which in recent times, thanks to the trend of nouvelle cuisine, has ended up on the menus of all the restaurants in the world, is appropri-ate and pleasant only in certain dishes and, moreover, only if it is fresh. A good chef knows how to combine this or that variety of rocket with his dishes, depending on how pungent the flavor is.

One of the chief typical dishes in Tuscany is called *pinzimonio*; in Lazio it bears the name *cazzimperio*. Despite how it may seem, there is nothing inappropriate or vulgar about the name of this dish: in fact it derives sim-ply from *cacio* (cheese). In ancient times, *cazzimperio* meant melted cheese with pepper, and in a gastronomic archaeological context you can of course encounter it even today in this sense. But it is worth recalling that, in the south of Italy, this word is currently used to mean *pinzimonio*.

Desserts Lazio's favorite dessert is *maritozzi*: leavened sweet buns with raisins, served with fresh cream. The gelato in Rome is exquisite. Gogol wrote enthusiastically about it to his friend A. S. Danilevskij on April 15, 1837: "In recompense the gelato is better than you could ever dream of. Not that loathsome stuff we had in Tortona, which you liked so much. Like butter!"

TYPICAL PRODUCTS OF LAZIO

Cheeses Pecorino romano cheese. Fior di Latte. Prized ricotta from Frosinone, made from the milk of cows who eat only clover: the clover gives the milk, and consequently the cheese, a particular density. Provola: a firm mozzarella. Provatura: cheese from buffalo milk, the largest mozzarella. Provatura is often confused with *provola*, because of the similarity of the names, and because both of these cheeses can be smoked and are often served breaded and fried.

Strawberries from Nemi. Artichokes, broccoli, sweet white onions from Marino, wild rocket, Onano lentils, Gaeta olives, Vallerano chestnuts, hazelnuts of Lazio. Homemade bread from Genzano and Lariano.

TYPICAL BEVERAGES

The local wines are the successors of Falernian, an acclaimed wine of ancient Rome: Malvasia, Trebbiano, and, recently becoming very trendy, Cesanese del Piglio and Fontana di Papa, produced in the famous region of the Castelli Romani, where the popes have had their summer residence since the Middle Ages.

The *sagra* of the white grape has been celebrated in the village of Marino since 1571, on the second Sunday of October. This feast was proclaimed for the first time by order of the pope to celebrate the success of the last crusade: the victory of the Christians over the Ottoman Empire fleet at the Battle of Lepanto.

Frascati wine, and in particular Est! Est! Est!, a white wine made from Trebbiano grapes from the Montefiascone region (province of Viterbo). Folklore tells of a German bishop who, on a pilgrimage to Rome, each day sent ahead a majordomo to scout out the best inns and to look for a wine worthy of the prelate. The majordomo would write the word EST! with chalk on the doors of certain inns to indicate the presence of good wine. Upon arriving in Montefiascone, he could not resist a triple exclamation, and wrote the agreed-upon word three times as testimony to the exceptional quality of the wine he had found. Since that time, the wine has been known as Est! Est! Est! The story, again, is legendary.

THE MEDITERRANEAN DIET

The Italian way of eating (popularly known as the Mediterranean diet) has the advantage of not being fattening. The uninitiated may be afraid of "getting fat from pasta," but in reality durum wheat pasta helps you stay in shape. And if pasta is not abused, if food is otherwise limited to vegetables, fish, and rare meat, then a lean body is almost guaranteed: that figure to which Italian Fascism aspired, since it valued mobility, speed, and agility. With a view toward transforming these goals into a dietary program, it adopted the ideas of the Futurists, specifically, those of Filippo Tommaso Marinetti (1876–1944). The aphorisms of Marinetti come to mind, with the admonition that heroic fighters should not eat soft foods; his program was laid out in a delightfully Futurist style: "We also feel that we must stop the Italian male from becoming a solid leaden block of blind and opaque density . . . Let us make our Italian bodies agile, ready for the featherweight aluminium trains which will replace the present heavy ones of wood iron steel."[1]

For the Futurists, the foremost enemy was "intellectual refinement," the heritage of Byzantium. The cooking of central and southern Italy, quick and light, could be considered the true, popular Mediterranean cuisine, according to Marinetti—and also according to Giuseppe Prezzolini. As the son of Sienese parents, Prezzolini, in a perfectly natural way, found in Tuscany the foremost pure Italian tradition:

I have summoned you as spokesmen of the Florentine table, the loftiest examples I know of that fare light, lean, savory, full of pith and flavor, fit for active wits, foes to sedentary obesity; lords of a table that never knew *risotto*, never conceived *maccheroni*, a table that execrates fats and reveres the spit and the griddle, with their lustral flames of wood and coal; a flame that fries you its fries without grease and roasts you its roasts without drip.[2]

The Tuscan specialty described by Prezzolini consists of light, lean meat, larks of field or forest, or thrushes threaded onto the skewer along with chicken livers, bay leaves, and small pieces of pork fillet seasoned with thyme, all of it alternating with toasted bread (*crostini*) and slices of bacon and cooked over a wood fire. An old recipe, still alive today.

Michel de Montaigne, in his *Journey Through Germany and Italy*, noted, "The people about here are not near such meat-eaters as we are."[3] Giacomo Castelvetro, in his work about the roots, herbs, and fruits of Italy, written in England, declares: "Beautiful Italy is not as abundant with meat as France and this island."[4] Bartolomeo Scappi, in his imaginary journey through Italy, wrote a summary description of Italian cuisine that is actually a catalog of fish dishes.[5] Contemporaries emphasized the prevalence of fish and seafood products as a common Italian characteristic. A sign of hospitality in ancient Rome and in medieval Italy was an offer of bread with fish sauce (*garum*).

Indeed, why shouldn't the population have taken advantage of the country's rich fish resources, since they were subject, among other things, to the strict rules of a religious calendar that imposed 160 to 200 meatless days a year (see "Calendar")? Surrounded almost entirely by sea, with abundant rivers and lakes, these people found in fish the chief ingredient of their diet: a wholesome, endless reserve of protein to sustain them in a healthy and economical way. Furthermore, over the centuries they had acquired a unique ability, still unparalleled today, to process all kinds of fish, transforming them into simple dishes at some times and elaborate ones at others.

Italian fish soups are a showcase of culinary perfection: the Sardo-Genovese *buridda*; the *cacciucco* of Liguria and Tuscany; the Rimini-style broth in Emilia Romagna; and all the soups taught to cooks in the Accademia del Brodetto (fish soup academy) of Porto Recanati, in the region of Macerata.

There are five hundred species of fish, seventy species of crustaceans, and thirty edible cephalopods living in the seas that surround Italy—the *mare nostrum* of ancient Rome. According to statistics, the average Italian ranks second in the world for fish consumption, after Japan. His average consumption is twenty-five kilograms of fish per year.

At 2:40 a.m. on a starry night in November, the wholesale fish market on Via Lombroso in Milan looks like the scene of a fashion show. Driving through the huge area by car, you see lights, crowds, action everywhere. Cars are parked in front of all the entrances of the main building. In the large hall the light is blinding; a wide corridor has been left in the center, and counters with "spectators" line both sides of the long "catwalk." The "spectators" look on with dead faces as they lie prostrate, sometimes sliding down off the counters. The spectators are tuna and swordfish, their protuberances turned toward us as we move down the "runway" amid a crowd of merchants, restaurateurs, wholesalers, and those who are just looking. With swordfish and hammerheads leaning threateningly out into the aisle, the scene recalls not only a fashion parade, but also a company of Cossacks with sabers drawn before an attack.

The most picturesque are the tuna, the large sturgeon, and the salmon, packed in polystyrene boxes, extended so that the head sticks out entirely from a hole on the left, while the tail protrudes by half a meter from a corresponding hole on the right—more or less like the lady in sequins whom the circus magician prepares to cut in half with his fake saw.

Each fish is officially assigned a commercial name, coupled with the Latin name, as required by law. Professor Renato Malandra, director of the market, knows not only the correct, official names of the fish but also their countless dialect variations, unique to each city and each village. The fish have the right to have two Italian names—two, but no more than two. The *molo* is the *merlano* (whiting), the *melu* is the *potassolo* (blue whiting), the *spigola* is the *branzino* (bass), the *busbana* is the *cappellano* (poor cod). The problem is that only one of these two names can be written on the cardboard signs that both fish market owners and itinerant fish vendors display on their counters. Writing any other dialect name for the fish in question is absolutely prohibited.[6]

The signs are replaced each day. The ones from the day before cannot be reused, since they have become soaked with ice and permeated by the fish smell; then, too, the price has changed. So each day the fishmongers make new signs; they are cunning when it comes to the rules, replacing one dialect name with another dialect name, trying to choose the one that will suggest a more superior variety. For example, they put a cardboard sign on the stand with the illegal designation *piovra* rather than the legitimate one *polpo* (octopus). Instead of *smeriglio* they write *palombo* (dogfish). Finally, instead of *pagello atlantico* they write *pagello fragolino* (both types of sea bream), which costs twice as much. Buyers swallow the cunning vendors' baited hook like hapless gobies.

Therefore, the director of the market, Malandra, must be an expert in psychology, in addition to his other skills. He is a university professor (two final-year students patter along behind him, having the honor of doing the nightly rounds with this luminary), a specialist in ichthyology, medicine, and helminthology, and a linguistics expert. It is his job to sort out and correlate the regional names of all these fish and shrimp, shellfish and invertebrates, snails and frogs. He knows how to deal with the unscrupulous itinerant vendors— hardened, chapped by wind, seasoned, and crafty—whose sector is protected by a solid trade union. It should be said that many of them inspire genuine admiration: they are outstanding, first-rate masters whose knowledge, manual dexterity, and work style is supreme virtuosity.

A man who holds the post of director of a market such as this, who spends every night except Saturday and Sunday on the job, must have solid skills in both the economics field (to decide quickly how to regulate complex fish bidding, to prevent financial crashes, the spoilage of merchandise, or the ruin of individual players) and the field of physical geography. He must be familiar with all the harbors where rate fixers accept the fish of the day and define the quantity of fish that can enter an Italian port on any given day, depending on the season, on the weather forecasts, on upcoming holidays, and even on the different days of the week, since more fish is consumed on abstinence days (see "Calendar").

The first requirement of the goods sold in this fish market is, of course, freshness—a freshness that is not defined by smell. In terms of smell, everything is always perfect, simply because in this market no merchandise smells. Well, maybe there's a very faint, salty aroma of seawater. Freshness, on the other hand (the absolute kind), is unmistakably clear. It is demonstrated when a fish picked up by its tail stiffens, like a stick, parallel to the ground: that's rigor mortis. The dorsal fin is erect, the muscles are tense. The eye must be bright and convex (although the eyes of fish that live in deep waters cave in immediately as a result of pressure, and this does not mean that the fish is not fresh).

Saltwater fish, therefore, are not sold alive: these types of fish, unlike freshwater fish, die quickly when removed from their environment. Not so with crustaceans. The market value of lobsters, crayfish, prawns, and shrimp depends on their vitality. Like bivalve shellfish, snails, and all related species, they must be alive to sell. As we pass the tanks and huge vats full of lobsters (the lobsters' pincers are taped so that they will not harm one another), the professor occasionally smacks the prisoners, who shake their antennae. You can see that they are alive and somewhat irritated.

On the "runway" of the fish market showroom, there's a crowd of specialists who have come from Milan, Bergamo, Brescia, Lodi, Cremona, and Pavia: restaurant owners and wholesalers. But the more numerous buyers are the street market vendors. These are the cheerful, rowdy, omnipresent fishmongers to whom Italian cities owe their unique, lively atmosphere. Their markets are the legacy of the Greek agora.

Around five or six o'clock in the morning, the itinerant vendors begin carrying the crates and tubs to their locations in the market, which differ depending on the day of the week. If you stroll through the piazzas of any city and look carefully under your feet, you will see that nearly invisible figures have been drawn on the pavement: these mark the spaces rented by the street vendors for the weekly market. Some of them have occupied their squares of space on the central piazza or on the main street of the city or village for three decades or more. The spaces are handed down from the dynasty's oldest member to the youngest.

Every Tuesday, after leaving the wholesale market around 6:30 a.m., the president of the provincial association of itinerant vendors, Ercolino Piva, cleans, slices, guts, and sells his fish—explaining in detail the various ways to cook them. This lasts from 7:20 a.m. until 2:00 p.m. in front of an ATM window (Ercolino's buyers often need to replenish their funds) on Via Eustachi in Milan. At 7:20 a.m. his line forms. There are mistresses from large, wealthy homes, difficult to manage, accompanied by their domestic help (the lady of the house will hurry to the office, the maid will put the fish in the refrigerator), journalists leaving the newspaper office early in the morning after a night shift, the elderly woman from next door who slips out for a piece of tuna, mothers (starting from 8:15) who have brought their children to the nearby elementary school, and an engaged couple who have come to buy two dozen oysters.

"Sapore di mare. L'arte di gustare il pesce fresco" (The taste of the sea: the art of enjoying fresh fish) is the title of a short article by Lina Sotis in the *Corriere della Sera* (spring 2006), which is dedicated to this local vendor: "A famous city haunt, offering magnificent specimens that live in the sea, is the mythical fishmonger Ercolino, who has a stand in the city's most famous markets . . . As we were saying, fish is in vogue."

The wholesale market has every tuna that exists. The *Thunnus thynnus* (bluefin, the kind the Japanese use for sashimi and sushi), caught during the *mattanza* (tuna killing)[7] among the Egadi Islands off Trapani in Sicily, not far from Favignana. There are also yellowfin tuna, albacore (these do not interest the Japanese, but do the Spaniards, for their traditional dishes), and bigeye. They all have different prices, and are in greater or lesser demand. Even the different parts of the tuna have different prices. Particularly prized is the *ventresca* (stomach muscle), followed by *tonnino* (dorsal muscle), and then by all the other parts (*tarantello*). There is a minimum size limit for tunas: fishing of smaller ones, those that have not lived long enough, is prohibited.

In general, the most prized element in all fish is muscle mass, and for this mass to be significant and the flesh supple, the fish must spend its life in an incessant struggle for survival, not vacationing in a guesthouse with three meals a day. It is even better when the muscle mass is suffused with sex hormones. Therefore, the best fish is that caught at the moment just prior to mating. Not after spawning: once the eggs or semen are ejected, fish become quite inedible.

We notice two rigid blocks, externally indistinguishable from each other: they are fillets of dried cod, or stockfish, a subject already covered in this book. Thus at the wholesale market there is the opportunity to observe the best species of stockfish, protected by the Slow Food Association: the *Gadus morrhua* (cod), on whose skin a lengthwise yellow stripe can be seen amid the many gray ones. To buy a slab like this you must pay a substantial sum. The other type of stockfish does not have the stripe; it is called *molva* (ling) and costs significantly less . . . except in cases where it is fraudulently passed off as the expensive type.

In the past, one of the most sought-after products at the Milan fish market was the *mosciame*, the dried dorsal muscle of the dolphin. But dolphin fishing in the Mediterranean Sea has been prohibited since 1980. So now *mosciame* may only be tuna.

The particular mine of national gastronomic wealth that deserves special mention is *pesce azzurro* (blue fish): herring, anchovies, sardines, mackerel, sardinellas, horse mackerel or scad, sand eels, and needlefish. The flesh of these fish is rich in polyunsaturated omega-3 fats and vitamin D. They are precious substances that can protect against thrombosis and various other illnesses. *Pesce azzurro*, a true medicine, prescribed in cases of psoriasis and rheumatoid arthritis, are a source of mineral elements and contain more calcium, iodine, phosphorus, fluorine, and zinc than other marine species. Moreover, these fish are caught mainly in the Adriatic Sea, so they are local, inexpensive, and reach the market the same day they're caught. This is important to the consumer, particularly because polyunsaturated acids decompose at high temperatures. Therefore, to maintain the incredible quality of *pesce azzurro*, it should be eaten raw, after a brief marinade, or baked for a short time in the oven or in foil. Only with these cooking methods are the beneficial acids preserved. These fish are good with pasta, the soft inner part of bread, and tomato sauce. Different varieties of anchovies are distinguished by the salinity of the waters in which they've lived: those caught in the Adriatic Sea have a less marked flavor, while the anchovy of the Ligurian coast is much more salty.

Every evening fishing lamps appear out at sea. The anchovy swims toward the light, drawn by the plankton that become more visible in the illuminated water. Once caught, the fish are immediately sprinkled with salt. Raw sardines, salted right on the boat, are the basis of a famous Venetian dish: sardines *in saòr* (in a sauce of onion, vinegar, raisins, and pine nuts).

Italian seafood cuisine is full of interesting products. Romagna boasts specialties such as clams, or *poveracce* (*Venus gallina*). Throughout Italy, and primarily in Naples and Sicily, *arselle* clams (*Tapes decussatus*, the checkered carpet shell) are eaten. A very common homemade dish is the delicious calamari, also called squid. Also popular are razor clams (*Solen vagina*) and scallops, or "sea combs" of St. James. In restaurants and on the market they are known by the French term "Saint-Jacques," but it would be more accurate to call them "Santiago," since these beautiful shells (well cleaned after the mollusk was eaten) were affixed to caps worn by medieval pilgrims on their way to the shrine of Santiago de Compostela. The second name for the sea combs of St. James, *capesante* (referring to the holy sign on the hat), goes back to that very tradition. Upon closer observation, this same flat shell with its broad wavy edge can be recognized in ornamental motifs that are found over the portals of both Catholic cathedrals and Orthodox churches, as a symbol of Christianity.

Very often mussels, giant squid, octopus, and *moscardini* (little octopuses) are present in Italian menus. Cuttlefish are often prepared, bought from the fish vendor or in the frozen food section of the supermarket, as well as sea truffles and tellins (both shellfish). Mantis shrimp (*canocchie*) or sea cicadas (*cicale di mare*) are not a rarity, nor are the magnificent crustaceans: shrimp, prawns, *mazzancolle* shrimp, scampi, crayfish, lobsters, crabs, spider crabs, and *moene* (sea cicadas during the shedding period).

The artistry of the Italian chefs who specialize in seafood is so renowned that the authoritative cooking expert Davide Paolini states that even the famous tempura of Japanese restaurants was introduced in Japan by the Italians.[8] According to his theory, the word "tempura" derives from *tempora*, seasons. Italian, Spanish, and Portuguese missionaries, finding themselves in Japan, observed the fasts "of the four seasons" (*tempora*), the quarterly three-day periods of prayer and fasting known as Ember Days, and during those times ate only fish. According to this expert, even the famous Japanese platter called the boat dish (so called in all Japanese restaurants in Europe and America, it is a small wooden boat, on the deck of which sashimi and sushi are displayed) recalls Italian and Portuguese ships. The Europeans also supposedly taught the Japanese to marinate mackerel with seaweed in special wooden molds, reminiscent of Portuguese sailing vessels.

Besides the huge consumption of fish, there is another almost universal feature of Italian food that is evident to both locals and foreigners: the love for raw, unprocessed vegetables.

This trend existed as far back as ancient Rome. In a comedy of Plautus, a chef explains why nobody has hired him: he charged handsomely, because his skill set him apart from other cooks who "slap barely seasoned grasses on the plate, almost as though the diners were ruminants." There follows a description of these "grasses": cabbages, beets, borage, spinach, garlic, coriander, fennel, black lovage (*Smyrnium olusatrum*), and mustard

(Plautus, *Pseudolus*, III). "The breath of our grandparents and great-grandparents reeked of garlic and onion," Marcus Terentius Varro wrote in his *Saturarum Menippearum* (fragment XIX), "but their spirit was one of courage and strength."

In the Middle Ages and in the Renaissance, foreign travelers were amazed at the excessive quantities of vegetables eaten by Italians. In 1581 Montaigne noted with astonishment in his travel diary: "We had artichokes, beans, and peas here, in the middle of March."[9] Costanzo Felici, in his treatise on botany (1569), advised against consuming raw tomatoes:

> The golden apple, so called in common parlance because of its intense color, or the apple of Peru, which is either bold yellow or vivid red—this one is either equally round or divided into sections like a melon—is also similarly sought after by gourmands eager for new things and also fried in a pan like the other, accompanied by verjuice, but to my taste it is more fine-looking than flavorsome.

He goes on: "The eating of salads is almost characteristic of gluttonous Italians (say those across the mountains), who have commandeered the food of animals who eat raw grasses."[10]

Fruits and vegetable foods were so important for the nourishment of the peninsula's population that scholars could not help but take serious note of it. At the end of the eighteenth century, that period of encyclopedias and scientific classifications, Giorgio Gallesio (1772–1839) completed a journey of exploration lasting twenty-five years, from north to south, through all the countrysides and villages of Italy. With the ardor of an enlightened thinker and the fanaticism of a collector, he aimed to observe, record, describe, and classify the principal varieties of existing fruits. His work, the *Pomona italiana*, which was published in installments between 1817 and 1839, has been reintroduced online and may be freely consulted in electronic and hypertext format.[11]

The largely vegetarian diet, coupled with Italy's generally charming customs and gentle climate, sent the romantic writers into raptures. Typical is Goethe's thrilled description of both lettuce leaves and the city of Naples and Sicily as the quintessence of *italianità* (the Italian spirit). In Goethe's imagination, southern Italy, with its light food, was the pearl of creation. "I won't say another word about the beauties of the city [Naples] and its situation, which have been described and praised so often."[12] Goethe is not even able to coherently describe this magnificent city: the only thing that he can say is *"kein Wort"* ("there are no words").

Italy boasts an ancient tradition of nutrition and dietetics inherited from the Arabs, primarily from the *Book of Agriculture* by Ibn Al-'Awwam (twelfth to thirteenth century). During the Middle Ages and the Renaissance, dietetics was associated with the principles of complementary humors (according to Galen), vegetarianism (according to Pythagoras), and the theories of the late-Roman cooking theoretician Apicius, who recommended the Mediterranean diet (that is, the normal dietary allotment of southern Italy, based on grains, wine, and olive oil).

Galen, a second-century Greek physician, remained topical until the eighteenth century. His theory is founded on the idea of balance among the four basic qualities: hot and cold, dry and wet (to which the poetic elements of fire, air, earth, and water correspond). Illness can be explained by the prevalence of one of these qualities with respect to the norm for any given age group (older people are cold and dry, younger people hot and wet). From ancient times through the Renaissance, an individual's state of health was thought to depend on a balance of humors in his body. An excess or a deficiency of one of the four humors—blood, yellow bile, black bile (melancholy), and phlegm—determined the appearance of an illness's symptoms. In an ideal world order, an ideal body, and an ideal dish, all elements should be present, in harmony with one another. All cuisines, then, are based on one's skill in combining ingredients. Only a few rare foods, foremost among them bread, are perfect in and of themselves. In most cases, the cook must correct the nature of the product based on a complex classification of foods according to the intensity of their quality. A number of classic dishes that are part of the Italian menu were formed in the light of such nutritional concepts, such as pears with seasoned hard cheese or slices of *prosciutto crudo* (cured prosciutto) with melon. Galen's remedies and the cooking treatises of the Renaissance advised against eating melon and pears in their natural state, since they were considered excessively wet and cold. Cheese and prosciutto, on the other hand, contain hot and dry humors: they must be combined with wet and cold humors, and then they may be eaten with gusto.

The final and fundamental Italian food principle is moderation.

The Venetian writer Alvise (Luigi) Cornaro (c. 1484-1566), following a period of illness and suffering, regained his health at forty years of age, thanks in part to his practices as a health fanatic. He had a tendency to overstate his age, and toward the end of his life declared that he was almost a hundred years old; nevertheless, only the date of his death, May 8, 1566, is certain. Cornaro noted in his *Discorsi intorno alla vita sobria* (*The Art of Living Long*):

> Oh, how profitable it is to the old to eat but little! . . . I, accordingly, who am filled with the knowledge of this truth, eat only what is enough to sustain my life; and my food is as follows: First, bread; then, bread soup or light broth with an egg, or some other nice little dish of this kind; of meats, I eat veal, kid, and mutton; I eat fowls of all kinds, as well as partridges and birds like the thrush. I also partake of such salt-water fish as the goldney and the like; and, among the various fresh-water kinds, the pike and others.[13]

Twelve ounces of solid matter and fourteen ounces of wine a day was, in Cornaro's opinion, the secret of longevity. "For I feel, when I leave the table, that I must sing, and, after singing, that I must write. This writing immediately after eating does not cause me any discomfort; nor is my mind less clear then than at other times. And I do not feel like sleeping; for the small amount of food I take cannot make me drowsy, as it is insufficient to send fumes from the stomach to the head."[14]

Naturally, Cornaro's self-satisfaction more than once inspired attacks of sadistic irony in those who came after him. Thus, a certain "Academic," in 1662, published a transposition of Cornaro's treatise in tercets, in macaronic Latin, signing himself "the walking corpse."

Medical research has confirmed that the Mediterranean diet does, in fact, prevent diseases prevalent in so-called affluent societies: atherosclerosis, stroke, obesity, and hypertension. There are countless contemporary manuals on the Mediterranean diet that bear titles such as "Eat Well to Live Better."

The majority of Italians are only halfheartedly interested in dietetics and alimentary chemistry: they keep one or two manuals on the subject at home pro forma; they remember their cholesterol periodically and are aware of its danger, but not so much that they go to the doctor to have it regularly monitored (as Americans do). Italy's two greatest certainties concerning nutrition are well established; they do not depend on short-lived trends and may be boiled down to the following creed:

1. Avoid junk food, represented by potato chips, Coca-Cola, snacks, and munchies that are bad for your health and above all, fattening.

2. Show no pity for pasta that's cooked even one minute too long. Overcooked pasta should only be thrown away. Pasta al dente is never fattening.

Today everyone aspires to be lean and slender and struggles against excessive weight. One cannot fail to observe that in social relationships in contemporary Italy, a trim, fit appearance, outward style, and above all a well-proportioned figure are key to a successful social identity. Gone are the days of Matteo Bandello, with the cult of full figures and excessive eating (in one of his stories, Bandello praised Milan for its "corpulence"; in another he applied the same epithet to Bologna). Gone are the days when the humanist and culinary theoretician Platina advised his academic friends Scaurio and Celio on how to eat in order to get fat. Distant, by now, are the follies of those dinners that the Church condemns, comparing them to the banquets of the rich Dives (from the Gospel story of the prosperous Dives and the poor Lazarus).

Italians today aspire not only to keep fit, but also to remain agile and active, free from postprandial stupor. This can be noticed at family meals as well as at official receptions. During the international summit attended by Tony Blair and Bill Clinton in November 1999, the Italian government, led at the time by Massimo D'Alema, organized a reception in Florence, in the Sala dei Gigli of Villa La Pietra and, as always, the then prime minister was aided in no small way by his friend and personal chef, Gianfranco Vissani. The menu created by Vissani was privately described as "characterized by lightness." It included creamed potatoes with lobster, *pappardelle* noodles with rabbit sauce and truffles, weever fish with fennel ravioli in orange sauce, and Florentine-style pumpkin for dessert. By contrast, at the Cologne summit, not long before, the same world leaders dined at the Museum of Roman Art, sitting at a transparent table, beneath which an ancient mosaic was visible. The Germans had orchestrated such a heavy dinner that soon afterward, at the concert of the city's Philharmonic, Clinton slept, Blair dozed, and D'Alema pinched himself to keep his head from lolling on his chest, while his wife, Linda, nudged him with her elbow from time to time.

The menu for the reception given by President of the Republic Carlo Azeglio Ciampi in honor of U.S. president George Bush (2003) appears utterly light, even imponderable: consommé in a cup, boiled rice, veal cutlet, and light pineapple cream. The wines were Montecarlo, Refosco, and Spumante Ferrari. After such a lunch, it is doubtful that anyone would fall asleep at a concert.

On the other hand, an overly serious attitude toward diet as an end in itself has always evoked laughter and ironic detachment, as in Gadda's *Cognizione del dolore* (*Acquainted with Grief*), 1963:

"They eat too much," the doctor opined to himself. "Half an apple, a slice of wholewheat bread that is so tasty to the tongue and contains all the vitamins, from A to H, no exception ... That's the ideal meal for a fit man! ... what am I saying ... for a normal man ... Anything more than that is simply a burden for the stomach. And for the body. An enemy illegally introduced into the body, like the Danai in the gates of Troy ..." (this is just what he thought) "which the gastrointestinal tract is then forced to reduce to a pulp, knead, and eliminate ... The peptonization of albuminoids! And the liver! The pancreas! The amidification of fats! The saccharification of starches and glucoses! ... a word! ... I'd like to see them! ... At most, in critical seasons, one may grant the addition of a few seasonal vegetables ... raw or cooked ... pods ... peas ..."[15]

All the more reason why esoteric diets do not enjoy great prestige nowadays. Experimental trends aren't terribly authoritative. Many would probably be horrified at the Bratman Test, publicized in the American and European press and on the Internet, whose first question reads: "Do you spend more than 3 hours a day thinking about your diet?" The test is intended to reveal the symptoms of orthorexia (*orthorexia nervosa*), a pathology described for the first time by Dr. Steven Bratman of the University of Colorado in an article devoted to the morbid fixation on healthful eating.[16] The International European Food Council warns that excessive attention to issues relating to one's diet and to the quality of foods is no longer a trend, but an illness. There is a specialized center at the Policlinico Umberto I hospital in Rome, to treat people suffering from eating disorders: there people are taught not to be too concerned about the quality of what they eat.

But in Italy, thank heavens, most people still tend to sensibly follow the culinary and gastronomic traditions of their forefathers (see "Slow Food"). It is a fine Mediterranean custom that Italians are unable and unwilling to give up.

Abruzzo and Molise

F arther south and east of Lazio, a harsh continental climate zone forms part of the Italian mosaic. Abruzzo is the ceiling of the Apennines, rising to almost three thousand meters, with the summit of the Gran Sasso (2,912 meters). Half the region is occupied by a national park protected by the state since 1872. Today it has grown to 44,000 hectares and is populated by Marsican brown bears (that is, bears typical of areas where the population of the Marsi once lived), Apennine wolves, Abruzzo chamois, deer, roe, golden eagles, otters, wildcats, alpine and sea choughs (sea crows), Dalmatian woodpeckers, and ravens. The first three of these animal species are practically nonexistent in the rest of Italy.

The climate in this area is frigid, so let the hot red pepper rage! Everything is pungent and spicy: from the strong, diabolical Centerbe liqueur to the intensely peppered meat that is eaten in Abruzzo. Up until a few decades ago, herdsmen and breeders were prevalent among the inhabitants. Only recently has industry in Abruzzo begun to develop more intensively, and to change the character of the region.

The abundance of proteins in the local diet clearly shows that this is a mountainous area. With all those mountains, it is difficult to talk about farming! Moreover, Molise, the ancient Samnium, is a land that has a high seismic risk. The economy is

based upon tourism and animal breeding (though actually an industry for construction materials, ceramics, and glass has also developed in recent years). As for animal breeding, cattle naturally cannot graze on such steep slopes, so Abruzzo is a grazing land for sheep and goats.

Sheep and goats, bucolic traditions that are almost ancient Greek. As in other regions of Italy, rejected lambs and unweaned kids end up on the table more often than not.

Abruzzo cooks are also wizards at cooking kid meat: according to Molise custom, it is stewed in red wine with rosemary, sage, bay leaves, and spicy red pepper.

What don't they say about the villagers here! Abruzzo is surrounded by eccentric, picturesque legends. From a historical and anthropological viewpoint as well, relations between people here have always had a particular distinction. No matter what the ruling power—Lombards, Normans, Swabians, Angevins, Aragonese, Spaniards,

Austrians, Bourbons—given the conditions of feudal backwardness, it was not these foreign conquerors who dominated the region, but the laws of poverty. Bandits were rife everywhere. It is understandable that the region's main typical dish is called *pecora alla brigante* (bandit-style sheep). More than any other social relationship, an ability to come to terms with the criminal elements was highly valued. And also with the charcoal burners, the *carbonai*, who throughout the year, in the dense forests, produced wood coal for sale (one of the local resources).

"From a strategic point of view, Abruzzo is notable for the fact that only one road leads there, extremely difficult for an army to traverse," says the Russian Brockhaus and Efron Encyclopedic Dictionary from the early years of the twentieth century. The Guelphs had earlier sought protection against their political enemies from the *carbonai* in Abruzzo, actually hiding in their huts to escape the Ghibellines in the twelfth and thirteenth centuries. On these mountains, Joachim Murat and the patriots fighting the tyranny of the Bourbons and French domination in Naples sought refuge from the king of Naples's troops. And those affiliated with the secret society that played such a large role in the history of the Italian Risorgimento, the Carbonari, took their name and symbols from the *carbonai*. Exalted as heroes by romantic writers, its adherents would enter history and the lexicon of European languages. Like the Freemasons, with whom they had much in common, the Carbonari shrouded their meetings in great secrecy, created a whole system of mystical rites, and developed their own phraseology, whose expressions were in part borrowed from Holy Scriptures, in part from their occupation as charcoal burners. The meeting place of the Carbonari was called the *baracca* (shack), the province where the encounter took place was called the "forest," the meeting itself a "lodge," a group of shacks a "republic." "Clearing the forest of wolves" meant liberating the country from tyrants. The symbol of tyranny was the wolf; they saw its greatest victim in Christ, symbolized by the lamb. The phrase "take revenge on the wolf that oppresses the lamb" became the society's watchword. Indicative, in the context of our culinary analysis, is this metaphor of the lamb, which is precisely the basic food of these areas.

It is fitting that an extremely widespread, typical Italian dish such as *pasta alla carbonara*, which takes its name from these same *carbonai* who cooked and ate it, was born here. Any self-respecting hermit cannot fail to have a supply of salt pork (usually pork cheek or *guanciale*, pancetta, or fatback) and goat cheese. That was all that was needed for pasta carbonara. A fresh egg could always be found in the woods, in the nest of some quail.

Pasta carbonara is sautéed in the same pan where cubed *guanciale* or pancetta has first been browned, that is, in pork fat, and then the raw egg is poured over it; the dish is sprinkled with grated pecorino cheese and seasoned with plenty of pepper, then heated a little more and eaten directly from the pan. Carbonara enjoys great popularity throughout Italy, especially in Lazio.

The Abruzzese population is used to ruggedly withstanding nature and is prepared to compete against it for its own vital space. One of Italy's major planning projects was achieved here, over a long period of time, like most major projects in Italy. The work was begun by the ancient Romans and completed in the year of Italy's unification (1860). The project involved the plain of Lake Fucino (later Lake Celano, Capestrano). The decision was made to reclaim vast stretches of land that could not be used for farming and prevent the flooding that submerged the region each spring (Lake Fucino is situated at a high altitude, in the crater of an extinct volcano).

The first major efforts intended to prevent flooding and drain the vast marshes around the lake were carried out by that great organizer Emperor Claudius in the first century A.D. After constructing the chief Roman aqueduct (Aqua Claudia) and the port of Ostia, Claudius had an underground sluice designed to drain water from the Fucino. Then a deviation channel 4,700 meters long was dug at a depth of 14 meters (eleven years of work, involving the labor of 30,000 slaves). The inhabitants of the region could finally breathe a sigh of relief: water finally flowed into the Liri River. It is true that maintaining this tunnel turned out to be quite complex after just a few centuries. And after more than a millennium and a half, the situation became absolutely disastrous: the underground channel was continuously obstructed, probably due in part to underground volcanic shocks.

In 1852, Prince Alessandrio Torlonia proposed draining the lake completely, though it was not a small one: 165 square kilometers. Having obtained the government's guarantee that the reclaimed lands would be his, he organized the excavation of a new underground tunnel, at a greater depth than the previous one. The work was completed after the unification of Italy and Prince Torlonia acquired vast holdings; there he settled colonists brought from neighboring regions (the Abruzzese have always been few in number). But at that point it was found that the general climate of the region had become harsher, precisely because of the elimination of that gigantic body of water: the famous centuries-old olive trees died, and only sugar beets could be grown on the reclaimed lands.

The character of the inhabitants of Abruzzo is suspicious, severe. People here are superstitious. It is strange, but historically accurate, that the approval of certain projects, including urban planning, was subject to a secret concordance expressed by magic numbers, surprising at times, such as ninety-nine. The capital of the region, L'Aquila (eagle), was established in the thirteenth century based on a plan personally designed by Holy Roman Emperor Frederick II of Hohenstaufen (or of Swabia). Emperor Frederick (1194–1250) was a patron of the sciences and philosophy, hosting French troubadours, German minnesingers, and Arab alchemists at his court. He was a painter and scientist himself, and spoke six languages, including Arabic and Greek. In his territories, religious tolerance toward Christians, Muslims, and Jews was imposed by law. He founded the University of Naples, where, according to his program, students in Europe for the first time began to study algebra and use Arabic numerals. Frederick was interested in esoteric doctrines, and assimilated notions of alchemy from the Arabs. The construction of the city of L'Aquila was completed only after Frederick's death, with funds collected from the proprietors of the ninety-nine castles surrounding the site.

The city was formally inaugurated in 1254, but by 1259 it had already been destroyed by order of Manfred, Frederick's illegitimate son, so that it would not go to his enemy, Charles of Anjou, who was about to conquer it. But the enemy (that is, Charles with his army) took possession of the ruins and the city was rebuilt according to the original plan, in which the magic number of ninety-nine was repeated. The city's main fountain consists of ninety-nine statues, representing the city's founding fathers. Water spurts from the open mouth of every founder. The city's main bell tower, in the Palazzo del Buongoverno, strikes ninety-nine times each evening. And there are ninety-nine churches in the city.

In Pescara, at the shrine of the Madonna dei Sette Dolori (Our Lady of the Seven Sorrows, pierced by seven swords), processions are held in which young girls carry lit candles, protecting the flame from the sea winds. Numerology, in these areas, is distinctive: often the number seven is encountered in sacred contexts, though just as often the number thirteen has a "magical" value.

At Campobasso, on Corpus Christi day, a grand procession, the Sfilata dei Misteri (Mysteries Pageant), is organized: the crowd carries wooden platforms (*macchine*, or stages) on their shoulders, thirteen in all, on which sacred performances of themes from the Holy Scriptures and the lives of the saints take place. At Toro, near Campobasso, on March 19, St. Joseph's Day (a day of mercy for the poor), the *sagra* of the Banquet for the Needy is held. According to the rules of the feast, the attendees are served thirteen courses. In the village of Rivisondoli, a living *presepio* (crèche) is arranged at Christmas; there, too, sacred representations are put on, with hundreds of participants and thousands of spectators.

The traditions of Abruzzo have been described by ethnographers and ethnologists numerous times, in the past as well:

> "Come, you drunkards, from the four corners of the wind. The land of plenty is open. You can drink wine without paying. But hurry, it won't last long. You can head for Avezzano, Sulmona, Bugnara, Raiano, Pratola Peligna . . ." As the Corpus Christi procession winds around, fountains of wine often spout in the middle of a piazza or in front of makeshift altars in the streets. The liquid is poured into a funnel from a third or fourth floor of the house, passing through special ducts of tin or cane, and comes out airy and lively, as if by magic, in the shape of a spiral or plume. Then whoever wants to drink, drinks . . . The same ceremony is performed in Raiano on the Feast of St. John.[1]

In Fossalto, on the first day of May, Maggio Grasso (Fat May) takes place: the crowd pours water over a man wrapped in branches and leaves (the *pagliara*), invoking the harvest with shouts of *"Rascia, Maje!"* ("Abundance, May!"). In the same period, other fertility-evoking rites associated with snakes are performed (mythical correspondence: the serpent, as a phallus, penetrates the earth's depths), or even rituals related to reminiscences of propitiatory sacrifices. At Cocullo, near L'Aquila, on the first Thursday of May, the procession of the *serpari* occurs in honor of St. Dominic of Foligno. Four sturdy parishioners carry on their shoulders a statue of the martyr, draped with live snakes. Behind the statue come young girls: each one carries on her head a basket containing five braided loaves of bread that will be offered to the snakes. Auspices about the future are drawn based on the behavior of the snakes upon seeing the loaves.

Just as the customs are exotic and the appearance of the celebrants is exotic, so, too, are the shapes and names of the region's pastas. In Molise and Abruzzo *maccheroni alla chitarra*, guitar-style macaroni, is produced, cut on a special apparatus that is aptly called a "guitar," which is built roughly like a musical instrument: a frame on which metal wires are stretched. It seems there are only two craftsmen left in the world who still make "guitars" for pasta. One of them, Gabriel Colasante, lives near Pescara, in the village of Sambuceto.

By pressing the pasta through the spaces between the wires with a rolling pin, square-cut strands are obtained. Artisans play this machine like a musical instrument, reaching a level of great virtuosity. The appearance of the pasta depends on how tautly the wires are stretched on the frame. With the wires somewhat slack, or placed on a diagonal, and using additional devices, you will get *maccheroni al rintrocilo* (made with the help of a toothed wooden rolling pin, the *rintrocilo*) or *della ceppa* (rolled around a stick, called a *ceppa*). Both the strings and the accessories are manufactured in bronze, in accordance with traditional technology. The cut pasta is left to air dry for fifty to sixty hours. Only then will it behave properly during cooking. Only then will its surface be rough enough to retain the sauces. And in Abruzzo these sauces can be so fragrant that it would be a crime to use the wrong pasta, which the sauce would not adhere to, allowing part of the wonderful flavor to be lost along the way.

Abruzzese cooks enjoy great success partly because they are able to prepare dishes correctly, and partly because they are unsurpassed masters in the use of spices, such as saffron, a typical product of the region. Saffron is collected from the stigmas of *Crocus sativus*. To produce a kilogram of the product, it takes two hundred thousand flowers and five hundred hours of work. Crocuses bloom in October and their flowering only lasts two weeks. One can therefore imagine the number of seasonal workers who are called upon for the saffron harvest during this brief but intense period.

The cultivation of saffron requires a lot of work, but it is also the most picturesque in the world. The inside of the flower's corolla is red, the petals are purple, the pistils yellow. In India and China, saffron has always been used both to prepare foods and to dye fabrics. And as we have already mentioned, the beauty of this spice suggested the legendary tale about the origin of risotto Milanese: a distracted artist who was painting the stained-glass windows of the cathedral in the sixteenth century is said to have dropped his paintbrush in the rice.

Of course it is just a tale. It is not difficult to date the appearance of saffron in Milanese cuisine: undoubtedly it was brought there by the Spaniards, who for years used it to flavor foods, having learned to do so from the Arabs. La Mancha is a region of Spain famous not only for the "Knight of the Rueful Countenance" but also for the cultivation of saffron. The Spaniards ruled in Milan from 1535 to 1706; hence saffron, too, must have found a place in Milanese recipes at the beginning of this period. And the legend of the stained-glass window painter dates the event to 1527: in short, roughly the same period.

The cultivation of saffron was introduced in Abruzzo long before Milanese cooking made it its own. Like many other important agricultural innovations in Italy, saffron spread thanks to the work of selection in monasteries (see "Pilgrims"). The monks had always been willing to experiment with new and promising crops. From the annals of the Dominican monastery of Gran Sasso, it appears that *Crocus sativus* was brought from Spain by the Dominican monk Domenico Cantucci around 1300. Cantucci was an inquisitor, and it is likely that his arrival caused the prior some agitation; but in the long run, his visit turned out to be incredibly propitious for the monastery. At Gran Sasso, Dominicans still cultivate saffron today. The cost of the finished product is as high as ten thousand euros per kilogram (more than the white truffles of Alba!).

In central Italy, saffron was already considered hard currency in the thirteenth century. In 1228, when the commune of San Gimignano repaid creditors who had financed the military operation for the conquest of the Castello della Nera, the debt was settled in cash and saffron.[2]

Not always, and not by everyone, were the merits of saffron considered indisputable. Goethe, for example, was of a different opinion: "A chicken boiled with rice is certainly not to be despised, but an immoderate use of saffron made it as yellow as it was inedible."[3] Alexandre Dumas, in *Le grand dictionnaire de cuisine*, considered saffron a downright dangerous substance: "The scent of saffron is extremely penetrating; it can cause violent headaches and even lead to death."[4] Still, saffron is irreplaceable in Italian cuisine. In Sardinia it is added to bread, in Abruzzo to guitar-style pasta (L'Aquila), rabbit, and sole. Without saffron the Sicilian cheese Piacentino di Enna could not be produced: its wooden molds are sprinkled with saffron so that the rind will be yellow. In recent times in Italy there have even been those who make saffron ice cream. In all eras, saffron has been used both as a dye and as a medicine. By gilding meat and rice with saffron, cooks in the Middle Ages improved both the appearance and the nutrition of the dish. In the sixteenth and seventeenth centuries,. L'Aquila sold saffron to Milan, Spain, and Marseilles. The precious pistils were one of the most sought-after items, since without this spice, neither risotto Milanese nor Spanish paella could be prepared. Knowing this, authorities have always tried to tax its sale. Saffron has not been expensive only in the twenty-first century: judging from a document that has come down to us, in the fifteenth century five hundred grams of saffron cost as much as a horse.

In general, the Abruzzese know how to add the right amount of spices to their dishes to get an aromatic, spicy taste without overdoing the aromas. It is popularly said that the taste receptors of Abruzzese cooks pick up more nuances of flavor than those of the average Italian. This reputation causes candidates from Abruzzo to be in high demand when selecting restaurant staff and appointing expert tasters. It is known that the Val di Sangro (in the province of Chieti) has given the world an entire constellation of distinguished chefs, working in the kitchens of great restaurants, hotels, and ocean liners. Many of them are emigrants or descendants of emigrants. Abruzzo was a depressed area up until the 1980s. The farmers of Abruzzo constituted almost half of those who were forced to leave Italy. In 1984 the situation began to improve: the L'Aquila–Rome highway was built, industry gradually began to develop, and the need to emigrate lessened. But as long as emigration was substantial, many Abruzzese found work as cooks in Switzerland and Germany, at the court of the emperor of Japan, and at the White House. An Abruzzese cook is a real treasure, distinguished by an almost religious devotion to his profession and by a particular gift (refinement plus originality) in measuring out the ingredients. Abruzzo belongs neither to the north or south of Italy nor, come to think of it, to the east or west. It is a unique region, a special case. Since its ingredients are modest, culinary salvation lies in the introduction of spices; it is therefore necessary for local chefs to develop subtle flair and culinary intelligence.

TYPICAL DISHES OF ABRUZZO AND MOLISE

First Courses *Maccheroni alla chitarra*, guitar pasta (called *crejoli* in Molise), with meat sauce of mixed veal, lamb, and pork, or pancetta and pecorino cheese. Spaghetti with garlic, oil, and hot red pepper. *Pasta alla carbonara*. *Ciufeli* and *tanne de rape* (pasta with turnip greens), similar to Puglia's *orecchiette* pasta with turnip tops. Pasta with mutton gravy, or with lamb gravy. Also mozzarella and fried potatoes with saffron.

Second Courses *Pecora alla brigante* (bandit-style sheep): skewers of adult sheep, which no one would eat in other localities in Italy. The cooks here, however, are capable of roasting this meat as well, thanks to their ingenuity and to delicious spices. *Castrato alla baraccara*: young mutton, from the high pastures of Tavenna, is cooked in a very large clay baking dish with olive oil, fresh tomatoes, onions, yellow sweet peppers, celery, parsley, and basil. This is called *alla baraccara* (shanty-style) because it was prepared at livestock fairs in makeshift shacks. Typical of the pastoral community are *torcinelli*: fresh, fat sausages made with lamb sweetbreads and intestines (liver, tripe), parsley, pepper, garlic, and lemon. *Annodate di trippa* (knotted tripe) can be made with the same ingredients: the casing is filled with vegetables and salt pork and then boiled. *Pamparella*: pork meat with garlic and red pepper, soaked in vinegar.

The specialty of Pescara is calamari stuffed with a mixture of shrimp, soft bread, garlic, and parsley, then cooked in white wine. *Scapece* of Vasto: slices of skate and dogfish marinated with vinegar and saffron. Pescara-style fish soup: scorpion fish, dogfish, skate, octopus, shrimp, mussels, tomato, onion, red pepper, and saffron.

TYPICAL PRODUCTS OF ABRUZZO AND MOLISE

Saffron of L'Aquila. Licorice, a specialty of Atri. *Ventricina*, a typical salami of Montenero di Bisaccia. Pork *guanciale* (cheek). Mortadella of

Campotosto, produced at Gran Sasso. This salami is also disrespectfully called "mule's testicles" because of its shape: a pair of elongated sausages, each of which contains a small column of fatback. Other specialties of Abruzzo are the *ventricina* of Crognaleto and the offal salami of Ortona.

Cheeses Hard pecorino cheeses from Farindola, Atri, and Penne. They are the best sheep's milk cheeses of Italy. Every shepherd and every dairy factory produces them according to their own recipe and their own norms for ripening (from two days to two years). In the town of Farindola, the stomach of the pig is used as rennet, cut into strips and marinated in wine, salt, and pepper for three months. The Fior di Latte of Boiano (Campobasso) is famous, similar to mozzarella, but produced with cow's milk instead of buffalo milk. Scamorza, an unfermented cheese, can be fresh or smoked. Both types are excellent breaded and fried. There is also the Scamorza *appassita* (a low-moisture variety) of Rivisondoli and Piano delle Cinque Miglia. Cheese *incanestrato* ("in a basket") is made in rush baskets, which impart a particular grassy flavor.

Other notable typical products: red garlic from Sulmona, carrots from Fucino. Fava beans, white beans, lentils. Spelt. Onions from Isernia (their *sagra* has been celebrated on June 28 and 29, the feast days of Sts. Peter and Paul, since 1254, when it was organized for the first time by order of Count Ruggero of Celano).

DEMOCRACY

In Aleksandr Herzen's words: "A sense of respect for themselves, for the individual, is particularly developed in the Italians; they do not simulate democracy, as the French do, it is inherent in them; and by equality they do not mean slavery for all."[1] In Italy, self-respect and satisfaction with one's place in the world are not dependent upon social status: it is a fairly well developed feature of the national character. One might say a lack of class conflict is characteristic of Italy. Obviously, there are exceptions: in particular, periods dominated by ideology have not infrequently given way to demonstrations of intolerance and antagonism. Even in the most ruthless times, however, antagonism and class struggle were kept within the bounds of relatively civil behavior, hardly ever leading to excesses, persecution, or atrocities. One need only think of the characters in the books of Giovanni Guareschi and the Don Camillo and Peppone series of films (released between 1948 and 1969). Relations between a diehard Communist and a shrewd priest, bound by an invincible mutual liking in spite of the most intense hostility, offer an excellent key for understanding the history of Italian society.

The roots of this moderate tendency toward conflict can be found in a widespread sense of pride, developed over the centuries thanks, among other things, to direct access to sources of survival: food products, warmth and sunshine, water, land. Such wonderful conditions ensure the individual a considerable degree of independence, with all its attendant joys: self-sufficiency, freedom from slavery, a profound historic memory, and a sense of aesthetics regarding both feast days and everyday moments.

This self-sufficiency comes with a critical attention to detail. The average Italian has a range of convictions for which he is prepared to burn at the stake. And these convictions do not have all that much to do with politics or ideology. The creed of the average Italian refers, above all, to the realm of food—a more personal, more accessible sphere of creation and individual self-expression.

This kind of creativity does not demand expensive foods. Those who know cooking are characterized, on the one hand, by a low regard for the "expensive," and, on the other, by a defense of the romantic notion of poverty, almost as if following the direction outlined by Leo Longanesi:

Poverty . . . is still the country's only vital force and whatever little or great that is still standing is only the result of poverty. Beautiful places, artistic heritage, ancient dialects, rustic
cuisine, civic virtues, and artisanal specialties are preserved only by poverty. Where it is
overcome by the addition of capital, that's where we witness the complete ruin of every
moral and artistic patrimony. Because the poor have ancient traditions and live in centuries-
old places in a poverty that has ancient roots, while the rich are recent, impromptu, the
enemy of all that preceded them and that humiliates them. Their wealth came easily, usually as the result of fraud, of shady dealings, always, or almost always, imitating something
created outside of here. Thus, when Italy is crushed by the fake wealth that is already
spreading, we will find ourselves living in a country whose face or soul we no longer
recognize.[2]

The gastronome Davide Paolini exalts the *poveracce*, mollusks (*Venus gallina*) considered inferior, known also by the names *telline* (tellins or cockles), *ostriche di pollo*
(chicken oysters), *filoni*, and *schienali*. Found on the sand at the water's edge near Rimini,
they are cooked in seawater and are sold in kiosks on the beaches of Romagna. According
to Paolini, *poveracce* are the culmination of culinary perfection: "Anyone who does not
agree that this is a dish truly fit for a king deserves to eat farmed bass, Cuban lobsters, or
the ubiquitous sashimi, made of fish fed with powder, for the rest of his life."

Those who really love Italian food do not aspire to be showy or flashy. Improbably
beautiful food arouses suspicion in the connoisseur. He knows that there are cooks who
specialize in preparing photogenic food, and that a dish created for a photo is unfit for
eating: it is bad even before it is sprayed with glue or shiny lacquer to make it glossier.

Anyone who loves Italian cooking also knows the society and is profoundly democratic. He knows that even the less elite social groups (fishermen, seamen, farmers) are
highly versed in matters of culinary art. They are separated from the culinary establishment only by language barriers. The food lexicon is made of predominantly local dialects:
in any location, cooking ingredients and preparation methods are better known to the
farmer or fisherman than to any city dweller. The locals can discuss food only in their language, which is not covered by any manual. All you have to do to learn is listen well and
make a guess.

There's no doubting that the Italians have an egalitarian attitude toward food. Here
the poorest people are invited to banquets on feast days; food is distributed in the main
piazza; tripe is served in luxury restaurants; the best restaurant is defined in accordance
with the principle "where the truckers stop"; and a coffee or a pizza is left *in sospeso* (on

account) for someone who can't afford it (see "Pizza"). All this is authentic and natural, like the relations between the waiter serving the meal and the *pizzaiolo* who makes the pizza.

Be careful, though: there is a certain threshold beyond which this respect suddenly disintegrates. As soon as the fundamental principles of the culinary code come into question, all hell breaks loose! A rigidity bordering on fanaticism, a fundamentalist intolerance, then emerges in the tolerant Italians. This is where democracy ends, or is at least transformed into majority rule. Here is a list of the Italians' rigidities, with which foreigners are easily at odds:

They will try to discourage unusual combinations of certain dishes or certain ingredients.
They will avoid serving you a cappucino, unless it's early morning.
They will try to dissuade you from having tea after a meal.[3]
They will make it difficult for you to get a cheese sandwich for breakfast.
No one will be happy to serve you spirits (vodka, grappa, gin, cognac) before the end of the meal.
No one will agree to bring overcooked pasta to the table to please a foreigner.
No one will let you have lunch either before 12:30 or after 2:00 in the afternoon.
They will not want to bring you wine that is not suited to the specific dishes you ordered; you will have to insist strongly.

An amusing case was described by the restaurateur Mario Zurla, owner and chef of the famous Pappagallo in Bologna:

"What was the worst day in your restaurant?" I asked Mario Zurla many years ago. He replied: "The day the Americans liberated the city. Don't misunderstand me. I was eagerly awaiting the Allied victory, and when an officer came to tell me that the staff of the American Fifth Army intended to celebrate the event with a grand dinner at my place, I experienced one of the most exciting joys of my life. The officer advised me that they would see to the ingredients: for once I did not have to worry about ration cards or resort to the black market. Maximum liberty as to the menu. Tortellini in broth? I suggested. Very good, the officer said. Then I suggested roast turkey. That too was very good. I added some *bollito*, *cotechino*, *zampone*, and lentil purée. The officer approved without objection. And to drink, what did they want? Hot chocolate, the American replied. I thought I would faint. Chocolate with tortellini, with *zampone*! It was like something from outer space! The officer realized that he had made a gaffe and immediately corrected himself: Oh, Mr. Zurla, if chocolate doesn't go well, we can have Coca-Cola with our meal. What reply could I make to this second gastronomic heresy? None. I said: As you wish. And out of love for my liberated homeland, I started cooking."[4]

Openly confessing his unpreparedness, the Russian critic Aleksandr Genis describes a similar incident in his biography:

Finding myself in Italy for the first time, after tasting everything I could, I finally went into a trattoria by the sea. The tiny octopus swimming in olive oil and vinegar enticed me. I ordered the dish, but before having time to taste it, I unfortunately remembered Hemingway. In Italy his characters often sipped drinks with exotic names: "Strega" and "Sambuca." Not suspecting that they were liqueurs, I ordered them from the owner of the place. His face darkened, and he grabbed his throat with both hands, which did not stop him from shouting loudly, "White wine, *stupido*!" I understood without a dictionary, but I was too late to correct myself. Throwing his apron on the ground, the owner stalked out of his trattoria. I hope he didn't rush out to drown himself, though I never saw him again.[5]

For Italians, these examples bespeak an ignorance so gross that it's nearly unimaginable. In cases like these, behaving democratically is impossible. The requests are senseless, not even worth talking about. But all in all, no one pays much attention to the combinations that occur to foreigners—particularly when these foreigners, Russians or Americans, say—are from another continent. They, in fact, can be given to combinations so arbitrary, so dissonant, as to leave Italians appalled:

This depicts food in the realistic way which only Americans ever attempt. Virginia ham glows in Technicolor from amid slices of pineapple. Steak sizzles among . . . mushrooms and cream billows over the chocolate cake . . . It all suggests the mood in which a perfect dinner should end. Sighing happily . . .[6]

It is difficult to imagine how far removed an Italian reading this description is from "sighing happily." In fact, one of the fundamental principles of a normal meal in Italy is that no other food is found on the table except that which everyone is currently savoring. The antipasto has no right to remain on the table if it is already time to bring in the first course. If one of the guests has not yet finished enjoying the prosciutto and salami, all the other diners must endure their hunger pangs and then eat their pasta cold.[7] The first course will not be served to anyone until the remains of the antipasto are removed from the table. The antipasto is like an overture that introduces the meal: it must be taken away and forgotten before the other foods make their appearance.

Cheer up. At least some manifestation of democracy can be sought in the culinary code. Here are the few, yet pleasing, signs of indulgence: When talking to the waiter, the diner may ask to add olives to his pizza instead of the capers called for in the menu. The diner can also say what kind of water he wants at the start of the meal: natural or fizzy. A decision must absolutely be made, and quickly. Still, freedom, as Karl Marx taught, is the consciousness of necessity. No one will comply with a dinner guest who decides to sprinkle his fish sauce with Parmesan.

To summarize: Freedom is reserved for one's personal life. When it comes to clams, there is a higher law. As recompense, any restaurant will offer a diner the opportunity to dress his salad himself with oil, vinegar or lemon, salt—incredibly democratic. He must remember, though, that there are rules even in this case. Wisdom has it that to make a good salad, a miser should see to the vinegar, a sprendthrift to the oil, a wise man to the salt, a judicious man to the pepper, and then a madman to the mixing.

The principles of the Italian culinary code are rigid. Its language, though, is democratic: simple, clear, and joyful, it is accessible to everyone. This is why politicians love to use food metaphors so much. The language of food is widely employed to manipulate the behavior of voters during the course of elections. Politicians' advisers recommend a widespread use of the food lexicon, which so quickly touches both the intellect and the heart.

Even during a pre-electoral battle between the countries' two main parties in 2005, the former mayor of Rome, Francesco Rutelli, leader of the Margherita Party, shouted at his party's assembly in order to portray the situation of conflict and discontent that had built up within the Left in the most accessible way: "For three years I pulled the cart, I ate bread and chicory to deliver to Romano Prodi a center-left coalition capable of winning. This is our joint reality. This has been the battle for years." "Bread and chicory," in Rutelli's metaphor, referred to the bitter ration of the worker, not very tasty but life-giving, capable of strengthening the political machine. Rutelli's partner, Romano Prodi, on the other hand, though obviously perceived by Rutelli as a fellow politico, is known by the nickname of

"Mortadella": a soft, fat salami, pleasant to the taste yet high in calories, which leads to flabbiness. This remark earned Rutelli the nickname "er Cicoria" (Chicory Man, in Romanesco dialect); and during a summit meeting of his party, on May 25, 2005, militants polemically distributed crusts of bread and chicory plants in Piazza dei Santi Apostoli in Rome.

During the D'Alema government, chicory played a leading role at the high-level presidential table. A chicory pie with sea urchins, made by the illustrious personal chef Gianfranco Vissani, was served to Gerhard Schröder on May 17, 1999, on the occasion of the Italo-German summit in Bari. More recently, this plant of the Asteraceae family leaped back into the headlines of all the Italian newspapers when, after the capture of the dangerous fugitive and mafia boss Bernardo Provenzano in Sicily on April 10, 2006, a saucepan with the remains of boiled chicory was found on the small cooking stove in his rundown farmhouse.

> It sends us back to an archaic food world, governed by simple gestures and honest flavors . . . things available to cows and people who have nothing—all they have to do is search through the weeds as millions of Italians did during World War II. The search for wild chicory holds up against affluence, the third millennium, emigration.

Thus *The New York Times*, in a front-page story, described the strange habits of Italian-Americans of New Jersey and New York: surrounded by trailer trucks and speeding cars streaking past one another, they park in highway turnouts and pick supplies of chicory plants. The health authorities' appeals—"Plants saturated by pollution"—fall on deaf ears. There's nothing to be done. The Italian-Americans have been looking for chicory *da sempre*—since time immemorial, as the Romans say, and they will continue to do it.[8]

The active use of the culinary code in election campaigns was exalted at one time by the shipowner Achille Lauro, a political Monarchist, nicknamed "Commander," who became mayor of Naples by buying votes in exchange for pasta. It was said bitterly and sarcastically in the city that during the course of the elections of 1953 "the grain mills worked harder than the printing offices."[9]

"The Vacca family, hired by mayoral candidate Achille Lauro, distributed pasta during the electoral campaign. The family next door, after receiving it and eating it for lunch, left the house to conduct propaganda for the PCI [Partito Comunista Italiano, the Italian Communist Party]. The Vacca family became aware of it. An altercation arose, which then continued dramatically with razor slashing. Four people . . . were seriously injured," the newspaper *La Stampa* reported on June 5, 1953. Also published in *La Stampa* during the months of Lauro's electoral campaign were the articles "Pastasciutta calda con contorno nuova arma 'segreta' di Lauro" (Hot pasta with a side of Lauro's new "secret" weapon)[10] and, aptly, "Nuovi incidenti a Napoli per le violenze dei monarchici" (New incidents in Naples as a result of Monarchist violence).[11] The article "Ricompaiono pasta e olio nella campagna elettorale Dc" (Pasta and oil reemerge in the DC electoral campaign) appeared in *L'Unità*, The Italian left-wing newspaper, on April 30 of that same year.

Thanks to pasta, olive oil, and tomatoes, the Neapolitan populace proclaimed the Monarchist Achille Lauro its first citizen. In the three months prior to the elections, the Christian Democrats, his adversaries, having learned of his citywide food distribution, had sent fourteen thousand gift packets to the city through Leopoldo Rubinacci, the minister of labor. But Lauro, responding to the distribution of dry rations by his competitors, decided to take a revolutionary step: he began distributing hot pasta dishes in Monarchist centers in Naples. Beginning April 8, 1953, a free mess hall began operating in the city at the Flower Market, serving a thousand meals per hour. A plate of pasta was distributed to anyone who showed a Monarchist Party card or had a special voucher, distributed by the Monarchists' electoral committee.

Snickering, people began calling Achille Lauro's Popular Monarchist Party (PMP) the "Pasta Macaroni Pomodoro" party. But this taunting was not enough to decrease his number of votes—on the contrary.

In other regions of Italy, especially in red Emilia Romagna, free pasta was unsuccessful. Achille Lauro tried to hold a rally in Piazza Maggiore in Bologna, but leaflets were distributed among the crowd: "Here in Emilia Neapolitan pasta doesn't catch on: we prefer our homemade tagliatelle." In Italy, tagliatelle, like the embattled tortellini of Emilia attacked by the Roman D'Alema (see "The *Sagra*"), were and still remain a symbol of Communist camp kitchens. It was the Communism that Mussolini termed "Socialism of the tagliatelle," in reference to the rallies held by revolutionaries who "furled up the red flags as soon as they saw a white tablecloth."

But that's how Communist propaganda work was done immediately after the war, in July 1948. To wish Palmiro Togliatti a quick recovery after the dangerous attempt on his life, a huge party was held in Rome at the Foro Italico stadium, which appeared to have lost its institutional solemnity for the occasion:

> The lawns and marble *piazzali* were teeming, their green and white expanses covered by a shrieking crowd that only the vendors of fritters, soft drinks, balloons, and propaganda leaflets were able to make their way through . . . Seamen from the Lido, on a cart repre-

senting a fishing trawler, were cooking fish stew and eating it, alternating the lyrics of "Bandiera rossa" with loud shouts of hurrah. Meanwhile the guests arrived, trooping through stands selling grapes and melons, orange drinks, ice creams, and sweet buns (*maritozzi*); sweaty and boisterous, they crowded on the steps of the stadium.[12]

Today, the culinary code is still part of the political experts' arsenal and is used widely in electoral campaigns, especially by the coalition of the Left.[13]

Campania and the City of Naples

Following the fall of ancient Rome, Naples was dominated by the Normans, the Swabians, the Aragon dynasty, the Angevin dynasty, the Bourbon dynasty, and the Savoy dynasty, but these foreign rulers did not leave many recipes in Neapolitan tradition and cookbooks (with the exception of *sartù* and baba).

For a long time, the world considered the cuisine of Naples and Campania the maximum, absolute expression of the Italian character (*italianità*). And indeed, it was in Naples that macaroni with tomato sauce, spaghetti with clams, and pizza were invented. Since the days of ancient Rome, the term *cene capuane* (Capuan dinners) has been synonymous with "extravagant banquets." On May 29, 1787, Goethe wrote of Naples:

> There is no season when one is not surrounded on all sides by victuals. The Neapolitan not only enjoys his food, but insists that it be attractively displayed for sale. In Santa Lucia the fish are placed on a layer of green leaves, and each category—rock lobsters, oysters, clams and small mussels—has a clean, pretty basket to itself. But nothing is more carefully planned than the display of meat, which, since their appetite is stimulated by the periodic fast day, is particularly coveted by the common people.
>
> In the butchers' stalls, quarters of beef, veal or mutton are never hung up without having the unfatty parts of the flanks and legs heavily gilded.

Several days in the year and especially the Christmas holidays are famous for their orgies of gluttony. At such times a general cocagna [*cuccagna*, feast] is celebrated, in which five hundred thousand people vow to outdo each other. The Toledo and other streets and squares are decorated most appetizingly; vegetables, raisins, melons and figs are piled high in their stalls; huge paternosters of gilded sausages, tied with red ribbons, and capons with little red flags stuck in their rumps are suspended in festoons across the streets overhead. I was assured that, not counting those which people had fattened in their own homes, thirty thousand of them had been sold. Crowds of donkeys laden with vegetables, capons and young lambs are driven to market, and never in my life have I seen so many eggs in one pile as I have seen here in several places.

Not only is all this eaten, but every year a policeman, accompanied by a trum-peter, rides through the city and announces in every square and at every crossroad how many thousand oxen, calves, lambs, pigs, etc., the Neapolitans have consumed.[1]

This region is fortunate for the fertility of the terrain, for its prominence, and for its climate. Here, outdoor life, no matter what the weather, affords a genuine physical pleasure. The climate is simply ideal, mild in winter and not too hot in summer, with a steady, pleasant breeze. The natural landscapes are remarkable and the day passes in contemplation: this is a paradise for tourists, with one of the most beautiful coastlines of Italy, the Amalfi Coast. Hippolyte Taine, who didn't like anything, found Campa-nia extraordinarily pleasing. On March 6, 1864, after leaving Naples, he wrote:

As far as Capua the country is a garden. Green crops as fresh as in May cover the plain. Every fifteen feet a branchless elm sustains a tortuous vine, the lateral shoots of which extend to another trunk, and convert the field into one vast arbour. Above this brown trellis of vines and the whitened branches of the elms rise Italian pines with their dark spreading cupolas, as if of a foreign and superior race . . . But how luxuriant the coun-try around! Vegetation rises to a man's height, and the atmosphere is so mild that we can leave the windows of the carriage continually open.[2]

Here the harvest is so abundant that it plentifully supplies not one but two metropolises (Rome and Naples), located in the same agricultural region. Unlike Rome (a papal city, and a tourist city, where the clergy rules), Naples was a true cap-ital of a kingdom. Stendhal wrote on December 6, 1816: "The Kingdom of Naples is confined to this one city, which alone among all towns of Italy has the tone and the bustle of a true capital . . . Naples, like Paris, is a great capital city; this, perhaps, is the reason why I find so little to record . . . Naples, alone among Italian cities, has the true makings of a capital; the rest are nothing but glorified provincial towns, like Lyon."[3]

Naples was the capital of a kingdom, with all the drawbacks this entailed. One of these problems, the turbulent Neapolitan crime, is known throughout the world. In Naples and its environs, unemployment was and still is high; how could it be other-wise? The city has never had and does not now have any industries. As a commercial port, it represents an outlet for impoverished regions and, consequently, does not offer serious employment opportunities for a population qualified to work. What is Naples famous for, and in what does it excel? As may be expected with a royal city, Naples has seen court-related trades flourish for centuries. Even today, the best tailors in Italy (and therefore in the world) can be found here; prestigious clientele from all over the world seek out Neapolitan manufacturers of men's clothing, including hat, button, shoe, and tie makers.

Moreover, intellectual life, which developed in part (though only in part) in salons and at court, has always been lively in Naples. Under Frederick II of Hohen-staufen (mid-thirteenth century), emperor of the Holy Roman Empire, one of the first universities in the world was founded there (1224), and named nowadays after him. The court was cosmopolitan, and moved continuously from Naples to Palermo and from Palermo to Naples; among its notables were Normans, Italians, Greeks, and Arabs. This group of distinguished intellectuals included jurists, functionaries, and clerks who were part of Frederick's bureaucratic apparatus. Poets were also plentiful. They formed one of the most unusual creative groups in the history of world litera-ture: the Sicilian school of poetry, centered in Palermo. Legend has it that Frederick's chancellor, Pier delle Vigne (who unfortunately later clashed with his master and was blinded and exposed to public mockery in a cage by imperial order), was the first to develop the sonnet, the fourteen-line poetic form that, in many ways, influenced the development of world literature. According to another version, the inventor of the sonnet was Jacopo da Lentini, a notary at Frederick's court. The Neapolitan intelli-gentsia enjoyed high esteem in Italy in the Baroque period and under the Bourbons, as well as during the years of Italy's unification and during Fascism. Even today, Naples often gives birth to literary trends, crowns philosophers with laurels, dictates fashions, and imposes taste.

The constant presence of baleful Vesuvius on one side of the landscape and Her-culaneum and Pompeii on the other seems like an eternal memento mori, leading to a unique philosophical depth. Here the soil is saturated with volcanic lava, a remnant of catastrophic disasters, but it also contains a rich natural fertilizer: seaweed. On this fertile ground, flavorful vegetables and fruit are grown, redolent of the sea and of the volcano: artichokes, apricots, apples, white figs, and incredible lemons. A particular variety of local tomato in Campania is the San Marzano, which is grown on vast farms and supplies a thriving cannery industry. It was in Campania that tomatoes began to be cultivated sooner than anywhere else in Europe, and Naples has created many sig-nature dishes with them: everything here is drizzled with tomato sauce. The fruit of Campania constitutes a third of all Italian fruit production. In addition, durum wheat, essential for the production of pasta, is grown here.

Campania also specializes in water buffalo breeding. Up until relatively recently, a marshy strip extended along the coast, from Rome to Naples. Those swampy areas were drained during Mussolini's dictatorship, but up until then, since it was impossible for cows to graze there, the inhabitants of Campania raised buffalo, which happily browsed on the sedge in those wetlands flooded by rivers. Buffalo in fact love to live in wet environments (they are often pictured in the paintings of Asian artists, in the midst of tropical landscapes). For this reason, there was no cow's milk in Rome or in Campania, only buffalo milk. Though this milk is not good raw, a wonderful masterpiece, a miracle of nature, is obtained from it: *mozzarella di bufala*, with all of its variants and subspecies (*ciliegine, bocconcini, aversane, trecce, treccine, cardinali, scamorze, provole*).

Everything involving the production of mozzarella is, of course, regulated: the process, the recipe, the weight. The *ciliegine* ("cherries") are little balls of twenty-five grams. The *bocconcini* ("morsels"), balls of fifty grams. The *aversana*, on the other hand, must be very large: five hundred grams.

According to a widespread conviction, mozzarella cannot be exported or stored, but should be eaten immediately on the spot, on the day it is made.

The writer Lidia Ravera recounts, in her piece dedicated to buffalo mozzarella:

> The "shop" opens on the most exposed square; there young girls, their hair pinned up under white bonnets, sell mozzarella, *bocconcini, aversana, trecce, treccine, cardinali*, yogurt, *scamorza*, smoked *provola*, ricotta, butter, ice cream, pudding. All made with buffalo milk . . . It is Sunday morning. The square is packed with cars. There is ferment. Buyers display anxiety: when the buffalo mozzarellas run out, there is no way to get more. Once those are depleted, everyone might as well go home.[4]

However, since enthusiasts of true mozzarella live everywhere, not just in Naples, a way of satisfying their demands had to be found, without departing too much from the canon. At five in the morning, no matter what the weather, at the terminal of the regional wholesale market (Via Mecenate), Milanese fanatics of real mozzarella wait for the refrigerated trucks that come from Campania after a night's journey. Even high-quality industrial mozzarella is good, of course: the kind sold in supermarkets in plastic bags, in its own preservation liquid, whose salinity is similar to that of tears. Truthfully, though, it is not exactly the same thing. Everyone knows that mozzarella should be eaten in the shortest time possible. To prolong its life at least a little, mozzarella (that is, Provola, its most solid variety) is smoked. It then assumes a dark brown coating, while the center remains bright and white.

It is better to eat mozzarella in its natural state, but sometimes it is prepared *in carrozza* ("in a carriage"), between two slices of bread whose crust has been removed: the whole thing is fried in butter after being floured and dipped in egg.

Mozzarella dominates Caprese cuisine. Since life on Capri is the height of earthly luxury and indolence, no one should spend hours at the stove, cooking. Thus the cuisine on Capri is light and spirited. The mozzarella balls are cut into round slices; large tomatoes are similarly sliced into rounds; basil leaves, sea salt, a pinch of oregano, and black olives are added; and extra-virgin olive oil is poured crosswise onto the colorful dish. It is dinner, it is lunch, it is divine grace—call it whatever your romantic fantasy suggests, but if nothing comes to you, the technical name of the recipe is *insalata caprese* (Caprese salad).

After the reclamation of the marshes, Campania acquired many new arable lands, fit to be planted with wheat and vegetables. The channels that run where once there were only swamps clearly show how freshwater abounds in the region, an invaluable asset for agriculture and for the lives of the inhabitants. Precisely because of this availability of good freshwater, the intrepid Maritime Republic of Amalfi lived sated and prosperous during the Middle Ages. It is thought that the best pasta in Italy, and probably in the world, is made in Amalfi (see "Pasta"). No wonder: an extraordinary pasta has always been produced as a result of good, abundant freshwater. Wheat was ground and the mechanisms for extrusion were activated using energy provided by rapidly flowing streams. Pasta, and white paper, is still produced today using local water here. In Gragnano, tourists are shown both traditional pasta factories and paper mills: the area is like Holland, a flat plain with windmills and water.

It is easy to see why a culture of great bread, radiant and unusual pastas, and, of course, pizzas (see "Pizza") was naturally created in Campania.

As far as the bread is concerned, it is made with durum wheat flour, a particular variety that grows only here in Campania, in South America, and in Russia. The flour is mixed with yeasts that mature on the surface of old wine and are called *crescita* (growth). Unlike Tuscan bread, the bread of Campania is acidic, and its thick crust conceals a rich soft mass that remains fresh for a long time.

The pastas in Campania (long shapes, for the most part) are served with shellfish, fish, or simply tomato sauce (the famous *pummarola*). In addition to traditional preparation, pasta in Naples is also baked in the oven.

———

Desserts also have an enormous importance in the cuisine of Campania. Desserts are rarely the main attraction of regional cuisine in Italy: only here in Naples and in Sicily. The passion for desserts in Neapolitan cuisine is a clear legacy of the Bourbon and Austrian domination, but a prosperous tourism has also influenced the rise of the local madness for pastry. Visitors go to Capri for the intense social life, and to Ischia to minister to the body in the warm mineral waters of spas. Tourists love desserts, and happily order them in the pastry shops. These pastries are difficult to prepare and require an elegant presentation. The light baba that oozes a sweet liqueur, the *susamelli* (S-shaped cookies), *struffoli* (fried honey balls), *raffioli* (cream-filled sponge cake), and *mostaccioli* (honey cookies), typical of Christmas. The springtime *pastiera*, made with cooked wheat—a symbolic ingredient, but at the same time also rich in vitamins.

The sea supplies Campania abundantly with fish, mollusks, shrimp, and crabs. It would be logical to suppose that fish and crab also provide food for Capri, Ischia, and the other islands in the Gulf of Naples, but that is not the case. The island cuisine is far less marine-based than coastal cooking. In general, those who come to Ischia get the feeling that the sea isn't there at all, as if the local cuisine were turning its back on the sea to face the mountains. The basis of the diet is the only animal that can be raised in a courtyard: the rabbit. The rabbit is the mainstay of Ischia's cuisine.

The island of Ischia, teeming with German tourists today, is where the giant Typhon was imprisoned underground for not having submitted to Zeus; he now continues troubling the sea from the nether regions, expelling sulfurous fumes from volcanoes. The sulfurous vapors have infused the curative springs, and tourists love to immerse themselves in these spas, where Roman patricians also took the cure. Thus invitations to sample Wiener schnitzel and *Kuchen* are displayed in German in all the restaurants today. But not to worry. Authentic Ischia cuisine still exists. *Bucatini* in rabbit sauce is a typical dish of Ischia. The secret of the dish lies in the fact that the *bucatini* are precisely that: *bucati* (pierced), so that the rabbit sauce (garlic, basil, thyme, marjoram, rosemary, red wine, tomatoes, olive oil, red pepper) will drench the pasta from within. The result is a tube of pasta with rabbit sauce in the center. Which, as anyone will agree, is very high-class. *Bucatini* are eaten with deafening sucking sounds, or slurping, as the British would say.

Antipasti Neapolitan *sartù*: a ring-mold of rice, giblets, mushrooms, peas, and mozzarella. The name derives from the French *surtout*, the tray that was placed in the center of the table (there are quite a few French words in use in Naples, since the kingdom of Naples and the Kingdom of the Two Sicilies were ruled first by the Angevins and later by the Bourbons, from the thirteenth century up until 1860).

First Courses Pasta with broccoli. Spaghetti with clams. Pasta puttanesca. *Paccheri*: a type of ribbed pasta similar to rigatoni, but bigger in diameter and shorter in length. Perfect for collecting the sauce thanks to their scored surface, at one time they were also called *schiaffoni* (slaps): a few were said to be enough to satisfy anyone.

Macaroni timbale with hard-boiled eggs, meatballs, and eggplant. Frittata with pasta and black olives. The head of a young goat, roasted in the oven with soft, crustless bread. Boiled anchovies in oil, garlic, and lemon, served cold. Seafood, especially raw clams and mussels with lemon and pepper. *Minestra maritata* (married soup): the soup's "marriage" consists of the union of meat and vegetables. In Italy, where soups are predominantly meatless and intended to be eaten on days of abstinence, "married soup," that is, with meat, is a rarity and an authentic local specialty. But apparently soup can not only marry, but also go crazy: *spigola all'acqua pazza* (bass in crazy water), a fish soup where the broth is called "crazy" after three good handfuls of barely ground pepper are tossed into it, is prepared in Campania.

Pizzas.

Second Courses Roasted peppers. Marinated zucchini with mint. Calzone and *caniscione* (types of pizza folded in two like a half-moon, with sealed edges). *Maruzze* (snails). *Mozzarella in carrozza* (breaded, dipped in egg, and fried). The famous beans of Neapolitan vegetable gardens, "slender as vermicelli, flavoursome, tender, and of course without a trace of string."[5]

Desserts *Zeppole* of St. Joseph, sweet fritters fried quickly, which are eaten for the saint's feast on March 19. The Christmas treats *susamelli, struffoli, raffioli, mostaccioli.*

TYPICAL PRODUCTS OF CAMPANIA

Mozzarella di bufala and the soft cheese *burrino in carrozza.* Apricots from the slopes of Vesuvius, white figs from Cilento, lemons from Amalfi and Massa, apples and pears from Salerno. San Marzano tomatoes, artichokes of Paestum, chestnuts of Montella, hazelnuts of Giffoni, walnuts of Sorrento and Irpinia. Neapolitan pastry and baba au rhum (also brought to Naples by the French).

TYPICAL BEVERAGES

White wines, formerly introduced by the Greeks. Taburno, Greco di Tufo. The Falernian that we recall named in Catullus's Ode XXVII:

> *Come, my boy, bring me the best*
> *of good old Falernian:*
> *we must drink down stronger wine*
> *to drink with this mad lady.*
> *Postumia's our host tonight;*
> *drunker than the grape is,*
> *is she—*
> *and no more water;*
> *water is the death of wine.*[6]

INGREDIENTS

Italians transform the ingredients for food preparation into poetic elements, elevating them to the rank of the most beautiful objects in the world. They know their products well and know the names of many varieties. It is very chic to be so well prepared as to be able to explain the difference between *Citrus limonum, Citrus lumia, Citrus medica, Citrus bergamia, Citrus limetta, Citrus decumana,* and so on, all varieties of lemons grown in Sicily.

This approach is the opposite, for example, of a certain French attitude that we find in the characters of Jean La Bruyère: "If you go into a kitchen and become aware of all its secrets; . . . if you see all these foodstuffs not on a sumptuously laden table, but in any other place, you would consider them scraps and feel repugnance."

Undoubtedly, the genetic tendency of Italians to be fascinated by commodities was not created out of thin air. This passion already distinguished the nation in the time of ancient Rome:

> I'll tell you the precepts themselves,
> but hide their author.
> Remember to serve eggs
> of elliptical shape,
> Since they're whiter

and better flavoured than the round:
They're harder-shelled
and the yoke inside is male.
Cabbages grown in dry soil
taste sweeter than those
From farms near town: tasteless
from moist gardens.
If a guest suddenly descends on you
in the evening,
To whose palate a tough fowl
might not be the answer,
You'd be wise to plunge it alive
in diluted Falernian:

That will tenderise it.

Mushrooms from the meadows

Are best quality:

others are dubious.

Healthy each summer he'll be,

who ends his lunch with black

Mulberries, picked from the tree

before the sun's strong.

Aufidius mixed honey

and strong Falernian,

Unwisely: since one shouldn't admit to empty veins

Anything that's not mild:

you'd do better to flood

The stomach with mild mead.

If the bowels are sluggish

Mussels and common shellfish

and tiny leaves of sorrel

Will clear the problem.

but not without white Coan wine.[1]

This unique sensibility of the ancient Romans toward the most minute details of their products and food acquisitions has amazed all historians, and of course historians of gastronomy: "In fine, what can we desire in a faculty susceptible of such perfection that the gourmands of Rome were able to distinguish the flavors of fish taken above and below the bridge? Have we not seen in our own time, that gourmands can distinguish the flavor of the thigh on which the partridge lies down from the other?"[2]

Not feeling the slightest repugnance (unlike La Bruyère), on the contrary, in an outburst of poetic enthusiasm and scientific interest, an individual who takes part in Italian table talk is capable of indulging in long debates, for example, on the right cuts of meat. It is a civilized conversation, given today's vapid, hurried times. If we continue at the rate we're going, most likely there will soon be very few people able to recognize, name, and prepare some rare beef or lamb part.

Rushed and hurried, many think that to create an adequate meal, it is enough to stop along the way and buy a part of the butchered animal's hindquarters. In the hindquarters there are chops, fillet, top round, and rump, as well as loin. That's where the tender meat is found, which is used to prepare cutlets, and bottom round; and then the rump and shank. In today's hurried, distracted daily life, the fore and hind shank and the rind are still used, for better or worse. Few know how to cook the shoulder, neck and *sottocollo* below the neck. Not to mention the *biancostato*, part of the ribs.

Specialists gladly tell which typical dishes (specifying the exact origin: region, city, or town) require a cut of meat that is not highly esteemed, such as chuck. Which typical dishes (for example, Genoese *cima*) cannot be prepared without breast of veal, which must be stuffed and then sewn with a needle and thread. Experts would like to know how *scalfo* (or *bollito*, *tasto*, *pancetta*, all regional names for flank) can be used and how to prepare the head, spinal marrow, tendons, tongue, lungs, heart, liver, rumen, tail, udder, brain, lips, spleen, kidneys, tripe, sweetbreads, offal, and testicles.

There is no end to these lists. The topside (top round), arm clod, and rump can be used for roasts in large cuts. The heart of the fillet, which is the best part, makes an excellent roast. A good cut for roast beef is the loin. Chuck, bottom round (silverside), heel of round, thick flank, and rump are the best cuts for braising. There is also the *bamborino* (flank that runs along the back part of the belly) and the cross ribs.

The neck, it seems, should be stewed. *Ragù* (meat sauce) and meatballs can be made from it. The boneless blade is cooked for several hours, and this is how *stracotto* (braised beef) is prepared, that embellishment and pride of the culinary traditions of Emilia Romagna and Sardinia. The *cappello del prete* (priest's hat) is made with zabaglione, while *cotechino* (pork sausage) is cooked *in galera* (in jail: the curious definition is due to the large, thin slice of beef that "imprisons" the *cotechino* once it's cooked and its casing is removed). In Emilia Romagna breast of veal with white sauce is renowned. Roast game, in Tuscany, calls for *barberina* sauce (dry white wine, broth, lemon juice, bread crumbs, and olive oil, seasoned with onion, parsley, bay leaf, salt, pepper, and nutmeg). As far as oxtail is concerned, the Roman oxtail *vaccinara*-style is one of the best, most popular, and most horribly awkward dishes of Lazio to eat (see "Eros").

As for entrails, from the conversation of those who know, it is clear that it is not enough to know the ABCs; a kind of doctorate is needed. Moreover, from the way beef is sold in Italy we can see how narrow traditional specialization is, and how much detailed knowledge professional butchers must possess. Indeed, two thousand years ago meat merchants were divided into *boari*, *suari*, and *pecuarii*, depending on whether they sold beef, pork, or poultry. This tradition has been maintained, and today there are still shops that sell cold cuts and chicken but not meat, since to be a butcher requires special preparation and training.

The stomach of the bovine has four chambers: rumen, reticulum, omasum, and abomasum. Each part is prepared according to a particular procedure, and when properly presented is a rare culinary pearl. Then too, *lampredotto* of baby calf (that is, the thin intestine full of semi-digested food) is a fundamental ingredient for preparing a well-known Roman dish like *pajata*. Spinal marrow (called *filone* in Piedmont) is essential for cooking a proper Piedmontese *finanziera*.

There is also regular veal (from an animal approximately 120 days old); if the animal is younger (up to ten weeks), it is referred to as a milk calf or baby calf. Both types of meat are pale, not too high in calories, and are not considered optimal for digestion. Veal is not recommended for small children, for example. Much better in flavor and nutritional value is the meat of *vitellone* (fatted calves twelve to eighteen months old) or beef (three to four years old: young bulls must be castrated, and the heifers should not have calved, since sex hormones adversely affect the digestibility of the muscle mass).

Held in less esteem is the meat of ox or cow (beef) four years old and more. The meat of the bull is of mediocre quality, while that of cows that have already calved, a dark, stringy, tough meat, is considered almost inedible.

Ovines and their cuts of meat are classified separately. With regard to ewes and rams and their offspring, cooking distinguishes milk lamb or spring lamb (*abbacchio*), that is, an animal no more than three months old, that has been fed only milk. The word *abbacchio* means "slaughtered with a cudgel" (*bacchio*), or "tied to a cudgel" (*ad baculum*); a lamb that is tied up is unable to browse and eat grass; thus it cannot compromise the exclusive quality of its meat.

Also popular in Italian cuisine is lamb (*agnello*) no older than ten weeks that is fed primarily with mother's milk, but has already started grazing. The paler its meat, the more prized it is. Once it has grown more mature, it is called an *agnellone*: this is a young ram, one year old, that has already been sheared twice. Its legs, ribs, tripe, and head are eaten. The adult ram, on the other hand, is not esteemed. In Italy it is felt that its meat "tastes wild" or, worse, "smells of mutton fat." The same is said of female sheep. Ewe meat, however, is used for sauces. One exception is *castrato*, the meat of gelded sheep, which are bred and eaten only in southern Italy, for the most part in Abruzzo and Molise.

Another branch of this science teaches how the names of the cuts of meat change from region to region, and also which parts may suddenly, unexpectedly, go from being a prized ingredient to scrap material. It all depends on the situation, it seems, and in some cases even on the style. Thus, getting into the specifics of how to make an authentic Milanese-style veal cutlet, we learn to our amazement that the expert discards an entire half of the butchered animal, and ends up eliminating yet another half of the remaining half (seven ribs):

> Pardon me for interrupting, but this ridiculous nonsense over quality meats must end. It is an unacceptable waste. Are you aware that we import the hindquarters from Holland and Germany, paying the price of the entire animal, and give the forequarters away to the vendors because they are too fatty and ruin our figure? We behave like someone who goes to a store to buy a complete suit, and then has only the jacket wrapped up, giving the pants away to the sales clerk. Pure madness . . .
>
> "Alfredo, how many ribs of a calf are used?"
>
> "Fourteen, seven on each side. There's an eighth, but I don't care for it: too close to the neck, too many nerves. The best are the first four; the other three have some strands of fat."[3]

All of this requires knowing and understanding the ingredients, loving them and protecting them, handling them intelligently and gently, knowing that an unwise move could destroy all the potency and value of a God-given asset. Carlo Petrini, founder of the Slow Food movement, recounts in his book the almost paradoxical case of an apprentice chef who was fired only because he allowed himself to hold and handle a knife in a different manner than that prescribed by the omniscient master chef:

> For example, Pierangelini told me how he had fired a young assistant on the spot, after a few days' probation, even though he had worked in important kitchens before then. The young man wouldn't hear of cutting fish by moving his hands as Pierangelini had taught him. Whether out of convenience or ineptitude, he stubbornly persisted in making the cut at an angle with respect to the work surface, completely different from what he had been shown.[4]

Not by chance, experts in ancient times advised this method to bring a prized wine out of the wine cellar: on the first day, move the bottle from the last step of the ladder to the second-to-last step, the following day from the second- to the third-to-last step, and so on until reaching the cellar door. Only in this way would the contents not be traumatized by abrupt fluctuations in temperature.

Puglia

The tableland of Puglia is Italy's granary. Here, 800,000 tons of durum wheat, 600,000 tons of tomatoes, 500,000 tons of table grapes, 300,000 tons of olive oil, and 200,000 tons of artichokes are produced each year.

The land is flat, crops grow with ease, and the climate is good, but it is not Campania: water is hopelessly scarce in Puglia. Neither the oil nor the wine produced here are of the highest quality. In exchange, however, they are abundant. Thirty-three percent of the entire national olive oil production and 30 percent of all of Italy's wine production is concentrated in Puglia. The low cost of local agricultural production is also due to the abundant supply of cheap labor, often illegal, coming from North Africa. These seasonal workers cultivate all kinds of fruits and vegetables in the flat, irrigated fields: tomatoes, zucchini, broccoli, peppers, potatoes, spinach, eggplant, cauliflower, fennel, chicory, kale (*cavolo nero*), capers, figs, almonds, catalogna chicory, mulberries (a specialty of Oria), lettuce, and legumes (fava beans, lentils, white beans). Puglia exports sun-dried tomatoes, a typical product of Ostuni and Fasano.

Oats are also grown here. The local wheat is an excellent ingredient for the production of pasta, so pasta and bread are at the forefront in Puglia's cuisine. Toppings for pasta can be meatless or meat-based (beef and horse) sauces, with tomatoes, goat cheese, and any kind of vegetable, even potatoes.

The landscape of Puglia is characterized by severe silhouettes of farms with high stone walls, formerly a defense against brigands and marauders. Normans, Moors, and pirates passed through this land. At the center of the farm stood (we cannot say "rose," since for security reasons the locals always tended to build structures that were not very high) the tower that housed the rooms of the landowners, more like a fortified stronghold than a dwelling in the common meaning of the term. The proprietors' tower was surrounded by the farmers' houses, stables, oil presses, granaries, cellars, and chapels. A moat ran all around the citadel. Today, many of these complexes have been restored, rebuilt, and turned into luxury hotels.

In addition to farms, orchards abound in the rural landscape of Puglia, laid out all around the city. Small farming towns were mainly designed around a radial type of plan, in order to facilitate entry and exit from the town (whereas military towns, from ancient Roman towns to St. Petersburg, were usually built on a chessboard plan, as a network of *cardones*, cross streets, and *decumani*, longitudinal streets).

No matter how small a given plot of land may be, a place will be found for both olive and almond trees, as well as for the cultivation of legumes. The last, a valuable source of protein, were often a guarantee of survival in times of famine. Until the end of the nineteenth century, the main legumes grown in Puglia were fava beans, chickpeas, and lentils. The twentieth century brought great changes: new plants, such as peas and white beans, became common. Also often present in the diet of Puglia's inhabitants today are puréed broad beans and chicory.

Turnip tops are everywhere, both growing in family gardens outside the city and for sale in large distribution chains. Turnip greens served and still serve as the base for the preeminent Pugliese dish, orecchiette pasta with turnip tops. (The Pugliese eat only the turnip greens that have not flowered: the opposite of the Friulians, who eat only the roots, feeding the leaves to the pigs.) The artichokes here are excellent and have no thorns; Mola's are particularly noteworthy. Recently, a trend of serving *lampascioni* has spread from Puglia into other regions of Italy: this is the common name of the wild bulbs of the species *Muscari comosum*, slightly more bitter than scallions, but lately much sought-after for elegant tables, boiled and seasoned with vinegar and olive oil.

The third pillar of Puglia's agricultural economy, after wheat and vegetables, is olive oil. The local oil is distinguished from that of Liguria and Tuscany, and from the oil of the lake region of northern Italy, by its fruitier aroma and higher acidity (that is, a lower quality). Fifteen percent of the world's oil is produced in Puglia. Experts are able to distinguish the taste of each local variety: the one produced in Foggiano, the one that comes from the province of Bari, and the one from the Salento Peninsula (in the provinces of Lecce, Brindisi, and Taranto).

The varieties of oil take their names not from the farms or estates, but from the cities: "oil of Trani," "oil of Barletta," etc. This type of designation is very common in Italy, where every city boasts its own gastronomic emblem, but it is particularly characteristic of Puglia, where the majority of the land is cultivated by city farmers, who in the evening return within the stone walls of their town.

The most famous "oil cities" are Giovinazzo, Molfetta, Bisceglie, Trani, Barletta, Canosa di Puglia, Andria, Castel del Monte, Ruvo di Puglia, Gioia del Colle, and Bitetto, all adorned with splendid Romanesque cathedrals (much more rarely, Gothic, as in Ostuni), and often with Norman castles.

The fourth pillar of Puglia's cuisine includes all the products of the sea. In the waters of the Adriatic, small fish are caught with nets and larger ones with harpoons, while in the Mar Piccolo of Taranto (an inlet of the Ionian Sea), colonies of oysters and mussels are farmed.

The towns of Puglia are rich in history: although the twentieth century has changed them, their old facade is still recognizable. In Barletta, Bitonto, Monopoli, and Polignano a Mare, centuries of poverty can be felt, as well as the memory of ancient Greece. Puglia (its southern part, Salento, with the city of Taranto, the ancient and powerful Tarentum) was part of Magna Graecia. Saracen lookout towers have remained from the period of Arab domination (eighth and ninth centuries), and their appearance has not changed since the time the Arabs fought Byzantium for control of this territory. The Angevins and the Aragons also left their mark on the local cuisine and dialect. In Faeto and in Celle di San Vito, a Franco-Provençal language is still used here and there today, having survived for a good eight hundred years, since the time of the Angevin conquest.

The domination of the Holy Roman Empire (starting in 1043) had a decisive influence on the development of Puglia's culture. At the beginning of the thirteenth century Frederick II of Hohenstaufen erected eight castles in Puglia, the most famous of which is the esoteric Castel del Monte; its construction is based entirely on occult codes, which experts are still trying to decipher. The castle looms in a remote, unpopulated moor, isolated from towns and cities. Other castles of Frederick's were also established in unusual places.

We have already encountered this extraordinary sovereign in Campania and heard mention of his eccentric urban planning philosophy in Abruzzo. Frederick did not build his castles as residences in a given area or for military purposes, but out of capricious personal choice, and he designed them exclusively for himself and his courtiers. Some said that Frederick chose his locations by following the spring and autumn migratory patterns of birds. Others thought this habit of bird-watching allowed Frederick to hunt more easily. Still others said that, by observing the birds' routes, he was trying to understand the unique structure of the world and of space.

Whatever the case, Frederick actually composed a treatise on the art of hunting that has come down to us today: *De arte venandi cum avibus* (The art of falconry). In calculating the routes of birds, Frederick took into account the celestial equator, the earth's axis, and the inclination of the sun's rays on the days of the spring and fall equinox. Castel del Monte, with its exacting geometric structure, is reminiscent of a calculus workshop. The scholar Aldo Tavolaro has reconstructed several designs of Frederick's, showing that the shadows projected by a vertical shaft (a gnomon) fixed to a certain point on the roof of the castle, depending on the time and day, form precise lines that confirm the emperor's zodiac calculations and measurements.

The unusual Norman castles, designed for aristocrats and astronomers, are found alongside some unique dwellings in the region of Puglia, the trulli. It seems incredible that people actually lived in these ancient domelike constructions, conical in shape, with no windows and a ventilation opening on top. But even more surprising is that these wigwamlike dwellings are still lived in today, in the villages of Polignano a Mare, Monopoli, Noci, Castellana Grotte, and especially in Alberobello, which has the largest complex of trulli, listed among the monuments declared by UNESCO as World Heritage Sites. Alberobello is a town made up entirely of rather large trulli, with hundreds of whitewashed cones that attract crowds of tourists. The trulli are rented to tourists in the summer, or transformed into luxury hotels. This type of dwelling was invented in the sixteenth to seventeenth centuries, during the Spanish maladministration of Puglia, but spread to numerous towns in the eighteenth and nineteenth centuries. Apparently the windowless houses were designed specifically to avoid the payment of taxes, since the various rulers of the occupants, Spanish as well as Bourbon, imposed a tax on every window.

Tourists who are architecture enthusiasts are also interested in the so-called *trappeti*, the ancient olive presses that are frequently set belowground in Puglia to protect the oil from harmful temperature fluctuations. Sheltered in caves of karstic rock with only one way in, these presses were protected from heat and from the cold winter wind, while the rock walls of the cave, strong and thick, cushioned the vibrations of the grindstones. The olives were poured into natural hollows in the rock, and the oil flowed along the natural grooves of the cave: the combination of nature and human labor was perfect. More than thirty of these underground presses have been preserved in the area of Gallipoli alone.

The main varieties of Pugliese olives are Cerignola (also called Belle of Cerignola) and Coratine. The first are common, especially in the southern area of the province of Foggia. The cultivation of these olives seems to have been introduced around 1400 by Spain. They can be either green or black and have a very substantial pulp; the weight of each olive varies from eleven to eighteen grams. The Coratine olives take their name from the town of Corato, but their very ancient origin is unknown. They are grown in the provinces of Bari and Foggia, but also in other areas outside Puglia. These olives are particularly rich in antioxidants (polyphenols); elongated and slightly asymmetrical, they weigh around four grams.

Wild landscape is still preserved in Puglia, and it comes together uniquely with more domesticated nature. This marriage is reflected in the distinctiveness of the local food. The cuisine of Puglia prefers raw products over processed ones. Bypassing oil production, the farmers and laborers of Puglia gladly eat their olives alone with bread. And what a bread! The bread of Altamura! Unlike in northern Italy, where they turn out crusty rolls that are delicious but stale in a day, the Pugliese make enormous round loaves intended to last as long as a month.

The tendency to eat unprocessed food is especially evident in the consumption of raw fish. In fish markets, for example, it is customary to set out plates of raw shrimp, cuttlefish, and mussels for customers who are waiting, to be eaten on the spot with a squirt of lemon. On the table of a Pugliese restaurant, as in Portugal, you will find raw *mazzancolle* (a type of prawn); raw octopus, freshly caught and vigorously clubbed on the stone pier; herring; sea urchins; starfish; and tellins (cockles). The fish (for example, mullet from the reef of Polignano) end up on the grill, but they don't stay there longer than ten minutes or so. Obviously, such eating habits would be unthinkable without a confidence in the excellent quality of the ingredients. In Puglia, there is no need to worry: the quality of its fishing and fish farming is recognized worldwide, and the water of Puglia's coasts, in the area where the Adriatic Sea and the Ionian Sea merge, is of a rare clarity.

The oysters of Taranto were praised as far back as Pliny's time. Under the emperor Trajan their collection was practiced according to industrial standards, but with the end of the Roman Empire and for a good 1,500 years after, breeding of the mollusks was discontinued and was resumed only in 1784 under Ferdinand IV of Bourbon, king of the Two Sicilies. Hatcheries were reestablished, based on the same technologies used in ancient Rome. The Taranto oyster is recognized by its green shell, squamous and very gibbous, and by the fragile edges of its valves, with a mother-of-pearl glossiness inside. These oysters, according to experts, stand up to those of Marenne and Arcachon. Even today, along the coasts of Puglia, colossal mollusk colonies are developed in enormous nylon tubes, the mollusks feeding on the precious mineral salts and algae carried to shore by the waves. After twelve to fourteen months, the mollusks are extracted from the nets and then chosen for sale.

In addition to traditional fishing with nets and lines, fishing by means of a *trabucco* is also practiced in Puglia. This method, once used by the Saracens, makes it possible to fish without moving away from the shore. The *trabucchi* are vertical nets, lowered from old ships no longer in use and anchored to rocks. The fishermen's work recalls an acrobatic act. Lying on a not very steady raft, the leader of the team, called the *rais*,[1] searches with a special tube to see what's happening down below. At that time the *trabucchi* are lowered to the seabed. Once a school of fish is spotted, the *rais* gives the order to raise the nets, which are quickly rolled up using a winch. These picturesque scenes—with all of their characteristic attributes, rafts, and hoists—have often inspired painters and attracted documentary makers. The fish caught this way are cooked whole in salt: this forms a dense shell around each fish, which keeps the juices, aromas, and flavors intact.

From this detail it should not be difficult to surmise that the region has its own salt. In fact, salt harvesting has been carried out in Puglia since the fourth century B.C. At Margherita di Savoia, a strip as wide as five kilometers, allocated to the production of salt, extends for more than twenty kilometers along the coastal plain. This is one of the largest salt marshes in Europe. Collected in enormous basins, the seawater is made to evaporate using natural and nonpolluting technologies developed over the centuries, separating out carbonates on the one hand and iron, calcium sulfate, and virtually pure sodium chloride on the other.

In addition to mussels and oysters, murexes, or trumpet shells (*Murex brandaris*), are also farmed in the region. The ancient Romans dyed their togas, initially those of the emperors and later on those of patricians and state officials, with a substance secreted by the hypobranchial gland of these mollusks. The purple was so expensive that rather than the entire toga, only a strip was dyed, and the result was a *toga praetexta*. Horace mocked those who wore the magistrates' toga for pure vanity:

> *. . . mocking that clerk's*
> *mad reward,*
> *Bordered robe, a broad-striped tunic,*
> *burning charcoal.*[2]

In 314 the Christian church discovered purple for itself and its prelates. Starting with Pope Sylvester I, it began to use this precious dye. The high cost of purple was determined by the hours of labor required to collect it: from ten thousand mollusks, 1.2 grams of dye were obtained. Taranto and the Phoenician city of Tyre competed at length for supremacy in the production of purple. Finally, it was the Italian purple that won for its intensity, with beautiful, subtle shades ranging from violet to scarlet.

Bari is an ancient commercial port, once the center of trade with Byzantium, and still the destination of pilgrimages due to the relics of St. Nicholas, bishop of Myra, which are particularly revered in the Christian East and housed in its cathedrals.

As in all regions where the presence of pilgrims was strong, here, too, the production of bread was one of the principal activities. It was already so in Horace's time:

> *From that point on Apulia begins to reveal*
> *Her familiar hills to me, . . .*
> *Though here's a clue: they sell what's commonly free*
> *There, water: but the bread's,*
> *the best by far,*
> *so wise Travellers*
> *carry a load on their shoulders for later, . . .*
> *Next day the weather was better, the road was worse,*
> *Right up to fishy Bari.*[3]

The large-loaved bread of Altamura, which keeps for a long time, is sold not only in Puglia but throughout Italy, both in supermarkets and in bakeries. Other types of street food are *puccia* (very soft bread stuffed with black olives) and *puddica* (a focaccia with chopped tomato and garlic). *Taralli* were created especially for traveling: crunchy, savory little ring-shaped biscuits, they are excellent with red wine. The popularity of this product is evidenced in the popular saying that sooner or later all conflicts in Italy are settled and resolved "with *tarallucci* and wine"—that is, ironed out in an amicable way. *Tarallucci* are smooth and shiny because they are dipped, unbaked, in boiling water for a moment, before being put in the oven.

Bakers in Puglia have always been masters, but they could not count on the support of the authorities, as was once the case in Tuscany or in Rome itself. In Puglia, those in power tried to make life difficult for the bakers in every way possible. Administrators in the eighteenth and nineteenth centuries stubbornly decided to impose stiff taxes on individually owned ovens! As good Italians, with some Greek genes to boot, the Pugliese naturally managed to get by, even in the nightmarish conditions created by the Bourbon government. Recall that Puglia responded to the tax on windows by building houses without windows. It responded to the tax on fires by building houses without stoves. Tourists in Puglia are invariably shown strange piles of stones along the edges of the roads. They are illegal public hearths. If the tax inspector discovered such a hearth, it was very difficult to identify its owner. The Bourbon government actually issued an ordinance that obliged the University of Bari to send officials specifically to inspect the territory and take a "census" of these illegal fireplaces.

People here manage to cook any food in primitive stone kilns. Bread is baked in ovens, molds are made in pans (*tielle*, a legacy of the time when Puglia was under Spanish rule), and sausages and meat cuts are roasted.

The region's typical pasta shapes are the famous orecchiette (little ears), which are locally called *chiancarelle* (the smaller ones) and *pociacche*. Orecchiette of durum wheat flour are made by hand, squeezing little disks of pasta between the thumb and forefinger.

In Foggia *troccoli*, a type of pasta that is produced with a special machine and that looks a little like the guitar-style macaroni of Abruzzo, is made. The specialties of Lecce are called *turcinelli*, while in Brindisi *staggiotta* (a local variant of lasagna), *fenescecchie*, and *mignuicchie* (little semolina gnocchi) are eaten. *Turcinelli* are served with cauliflower and anchovies, the *trucioletti* of Brindisi with squid, mussels, and basil.

Spaghetti is served with sea urchins. In 1647, a small revolution even flared up in Bari over pasta: the city's residents rebelled against the Spanish rulers, who had planned to impose a tax on pasta based on popular consumption and had sent inspectors house to house to verify it. The city rose up in revolt—an actual riot with looting and killings—until the Spanish governor was forced to repeal the hated tax after less than a week.

TYPICAL DISHES OF PUGLIA

Antipasti *Muersi*: toasted white bread with broccoli and peas, seasoned with oil and hot red pepper. Mussels *arracanate* (covered), anchovies *arracanate*: anchovies, boned, placed in a pan and layered with bread crumbs, garlic, mint, capers, oregano, and oil and baked in the oven. *Cardoncelli* (boiled cardoons). *Calzoni*, or *panzerotti*: pizzas folded in half and pinched along the edge, with onion, tomato, garlic, olives, and anchovies, but fried in oil instead of baked in the oven. In Salento, this dish is called *puddica*. *Cappello* (hat): a timbale stuffed with eggplant, fried zucchini, sliced meat, hard-boiled eggs, and cheese.

First Courses *Ciceri e tria*, a legacy of ancient Rome, common in Salentino: pasta with chickpeas, namely *tagliatelle* of durum wheat with chickpeas and onions cooked together in boiling water; it is said to have existed for two thousand years. Orecchiette with turnip tops. *Minestra maritata* (married soup), the same one found in Neapolitan cuisine, in which vegetables and meat are boiled together (thus they "marry"). The boiled vegetables alternate with layers of salt pork and pecorino cheese. The entire dish is topped with meat broth and baked in the oven.

Second Courses Meat dishes are scarce, but very high in calories; for this reason the most famous one is candidly called *bombetta* (little bomb). It is a pork meat loaf stuffed with cheese. Sometimes lamb intestines are filled with cheese, then packed into the *teletta*, the thin mesh that surrounds the pig's stomach, and stewed: the result is called the *quagghiarebbe*.

Vegetables are so much a part of Puglia's tradition and domestic economy that even after eating it is customary to offer raw carrots, celery, and artichokes, known as a *pinzimonio* (olive oil dip). In other regions this *pinzimonio* is eaten at the beginning of the meal, as an appetizer: here, instead, it is served as dessert.

Desserts *Caciuni*, pastry ravioli with honey fried in oil and filled with chocolate, boiled chickpeas, *vincotto* (reduced wine must), and cinnamon.

Susamelli: cookies with orange peel, tangerine and lemon juice, cinnamon, chopped roasted almonds, vanilla, and must wine, sprinkled with sugar.

TYPICAL PRODUCTS OF PUGLIA

Vincotto (cooked wine), made from two varieties of grape: Negroamaro and Malvasia Nera, which grow in the province of Lecce. The grapes are left to wither for about thirty days on vine branches or on wooden frames before being pressed; the must is then cooked slowly (for more than twenty-four hours), until it is reduced to a fifth of its initial volume. The syrup thus obtained is poured into small wooden casks, the lees are added, and the mixture is left to age for a period ranging from one to four years. It will be used to top desserts such as *cartellate*, very thin dough fritters dusted with cinnamon, or *pettole*, flour- and potato-based doughnuts that are eaten hot after being dunked into the *vincotto*.

Canestrato of Foggia, a cheese produced and stored in baskets (*canestri*). Burrata cheese of Andria. Tarantella salami of Taranto. *Lampascioni* (wild bulbs). Altamura bread.

EROS

Often in describing food, gourmets use the language of seduction, alluding to the associations between eating and sex. Though never spoken of directly, when a discussion takes a gastronomic turn the air is charged with joyful electricity, subtly exciting those taking part in the conversation. Throw in the overindulgence associated with eroticism and you have an explosive mix, exploited in literature since distant times: Petronius, Rabelais, Boccaccio. The Brazilian writer Jorge Amado, joining the themes of cooking and the boudoir, gave us a magical image of Brazil, and in particular of the city of Bahia (in *Gabriela, Clove and Cinnamon* and in *Dona Flor and Her Two Husbands*). Jean-Anthelme Brillat-Savarin (1755–1826), a gastronome and great expert on sensual pleasure, wrote in the *Physiology of Taste* (1825):

> Those who are fondest of friandises have delicate features, smaller, and are distinguished by a peculiar expression of the mouth.
>
> Agreeable guests should be sought for among those who have this appearance. They receive all that is offered them, eat slowly, and taste advisedly. They do not seek to leave places too quickly where they have been kindly received. They are always in for all the evening, for they know all the games, and all that is necessary for a gastronomical soirée.
>
> Those, on the contrary, to whom nature has refused a desire for the gratifications of taste, have a long nose and face. Whatever be their statures, the face seems out of order. Their hair is dark and flat, and they have no *embonpoint*. They invented pantaloons.

Women whom nature has thus afflicted, are very angulous, are uncomfortable at the table, and live on lenten fare.

This physiological theory will, I trust, meet with not many contradictions: any one may verify the matter. I will, however, rely on facts.

I was sitting one day at a great entertainment, and saw opposite to me a very pretty woman with a very sensual face. I leaned towards my neighbor and said, that the lady with such features must be *gourmande*.

"Bah!" said he, "she is not more than fifteen; she is not old enough—let us see though."

. . . She not only ate what was set before her, but sent for dishes which were at the other end of the table. She tasted every thing, and we were surprised that so small a stomach could contain so much. My diagnostics succeeded and science triumphed.[1]

Brillat-Savarin then goes on to tell of meeting the young woman again two years later. She had been married a few days earlier and had become even more fascinating and coquettish, since she displayed all the charms that fashion now allowed her to exhibit. Whenever an admirer of the fair sex passed beside her, her unfortunate husband would quiver with jealousy, and not long afterward, in order to put an end to his suffering, he took his young wife and moved away.

Brillat-Savarin is a Frenchman. His philosophizing is universal. But Italy, the most Catholic of all the Catholic countries, has its own specific nature. The attitude of Italians toward eroticism has always been dominated not by the working of licentiousness, but by the allure and seduction of forbidden fruit. Half the liturgical year in Italy consisted of days of abstinence. During these periods priests required the faithful to observe sexual abstinence, both by direct prohibition—conjugal relations were forbidden—and by indirect action: anyone who fasts from morning to night doesn't get certain ideas. But it is inherent in the mechanism of eros that resistance strengthens attraction. Thus not only did chivalry flourish luxuriantly in Italy, so much that it became a model throughout the world, but so did the language of fasting and abstinence: it now became a substitute for obscene expressions. It was most likely in accordance with this principle that someone first got the idea of calling the male member *pesce* (fish) or *cavolo* (cabbage): foods associated with days of fasting. The same organ is also called *baccalà* (cod) in Italian: in the image of dried cod, the idea of "Lent diet food" is associated with the idea of rigidity.

When fasting, the thoughts of both sinners and the righteous naturally revolved around food. Hippolyte Taine recounts stories of the parishioners of the church of the Aracoeli, on the Campidoglio in Rome:

> During Lent the sermons turned entirely on fasting, and on forbidden or permitted dishes; the preacher gesticulates and walks about on a platform describing hell, and, immediately after, the various ways of preparing macaroni and codfish which are so numerous as to render flesh-eating gourmands quite inexcusable . . . Unlike the German or Englishman, the Italian is not open to pure ideas; he involuntarily incorporates them in palpable form; the vague and abstract escape or repel him; the structure of his mind imposes definite forms on his conception, a strong relief, and this constant invasion of precise imagery, which formerly shaped his art, now shapes his religion.[2]

Some "fat" foods (meats) are unforgivably fat, but others, if you don't put too fine a point on it, can also be eaten during Lent. Thus was born the indulgent attitude toward tripe, permitted on fast days that are not too strict. Tripe may be meat, and may not. It depends on how you look at it. Generally speaking, during Lent there was a subtle desire to deceive someone: if not God, then at least oneself. What is a "false capon"? Apparently, a capon made of vegetable purée. One senses the extent to which ritual in these cases is made absolute in the Italian conscience, the ultramundane solidified. "Within a few days a sausage vender on the Corso arranged his hams in the shape of a sepulchre; above it were lights and garlands, and in the interior a glass globe filled with gold-fishes.— The principle is to appeal to the senses," writes Taine with regard to the way in which the Church "intimidated" parishioners in Rome during Lent.[3]

Eros appears constantly in the Italian culinary code. Overly pious devotion inevitably ends up instilling forbidden erotic thoughts in the minds of the faithful. Thus, in Fellini's *Amarcord*, it is not the zeal of a pastor of young souls that prevails in the insistent questioning of the priest who hears the children's confessions, but a reprehensible voyeurism. Taine writes:

> I entered a church one day and saw a priest engaged in instructing forty little girls of about seven or eight years of age: they looked about inquisitively with sparkling eyes, all whispering together like tiny little mice, and their roguish animated little heads in constant motion. With a mild paternal aspect he went from bench to bench, restraining his excited little flock with his hand, always repeating the word *il diavolo*. "Be careful of the devil, my dear little children, the devil who is so wicked, the devil who devours your souls," etc. Fifteen or twenty years from this, this word will surely arise in their minds, and along with it the horrible mouth, the sharp claws of the image, the burning flames, and so on.[4]

Catholicism inspires a philosophy of a constant sense of sinfulness in the faithful in order to grant rare moments of catharsis, of joyful absolution: that enthusiasm that possesses the faithful after confession, just at the moment when the "food," namely communion, is distributed. Permission to forget their sins coincides with the sublimation of the food's forbidden eros.

Wherever you look, the lexicon of cooking is erotic. The whole world is familiar with the dessert tiramisù. A colorful legend has it that tiramisù was a favorite of Venice's courtesans, who needed a "pick-me-up" (the literal translation of the dessert's name) to fortify themselves between their amorous encounters; another version says it was their male visitors who required the pick-me-up. Also renowned are Perugina Baci. Few know that in 1922, when these chocolates were created, a Futurist poet was invited to concoct a name, something that was often done in those days. Trying to come up with some popular tradition, the Futurist immediately found the very aggressive name *cazzotti* (punches), and only after a few years did the owner of the factory, Giovanni Buitoni, rename them *baci* (kisses), slipping a card with a sentimental saying into each individually wrapped chocolate.

In the crisp and vivid Tuscan tongue, the ability to *ingravidarsi*, or become pregnant, is even attributed to a sandwich which has sinned with a slice of prosciutto: "She has been up and prepared: four boiled eggs, two *panini gravidi* (what nations deficient in sexual fancies call *sandwiches*), a nice round slice of goat's milk cheese, and a flask of native wine."[5]

The flavors of ice cream in a cone "marry," as do the greens in a salad.

As we've seen, "married soup," that is, vegetable soup with meat, is found in Neapolitan cuisine. The vegetarian element is penitential and God-fearing, so vegetable soup is guilt-free. When meat ends up in this meatless soup, it produces a change that is perceived as a loss of virginity; hence the idea that the soup is "married." The meaning of *maritozzi* (husbands) is analogous: sweet buns whose shape is decidedly phallic. And altered food products, even in court, are officially called adulterated.

The names of certain food preparations take on a double meaning, in vulgar parlance, that refers to the erotic sphere. Allusions to "dunking the biscuit" or "stirring the polenta" are sexually explicit, according to the dictionaries. But even in the literal sense, these procedures trigger particular associations. In the painting *La polenta* by Pietro Longhi (Ca' Rezzonico, Venice), hot, scantily dressed serving maids can be seen pouring soft polenta from a cauldron onto a white cloth spread on the table. Both the seductive allure of the female body as well as the fervor of the collective movement, the stirring and ladling, are rendered in the painting. An equally vivid sensuality is concealed in another Venetian work, this one theatrical: the dialogue between Rosaura and Arlecchino in the comedy *La donna di garbo* (The admirable woman), 1743, by Carlo Goldoni. Here Rosaura promises to prepare for Arlecchino a rich polenta:

"Look: we'll wait until everyone is in bed, even that eagle-eyed Brighella, whom I can't stand; then very softly we'll both go to the kitchen . . . When the water begins to murmur, I'll take some of that ingredient, beautiful as gold dust, called cornmeal; and little by little I'll add it to the cauldron, in which you with a knowing rod will make circles and strokes. When the substance thickens, we'll remove it from the fire, and both of us in concert, a spoon for each of us, will move it from the cauldron to a plate. There from hand to hand we'll top it with an abundant portion of fresh, yellow, creamy Butirro cheese, then equally buttery, yellow, and well-grated hard cheese . . ."

"Oh, hush, my dear, you're making me swoon."

The word "polenta," not surprisingly, often replaces the word "Madonna" in exclamations ("Santa polenta!"), since it is forbidden to take the Madonna's name in vain.

Literature and the visual arts give us many impressions like this. But even normal, everyday life or a simple evening in a trattoria can lead us to similar associations. The fact is that many Italian dishes are difficult to eat and force us to drabble. This is probably their greatest attraction.

It is not easy to wrap spaghetti around a fork, especially when it is dripping with red sauce. Before Italian cooking was introduced to tomatoes (prior to Columbus), Neapolitan vermicelli and macaroni were not seasoned with *pummarola*. Even much later, at the end of the eighteenth century, Goethe wrote of spaghetti eaten directly with the hands, along the street: it was a convenient food, which did not get you dirty. But now, it's torture.

Just think about *pasta all'amatriciana*, which is also called whistle-style pasta by some cooking historians, because if you suck it too frenziedly, the pierced noodle (*bucatino*) bathed in sauce emits a hissing sound that does not sound very polite. While enjoying the dinner as well as the refined conversation, it is imperative to keep an eye on jackets, ties, shirts, and blouses at the same time, since the *bucatino* is unforgiving:

And since bucatini must be slippery as eels, someone will easily end up with sauce on the tablecloth, or on his shirt, or tie, or trousers, or on the carpet. But no true pasta eater will allow the joy of the moment to be disturbed by these inevitable accidents. No talcum powder, which with its scent would ruin everything. We'll sprinkle that on later. The ideal thing would be to roll up the bucatini while sitting comfortably bare-chested in the shade of a pinewood, followed by the watchful eye of a faithful dog.[6]

Thus Aldo Buzzi, meditating on the relationship between pleasure and inconvenience, develops the theme of the joy inherent in the eating process, carrying the idea to its extreme consequences, to the point of having to undress and invite the dinner guest to more intimate relations, unrestrained by modesty. Better if this dinner companion is someone who loves you unconditionally, such as a boyfriend, girlfriend, or your faithful dog!

It's awkward eating a huge pizza and smearing sauce all around. It's not clear how to hold it: with your fingers, maybe, getting it all over your hands? Cut it into triangular slices and furl it, tucking the strands of piping hot mozzarella inside?

It's troublesome to peel a shrimp or prawn covered with tomato sauce, fishing out the meat and leaving the shell in the sauce. It's extremely distasteful to extract what little meat there is from a slippery oxtail, firm in the middle, that leaps away, squirting treacherously; not to mention having to do so blindly, since oxtail *vaccinara*-style is served submerged in a fiery red sauce at the very bottom of a tall ceramic container. It's cumbersome to remove mollusks from the shell. It's almost always difficult to eat fish. In a fancy restaurant they show you the whole fish first, then they take it away and fillet it, but in an ordinary trattoria (the kind of restaurant more commonly preferred by the majority of Italians) they are apt to serve it whole, with the skin and all the rest: it's up to the customer to remove the bones. You have to use your wits to eat even the simplest meal—whether a focaccia with olive oil or a seasoned, big-leaf salad—without staining your tie or shirt.

This creates a blend of difficulty and satisfaction that is almost amorous, almost passionate. The struggle to do one's best in public is neither an art nor a diversion for Italians; it is a proof of civility, a demonstration of national and geographic belonging. At the restaurant, tables are so close to one another that they couldn't be any closer, so the display of virtuosity is offered not only to one's own table companions, but also to those at neighboring tables.

Even when the food description is not directly related to the idea of eros, the most effective stories about the delights of dining elevate the feeling to such a temperature, to such an intensity, that the pleasure can no longer be expressed in words ("Oh, hush, my dear, you'll make me swoon . . ."), but can only pour forth in music or song. The progression from such passion to eroticism is just one short step, as Andrea Camilleri writes in *The Snack Thief*:

> He was early for his appointment with Valente. He stopped in front of the restaurant where he'd gone the last time he was in Mazara. He gobbled up a sauté of clams in bread-crumbs, a heaping dish of spaghetti with white clam sauce, a roast turbot with oregano and caramelized lemon, and he topped it all off with a bitter chocolate timbale in orange sauce. When it was all over he stood up, went into the kitchen, and shook the chef's hand without saying a word, deeply moved. In the car, on his way to Valente's office, he sang at the top of his lungs.[7]

Eros, and how! To a lover of good food a successful dish is a pleasure superior to erotic bliss, a sublime joy that makes him forget problems at the office, as well as any personal troubles. A joy that elevates existence to a height beyond which there is nothing more to be desired and the cheerful acceptance of the hour of death appears to be the only dignified way out of the ne plus ultra. Turning again to Camilleri's *The Snack Thief*, we find many descriptions of this kind:

> Actually, he knew exactly where he would go . . . When he arrived at the trattoria in Mazara, they greeted him like the prodigal son.
> "The other day, I believe I understood that you rent rooms."
> "Yes, we've got five upstairs. But it's the off-season now, so only one of 'em's rented."
> They showed him a room, spacious and bright and looking straight onto the sea.
> He lay down on the bed, brain emptied of thoughts, chest swelling with a kind of happy melancholy. He was loosing the moorings, ready to sail out to the country of sleep, when he heard a knock on the door.
> "Come in, it's unlocked."
> The cook appeared in the doorway. He was a big man of considerable heft, about forty, with dark eyes and skin.
> "What are you doing? Aren't you coming down? I heard you were here and so I made something for you that . . ."
> What the cook had made, Montalbano couldn't hear, because a sweet, soft melody, a heavenly tune, had started playing in his ears . . .
> The pasta with crab was as graceful as a first-rate ballerina, but the stuffed bass in saffron sauce left him breathless, almost frightened.
> . . . "If one ate something like this at death's door, he'd be happy even to go to Hell," he said softly.[8]

When table companions in a public place want to avoid erotic suggestions, the best choice is risotto. And risotto is precisely what many residents of Milan order frequently in restaurants. (To be clear: residents who are not necessarily natives of Milan. The natives, in fact, often prove to have primitive carnivorous instincts and express them by sucking the marrow in osso buco.) But a particular category of Milan's residents, or of Milan's weekday residents, is composed for the most part of people from the towns and villages of the north: people who are reserved, restrained, obsessed with convention, who come to the city at an already mindful age to look for a prestigious job and top wages, and try to suffocate their deep sensuality, burying it in the subconscious and excluding it from their outward, visible behavior. (From the depths of the subconscious, of course, it screams out even louder . . . but we digress.) These people—the people sporting jackets and ties and careers—frequently order rice in restaurants, or risotto, the characteristic Milanese dish. Planted by the Spanish in regions that later came under Hapsburg rule, rice has remained the traditional dish here and is psychologically associated with spartan severity, organization, and industriousness. With its petite grains, it is perceived on an aesthetic level as something refined, elegant.

Risotto is a traditional element of the formal business lunch and is the dish most frequently eaten around strangers. It is the opposite of pizza. Pizza is the food of friendship, of familiarity. People who already know each other and are connected by mutual fondness eat pizza together. If you don't know each other very well, it is difficult to avoid a sense of awkwardness, since everyone eats pizza sloppily—some with their hands, sticking their tongues out to catch strands of mozzarella. Spaghetti, too, involves scenarios of sucking and slurping that border on the amorous. It can even be seen in Walt Disney cartoons: in *Lady and the Tramp*, Lady and Tramp dine in an Italian restaurant before their wedding, sucking up the same strand of spaghetti from opposite ends. It's the ideal romantic dinner: spaghetti and meatballs! While risotto, from an erotic point of view, is sterile.

Basilicata

Basilicata is a solitary, silent place, a mountainous region, once covered with forests and populated by shepherds, that received its name during the time of the Byzantine rule. The name is derived in fact from the Greek *basilikos*, the term used to identify the region's Byzantine rulers. But in the Roman era the historical name of the region was Lucania, from the Latin *lucus*, woods. Wooded areas, then, were at one time common in this territory, before indiscriminate deforestation opened the way for rivers, which each spring descend from the mountains, eroding and scoring the landscape with gullies. This same disaster—the disappearance of trees due to uncontrolled, senseless exploitation of forests—has also destroyed neighboring Calabria.

Landslides multiplied, while roads, until recently, were virtually nonexistent. These places are so out of the way that they have always been an ideal hideout. Criminals and fugitives as well as honest men hid in Basilicata. In the seventh century, Christian monks came here from the Middle East and Africa to escape the Arabs and Persians. Religious dissidents, the iconophiles, fled from Constantinople, under the iconoclast emperor Leo III the Isaurian (in power from 717 to 741). Christians from nearby Sicily fled when the island found itself dominated by the Arabs. In Matera, all the land is riddled with caves where the Christians once hid from their persecutors and built underground churches. Today the region houses an archaeological wonder,

protected by UNESCO: 137 churches with frescoes painted between the eighth and thirteenth centuries.

It is a land of veritable poverty. It was in these very places that Carlo Levi, sent into confinement during Fascism, wrote *Cristo si è fermato a Eboli* (*Christ Stopped at Eboli*), a dark tale of poverty, superstition, and disease. From Levi's book it appears that the majority of Lucanian farmers survived, from autumn to spring, by eating nothing but bread that was made in November and kept in the pantry: hard, heavy round loaves, very different from today's fresh, crunchy Italian bread, bought in the morning at the local bakery. Rarely did the inhabitants of Basilicata eat lamb (only if someone in the family fell ill, or if the village celebrated a wedding, the birth of a child, or the feast of the patron saint) or mutton (one in twenty, at Christmastime).

There are few tourists in Basilicata. They have not yet discovered the region. All in all, one does not come across many recipes from this region, even in cookbooks. Yet

Cicero, Martial, and Horace once praised the spicy sausage from the area, back when it was called Lucania. The Roman epicure Apicius, in particular, was enthusiastic about the choice Lucanian sausages and gives us the ancient recipe: "Fill the casing with well-pounded pork, and add ground pepper, cumin, savory, rue, parsley, bay leaves, and lard, then hang it close to the fire." Every family raised pigs, the poor man's livestock. Even today there is at least one pig on every farm. From that meat come the excellent Lucanian sausages *pezzenta* and *cotechinata*, the same that were celebrated by seventeenth-century poets such as Giovan Battista Lalli in his *Franceide* (1629):

> *The people of Basilicata sent*
> *the fattest animals of the grubby herd,*
> *that large and small, when added up,*
> *numbered one thousand five hundred,*
> *in addition to plentiful cured meat*
> *aged a long time and slowly smoked.*[1]

In Basilicata pepper and spicy peppers reign: hot pepper, or *peperoncino* (in turn divided into two varieties: the small *diavolicchi*, little devils, and the long "cigarettes"), red pepper, Indian pepper, paprika, chilies, and Tabasco. Almost all these crops were introduced into Italy from the New World, and today the cuisine of Basilicata would be unimaginable without them. It is no wonder that dishes created here include *penne all'arrabbiata* (with tomato, pancetta, onion, garlic, hot red pepper, and pecorino cheese), Potentina-style pepper chicken, peppered potatoes, and the not-very-nutritious vegetable soup with soft bread ironically called *pancotto* (cooked bread) and *acquasale* (saltwater).

One of the typical products of Basilicata is honey. Bees create honey from lavender in Liguria, from acacia flowers in Lombardy, and from rhododendron and heather in Calabria. Prevalent in Basilicata instead is the famous *millefiori* honey, which the bees distill from a thousand plants and flowers: citrus, chestnut, eucalyptus, sunflower, and thyme.

TYPICAL DISHES OF BASILICATA

First Courses *Pancotto*: fairly liquid bread soup with onion and pepper, topped with hard-boiled eggs. *Lagane* (fettuccine) with beans: the so-called bandits' pasta, with fava beans, tomatoes, and garlic, which requires neither a colander nor a frying pan to prepare, since it all cooks in a pot, in just water.

Second courses *Capuzzelle*: lambs' heads roasted over the coals. *Gnummerieddi*, lamb intestines seasoned with pecorino cheese, fatback, parsley, and lemon, wrapped in mesh so as to form cylindrical little bundles. Fava beans with potatoes, artichokes, and onion on a good slice of homemade bread (*ciaudedda*). Peas boiled with chicory. *Ciammotta* (vegetables fried separately and combined at the end).

TYPICAL PRODUCTS OF BASILICATA

Caciocavallo Podolico cheese, produced with the especially fatty milk of the Podolico breed of cows that grazes freely in the fields and feeds on clover, mallow, juniper, lingonberry, wild strawberries, and dog rose. This cheese, which has a typical "pouch" shape, derives its spicy notes, its aroma, and its color from seasonal forage: in the spring it acquires a characteristic pinkish color as a result of the wild strawberries that the cows have eaten.

Cacio ricotta, a juniper-fire-smoked cheese. The cheeses Moliterno and Filiano, made from sheep's milk. *Ricotta forte* from Matera, aged a month, with pepper. Lucanian sausage, extolled by the ancient Romans. Matera bread.

RESTAURANTS

People can find something to eat in restaurants, trattorias, after-theater clubs, pubs, pizzerias, taverns, inns, bars, dairies, bakeries, pastry shops, cafés, tearooms, wine bars, workplace cafeterias, roadside stands and autogrills, fried food shops, rotisseries and delicatessens, wineshops, sandwich shops, kiosks, market stalls . . . and even behind a counter, in the back of some shops and stores. The "gastronaut" Davide Paolini writes:

> The back of a shop, with a large table, has become a must for refined palates. Light fried gnocchi, increasingly rare to sample, with *culatello*, to be enjoyed while standing in front of the counter of a historic *salumeria*; later savoring, in a sitting room that was once an ancient slaughterhouse, a soup of white beans, fried polenta with creamed baccalà, veal *guanciale*, sour cherry tart, and the house *fiordilatte* ice cream.[1]

People come to the bar, first of all, to have breakfast.

Tourists expect that having breakfast will be the simplest thing in the world and do not expect any particular hassles. So the foreigner who comes up against breakfast *all'italiana* for the first time (not the international breakfast served at hotels) usually experiences culture shock. The majority of this trauma assails the newly arrived visitor on the morning of his very first day. Breakfast, in Italy, is a terribly meager meal. Indeed, it isn't a

meal at all. Often the visitor is taken out on an empty stomach, then brought to a bar where he isn't even invited to sit down, but is made to swallow a sip of very black coffee with a rather insubstantial brioche: and so the day has begun.[2] And if, in reply to the question "What would you like for breakfast?," the guest should stammer, "Something simple is fine, a cheese sandwich," then it's his hosts who experience culture shock. Italians are capable of eating cheese only at lunch, or at the end of dinner.

During breakfast (barely a thimbleful of boiling aromatic coffee and a croissant, often with no filling, whose only salient features are its fragrance, its appearance, and its softness), which is eaten standing up at the counter, leafing through the newspaper, the foreigner nevertheless has a way out that may not even occur to him. He can always order a cappuccino. Anyone in his situation should do just that. And if the ingenuous soul postpones the pleasure till afterward ("Later in the day, there will still be time"), it shows he has no idea how inappropriate it is to order a cappuccino in the afternoon or evening.

Cappuccino is a symbol of the Italian way of life, so much so that in the European Union it was given the designation STG (Specialità Tradizionale Garantita, or Traditional Guaranteed Specialty). Cappuccino is made with a first-class espresso: the best quality coffee, just roasted, and high-quality fresh milk, never preserved. It is heated "by ear" until it begins to simmer, definitely never reaching the boiling point. After heating the cup at room temperature, a drop of cold milk is poured into it. One should not be in a hurry when making cappuccino. There is a special ritual that consists of tapping the milk pitcher, allowing the foam to be deposited, setting it aside, then shaking it again. And you must drink it slowly, with no rushing. This is why real Italians don't drink cappuccino as often as they would like. In the morning, in the two free moments he has at the bar counter, an Italian sips his tiny dose of espresso and is ready to go to work.

Italians are aware that German breakfasts—bread, jam, salami—exist in the world, and even the British breakfast of eggs, bacon, and porridge. But these meals are incredible to them: every time they hear somebody mention this, their gestures and words express unspeakable wonder.

After breakfast, the industrious, hardworking, busy people disappear from the bars, and the space belongs entirely to those who have nothing to do: ladies out for a walk, or tourists who are unfamiliar with the local rhythms and order the wrong thing. For clerks and managers, who are always in a rush, the bar in mid-morning offers a five-minute break to enjoy orange juice and peanuts. The same enthusiasts of productive work and business affairs return for two minutes after lunch to drink, while standing, the prescribed sip of coffee. It is a widely held conviction that the restaurant where one has had lunch, even if excellent, will hardly ever serve coffee equal to that at the bar: there the espresso machine, well heated, produces many more servings, and is better able to preserve the fluids and aroma of the coffee's essence as they pass through the crucible of the great machine to settle on the bottom of the cup in the form of a darkish dew. Even after having lunch at home, it is reasonable to go downstairs and have coffee at the bar. Who can prepare a decent coffee at home? Ridiculous to attempt it.

According to an adage, the ideal coffee can only be achieved when all five magical m's (mixture, milling, machine, maintenance, and mastery) are at the maximum level.

After three in the afternoon, the bars, according to a ubiquitous and obligatory evolutionary cycle, are decidedly deserted, but new faces appear around six, during happy hour (happy for the office employees, who are finally liberated). The customers pay only for the aperitifs (a beer or a bitter: Campari, Aperol, etc.) at this time, which is what they really came for. Peanuts, snacks, and various goodies (*sfiziosità*) are offered on the house.

Later on, the bars empty again, and people reappear around ten, to have coffee after dinner at a restaurant, a family meal, or an evening with friends. Sometimes, in the evening, people come to have a *caffè corretto* (a "corrected" coffee, laced with a liqueur) or even an *ammazzacaffè* (coffee killer), that is, a bitter, grappa, or Sambuca, to remove the taste of coffee from the mouth, so inappropriate in the evening hours.

Restaurants were created to feed pilgrims and other wayfarers. This is evident from the word itself: *ristorante*, namely, a place of *ristoro*, of refreshment and restoration. Here the body is restored. In Italy, there is very little stage or film decor in restaurants: it is not Moscow or Hollywood. And yet, there are restaurants whose fame is owed mainly to a certain theatrical formalism that is quite attractive to tourists: the Ambasciata in Quistello, near Mantua; Il Ristorante del Cambio in Turin; Villa Beccaris in Monforte d'Alba; Meo Patacca in Rome; Gualtiero Marchesi in Erbusco, near Brescia. Serious, ultra-traditional restaurants follow the canons—indications in books and historical chronicles—sometimes quite tediously and to the letter. In Pellegrino Artusi's hometown of Forlimpopoli (Romagna), the menu in his restaurant, Al Maneggio, includes specific references to the pages of his famous book of recipes. The reputation of a restaurant can be based on the fact that it is described in a famous novel, or that a very popular film was shot there. A Sicilian chef writes in the menu that in his preparation the pear and Bronte pistachios recall Tchaikovsky's "Arabian Dance," the baroque caponata a Hungarian song by Bartók, chocolate the notes of Brahms . . . it's like being in a conservatory.

Not to mention the restaurants in tourist areas, where people come to admire the monuments, castles, and museums. The food, in many of these restaurants, is a secondary matter. In recompense, however, they offer views of phenomenal beauty: terraces, balconies, wisteria, lake scenes.

Of course, even in Italy there are exceptionally chic premises, programmatically devoted to nouvelle cuisine, which are tiring and give the feeling of being a waste of time. Some menu items (egg yolk marinated with honey mushrooms and rape; basil pesto—a normal recipe but, for some reason, with sultana raisins; creamed corn topped with a layer of foie gras; rice custard with sea urchins and coffee sauce; breast of pigeon in puréed Chinese dates; purée of honey with goat cheese mousse and a sprinkling of white Alba truffle . . .) sound like counts of an indictment.

In which restaurant is one safe from foolish snobbery and tiresome solemnity, yet simultaneously protected from mistreatment or incompetence? How to choose the right place? Not to worry; the best restaurant critics who publish their weekly columns in the major national newspapers suggest ways. Above all, it is advisable to follow the promptings of friends and acquaintances, the suggestions of hotel staff and taxi drivers. Gastronomic guides, as a rule, are imperfect (the list of inns that are part of the Slow Food Association is, in a sense, an exception). In general, the restaurants recommended by Michelin and other similar guides are in the French model: white tablecloths, staggering bills. Such elegant, urbane cuisine may be successful in Italy, but only in a limited social circle: across from the Stock Exchange, at the Senate, and in the more exclusive tourist locales. In these restaurants the dining rooms are separated from the kitchen by a transparent wall. Dozens of chefs and assistant chefs flash before your eyes, wearing trendy aprons and caps. At the table, the sommelier approaches twenty times, in addition to the waiter, with his recommendations. In short, insane operating costs and little sense of humor.

Salvation lies in observation. Carefully study the situation in the city's streets, on the main roads, along the traffic flow. If a pair of elderly women come out of a modest trattoria smiling, this is a good sign: elderly women are demanding and do not like to throw money away. On any highway in the immediate vicinity, you will find food stops for truck drivers. See which has the greatest number of trucks parked in front of it at lunchtime, and enter without fear. As a rule, these places are not bad: truck drivers, serious people, do not let themselves be taken for a ride.

The name of a place also says a lot. It is felt generally that restaurants whose name includes the preposition *da* (at so-and-so's place)—"Da Peppino," "Da Vasco e Giulia,"[3] and so on—are reliable. Again except for laudable exceptions, one should be wary of places whose name does not bear the word *osteria* but rather the affected, pseudoantique *hostaria*. Anyone who glimpses such obtuse witticisms as "In wine, wisdom; in grappa, strength; in water, microbes" on the menu, or framed mottos on the walls that read "Melons, like men, soften over time," "Credit is only given to ninety-year-olds accompanied by their parents," and other banalities that immediately set your teeth on edge should consider himself forewarned. Anyone with knowledge of the typical dishes of a region (to which this entire book is dedicated) understands that a simple reading of the menu can safeguard against many misfortunes. If on Ischia we are offered a menu designed to include "1. Pasta alla Norma, 2. Agnolotti . . . " it is best to get up from the table and leave immediately.

The ritual of choosing the dishes at a restaurant is the highlight of the evening and the culmination of friendly conversation, a dialogue with table companions and with the waiter or restaurant manager, which confirms and elevates the gastronomic class of the entire table. Such talk gives us a wealth of new information and enriches the stores of our language with new dialects.

Reading the menu is useful and enjoyable because reading is always useful and enjoyable. Nevertheless, to choose well, it is best to consult with the waiter, and also have a look at the "chef's specials": on a piece of paper stapled to the menu—sometimes in crooked writing that is not quite legible—the restaurant suggests additional dishes, made with the best "bargains" they were able to buy that very morning.

They immediately bring bread and wine to the table, then go off to boil or roast the rest. They also bring water, after discussing whether it should be carbonated or not, thus highlighting affinities and differences among those at the table.

In some restaurants the first thing they bring to the table, by way of "compliments of the house," is pizza or focaccia. Not infrequently the appetizers end here. In reality appetizers are not customary in regional cuisine. The custom of the introductory course came to Italy from France and caught on mainly in Piedmont, where anchovies in green sauce, vegetables fried in batter, and veal in tuna sauce are usually served at the beginning of the meal. In most cases appetizers, both at the restaurant and at home, are a mark of extravagance, a sign of celebration. The tradition of being obliged to serve appetizers became widespread in Italy in the 1960s.

Regional cuisine reacted in its own way to this innovation. Wherever appetizers are served in simple, unpretentious Italian inns and trattorias, they are more often than not typical local products or dishes: marinated olives, sweet-and-sour pearl onions, mushrooms in oil, stuffed olives, stuffed mushroom caps, bruschetta with truffles or capers, or vegetables in oil (small artichokes, peppers, eggplant, zucchini, dried tomatoes, white beans). Freshly sliced prosciutto, *crudo* (cured) or *cotto* (cooked), mortadella, salami, Bresaola sausage. Seafood salads, which can be with or without sauce, cold or warm. Oysters. Marinated mussels. *Tuna bottarga*. Mozzarella with a drizzle of oil, mozzarella and tomato (Caprese), Parmesan, salted ricotta; focaccia in Liguria; in Puglia, garlic shoots boiled and dressed with oil and vinegar.

In any case, the "authenticity" and simplicity of both the setting and the menu was prized back in Dickens's time:

> In not the least picturesque part of this ride, there is a fair specimen of a real Genoese tavern, where the visitor may derive good entertainment from real Genoese dishes, such as Tagliarini; Ravioli; German sausages, strong of garlick, sliced and eaten with fresh green figs; cocks' combs and sheep-kidneys, chopped up with mutton-chops and liver; small pieces of some unknown part of a calf, twisted into small shreds, fried, and served up in a great dish like white-bait; and other curiosities of that kind. They often get wine at these suburban Trattorie, from France and Spain and Portugal.[4]

The antipasti can also be hot: various *zuppette* (light soups) of fish or seafood in tomato sauce, or thinly sliced meat.

Unlike the starters, first courses, namely, pastas and risottos, are essential and are served at any restaurant in Italy. If the first course is neither pasta nor rice, but a vegetable or meat soup, it is considered a rarity and a line or two about it will be noted in the margin of the menu. This absence of liquid soups on the traditional Italian menu often makes things difficult for foreigners from the north, for whom a lunch without soup is not a lunch. Everyone knows that for Russians, soups are the foundation of the diet. But, as we can see, its absence is also distressing for inhabitants of Germany, such as Heinrich Heine:

"First course: no soup. A terrible thing, especially for a well-born man like me, accustomed, since his youth, to having soup each day and who until that moment could not conceive of a world in which the sun did not rise in the morning and soup was not served at midday."[5]

Tourists must bear in mind that in Italy pizza is not considered a first course (see "Pizza"). Usually people order pizza (if they are not very hungry) or else a "normal" meal, with a first course, second course, and fruit.

The second courses on the menu are divided into two categories: fish and meat. Depending on the place, the fish dishes may be *baccalà* (dried cod) Vicenza-style, fish *in saòr* (fried and then marinated), fish in foil, or fish cooked in a thousand other ways. Meat dishes are prepared in a particular way each time; for example, game *alla cacciatora*, or hunter-style (stewed in a liquid sauce with tomatoes, wine, and spices), stew with Barolo wine, saltimbocca (pieces of lean meat or roulades fried in hot oil), or rabbit with rosemary and Taggia olives.

Side dishes, in Italian restaurants, are ordered expressly and are often served on a separate plate. Mixed salads or other vegetables, such as baked chicory, grilled eggplant, eggplant baked with mint, and spinach molds, are usually preferred over potatoes, which are less common here than in other national cuisines.

Desserts are often the pride of restaurants, but they are ordered more frequently by tourists unable to resist them than by local residents. The locals are accustomed to stoically overcoming the sugary temptation and try not to look at the dessert cart when it comes by. Among the most obvious desserts of any restaurant are macedonia (fruit cup); tiramisù, which has by now been around the globe and has lost all its exotic attraction for tourists; and zuppa inglese (trifle), neither a soup nor an exact replica of the English dessert, but a sponge cake thoroughly soaked in liqueur, with cream and chocolate.

After the seasonal fruit, the cheese cart is finally brought to the tables. This moment is the apotheosis of gourmandizing, of exchanging information, of satisfying curiosities, of attention to the typical products of distant regions. At a restaurant or a friend's home, it is usually possible to taste cheeses that you would never think of buying in a store—and which you might from that moment begin to adore and later buy.

The order of the courses in restaurants is sacrosanct, incontestable. To assail it would be tantamount to a revolution.

An amusing attempt to subvert the customs and habits of Italians was the Backwards Dinner, held by avant-garde artists at the Politeama Rossetti of Trieste on January 12, 1910, the first of many propagandistic evenings that Marinetti's Futurist Cookery movement organized during the thirty years of its history. During this dinner, dishes with arcane, polemical names were served, though, in reality, there was nothing really new about them: for example, "blood clots in broth," "roast mummy with professor's liver," and "jam of the glorious deceased." The most astounding aspect was the reverse order in which the courses were served, beginning with coffee and ending with antipasto.

A classic dinner, however, always ends with an espresso. A person may drink it or not; it's a personal matter. But giving the waiter prior notice at the beginning of the meal that coffee will be ordered and drunk after dessert is an eccentricity that would only occur to a tourist. A delightful story on the subject is contained in Galina Muravieva's comparative analysis of customs:

> "For me, spaghetti, steak, and coffee, please," a Russian woman orders in an Italian restaurant. Her Italian friends laugh.
>
> "Why are you laughing?" The Russian woman, piqued, doesn't understand. How can we help laughing: you ordered your meal and coffee at the same time.
>
> Don't you understand? Coffee is not just the ending of a meal, it is something distinct from lunch or dinner. With coffee, you don't eat anything, and after coffee, at most you may drink something: brandy, cognac, or the like. The Italians, like other Europeans, like to move to another place to drink their coffee, for example, to another room or, if dining in a restaurant, to a bar. You can also drink coffee at the restaurant, but it is ridiculous to order it right away.[6]

Often restaurants may have a social reputation and history that is more valued than their cuisine. It is interesting to dine in Roman restaurants near the Parliament, because they are "parceled out" among the parties and the gastronomic rituals celebrated in each of them are rich in symbols, which are curious to decipher and understand. When the Christian Democrat Party still existed, its parliamentarians dined in a restaurant run by nuns known as the Travailleuses Missionaires. Deputies and senators of this historic Italian party, in fact, lived in accordance with Catholic rules: and so their meals were served to them by nuns. The sisters, at the beginning of the meal, arranged a moment of meditation in the dining room and prayed together with their customers. Having been prepared in this manner, the diners felt that they were absolved in advance from a certain sinfulness in their dining, a pleasure . . . gluttony . . . extravagance . . . almost as if they had been granted an indulgence.

In past decades, an excellent coffee could be had in Rome at the Communist bar Vezio, near Piazza Campitelli, in the ghetto. Now the bar has been moved. Who knows if portraits of Lenin and Stalin hang on the walls along with postcards of Red Square and various other Soviet kitsch symbols?

Pastry and confectionery shops are places for the rich. Well-known are the elegant pastry shops Cova on Via Montenapoleone in Milan (since 1817) and Sant' Ambroeus, also in Milan, under the arcades of Corso Matteotti. In Genoa the confectionery Romanengo Pietro fu Stefano (in existence since 1780) is renowned: here chocolate bars, candied fruit, pralines, and sugared almonds are prepared by hand in accordance with exclusive recipes.

Cafés do not always manage to reproduce the ancient noble prototype of the refined, uncommon haunt, but often they strive to equal it. In the old historic centers there are the literary cafés: Pedrocchi in Padua, 250 years old; San Marco in Trieste; the Caffè dell'Orologio in Modena. Then there are cafés for gourmets: in Turin the Caffè Torino, the Neuv Caval'd Bròns, the San Carlo, and the tiny Bicerin, on Piazza Consolata. This is where the Turinese specialty of the same name was born, which includes coffee, chocolate, boiling milk, and sweet syrup, and which can be drunk in three different ways: *pur e fiur* (coffee and milk), *pur e barba* (coffee and chocolate), and *'n po'd'tut* (a bit of everything). Originally this drink was called *bavareisa*; then the artificially anonymous term *bicerin* prevailed, indicating a glass cup with a metal holder, identical to those in which tea is served on Russian trains.

Trattorias are found on the *tratte* (tracts), along stretches of road. That is, they are the premises where travelers stop along the way. Up until a few years ago, there was a large number of Tuscan trattorias in Milan, for some reason. The restaurant Bagutta, located in the "fashionable triangle," as chic and expensive as it is, is still a Tuscan trattoria in terms of its cooking and decor. Writers love to meet in this spot, which has been open since 1924 and protected by the Ministry of Culture since 1991; the Bagutta literary prize is awarded there, and the walls are adorned with artistic and literary memorabilia. At the Antica Trattoria della Pesa, open in Milan since 1880, everything is folksy instead: the decor, the food, and the dialect.

Restaurant managers may have the most original traditions and gimmicks. In some places, like Il Pallaro in Rome, near the Campo dei Fiori, you can't order food according to your own taste or reject what you can't finish, because they bring the same dishes, beautifully cooked, to everyone, in Pantagruelian quantities. The customer is overfed but satisfied, and the joyful experience must be booked a month in advance.

If a locale is open until late at night, it is called a *dopoteatro* (after theater): one example is the Biffi Scala, near the Teatro alla Scala in Milan, or the Santa Lucia, also in Milan's center. You can go there at eleven or even twelve: no one is sent away, but, in terms of food, they'll serve you a *risotto al salto*: the saffron risotto left over from dinner, sautéed in a pan.

From a historical point of view, restaurants with a particularly judicious wine cellar should be called *osterie* (taverns). They are characteristic of port cities. The Antica Osteria del Bai in Genoa, to name one in particular, has existed since the eighteenth century. Today it is an elegant locale, famous for cuttlefish *in zimino* (in a sauce made of spinach, garlic, parsley, and chard).

In northern Italy *latterie*, or dairy shops, abound. At one time, every block had its own dairy shop, where besides selling milk they served meat, fish, and vegetables. They are wonderful places—at least the few that have survived to present day.

The existence of *fiaschetterie*, or wineshops (not to be confused with the Roman *fraschetterie*, wine bars), comes from the region of Chianti and has gradually spread throughout Italy. The Chianti bottle is called a *fiasca* (flask), and a *fiaschetteria* is a place where there are many flasks. Giannino in Milan (in the Vittoria area), known since 1899 and now a deluxe restaurant, started out as a *fiaschetteria*. Giannino's cuisine is Tuscan.

Taverns date back to ancient Rome and Greece.

Places that serve tea, in the absence of an Italian term, are pretentiously referred to by the English term "tearoom." The tea ritual is so rare, so aristocratic, that even Italian high society does not always have enough *bon ton* to indulge in it. But if they do, it is at five o'clock in the afternoon. The tea is brewed strong, as the English prepare it. The most affected ladies schedule appointments in a tearoom for five o'clock. A trace of lemon in the tea is a symbol of high aristocracy, recalling the counts and countesses in a song by Giorgio Gaber and Enzo Jannacci: "A slice of lemon in the tea . . ." Asking for tea at the end of lunch or dinner in an ordinary restaurant, as Russian tourists often do, is wasted effort: you get a teapot of boiling water and a sorry teabag.

Cantine, or wine bars, are places where you can drink wine and have some bread and cheese. Like most other places, some wine bars have kept to their mission, while others have been transformed into restaurants, at times quite lavish. There are wine bars that have existed for several centuries, such as the Ca' de be' (the place to drink) in Bertinoro, Romagna, not far from Predappio, a powerfully alluring destination for the history buff: Mussolini is buried not far from there.

Enoteche (wineshops) can be unforgettable, such as the Enoteca Pubblica della

Liguria e della Lunigiana, in the high-vaulted basements of the seventeenth-century Palazzo del Comune in Castelnuovo Magra, where art exhibitions are held. Or the illustrious Enoteca Pinchiorri in Florence's historic center, which is recognized as the best in Italy by the most rigid gastronomic experts.

In the center of Tuscan cities there are shops, *mescite*, also called *vinaini*, where unbottled wine is sold from the barrel. In many cities in Liguria, Campania, and Sicily people love the *friggitorie*, where fried foods are sold to take home or eat along the street. There you can get something savory or something sweet. The *rosticcerie* (rotisseries or delicatessens) have a similar function.

In thousands of villages, in hundreds of thousands of places, you can enjoy wonderful food directly from the producer. You can also go directly to the farms for that purpose.

In stalls in the historic center of big cities, at the market, or in small villages, you can buy every kind of street food: chestnut cake, roast chestnuts, roast corn on the cob, watermelons, and so on, and it is these stands that give the city such a warm, human, unique feeling: the watermelon vendors, the lupine vendors, the cooked-pear vendors. These are the few individuals who remain constant in a landscape of rapidly changing features, as we all become acquainted with the third millennium, now no longer the stuff of science fiction.

Or we can plunge into the mountains and hills of Piedmont, in the Langhe, and clamber up the hills, looking for a particular farm in order to have lunch or dinner and at the same time support the rural economy by participating in the program Turismo del Vino e Dei Sapori (Tourism of Wine and Tastes). It is an essential effort for the salvation of those farms, which would otherwise be forced to close. Besides being of clear benefit to farmers, this type of tourism secures great satisfaction to all participants (see "Slow Food").

But the best thing someone who wants to eat outside the home in Italy can do is travel 240 kilometers away from one's home city, follow a winding road along a lake, climb up 1,500 meters along a snaking, unpaved track in the Ossolan Alps, and end up right at the hut of a herdsman who keeps a hundred cows and produces a hundred Toma cheeses per year. There they will serve you potato gnocchi and *neccio* (a local focaccia) with butter, sage, and cheese or with grated smoked ricotta. They will prepare a dish called *cuchela*: red potatoes cooked with pork ribs or slices of pancetta. They will offer you the local cheeses. No need to think twice: go and eat at a place like this.

Calabria

alabria, which lies between the Ionian and Tyrrhenian seas, has always held great strategic importance because of its position and has always been the target of foreign conquerors. Its land has frequently been the scene of battles between various conquering peoples. And the Calabrians, without much resistance, assimilated the language and customs of their invaders, and appropriated their culinary cultures, with all their oddities and superstitions. In some areas of Calabria, farmers still read omens from a pig's entrails when it is taken to slaughter, as the Etruscan haruspices did. And like the ancients, they believe that it is possible to guess whether a boy or a girl will be born by interrogating the stars. Even today, they see to it that the formal Christmas and Epiphany dinner consists of exactly thirteen courses, not one more, not one less. For St. Rocco's Day, you can bake bread dough in the image of any ailing body part, and it will heal without any medical intervention. While kneading the leavened dough, women were expected at one time to dance and shout incantations to drive away the evil spirits. The bakers who were kneading the bread could not be approached without having first requested permission from St. Martin. In Calabria there are still some who trace a magic sign of protection on the loaf before it enters the oven: a triple cross.

The ethnographer gathering all this material must suddenly stop in bewilder-

ment. For Calabria hosts a phenomenon even more arresting than these rituals: a mirage, right before his very eyes. It is called the Fata Morgana effect, referring to the magical fairy Morgan le Fay. From the port of Reggio Calabria, on very hot days, an entire city with houses and palm trees can suddenly be seen clearly, rising above the sea. According to scientific explanation, they are the buildings of the city of Messina that "fly" across the strait as a result of water vapor and fluctuating warm air, saturated with moisture.

Some Calabrian customs deviate quite a bit from widespread Italian ritual. Throughout Italy breakfast usually boils down to a sip of coffee, or something extremely light. In Calabria, on the other hand, it is a very substantial meal. Unique in all of Italy, Calabrians consume a real English-style cooked breakfast. In the morning they may eat a specific meat pie, the *murseddu* (from the Spanish *almuerzo*, breakfast), a shell of leavened dough with entrails, liver, pancetta, salt pork, and salami with hot red pepper. Often such an abundant breakfast is consumed in the company of friends and relatives, in a trattoria. Others eat a brioche filled with ice cream (a rather exotic variant) instead, in the course of their morning travels. It is definitely part of the southern tradition to eat while walking in the street: in the early morning, in the piazzas and narrow streets of Calabrian towns are stands where you can buy *arancini* (rice balls), *panzerotti* (folded, fried pizza), fritters, pizza, and stuffed focaccias.

From the eighth century B.C. until the third century B.C., Calabria, like Puglia and Sicily, was part of Magna Graecia. It was the Greeks who founded Reggio Calabria, Sybaris (populated by dissolute Sybarites), Crotone, and Locri. Five hundred years after the Greeks, the Romans arrived in Calabria and had high regard for the local wines. After the fall of the Roman Empire, Calabria was ruled in turn by the Germans, the Goths, the Lombards, the Byzantines, the Normans, the Franks, the Swabians, the Saracens, the Spanish, and the French, until the power of the terrible Calabrian mafia, the *'ndrangheta*, began to assert itself, succeeding the numerous foreign rulers in the second half of the nineteenth century. The sparse, scattered population maintained political neutrality, developed few relationships, and led a silent, dismal life in houses similar to hermitages.

Indeed, this region is ideal for anchorites. In the area of Sybaris, at a vast distance from northern monasticism, Cistercian monasteries began to be established in the eleventh century. The Cistercians, at the time, had broken away from the Benedictine order to observe asceticism more strictly and follow the austere rule of St. Bernard. Calabria was so poor that asceticism was part of everyday life there. The cenobitic life of the Sybaritic monks certainly did not evoke the extravagance of the ancient Sybarites. Working very hard, unsparingly, the Cistercians introduced many agricultural innovations into local life and developed a regular dairy farming industry in Calabria.

Nevertheless, despite this contribution of Nordic know-how, Calabrian life on the whole remained immune to external influences. The Calabrian population's custom of isolating itself on mountaintops—eating the fruits of the land and breeding with little diversity—was too ingrained. The main vegetables grown in Calabria are eggplants and peppers, while in the orchards citrus fruits predominate, especially oranges. These oranges were introduced in Calabria, as in Sicily, by the Arabs, who brought them from India and China.

Eggplants also came from the Arabs. In northern Italy they are not generally grown, because it is too cool and the eggplants grown there have no flavor. By contrast, under the burning Calabrian sun they develop fragrant juices. There is a great wealth of variety in the Calabrian eggplant domain: Asmara, Nubia, Larga Morada, Slim Jim, Black Beauty, the so-called Violets (*Violette*), and the enormous variety called "Mostruosa di New York."

Until the end of the nineteenth century, eggplants were looked upon with suspicion in Italy. Just as cucumbers are subject to ostracism today, considered indigestible, so eggplants were once accused of all kinds of sins. At one time it was thought that they were responsible for indigestion, madness, and psychic disorders. The popular interpretation of their name *melanzana* as *mela insana*, or "unsound apple," speaks volumes. In short, it took crusty, obstinate Calabrians to stubbornly keep on using eggplants for centuries, growing them, caring for them, and loving them.

By an irony of fate, one of the rare dishes invented by Calabrians has become famous by the name of "eggplant parmigiana," even though Parma's role here is clearly rather marginal. In fact this dish, which is simply named after the Parmesan cheese sprinkled on the fried eggplant, is not prepared at all in Parma. And the Parmesan in Calabria, of course, was not brought from the north, but obtained here, in the Cistercian dairies, where the Calabrian monks produced it in accordance with the northern recipe.

In addition to eggplant, fava beans are used heavily here, as are broad beans and white beans. These vegetable protein foods are consumed in winter, during the cold season. But beans here are not cooked in the same pot with meat, as in the north. One type of protein is considered to be sufficient. Along with these beans are cooked vegetable dishes with tomatoes, celery, catalogna chicory, and abundant olive oil, or with cabbage and potatoes. The beans are first marinated with spices for almost twenty-four hours. This, too, is an ancient Roman method, and a medieval recipe: in short, a culinary relic, a kind of gastronomic archaeology.

But the main source of protein in the diet of Calabria's inhabitants is fish. Calabrian fishermen work in ideal conditions due to their access to two seas: they can afford to choose where and when the fish are biting best, and where there are fewer storms, in the Tyrrhenian or Ionian waters. Particularly important for the economy is swordfish fishing, practiced by fishermen from the ports of Pizzo, Palmi, and Scylla—the rock with the six-headed monster from whom Ulysses perilously escaped while six of his sailing companions were devoured:

> *Deep-set that cavern lies; no archer stout*
> *Might from his hollow ship an arrow send*
> *Into its depths, where, barking fearfully,*
> *Scylla her habitation hath. Her voice*
> *Is like the yelping of some new-born whelp;*
> *Her form is that of monster dread. Nor God*
> *Nor man would joy to meet her face to face.*
> *Twelve dangling feet she hath, and six long necks,*
> *On each a fearful head with triple row*
> *Of thick-set teeth environed with black death.*[1]

Throughout the year, sardines and herring are caught between Scylla and Charybdis, but in May and June in the Gulf of Sant'Eufemia everyone mobilizes for the most important moment of the season. The arrival of the swordfish! Individual specimens may reach a length of four meters. As a rule, customers pay for the fishermen's catch in advance and wait patiently on the shore for the evening fish delivery.

Each year, in Bagnara Calabra (which according to the latest census counts two thousand professional fishermen out of eleven thousand families), a picturesque swordfish *sagra* is held on the first Sunday in July, attracting crowds of tourists both from Calabria and from nearby Sicily. During the *sagra* the priest blesses the *ontre*, the traditional boats of swordfish fishermen. The feast day takes place when schools of these fish, hurrying toward warmer waters in which to deposit their eggs, must pass through the Strait of Messina. Though it is true that the fish are at home in these waters, the strait has always been troublesome for humans. The frightening tales about Scylla and Charybdis did not enter Homer's story by accident: the currents in the violent strait change direction at any time of day, so only the most expert sailors and fishermen are able to cross it with their boats.

Antonio Mongitore, a historian who lived in Sicily in the eighteenth century and authored the detailed study *Biblioteca sicula* (Sicilian library), described the preparatory rituals of going after swordfish. In the center of the *ontra*, or boat, stands a twenty-foot mast with an observation platform. From this platform the ship boy sights the prey. Two mighty harpoons are tied to 120-foot-long ropes. From high on the platform, the spotter shouts, and the tracking begins. The swordfish are mating at this time, so often the fishermen catch them in twos. A surefire strategy is to harpoon the female first. The male will not abandon her, and he, too, becomes easy prey. Domenico Modugno wrote a song about this sad tale: "Lu pisci spada" (The swordfish), 1956.

In Bagnara Calabra, on the day of the *sagra*, a fire is lit right in the main square, Piazza Marconi. *Pennette* pasta is prepared in a sauce of *scozzetta*, that is, the flesh found under the neck of the swordfish. The fishermen eat the most tasty parts, the fins, right on the boat, while out fishing. In the main piazza of the village, slices of swordfish are grilled and guests are also offered the famous raw swordfish roulades. Swordfish here is cooked in tomato sauce *ghiotta*-style (in a pan) or *in salmoriglio*: marinated in olive oil, salt, garlic, oregano, capers, and parsley, and then grilled.

The harpooners also hunt tuna, just as the protagonist of *The Old Man and the Sea* by Ernest Hemingway hunted marlin. A typical local dish, *maccheruni* with *ventresca* (stomach muscle), is made from tuna.

Antipasti *Mustica*: baby anchovies in oil. *Mustica*, like eggplant and, in some cases, fried sardines, is sun-dried with hot red pepper and preserved in oil and wine vinegar with herbs.

First Courses *Minestra maritata* (married soup), containing both vegetables and meat (also encountered in Campania and Puglia, and mentioned in "Eros"). Soup of herbs and vegetables with sausage, pork rind, and cracklings. *Macaroni alla pastora* (shepherdess-style), topped with ricotta.

Licurdia: onion soup with red pepper, prepared under the Aragonese towers of Pizzo Calabro.

Lasagne chine (stuffed lasagna). The noodles are baked in the oven, alternating with layers of meatballs, hard-boiled eggs, Scamorza, mozzarella, grated pecorino, and a sauce of artichokes and peas.

Pitta: the local variant of pizza; there is also *pitta chicculiata*, with fresh tomatoes, olive oil, and hot red pepper, and *pitta maniata*, closed up and stuffed with hard-boiled eggs, ricotta, Provola, *soppressata* (salami), and the usual hot red pepper.

Second Courses Stuffed kid, boned and filled with vermicelli with *ragù* sauce. The meat sauce is prepared with the young goat's own internal organs (heart, liver, lung). It is baked in the oven with salt pork and herbs.

In Diamante, fritters of *jujume* (sea anemones). In the town of Polistena they prepare kid the way the ancient Greeks did. The city of Vibo Valentia is famous for penne pasta with *'nduja*, a soft, spicy sausage with red pepper. Also popular in Calabria is *cuccia*, an ancient Roman dish of kid or lamb with wheat or corn. Eggplant *involtini* (roulades): thin slices of fried eggplant wrapped around a filling of pancetta, garlic, parsley, and cheese with soft bread, pitted olives, anchovies, garlic, and oil. These *involtini* are cooked on the grill, or stewed in a sweet-and-sour sauce with sugar, vinegar, chocolate, and pine nuts.

Morseddu: a pie with entrails, tripe, heart, lungs, and spleen. The filling must include red wine, tomatoes, red pepper, and herbs. *Tiana*: lamb baked in a clay pan with potatoes. *Mazzacorde*: sausage of lamb intestines. Swordfish in tomato sauce, *alla ghiotta*, in a pan, and *in salmoriglio*, on the grill. Calabrian-style tuna, roasted with capers. *Alalunga* (albacore, the most prized variety of tuna) in sweet-and-sour sauce.

Desserts *Mostaccioli* or *'nzudda*, sweet pastry with honey (flour, honey, anisette, a dab of butter, and nothing more). They are made for the Christmas holiday in the shape of fish (a Christian symbol) or a pastoral crozier.

TYPICAL PRODUCTS OF CALABRIA

Cheeses Caciocavallo Silano, Calabrian ricotta (from sheep's and goat's milk, coagulated with fig latex, in barrels made of fig-tree wood), Butirro. Another soft cheese, aged instead in small rush baskets, is Giuncata of Morano Calabro. Crotonese, of sheep's milk.

The above-mentioned salami called *'nduja*.

Calabrian tangerines (*clementine*). Bergamot oranges. Citrons. Zibibbo grapes, grown in Pizzo Calabro. Watermelons of Crotone, a city of Magna Graecia, the cradle of Pythagoreanism. They are incredibly juicy, because the soil here is clay: strips of compact soil alternate with layers of hard sand, so the water does not go very deep but flows into the sugary juice of these enormous watermelons.

Red onions of Tropea.

Licorice.

TYPICAL BEVERAGE

Orange liqueur.

PIZZA

We know that pasta plays a role as the gastronomic emblem of Italy, both in the Italians' eyes and in the eyes of foreigners. What about pizza, the second most popular Italian dish? Can pizza be called an Italian symbol, in the same way pasta is?

Well, no. It would be more accurate to say that pizza is a symbol of America or a symbol of international fast food. In Italy, pizza's importance and consumption of it is far more limited than what is believed abroad.

The name "pizza" has been traced back at times to the Greek *plax*, a flat surface or table, and at other times to the Latin *pinsere*, to crush or grind. A similar idea—the "edible table" of Virgilian memory—was known both in ancient Rome and in almost all the culinary traditions of the world. The Mexican tortilla, the Arabic pita, the Indian chapati, and the Georgian lavash are variations of the same approach: putting an oily filling, which stains, on an edible "plate" to protect the hands and clothing. In Naples snail soup was ladled into the crusty end of a bread that had been hollowed out. This same principle is also the foundation of American (and international) fast food: hamburgers and hot dogs.

Pizza, as it is understood everywhere in the world (round, covered with red sauce and cheese), was invented in Italy at the end of the nineteenth century. In 1889 Don Raffaele Esposito, owner of the famous pizzeria Brandi in Naples, presented his customers with an edible version of the patriotic tricolor (a pizza with red tomato, white mozzarella, and green basil), in honor of the queen of Italy, Margherita of Savoy. The queen herself

appreciated the dish very much, and from then on the pizza took her name, Margherita. But at the beginning of the twentieth century, pizza, exported to the United States by Italian emigrants, became a phenomenon not so much of Italian but of American culture, and as a result an integral part of unremarkable popular food. In 1905 the first Italian pizzeria opened in New York. Following that, pizzerias began to appear everywhere, even in northern Europe. In Italy, pizza continued to remain a local specialty of two or three southern regions. Only after World War II did the Neapolitan creation ricochet back home from abroad, disembarking with the ships of Allied soldiers from the United States. Contributing significantly to the spread in its popularity were Italian-Americans who had become popular in Italy, such as Frank Sinatra and Dean Martin, who sang about pizza in his famous "That's Amore": "When the moon hits your eye like a big pizza pie . . ."

In postwar Italy pizza caught on as a festive food, a cheerful collective meal, and an alternative to pasta, which is so distinctly domestic. For today's Italians, choosing between pasta and pizza means choosing between staying home and going out—that is, between time spent with the family (keywords: family, mother) and social time (keywords: friends, companionship).

The contrast between pasta and pizza is underscored in the homespun philosophy fed to us by the glossy magazines. According to the nation's psychologists, pasta is associated with mother and family, since it is eaten daily at home. Pizza, on the other hand, is associated with lovers, since it is very difficult to prepare at home and requires going out.

Naturally, the historian of gastronomic culture will object that, in ancient times, pasta wasn't cooked at home either, but was bought already prepared in the nearby tavern. Neapolitans, Romans, Sicilians, Emilians, and Genoese did not like being shut in at home and preferred the precious human contact found in trattorias. Goethe described macaroni not as a component of the domestic diet, but as a social event:

> Though people here lack our well-equipped kitchens and like to make short work of their cooking, they are catered for in two ways. The macaroni, the dough of which is made from a very fine flour, kneaded into various shapes and then boiled, can be bought everywhere and in all the shops for very little money. As a rule, it is simply cooked in water and seasoned with grated cheese. Then, at almost every corner of the main streets, there are pastry-cooks with their frying pans of sizzling oil, busy, especially on fast days, preparing pastry and fish on the spot for anyone who wants it. Their sales are fabulous, for thousands and thousands of people carry their lunch and supper home, wrapped in a little piece of paper.[1]

Dickens, too, noticed this, not in Naples, but in Genoa, and the sight did not arouse any joy in him: "Beneath some of the arches, the sellers of maccaroni and polenta establish their stalls, which are by no means inviting."[2]

Nevertheless, it's worth repeating that this banal cliché (pasta = hearth and home, pizza = sociability) faithfully reflects today's reality. Pasta is now eaten at home with the family. In Italian homes it is cooked much more often than any other first course. In the lexicon of gastronomy, pastas in broth are called *minestre*, soups. Pasta is served as a first course if it is topped with light vegetable sauces. If the sauce is chock-full of protein-rich ingredients (such as meat, fish, shrimp, mussels, or wild boar), then it naturally becomes a main course instead.

After World War II, the proportion of working women increased nationwide, and a behavioral model was established for European families in which everyone is away from home for the entire day. Today, few Italians manage to go home for lunch, even though a lunch break sometimes lasts three hours. Pasta is therefore reserved for the evening, when everyone finally gathers around the family dinner table. We live in an age when the abundance of electrical appliances and the availability of ready-made and frozen sauces make work easier in the kitchen. Nevertheless, thanks in part to the assimilation of foreign models (from the Italian-Americans: pasta is family, home), the ritual of pasta-making is notoriously associated with a huge pot in the family kitchen, along with discussions about what to pair with what, choices regarding sauces and shapes, and exchanges of views that sometimes lead to disputes of culinary principle.

Pizza, on the other hand, which returned to Italy at the end of the war, at the same time that everything American became fashionable, is a cheerful, carefree ritual food, which does not require either effort or memory! There are more than seven hundred pasta shapes, while there are only ten classic pizzas. You can't go wrong when you order them. As for the nonclassic versions, it isn't necessary to remember them, since they generally bear the name of the pizzeria, or a trendy song, or the girlfriend of the *pizzaiolo*, who puts whatever comes to mind on it. Anyone who doesn't like it doesn't have to order it.

Pizza is a truly social food. It is unrealistic to try to make it at home, given that it traditionally requires a wood-burning oven heated to 485 degrees C, with an incandescent vault. Just try making it at home without burning down the whole neighborhood!

Transforming a frozen pizza into an edible pizza is an absurd idea to Italians. To have pizza for supper, you either go to a pizzeria and eat it on the spot (which is more expensive) or, provided you can run home in less than two minutes and find everyone already seated at the table with their napkins tucked around their necks, you buy the pizzas hot, packed in flat cardboard boxes that give off an aroma of basil, garlic, and oregano; burning your hands, you then rush home to eat them at an insane speed so they won't get cold. The second option is, of course, cheaper, but the diners will know that they have been deprived of part of the pleasure of the experience.

Going out for a pizza is an ideal diversion for young people, as well as for those on a budget. A pizzeria, naturally, is less expensive than a restaurant, though neither is it as economical as one might expect, given the insignificant cost of the ingredients. Apparently, it is not the price of the ingredients that matters. Other factors affect the cost of an evening in a pizzeria. The customer pays for the decor of the place (the oven with its visible fire, the glowing embers, the rustic furnishings), and also helps to pay the pizza maker's high salary. Among cooks, pizza chefs are the highest paid. They don't "work";

they are masters on tour. In many places pizza is served only at night: which means that the *pizzaiolo* will only perform his solo concert then.

The pizza maker must have been born in Naples (or at least pass for a Neapolitan). He must be hieratic: like a celebrant, he performs every gesture in the public eye. To this guardian of sacred truths are entrusted the proportions of the ingredients, measured meticulously, down to that pinch of flour that is thrown under the dough in the pan (the famous pinch is recorded in all pizza recipes, probably because of its assonance: *pizza-pizzico*). The *pizzaiolo* also knows the baking times, those fractions of seconds needed for the pizza to be thoroughly, though not overly, baked. He controls his gestures to perfection: he tosses the dough in the air, stretches it, twirls it, tosses it back up . . .

The dough must be stretched by hand, not rolled out with a rolling pin. This is one of the fundamental secrets of pizza, or so says Gianluca Procaccini, 2001 winner of the pizza-cooking contest held in the town of Salsomaggiore. His victory was owed to a virtuoso execution of an individual variation of *pizza ai quattro formaggi*, or "four-cheese pizza." In his masterpiece, Procaccini introduced Camoscio d'Oro, Crema di Formaggi, mozzarella, and mild Gorgonzola instead of the classic cheeses.

Pizza invites the entire group of diners to have fun. The dialogue between customers and restaurant staff is ceremonial and playful. The ordering of pizza is sort of like a game of eeny, meeny, miny, moe, and conducting the verbal game is the talkative waiter, the exact opposite of the pizza maker who, solemn, and priestlike, remains silent while tending to the oven.

At the moment of decision, the customer deals in watchwords, code names. The basic types of pizza are margherita, marinara, *capricciosa*, Sicilian, Neapolitan, four seasons, four cheeses, Roman, *diavola*, and *ortolana*. For an Italian, this is the alphabet; it is impossible not to know the composition by heart: the list of ingredients on the menu is superfluous.

Napoletana (Neapolitan): tomato, mozzarella, anchovies, oregano, capers.

Marinara: simply a disk of dough spread with tomato and garlic.

Capricciosa: mozzarella, mushrooms, small artichokes, *prosciutto cotto*, olives, olive oil.

Romana (Roman): tomato, mozzarella, anchovies, oregano, olive oil.

Quattro stagioni (four seasons): usually the same ingredients as *capricciosa*, but in separate sections, not mixed together.

Diavola: tomato, mozzarella, spicy salami, oregano, olive oil.

Quattro formaggi (four cheeses): provolone, Parmesan, Gruyère, pecorino.

Siciliana (Sicilian): black olives, green olives, anchovies, capers, caciocavallo cheese, tomato.

Margherita: tomato, mozzarella, basil.

Ortolana: mozzarella, eggplant, peppers, zucchini.

There are also pizzas named for their ingredients, such as *pizza alla Parmigiana*, with Parmesan and ricotta, or *pizza al prosciutto*. Calzone is a pizza folded in half and pinched closed around the edges, like an oversized ravioli.

Cheerfully eating this wonderful, almost childish food, the patron often enjoys additional playful moments in sharing the food with others. This corresponds well with Neapolitan traditions, which stress a particular ethic of personal, everyday compassion. It can be seen, for example, in the famous *caffè sospeso*, a coffee paid for in advance and held for someone who can't afford it.

The poet and screenwriter Tonino Guerra, a friend and longtime collaborator of Federico Fellini, told this story to listeners of the radio station *Moscow Echo* on September 4, 2005:

> We go into a cafe near the station. Two guys arrive and say, "Five coffees—two to drink here, three left *sospesi* [suspended]." They pay for five coffees and drink their two. I ask De Sica: "What is this suspended coffee?" He says, "Wait, you'll see." Then more people come in—some girls; they drink their coffee and pay normally. Three lawyers come in and order seven coffees: "Three we'll drink, and four suspended." They pay for seven, drink three, and leave. Then a young man orders two coffees, drinks one, pays for two, and leaves. De Sica and I sit there chatting until noon. The doors are open. I look out at the piazza, flooded with sunlight, and all of a sudden I see a dark shadow approaching the door. When he's right in front of the door near the bar, I see that it's a beggar. He pokes his head into the café and asks: "Is there a *caffè sospeso*?"

Like the *caffè sospeso*, there was also once a *pizza settimanale* in Naples, the pizza that the needy were allowed to eat in a pizzeria once a week: the customers of the place paid for it, leaving a cent or two at a time. In practice, the system of "pizzas for the poor" in Naples was at times a cover-up to disguise usury, and the sums involved were not pennies. In any case, Neapolitan beggars in the past could firmly count on a bowl of pizza crusts every night, left over by customers.

These authentic Neapolitan rituals and rites of the sacred celebration of pizza are unheard of outside the confines of Naples, unknown to customers of those common eateries in the north where the name "pizza" may bring to mind a soggy, wobbly dough, soaked in oil.

What an authentic Neapolitan or Roman connoisseur calls pizza is a fine work of art, precise and dry, not oily, with a golden center and scorched edges, covered with a light layer of sauce *sub conditione* (subject to particular condition, not improvised). Neapolitan pizza was designated as a Traditional Specialty Guaranteed in the *Gazzetta Ufficiale* of Monday, May 24, 2004. Three full pages are devoted to the production and presentation of this dish, and all the steps that must be taken to prepare it are described and regulated.

In June 1999, the administrative body of Brussels that regulates the daily life of the countries of the European Union attempted to limit the temperature of wood-burning pizza ovens by law, restricting it to 250 degrees C. This triggered such a revolt in Italy that the Belgians had to back off and remove the proposed bill from the agenda. Today wood-burning ovens, in which the temperature can and must reach nearly 500 degrees C, are once again permitted. Then, and only then, does the characteristic smoky flavor develop that distinguishes real, authentic pizza from imposters.

Sicily

The ancients considered Sicily the birthplace of gastronomy. The Athenians used Sicilian cookbooks. Plato, speaking through Socrates' voice in his *Gorgias*, recalls a certain Mithaecus "who wrote about Sicilian cuisine."

The works of another Sicilian writer-gastronome, Archestratus of Syracuse, have also come down to us in the compilation of Athenaeus (third century A.D.). This sublime master was not fond of excessive condiments and wanted to create an impeccable cuisine, without superfluous substances, without unwarranted fats and sauces:

> *Inopportune and excessive*
> *by far for me are the other additions*
> *of too much cheese, oil and grease,*
> *as if preparing a meal for cats.*

The recipe in his *Gastronomy* for Sicilian tuna (the fish locally known as *amia*) is elegant and essential:

> *. . . wrap it in fig-leaves*
> *with a very little marjoram. No cheese,*

no nonsense! Just place it
tenderly in fig-leaves
and tie them on top with a string;
then push it under hot ashes,
thinking wisely of the time
when it is done,
and don't burn it![1]

Sicily is an island of contrasts, of sumptuousness and poverty, a crossroads of cultures. Here, everything is carried to excess: the sunlight, unbearable (for a foreigner)
without dark glasses; the blue of sky and sea; the green of cultivated estates; the fra-
grances. Here the immediacy and sensuality of life is almost too intense to take in all
at once; Sicily must often be experienced through recollection or from a distance. It is

saturated with the past, a past that imbues the warm flesh of the present. In Agrigento, in the Valley of the Temples, we can spot a shepherd leading his sheep through the Paleochristian necropolis. Lambs fall into tombs hidden by shrubs and the shepherd pulls them out, catching them with the crook of his staff. The staff is a genuine pastoral crozier with a hooked end, just like a bishop's (the shepherd of Christianity). The sky is blue-green, and the background is formed of Greek columns.

Appetizing images of food appear both in daily life and in literature. Just think of *Il Gattopardo* (*The Leopard*) by Giuseppe Tomasi di Lampedusa, or the novels of Andrea Camilleri (see "Joy"). Food metaphors are used constantly in songs, and acts associated with food enrich the local religious tradition, which is wild and riotous to the point of being paganistic. Halloween, for example, was not invented by the Americans: a thousand years before the discovery of America, the eve of November 1, All Souls' Day, was celebrated in Sicily with macabre tricks and eating *ossa dei morti*, bones of the dead, made of almond paste and sugar. On St. Martin's Day (November 11), *muffolette*, fennel rolls with ricotta, were made (and still are). For the Feast of the Immaculate Conception (December 8), special fritters called *sfinci* appear. On December 13, for the feast day of St. Lucy, the martyr's gouged-out eyes, replicated in meringue and candied pumpkin, stare out at customers from all the bakery windows. Sicilian Christmas desserts are legendary: *buccellati*, with figs, almonds, walnuts, pistachios, and grated chocolate; *mustazzoli*, cream puffs filled with fig jam; and *cucciddati*, cookies that represent the sun. Cannoli filled with ricotta cream, chocolate, and candied fruit, sold throughout Italy but created in Sicily, should be prepared and eaten only during Carnival time. On St. Joseph's Day (March 19), complex compositions of breads and desserts are displayed in homes, on altars or tables; these include *la Spera*, bread shaped like a monstrance (which symbolizes the body of Christ); *il Cuore*, a heart (with the initials of Jesus, Mary, and Joseph); and *la Croce*, a cross (symbol of the Passion). The entire arrangement is displayed as an elaborate iconostasis and also includes pastorals with the lily (symbol of purity), breads of Christ with cyclamens, breads of Mary with roses, and a number of other sweets made of sugar, marzipan, and chocolate.

At a time when the ancients still worshipped the Mother Goddess on the shores of the Mediterranean, Sicilians baked ritual votive breads in her honor. Later the coast was colonized by the Greeks. The female cults gave way to Dionysian cults, and wine, wheat bread, and cheese became fully integrated into Sicily's rituals and daily life. The Romans, the new conquerors, raised geese there, saviors of the Roman state, and taught the local inhabitants how to cook them for festive banquets as well.

After the Romans, Sicily was dominated by the Byzantines, who spread the custom of cooking complicated stuffed and sweet-and-sour dishes. The Arabs (from the ninth to the eleventh centuries) were responsible for a true revolution both in everyday life, as well as in the island's food industry. With the Arab conquest, apricots, sugar, citrus fruits, melons, rice, saffron, sultanas, nutmeg, cloves, pepper, cinnamon, fragrant jasmine, figs, and carob—all mainstays of today's cuisine—became part of the islanders' lives.

The conquerors from the north—the Normans and Swabians—joined forces with the brilliant Sicilian cooks to create the best meat recipes. The Spanish enriched the island's cuisine, first with a passion for flamboyant color and aesthetics and second with everything they were able to bring from the New World. The Spanish brought cocoa, corn, turkeys, and tomatoes to Sicily. Here and there, the legacy of cooks in the service of the French royal house can also be found, as the Bourbons ruled Sicily in the eighteenth and nineteenth centuries. The French passed on to Sicilians a passion for onions. They also introduced an exuberant, sumptuous cuisine, whose tradition has remained alive, uncontaminated by simpler popular customs. Even today, restaurants in Sicily seem almost Parisian. They are luxurious and exclusive, far from the universally Italian type of simple trattoria, and they love to develop menus in accordance with elitist experimental cuisine.

Nevertheless, an exclusive restaurant on a Sicilian street is surrounded by a sea of stalls and itinerant vendors, there for the joy of a crowd that eats all day long. Street food has some wonderful advantages: unlike restaurants, it offers affordable prices, it does not require too much time, and it is available at any time of the day or night. *Polipari*, boiled octopus vendors, abound on Palermo's seaside promenade. Also typical of the city are the *panellari*, purveyors of bread and *panelle*, thin fried fritters made of chickpea flour, traditionally accompanied by bread. Everywhere you go there are *friggitorie*, or fried food shops. In Messina *focaccerie*, focaccia shops, are popular. In Catania, you encounter vendors of flatbreads on every corner: these *schiacciate* may be filled with cheese, anchovies, onions, and tomatoes (the most common Sicilian version) or with black olives, Tuma cheese, and cauliflower (the local variant). In Syracuse and Ragusa these stuffed focaccias are called *scacce* and they can be sweet as well, in which case the filling consists of ricotta and coffee cream.

In the farmer's markets Piscaria and Fera 'o Luni in Catania, you wonder how nature can generate such an improbable palette of colors. And you wonder if the vibrant color of the local vegetables might be due to Etna's lava, to the particular mineral substances dissolved in the soil. In a quick trip through the market, you can buy fish and sardine patties with onions, soft crustless bread, parsley, and caciocavallo cheese, floured and fried in hot oil (sardines *beccafico*-style). In the port of Catania, the *friggitoria* Stella has an old-fashioned, unpretentious look, with humble white tiles on the walls. Everything that is sold here is eaten without silverware: crispy fritters with fresh ricotta (*sfinci*), sweet rolls with chocolate and cream (*iris*), rice balls (*arancini*). They also cook veal innards (namely, heart, liver, lungs, kidneys, trachea—*caldume*, or *quadumi* in dialect) at the port and sell pork jelly with lemon (*zuzo*).

Palermo, like Catania, is a paradise for street food. The traditions of the Arabic market are still alive here. At the market and in the streets of Palermo, flat fritters of chickpea flour (*ciciri*) are fried in hot oil, then placed between thin slices of bread. Starting with breakfast in the morning, you can buy the famous *sfincione*, a spicy pizza, spread with anchovies, onion, black olives, and cheese. Later, toward afternoon, *stiggiole* begin to be sold: intestines speared on a stick and cooked on the grill. The same stalls usually offer *frittole*, meatballs made with boiled, seasoned pork rind, sprinkled with lemon juice and wrapped in waxed paper. Spleen sandwich (*panino con la milza*) is a speciality of Palermo that can be found at any time of the day or night. A *focaccina* is called "pure" or "virginal" (*schietta*) if it is seasoned with lemon, and "married" (*maritata*) if it is sprinkled with cheese.

Not to be missed, too, are the wonderful *benedettini* (benedictines), fried rice fingers with honey and sugar. As is evident from its name, this sweet, like so many other recipes that have become a part of life for all laymen in Sicily, was introduced by the Benedictine monks. The crowds along the street eat their fried food in waxed paper, while a select few enjoy foods served on precious porcelain plates and white tablecloths. How different the rich Sicilian cuisine is from the rest of Italy's democratic diet! It is a cuisine of aristocratic families, of abbots and abbesses. In Sicily the second-born, deprived of an inheritance according to the laws of primogeniture, took religious vows, but did not completely renounce life's pleasures as a result of this. Life smiled even more amiably on these younger sons and daughters, relieving them of concerns, ensuring their freedom and leisure, and also ridding them of hassles related to the upkeep of the family estates.

A tradition of sumptuous cuisine was thus developed in the abbeys and monasteries. Nothing could equal the lavishness of the Sicilian Benedictine monasteries. They were the world's richest. The Abbey of San Nicola in Catania was the most important Benedictine monastery in the world after that of Montserrat in Spain.

The Benedictine monks perfected the macaroni timbale described in *Il Gattopardo* by Giuseppe Tomasi di Lampedusa, replete with veal, prosciutto, chicken gizzards, vegetables, and hard-boiled eggs, in the spirit of the opulent table of ancient Rome. The monks were also the first to make *arancini*, the rice balls that are famous today as a specialty of papal gastronomy, both here and in Rome. Another creation that can be traced back to the monks is that of the breaded, fried olives with a complex stuffing that later, after being made famous by the monasteries in the Marches, entered the encyclopedias as a specialty of Ascoli (*olive ascolane*). The monks also created stuffed cannelloni in sauce, arranged in a baking dish and baked in the oven under a thick layer of béchamel.

How much leisure they must have had to come up with such refinements! Naturally, it was the chief cooks of the monasteries who had the most free time to engage in these activities. They viewed culinary experimentation as a path to holiness. It was these devout God-seekers who created such wonders as Sicilian *cassata*, filled with candied fruits, whipped ricotta, and vanilla mousse.

Cassata was born in Palermo in the eleventh century, and its recipe was improved until it reached its current state of perfection, before the end of the nineteenth century. The history of *cassata* developed alongside Palermo's. On June 14 of the year 827, the Arabs landed in Mazara del Vallo and occupied Sicily, proclaiming the emir's residence, Palermo, a free port: troops returning from military campaigns could enjoy a rest there, and a moratorium on the Koran's rules was proclaimed. In Palermo, soldiers were allowed to savor in advance the delights promised by Mohammed to those valiant warriors who fell in battle. Alcoholic beverages were permitted and, to distill them, the Arabs themselves brought special vessels called alembics. Vendors of sweets abounded, and tents with belly dancers from the Orient enticed passersby. The new Arab delicacies—citrus fruits and sugar—were eaten more in Palermo than in any other Saracen colony in Sicily.

When the Normans invaded Sicily in 1060 and entered Palermo, a melting pot of very different cultures created a felicitous cultural stew, reflected in the culinary sphere as well. Thus an insanely caloric Easter dessert appeared to commemorate the victory of the Christians over the Arabs: the *cassata* (from the Arab *quas-at*, cauldron), whose recipe was tested and perfected by Norman nuns under the guidance of the noblewoman Eloisia Martorana. It is made of almond paste, sheep's milk ricotta, and candied fruit; decorated with cannoli, colorful wafer florets, and silvery confetti; topped with sugar frosting; and given sugar trim on the sides.

Cannoli had a life of their own for centuries before they were used to decorate the *cassata*. Cicero had already thought to praise them when he was quaestor in Sicily: *Tubus farinarius, dulcissimo edulio ex lacte factus*, that is, "A pastry tube, a very sweet edible, made with milk."

Though *cassata* was conceived as a ricotta dessert for Easter, its appearance is not at all devout, but rather full of repressed eroticism, which is not surprising given the cloistered environment in which it was created (see "Eros").

In the sixteenth century, the Spanish introduced chocolate and sponge cake to Sicily. In the nineteenth century, it became fashionable to decorate the *cassata* with candied fruit, soaked in thick syrup for exactly forty days, in accordance with religious symbolism: that is, for the entire duration of Lent. These fruits tinted the surface of the *cassata* with vibrant colors that stood out against the whipped cream background. Subsequently, *cassata*'s distinction spread throughout the world—thanks in part to the long journeys of Italian emigrants.

In his very interesting article "Marilyn Monroe e la cassata siciliana," Roberto Scarpinato, magistrate and deputy prosecutor (Anti-Mafia Special Directorate) at the Public Prosecutor's Office of the Republic of Palermo, describes the complex implications of *cassata* in the context of the Sicilian world, particularly against the backdrop of the mafia and its complicated supremacy struggles and power games.

Just as the thin wafer of the Host contains the bimillenary history of Western Christianity, so the *cassata* encompasses the entire history of Sicily, from the "Paleolithic" recipe, through its Greek, Arabic, Norman, and Spanish reincarnations, until the present-day figure of the "poor *cassata* . . . it, too, brutalized by the dark malevolence of power":

> When we talk about power in Sicily, we cannot fail to mention the role of *cassata* in the mafia world . . . At the end of the meal it, the *cassata*, arrives at the table greeted by cries of wonder: I'll leave it to you to imagine how magnificent mafia *cassata* is. Once the *cassata* has been savored, the unsuspecting designated victim is surrounded by friends who, acting affectionately, without rancor, nothing personal for heaven's sake, choke off the last mouthful in his throat by tightening the noose around his neck.[2]

The same Sicilian pastry chefs made another treat famous: marzipan. The art of shaping figurines of almond paste was also brought to Sicily by the Arabs. The almond paste itself may well have been made elsewhere, but to make it suitably moldable, orange flower water must be added. Without it, nothing can be produced. And orange trees bloom in Sicily.

After properly distilling the orange flower water, the almonds are crushed in a mortar and sugar is added to the mixture. One must work quickly, or the paste hardens and crumbles. The Benedictine nuns of the convent of Martorana, in the best traditions of Sicilian "religious pastry making," began shaping figurines of little angels and the pierced heart of Our Lady of Sorrows, and coloring them with extracts of roses, saffron, and pistachios. Some works assumed an inexplicably profane aspect, for example, girl's breasts crowned with cherries, perhaps inspired by the martyrdom of St. Agatha of Catania.

The art of marzipan figurines conquered the hearts not only of the sisters of Martorana, but of all the wizards of the local cuisine. It reached extraordinary heights during the Baroque era, which is not surprising, since it is founded on the same stunning deception that informed the Baroque aesthetic. Marzipan fruits are sold throughout Italy today, made so skillfully that it is impossible to distinguish them from the real thing. Contests are held in Sicily to crown the most skilled marzipan creator, such as the competition that takes place in Palermo on January 20, St. Sebastian's day. Who will mold an edible saint, pierced by arrows? And the most inviting roast goose?

In Bourbon times landed property in Sicily was represented by enormous estates, or latifundia, belonging to the king's barons: a system inherited from Norman feudal times. Such huge estates, of course, meant large fields of wheat to cultivate, and therein lies the uniqueness of Sicilian agriculture compared to that of other regions. In the Apennine Peninsula, areas where wheat could be successfully grown were few. Since it offered this possibility, Sicily made up for Italy's acute shortage of wheat and enjoyed the security of a monopoly.

Over the centuries, arable lands in Sicily increased, at the cost of atrocious deforestation. Given the totally agricultural nature of the island's economy, the owner of a large latifundium not only prospered, but was rich as Croesus.

In no other region in Europe were aristocratic origins so highly esteemed. The barons in Sicily enjoyed an authority that exceeded that of the *padrini* (godfathers). The jury is still out as to who were more respected by the island's inhabitants: the nobility or the mafia. In the aforementioned article "Marilyn Monroe e la cassata siciliana," the prosecutor Roberto Scarpinato provides a lapidary assessment of Sicilian society:

> A society, today as yesterday, based on the cornerstone of the patron-client relationship, in which the culture of rights remains elitist and fragile with respect to the hegemonic one of *"Baciamo le mani"* [we kiss your hands], of the clan, of the tribe, of submission to the powerful who are asked for favors and protection in exchange for selling or relinquishing one's own rights as a citizen.[3]

Scarpinato's characterization helps us understand the many nuances of the Sicilian tales that the whole world has come to know through literature and film. This article about Sicilian desserts, written by a prosecutor, provides us with valuable information on the cultural and political panorama of the island's life—much more so than *The Mafia Cookbook* by Joe Cipolla, who was a cook for three generations of mafia bosses. First, because Cipolla talks mainly about the American mafia, and second, because his book is written in a jocular, anecdotal vein, with recipes such as chicken Valachi (the reference is to Joseph Valachi, an early mafia informant), pigeons *alla lupara* (shotgun-style), and *caponata* Al Capone.

Whatever the case, Sicilian nobles enjoyed and still enjoy enormous economic privileges. In the first place, they have always had the opportunity to produce and sell oranges, wheat, and almonds in huge, industrial quantities. Indeed Sicily, at one time so rich in wheat as to merit the appellation "granary of Italy," naturally became an area of great pasta and couscous consumption (around Marsala and Trapani). The local wheat, of excellent quality, proved ideal for producing the couscous introduced by the Arabs. Here it is cooked and served primarily with fish (another region that counts couscous among its typical products is Sardinia, where it is eaten not so much with fish as with meat sauces and vegetable *ragùs*).

In the center of Sicily, prickly pears (*fichi d'India*) are often eaten. The name was given to this cactus when it was introduced in Sicily because of the common confusion of the Indies with the Americas. In addition to offering such sweet fruit, prickly pear plants are used to surround houses with spiked living fences. Moreover, cochineal insects (*Coccus cacti*), who are important for the production of scarlet dye, breed on this plant. And finally, *mostarda*, an excellent dish with cooked wine, prickly pears, and mustard, is popular.

In the province of Agrigento the almond tree is prevalent. During the period when the almond trees bloom, around New Year's Day, the entire southern part of Sicily appears to be covered with white lace and an unforgettable fragrance. Almond milk is served in bars and cafés just as cappuccino is served in the north, or mixed with coffee instead of cow's milk.

Sicily is bathed by three different seas, and fish of three different provenances are consequently found in its markets. In the Ionian Sea, swordfish is caught. On the north shore, along the ancient coast of the Cyclops, grouper, sawfish, white bream, a special variety of mackerel, and albacore tuna are found. On the south coast snapper (dentex) is caught, and seasoned with mayonnaise made with Agrigento oranges. In the bay of Syracuse and in the waters of the Egadi Islands, particularly in the Bay of Favignana, the *mattanza* (mass killing) of three-meter-long tuna is celebrated, unchanged since the time of the *Odyssey*. The rituals of this harpoon fishing recall those of Calabria and Sardinia, and they, too, date back to Byzantine times. After harpooning the fish, fishermen, in Sicily as in Calabria, shout incantations in Greek: echoes of a Byzantine ritual. These cries, incomprehensible to the local peoples, as well as the practice of harpoon fishing itself, were imported from Byzantium. The Byzantines also happily ate tuna from the Black Sea and Spanish tuna. Euthydemus, the Greek author of a treatise on salted meats and vegetables, wrote:

> The *thymnia* or female tuna is found in Byzantium in particular. Take the tail, cut it in pieces and roast it until thoroughly done. Sprinkle it with nothing but salt, moisten it with oil, and soak it in a strong brine. If after that you wish to eat it without a sauce, it is an excellent dish which would give the gods an appetite, but if you serve it moistened with vinegar you take away all its merits . . . Byzantium is the mother of salted tuna, of mackerel which is a bottom dweller, and of angelfish, which is very nourishing, but . . . the little town of Patio is the respectable nurse of *cogoils* [large mackerel or hake]. The merchants of the Abruzzi, of Campania, and of the good city of Tarentum go to Cadiz for marinated *orcin*, stored in large jars in triangular pieces. A chunk of tuna from Sicily that is to be salted in a jar makes me scorn *coracin* that is sought far off in the Pont and those who praise it highly.[4]

But the Byzantines were simply crazy about Sicilian tuna, so much so that they bought up almost all the local catch, which they then preserved. Sicilian fishermen do battle with the tuna accompanied by the chanting of ancient songs, the *tonnarotti*, that sound cruel and solemn. According to Palermo's recipe, the tuna meat is quickly grilled after being marinated in wine, olive oil, vinegar, and rosemary. In addition, tuna can be browned in a pan with tomato and basil (marinara-style).

The abdomen of the female is filled with *bottarga*, roe, a favorite ingredient in Italian cuisine. The *bottarga* is eaten with oil, garlic, and parsley, and is used to prepare spaghetti sauces. The eyes of the tuna (*occhi rassi*) are salted separately in small casks with red pepper and dill. Much prized is the *ventresca*, or belly (the muscle of the ventral part of the tuna), what the ancient Greek gourmands called the hypogastrium. The roasted testicles and gonads (*lattume*) of the tuna are also eaten. The stomach and esophagus are washed, salted, and served with boiled potatoes. According to the fishermen, the tastiest part of the tuna is the heart: they brown it lightly salted, after letting it rest two or three days. Focaccias are mixed with the tuna's blood (they are well-known in Sardinia also, where they are called *fugasse*: a rare, unusual food). From the sun-dried tuna fillet *musciame*, or *musciuma*, or *mosciame*, is produced, which, softened with oil and lemon, is used as a dressing for salads. It is also enjoyed sliced on bread, adding arugula and sliced tomato. Finally, not even the tuna's head is wasted: ground up, it is used as fertilizer. It is not unusual to encounter a big tuna bone in a garden. This is not surprising: since ancient times, tuna has everywhere been called the "sea pig," because every part of its body is processed and, as with the pig, no part of the tuna is discarded.

Tuna meat is cubed and preserved in oil for industrial production. First the tuna are bled until they become pale and dry: that way, the canned food takes on an ascetic quality and stops resembling the fish itself. From a psychological point of view, it is easier to consume a food like this rather than blood-red flesh. As a result, canned tuna is very popular. Those who operate fine restaurants challenge its popularity:

> The tuna that we eat by opening a can has nothing in common with the red-blooded tuna of the Mediterranean. And this, too, occurs "by law." A 1981 decree of the President of the Republic also authorizes using similar fish as tuna: yellowfin tuna, bonito, mackerel, little tuna, skipjack . . . The real tuna of our seas is firm and dark, and if you can break it with a breadstick there is really something wrong. But advertising has taught us otherwise.[5]

In addition to growing grains and fruit and fishing, the Sicilian economy, like that of Puglia and Romagna, depends largely on salt harvesting. Sicilian salt began to be harvested at the dawn of history. The Phoenicians, Greeks, and Romans imported salt from Trapani. Later the trading of Sicilian salt passed into the hands of the Arabs, and around the same time the Normans became interested in Sicilian salt for the purpose of exporting it to the other end of the world. The Sicilian salt brought by the Normans was used in Brittany, in England, and in the countries of the Hanseatic League. The Norwegians sprinkled Sicilian salt on cod and herring, which were then transported from the Lofoten Islands to Liguria, and from there to the rest of Italy. The Genoese merchants had large amounts of salt sent to Genoa, and from there they transported it by land into the heart of the European continent. The salterns of Trapani assured Sicily the same prosperity that today is happily enjoyed by energy-producing nations. Only after the introduction of alternative methods of food preservation, such as freezing, lyophilization, pasteurization, and sterilization, did the exportation of Sicilian salt experience a crisis. Nonetheless, the local large crystal salt continues to be in demand, especially for cooking. As we know, in Liguria it is customary to sprinkle the surface of a local specialty such as Genoese focaccia with Sicilian salt.

In addition, Sicilian salts have different origins, and therefore different flavors. Sea salt is harvested in Trapani and Marsala (in Augusta the famous salt marshes have given way to oil industries), while rock salt is extracted from the mine in Cattolica Eraclea.

Mussolini sent intelligentsia who were hostile to his regime into confinement on the island of Lipari. During the Fascist period a unique colony was created on the island, a breeding ground for dissent and an ironic love of freedom. Today the island is one of the most popular tourist destinations: at the beginning of the summer season, in particular, vacationers can enjoy the local speciality, sea urchins, accompanied by cold white wine. Only the gonads of the urchins, the sexual glands, are eaten, and their consumption thus becomes possible only in the period in which they are mature, namely, in the spring and early summer. Just the time when flocks of writers, worn out from their exhausting work, begin thinking about their first brief summer respite. The islanders fish for, among other things, squid and needlefish, which usually live in the open sea, far from the coast. They also fish for turtles during their migrations in January and February, just when proteins are scarce in the island's natural economy. Turtles, like other sea products, are prepared in a sauce made of diluted must, with garlic, onion, parsley, capers, and almonds.

An interesting product of the islands is *cicerchia*, or chickling vetch, a legume

(*Lathyrus sativus*) now grown in only a few areas of Italy: the Marches, Tuscany, and the Aeolian Islands. The Romans also loved chickling, though it was later replaced by chickpeas. Calamint, a relative of mint, is also grown successfully on the Aeolian Islands. Along with the small local tomatoes, calamint is the main adornment for a colorful, aromatic omelet. The main crop of the Aeolian Islands is capers.

Among the dishes of Aeolian cuisine, *mustarda sicca*, or dry *mostarda*, is striking. Must and starch, walnuts, almonds, and wild fennel seeds are boiled, then sun-dried. This mustard does not resemble that sweet, spicy, rather liquid specialty of Cremona and Carpi, which in the north accompanies *bollito* (boiled meats). In Lipari boiled meat is not imaginable: it would be unthinkable given the southern climate. Consequently, the product that here assumes the fine name of *mostarda* is a completely different gastronomic specialty: a dry sweet cut into cubes.

A local crop that is as rare as it is important is the delectable, tasty pistachio. This is the "Bronte red" variety, ruby red on the outside and emerald green on the inside. An ice cream of incomparable taste is made from the ground pistachios, mixing them with cream, warm milk, sugar, and starch. But pistachios are not only suitable for dessert: a fantastic, typically Sicilian dish is penne pasta with cream of pistachio (onion, garlic, olive oil, pancetta, meat broth, ground pistachios, brandy, cream, salt, and pepper).

The pistachios in Bronte grow directly on the volcanic lava, alongside the terebinth, a similar plant (*scornabecco*, or turpentine tree, *Pistacia terebinthus*) from which precious resins used in folk medicine are gathered. Pistachios produce fruit in alternate years, lately in odd years in Sicily. Growing pistachios here is difficult because of the inaccessible terrain on which they are planted. As a result Italian pistachios are much more expensive than those from Iran or Turkey. Poor profitability might have led to the complete disappearance of the pistachio in Sicily; the fact that this has not happened, at least for now, is thanks only to the support of the European Union, the Ministry of Agriculture and Forestry Policies, and some private devotées. The fate of Sicilian pistachios is in their hands, and if the market survives, it will be due to Slow Food's protection (see "Slow Food").

Another famous product typical of the islands of this region, more universally sought-after than pistachios, is capers. The best ones, the largest and juiciest, grow on the island of Pantelleria, located a short distance from Africa. These same capers from Pantelleria were praised by Pliny the Elder in his *Natural History*. In 1560, Domenico Romoli, known by the nickname of Panonto, in his celebrated cooking treatise *La sin-*

golare dottrina (The singular doctrine), extols the healing virtues of capers, affirming that "those who eat them will have no spleen or liver pain," and adds that capers have an aphrodisiac effect.

Ice cream is an authentic Sicilian specialty. Here it is said that Sicilians were the first in Italy to learn of it, thanks to their Arab invaders. From here it was transported to Tuscany, and then circulated throughout the world. There is another theory, however: Catherine de' Medici, arriving in Paris in 1533 as the fourteen-year-old wife of Henri d'Orléans (subsequently king of France under the name Henri II), brought along her personal designer and architect, Bernardo Buontalenti, whose hobby was inventing desserts. Ice cream was supposedly one of his inventions.

The Sicilians, of course, insist on their primacy, and extensive research would be required to verify it. One thing is indisputable: the prototype for ice cream was sherbet or sorbet, the Sicilian *sorbetto* (from the Arabic *shar'bet*). Sorbets were not complicated to prepare: they were made with fruit juice mixed with snow from the mountains. The main problem, in ancient times, was to find the chief ingredient. Where to find ice at the time of the Renaissance? The Sicilians resorted to Etna. At the end of winter, they had huge balls of snow rolled down from the top of Mt. Etna to underground caves, where the layers of snow were alternated with layers of felt so that they would melt more slowly and would not solidify into blocks of ice. Thanks to this stratagem, the Sicilians sold packaged snow to all the cities of Italy during the summer and even exported it abroad, though not very far: to Malta.

Wine must, wine, and honey were added to the sorbet. This treat could be kept up to two days in caves or in wells. In the seventeenth century sorbet began to be enriched with butter and cream, and the result was a new dessert, at that time called *parfait*: perfect. If a little skimmed milk was added instead, the mixture was called *mantecato*, creamed or thickened. This time, too, it was the cooks in the monasteries who engaged in these experiments. By now it was no longer sorbet, but the end result we know well. Today ice cream is eaten on all continents. From Sicily gelato was very quickly brought to Paris. In 1686, the Sicilian pastry chef Francesco Procopio dei Coltelli opened a famous café-gelateria, Le Procope, in the Latin Quarter of Paris (St. Germain); it still exists today, and Benjamin Franklin was known to have frequented the prodigious locale.

It is easy to believe that these refreshing delights really were invented in Sicily. The plentiful snow, cheaply obtainable, allowed the Sicilians to initiate the production of a continuous stream of ice cream and other ice-based desserts. But the history of ice cream was to take an unpredictable turn from there. Starting in the nineteenth century, and particularly in the twentieth, the production of refreshing beverages and desserts on an industrial basis shifted to small artisanal concerns in the Veneto region. In that period an accelerated process of industrialization was under way in Italy, which threw the old workshops of mechanics and metalworkers into crisis. But it's no accident that Italians are famous for the art of coping (*arrangiarsi*) and for their flexibility, even when it comes to creating work. With impressive speed, alternative activities were organized in machine shops and forges: mini-units for the production of gelato, made mostly of cream. Having mastered the art of itinerant ice cream making and created convenient icebox-pushcarts, Venetian mechanics set out each summer to look for work, transforming themselves into strolling ice cream vendors and loudly hawking their goods on Italy's beaches and promenades. By the beginning of the twentieth century, 80 percent of the itinerant ice cream trade was in Venetian hands. In many places, however, the retail sale of ice cream and ice on the streets was prohibited, for hygenic reasons. So then the Venetian mechanics opened *gelaterie*, small ice cream shops and kiosks: not surprisingly, reminders of the lagoon city are still present today in the names of many ice cream shops found throughout Italy's villages and beaches: Café Venezia, Pasticceria Rialto, Bar San Marco.

Meanwhile, Sicilian confectioners had not stopped experimenting with fruit sorbets. After several centuries and much trial and error, Sicily now offers the world frozen desserts that are extraordinarily delicious and varied. It is generally thought that granitas are made with crushed ice; this is true in all of Italy except Sicily, where granitas are made by a unique process that never allows the mixture to become ice, but keeps it creamy and semi-liquid thanks to the high sugar content. Granita is often served with whipped cream or brioches. A specialty of Messina is mulberry granita. Once picked from the tree, the mulberry fruit can be kept for only a few hours, after which it becomes unfit to eat. But whipped with ice it keeps in the refrigerator until the end of the day, sometimes more than twenty-four hours. There is also almond *gremolata*, a frozen almond cream with crushed cookies. Also very popular among tourists are *spumone* or *spuma*: ice cream whipped with *crema cotta*, or "cooked cream," a kind of custard.

Various cities have different flavors of ice cream: for example, jasmine ice cream is popular in Trapani. Not infrequently in Sicily, and also in Calabria, ice cream is eaten for breakfast: at the bar one buys a brioche filled with ice cream, or with lemon *gremolata* (a granular water ice made from sweetened fruit syrup), or with almond *spuma*. A breakfast so refreshing, and at the same time so caloric, can provide a reserve of energy that lasts throughout the entire workday.

Antipasti *Mustica* (baby anchovies in oil). *Arancini*, rice balls, filled with cheese and *ragù*, peas, prosciutto, and sauce. *Caponata*: stewed vegetables in a pan, prepared separately and mixed at the table with olives, anchovies, and capers before serving. *Maccu*: purée of fava beans with wild fennel (a similar purée is known in Calabria, where it is called *macco*).

Salad of oranges with oil, salt, and pepper. It makes a striking side dish. Sicilian oranges are especially prized in Italy. It is said that the oranges that grow near Etna—Tarocco oranges, with the reddish, freckled rind and scarlet pulp—absorb micronutrients from the soil surrounding the volcano, which are rarely encountered in nature and which protect against cancer. Though we don't know how much factual basis there is for this idea, many believe it.

First Courses Pasta with *sparaconci* (wild asparagus). Nine specialties for the nine provinces of Sicily: macaroni with red sauce and eggplant, Agrigento; *cavatieddi* (gnocchi with pork sauce), Caltanissetta; spaghetti Trapanese-style, Trapani; small rigatoni with *maccu*, Ragusa; fried pasta Syracuse-style, Syracuse; pasta Norma, in honor of Vincenzo Bellini's opera, with fried eggplant cubes, tomato, and salted ricotta, Catania; *frascatula* (durum wheat polenta) with zucchini and potatoes, Enna; *quadrucci* with swordfish sauce, Messina. In Palermo *pasta con le sarde* (pasta with sardines) is made, bucatini served with sardines, anise, raisins, pine nuts, and saffron.

Also popular in Sicily is pasta with *muddica*, toasted crustless soft bread, flavored with anchovies mixed with oil, tomatoes, and parsley.

Second Courses Fish. *Pescestocco alla ghiotta messinese*, Messina-style stockfish in a pan.

Desserts Typical Sicilian cookies: *cuddureddi chini* (with hazelnuts and honey), *mastrazzola* (with honey), almond cookies, orange and lemon cookies. Cannoli and ricotta cakes, *sciauni* (with ricotta), *chiacchiere* (sweet fritters), *mastrazzoli* with honey, peach desserts. Almond milk, frappès, granitas, mulberry granita and nougat ice cream, mousses, and *gremolate*.

TYPICAL PRODUCTS OF SICILY

Preserved fish: swordfish from the Strait of Messina, and tuna.

Ragusa cheese shaped like a parallelepiped.

Red Tarocco oranges. Grapes, prickly pear, Bronte pistachios, sweet Zibibbo grapes. Capers from Pantelleria. Watermelons from Ragusa. Carob, found mainly in Rosolini. The seeds of the carob (*keratia* in Greek), which have the shape of a jewel, are always identical and always perfect, to the extent that they were used as weights in goldsmiths' scales, providing the etymological origin of the term "carat." There is a popular belief that treasures lie buried under the carob roots.

Almond paste. Mafalda bread, sprinkled with sesame seeds. Soft *torroni* (nougat) of almonds and chocolate. Desserts and cookies intended for religious feasts. Almond milk in cartons. Sicilian *cassata*.

TYPICAL BEVERAGE

Marsala, a sweet wine "discovered" by the English merchant John Woodhouse in 1773, as a valid alternative to Madeira or sherry.

TOTALITARIANISM

talian Fascism, which rose to power in 1922, used the accessible language of the culinary code to speak to the people. As we have seen, in order to intimidate them, Fascists told the Italians that the enemy ate five times a day (in fact, the British have four meals: breakfast, lunch, tea, and supper or dinner). Italians, always moderate and used to eating two or at most three times a day, were left to infer from the frequency of these meals just how powerful their enemy was. During the same period, the Fascists made dissidents drink castor oil, purportedly to strengthen internal discipline. With that, a sacred process of physiological and social life (the ingestion of food) was symbolically transformed into an execration, and digestion into torture.

The authorities, intoxicated by their own brute force, attacked the primary symbol of the Italian culinary code: pasta. The Futurist Filippo Tommaso Marinetti, ideologue of the regime, took up a revolver and shot into a plate of spaghetti carbonara.

An actual campaign for the establishment of an avant-garde table, with theories and concrete proposals, only began on December 28, 1930, however, when Marinetti published the "Manifesto della cucina futurista" in the *Gazzetta del Popolo* of Turin, subsequently reprinted the following January in Umberto Notari's *Cucina italiana* (Italian cooking).

Publication of the policy statement had been anticipated on November 15, 1930, with an evening at the restaurant Penna d'Oca in Milan, a meeting place for the most

famous and successful Lombard journalists of that time. On that occasion the author from Alexandria, Egypt, had issued a resounding challenge to pasta, which was described in emphatic, scornful terms as "an absurd Italian gastronomic religion": "In contrast to bread and rice, pasta is a food which is swallowed, not masticated. Such starchy food should mainly be digested in the mouth by the saliva but in this case the task of transformation is carried out by the pancreas and the liver. This leads to an interrupted equilibrium in these organs. From such disturbances derive lassitude, pessimism, nostalgic inactivity and neutralism. An invitation to chemistry . . ."[1]

Following the same impulse that led him to rail against gondolas and moonlight, Marinetti wrote:

It may be that a diet of cod, roast beef and steamed pudding is beneficial to the English, cold cuts and cheese to the Dutch and sauerkraut, smoked [salt] pork and sausage to the Germans; but pasta is not beneficial to the Italians. For example it is completely hostile to the vivacious spirit and passionate, generous, intuitive soul of the Neapolitans. If these people have been heroic fighters, inspired artists, awe-inspiring orators, shrewd lawyers, tenacious farmers it was in spite of their voluminous daily plate of pasta. When they eat it they develop that typical ironic and sentimental scepticism which can often cut short their enthusiasm.[2]

Rice was ultimately saved from the worldwide conflagration started by the Futurists: the national associations of rice producers were among the main supporters of the Fascist revolution.

What aroused the greatest interest in the Futurist manifesto, however, was the crusade against spaghetti, which was given ample and controversial coverage in the press. *La cucina italiana* started an opinion poll welcoming interventions by exponents of the culture and distinguished physicians of the time. Other viewpoints found a forum in the *Giornale della Domenica* of Rome, the *Gazzetta del Popolo* of Turin, the *Secolo XIX* of Genoa and even *The New York Times* and the *Chicago Tribune*, while some humorous newspapers like the *Guerin Meschino* and the *Marc' Aurelio* had a great time with cartoons and jokes . . . Not everyone was in agreement about banning "a dish which Italy could boast of throughout the world." The poet Farfa, for example, described ravioli as "love letters in a romantic envelope," while Futurists of Liguria, in the magazine *Oggi e Domani* (in the first issue of 1931), wrote a letter of entreaty to Marinetti to at least spare *trenette al pesto* in his anti-pasta crusade. The women of Aquila emerged from their usual apathy to sign a solemn petition in favor of pasta, and popular marches took place in Naples in defense of vermicelli, the dish loved by Pulcinella.[3]

It should be said that most people never managed to fully accept the polemical statements of the Futurists. Judging by some of their rhymes, it seems that propaganda was one thing, but deep inside even the proponents of these dictums adored pasta. Photomontages appeared in many of the tabloids in which the father of Futurism was immortalized as busily gobbling down spaghetti. The caption of a humorous cartoon of the 1930s reads:

> Marinetti says "Basta,
> enough, a ban on pasta."

Then we discover Marinetti
devouring spaghetti.

Behind the desire to subvert tradition and wean Italians from pasta (an impossible, suicidal plan) lay the brutal arrogance of power, as well as a certain political logic of the cult of personality associated with Mussolini. From a political-economic point of view, Italy stood to benefit if its population stopped preferring pasta over bread. The fact is that pasta is made exclusively with durum wheat, which is not produced in sufficient quantities in Italy and must therefore be imported from other countries, including America. Fascism, which had destroyed diplomatic relations with foreign countries and consequently cut off the importation of durum wheat for reasons of principle, reduced Italy to starvation. Even soft wheat began to be in short supply. Given the situation, the wheat that came in on American ships after 1945 became the main subject of the ideological debate among the political parties, in what had by then become the Cold War (see "The Later Gifts from America").

In the language of the food code, Mussolini's personality does not sound very attractive. Il Duce, as befitting a dictator (Hitler and Stalin were exactly the same), did not have a big appetite. He ate negligently, drank three liters of milk per day, and munched on fruit in between. It is not surprising that he suffered from stomach problems all his life. His regime was described as "a dictatorship of ricotta." And who coined this expression? The chief of Mussolini's police force himself, Guido Leto, who was dissatisfied with Il Duce's soft character, the weakness of the dictatorship, and, perhaps, its break with authentic Italian spirit: Italian food culture scorns sour dairy products such as fresh ricotta.

In many respects, the Fascist party inherited the ideas and aesthetics of the Futurists. The Futurists were interested in the industrialization of the country, while nature and the countryside were hugely alien to them. One of Italy's worthiest assets was deemed extraneous: the expanse of cultivated land (*ager*) along with all the people who live and work on it, contemplate it, dignify it, and enjoy it.

Like other regimes committed to industrialization, Fascism also began to destroy the structure of traditional family life, liberating men and in particular women from the bonds of domestic slavery:

Thanks to the achievements of the modern food industry (canned, frozen, and prepared foods), the time spent in the kitchen, the results, the very standard established by plan in accordance with models of political discourse, could be beaten, burned, overdone in the preparation of foods and meals as well . . . The housewife was no longer cooking for her husband, son, lover, whatever, but for the State, since those at the table were citizens first, and individuals second.

That is how the eminent Italian Russianist Gian Piero Piretto describes a similar transformation of daily life in the Soviet Union.[4] This transformation of society, in many cases, offered single individuals a further chance for emancipation (fortunately), but in many cases (unfortunately) it alienates the person from simple common sense.

Totalitarian powers tend to suppress even the weakest sex drive. This tendency is once again reflected in the language of the culinary code (see "Eros"). In Soviet Russia, suspecting someone of frequenting restaurants meant suggesting that the person had turned to a dissolute life. If the protagonist of a Soviet film went to a restaurant, the building manager immediately suspected he was "secretly seeing a lover." And in Ernst Lubitsch's film *Ninotchka*, an intelligent farce that pokes fun at the Soviet Union's revolutionary austerity, the heroine, played by Greta Garbo, begins to doubt the foundations of Socialism, and at the same time discovers the joys of eroticism after tasting a delicious soup in a charming French restaurant. The film's subtle irony lies in the fact that this scene takes place in a proletarian trattoria. But it is the moment of pleasure in consuming food that in itself conveys a liberated, antitotalitarian note.

Dictatorial regimes create cookbooks approved by censors, intended not for housewives, but for collective food services. The ingredients are measured by the bucketful, and the illustrations display impressive images of gigantic metal mixing machines and alembics. This is why Fascists dwelled on pasta, which is the symbol of a homey meal, easy to prepare for the family, but impossible to cook decently in bulk. Fascist propaganda demanded that people reduce their consumption of pasta and increase that of bread. To obtain the desired quantities of soft wheat (that is, wheat unsuitable for pasta, but suitable for bread), Mussolini proclaimed a new state program. According to this program, agrarian collectives were to be formed (whose model strongly resembled the Soviet *kolchoz*).

Italians were offered a grand objective: the battle over wheat. Championing the ideals of virility, autocracy, and nationalism, Il Duce had himself photographed—hairy naked chest and all—in farmyards in Littoria or Sabaudia (the names of the agricultural-industrial towns founded by him in newly reclaimed lands). In so doing he set a public example for the threshers, identifying himself with their difficult labor. Specially assigned men recorded the quantities of wheat threshed by Il Duce and news of his undertaking reached the newspapers. Meanwhile, high duties were imposed on wheat imports. The

Agricultural Ministry declared its goal of transforming Italy into a self-sufficient country in the production of wheat.

It is telling that the Italian villages did not profoundly assimilate either the Fascist ideology or its aesthetic. The new way of life had to be modeled on virgin land, which was obtained by reclaiming the marshes. When virgin lands could not be plowed because they were marshy, they were drained. The foremost objective of the regime became the development of reclamation at the state level. Mussolini had the unhealthy, malaria-infested Paludi Pontine, south of Rome, eliminated. He also undertook colossal efforts in Sardinia. Here, evidently, the native population was not considered loyal enough to be entrusted with the project of the century, so entire villages from the Veneto—which over the centuries had gathered a lot of experience in draining and restoring wetlands—were transferred to western Sardinia.

Not far from the marvelous city of Alghero in Sardinia, you can still visit one of Mussolini's collectives, Fertilia (an auspicious name). These places were irresistibly described by William Black.[5] Currently, as I had the opportunity to observe in September 2007, these sites are no longer surrounded by undulating fields of wheat or populated by dashing young Fascist countrywomen crowned with garlands of its golden ears. But in the past the *kolchoz* of this area were an oleographic illustration of the Fascist primer. Fertilia was built in an architectural style typical of totalitarianism that Black humorously describes as "a curious hybrid of St. Trinian's and a Tyrolean mental asylum."[6] Nowadays, I observed, it is quite deserted, though the center of Fertilia is still made up, as it was seventy years ago, by the massive former Casa del Fascio (the local public headquarters of the Fascist party) and two column formations with associated structures. The streets are symmetrically aligned, whereas in most Italian cities, harmony is born from asymmetry. In Fascist projects, instead, geometry reigns, strict linearity: standard houses, with enough room for families planned by the regime, seven children each; communal storehouses for the harvest. In Fertilia growers had to hand over every last ear of wheat to the agricultural colony, and the harvest was then sold by the authorities. A nearby town, outwardly identical, was called Mussolinia; after the fall of Fascism, it was renamed Arborea. As an experiment, the regime was less rigid in Mussolinia than in Fertilia, and the majority of the harvest was left to the families. As a result, there were granaries attached to the houses in Mussolinia.

The Fascist regime prescribed breeding cows for milk and butter (it was the dictatorship of ricotta, after all). But in regions where breeding was limited to flocks of sheep (for example, in Sardinia), raising cattle never caught on. Wheat did not produce good harvests everywhere, because it cannot grow under just any climatic conditions. In some areas, vegetable gardens were even planted with wheat, as required by the state, and as a result tomatoes began to be in short supply. One must admit that it took the full genius of a dictator to produce a tomato shortage in Italy! The consequences of this shortage were most unfortunate for cooking: How could one make pasta sauce?

But since Fascist authorities had declared war on pasta, no one at the state level was concerned about it. Nor were they troubled about the fact that the state's reconversion of food production was leading to tragic consequences: there was not enough food to go around. At that point the Ministry of Propaganda went into action, with the publication of this poster: a man with a napkin knotted around his neck, eating pasta, with a roast chicken, fruit, and a bottle of wine next to him, and a soldier in a khaki uniform, who approaches the glutton from behind and strangles him, saying: "The man who eats too much robs the nation."

Affluent families, many of whom secretly opposed the regime both idealistically and aesthetically, responded to the violation of the food code with provocative acts. Thanks to their money, they could buy products abroad, so dinners consisted of French Champagne, foie gras, caviar, Scotch salmon, and English whiskey. It was especially chic for these *frondeurs* (the term refers to La Fronde, a seventeenth-century French rebellion against royal authority, and has come to mean any malcontent or rebel) to invite some Fascist party leader into their ardent aristocratic society as a guest of honor. The secret agent and gastronome Federico Umberto D'Amato, in his book *Menu e dossier* (*Menu and Dossier*), describes a dinner of this kind, and records the words that the Fascist official later pronounced to justify his attendance, when the matter was discussed at a party meeting: "I accepted the invitation only to ascertain to what extent So-and-so's anti-national activity goes."[7]

After the war, the powers of the First Republic demonstrated much more psychological subtlety, accessibility of language, and mastery of the Italian food code (see "Democracy") in communicating with the masses. There were still a few notable times when communication broke off and the authorities erred by sending the wrong signal to the population. This happened in 1959, and almost led Italy to a revolution—the one that Italian Communists had unsuccessfully invoked for so long. In that year the country found itself on the brink of a popular revolt because of Health Minister Camillo Giardin. In 1959 one of the first instances of the adulteration of food products was debated in Parliament. During the debate, Minister Giardin ardently praised the progress of science and the food industry and used his eloquence and ardor to describe the bright prospects for the conquest of space: "On future space flights," he proclaimed in the hall of the Senate, man "will be scientifically nourished by his own excrement, transformed into scientifically pure foods."[8] It was not a good idea. Not at all. And the opposition took ample advantage of the minister's gaffe. The vivid line "We are a nation of fifty million aspiring space explorers"[9] was sarcastically and lengthily declined in all its inflections by the opposition's press.

Sardinia

Many tourists only visit the part of the Sardinian coast that has been paved over in the last forty years, and so they don't get much of a feel for the aroma of Sardinian cuisine. Real Sardinian food is found precisely where there are no tourists: among the local shepherds who, in the summer season, go up to the mountains to live without their family, without kitchen utensils, without shops, without a freezer, roasting the meat of suckling pigs, goats, and sheep over a fire with herbs and myrtle leaves.

The holiday roast *carraxiu*-style, a specialty invented in Villagrande in the province of Nuoro, eclipses the inventions of François Rabelais. According to the ethnographic descriptions, you take a young bull and stuff it with a kid; the kid is stuffed with a piglet, the piglet with a hare, the hare with a partridge, the partridge with a little bird. After sticking one animal inside the other, the town cobbler is called to sew up the tough hide of the young bull using thick waxed twine. In some locations in Sardinia this dish is called *malloru de su sabatteri* (cobbler's bull). Only Sardinian experts skilled at cooking meat over the fire are capable of roasting such a "nesting doll" uniformly.

Compared to this, other dishes, such as *pastu mistu*, which consists of stuffing a turkey with a chicken or a hare with a rabbit, are child's play. All these foods are

reminiscent of ritual sacrifices, of hecatombs. The local folklore has it that ritual incantations had to be pronounced when preparing them. In Lula, in the vicinity of the Franciscan monastery, the residents move to a "sacred clearing" during the feast of St. Francis in October, and in the village of Paulilatino they move to a "sacred well" for the feast of St. Christina at the end of July, spending nine days there in prayer (the novena). The buildings around a sanctuary, meant to serve as lodging during those novena periods, are called *combersia* (possibly from the Sardinian *combessa*, a lean-to shelter with a sloping roof). During those nine days, the entire village attends the solemn slaughter of animals and the preparation of traditional food. "A real hecatomb outdoors, or maybe near or within nuragic monuments, almost as if to stress the continuity with a past that is chronologically distant but very much alive in the consciousness of the islanders."[1]

Cut off from the rest of Italy for fifteen hundred years (from 1800 B.C. to 300 B.C.), the island was home to a distinct warrior civilization, which fought and traded with the Phoenicians, Etruscans, and Greeks, and left behind on Sardinian soil the stone structures known as *nuraghi*: enigmatic conical bastions. Only in the third century B.C., when Sardinia was conquered by the Romans, did it create the original culture that survives today.

The traditions in Sardinia are archaic. If you look at the natural environment—emerald sea, the streams and mountains—you think you are in a terrestrial paradise. This is Sardinia's problem. Everyone covets such a paradise, and the Sardinians have had to defend themselves against some invader or another through the ages. In addition to the more notorious groups who attacked Italy (the Phoenicians, Carthaginians, Greeks, Spaniards, Normans, and Arabs), the island was targeted by Pisa, Genoa, the Papal State, the Aragonese, the Austrians, and the Savoys as well. Add to this raids by pirates, and a scourge that marked the history of the island for centuries: kidnappings. Banditry, to a lesser extent, still survives today; to realize its importance, you need only visit the Santuario del Bandito (Shrine of the Bandit), a place of religious pilgrimage, which stands in the heart of the Sopramonte Massif, in Lula. The old Russian Brockhaus and Efron encyclopedia reads:

> The culture of the conquerors was never able to subjugate the wild, indomitable savages who lived in inaccessible gorges and caves. Even the Romans, who conquered the island in 238 [B.C.], failed to definitively break the mountaineers' resistance; in the slave market, Sardinian prisoners were the least prized because of their hardened nature, their ineptitude at forced labor, and their lack of dependability.

The Sardinians' peculiar language owes much to their surly nature, brusque and taciturn, which other Italians are unable to understand. Many of their word roots were borrowed directly from Latin, but transformed by a phonetic evolution so unusual that it is definitely impossible to grasp their meaning.

The Sardinians are stubbornly attached to their remote caves, the forests, the steep mountains in the central part of the island, the Barbagia, where, according to a curious statement by William Black, "mean-eyed, gun-toting sheep wait on every corner."[2] The attacks and enemies, in any period of time, came from the sea: it is not surprising that the Sardinians, even in times of peace, avoid the sea. The dishes most typical of Sardinia (except for lobster) do not belong to the category of seaside cuisine, but to that of the mainland. Essential to local life is *carasau* bread, also known as *carta da musica*, or music paper, which is excellent for travelers but involves a rather laborious preparation. Flour is mixed with yeast and salt; the dough rises slowly, then the sheets, inflated by warmth, are baked in the oven. Once removed from the oven and allowed to cool, the sheets are cut horizontally into two layers. One side of each disk is naturally smooth, while the other is rough and porous where it was cut. This is necessary so that the liquid condiments, olive oil and sauces, can be soaked into the bread. After cutting, the sheets are returned to the oven to bake a second time; the second baking, the *carasatura* phase, makes it crisp.

These paper-thin breads are sold in packages of twenty. Like all breads of nomadic peoples (for example, the lavash of the people of the Caucasus), they serve as both dish and napkin. They are topped with anything you want and, if sprinkled with water, the dough becomes pliable again and can be rolled up to make a stuffed roulade. *Fratau* bread is made from *carasau* bread. First it is soaked in unsalted water (or broth) for thirty seconds. Then it is placed on a hot dish, so that the sheet softens. It is covered with tomato sauce, sprinkled with grated pecorino cheese, and topped with a fresh raw egg.

Even the pasta here is unusual and terribly laborious to prepare: the wives of shepherds and sailors, left at home, once busied themselves for entire days making dry pasta. Some pasta shapes show a supreme indifference to the expenditure of working hours, such as the *filindeu* (God's threads), very fine spaghetti braided or knotted manually, one by one, to form bows. Similarly laborious is the production of another shape, the *malloreddus*, also made by hand with saffron dough, ribbed on the surface, and with an interesting curvature on the inside. The *malloreddus* easily soaks up the sauce and retains the grated cheese well. The saffron, naturally borrowed from the Arabs, was at one time prized for its antiseptic qualities and as a vitamin source.

Another nutritious product is mullet roe (*bottarga*), which is pressed into amber-colored bricks of three or four kilos, salted, and dried. It is obtained from the sea but preserves well enough to be used in the central part of the island. *Bottarga* is a product of the port of Cabras, in the middle of the western coast of Sardinia, where the sea is plentiful, teeming with fish, and particularly abounding in mullet. At Cabras there is a salt lake fed by seawater, so there are excellent salt marshes at hand. No less than 80 percent of the *bottarga* sold in Italy is produced there. *Bottarga* is eaten sliced or crumbled onto pasta. It is as rich in vitamins as old, nauseating cod liver oil, at one time the bane of every vulnerable child made to swallow this terrible substance. *Bottarga* is thankfully much tastier.

Some traditional Sardinian products are of such darkly decadent taste that even the government thought it was its duty to intervene to protect consumers. Without success, however: bans, as we know, only intensify interest. A case in point is Casu Marzu, otherwise known as Frazzigu, Becciu, Fattittu, or Gompagadu (that is, jumping cheese): the dialect forms vary depending on the location. This cheese is even more putrid than the pit cheese of Romagna. I tasted this cheese personally (though it's not allowed to be sold, it was offered to me by a local producer): it's true, as the widespread saying goes, that first you smell it with your nose, then you hear it with your ears (as the worms crawling in the cheese jump noisily onto the table), and only afterward do you taste it. Assuming, of course, that you have not lost the urge to. And assuming your finances will allow it: a small-sized one of these rotten cheeses can cost up to 150 euros at auction (furtively, since its sale is now prohibited).

The Sardinian's heart is devoted to the land, but he often works at sea.[3] Here big gray mullet are caught and cooked whole on the grill, rather than stewed or marinated, according to island tradition. Even the eighty-kilo dentex known as the *lupo marino*, or sea wolf, is cooked on the grill or over a fire. It is curious to learn that there is a stretch of coast in Sardinia, from Capo Caccia through Alghero and as far as Bosa, where lobsters are so abundant that, even in relatively recent times, people simply tired of eating them, and were content with vegetables and potatoes on holidays, to finally get a rest from the crustaceans. These lobsters are so big that they are called elephantine: *Palinurus elephas*. Today, the local population does not eat lobsters, but catches them to sell.

The stretch of coast where lobster catching is practiced is populated by Catalans. Catalonia, in fact, is a stone's throw away. Even the dialect here is Catalan, and the city of Alghero, whose current name means "place where there are many algae," was called Barceloneta ("little Barcelona") up until the sixteenth century. Therefore, the local population has a seafaring mentality, and does not cling, like the other inhabitants of the island, to a terra firma philosophy. The city of Alghero, with its ancient, winding narrow streets, was taken from Genoa by the Catalans in 1354 after a year of siege. At that time the Aragonese kings lost no time in conquering a piece of Sardinia here, a piece of Sicily there, and Pedro IV, a particularly skilled and fortunate commander, became famous for pinning new, gratifying flags on his military maps.

In the Catalan part of Sardinia, unique specialities, such as donkey stew, are well known. Donkey, as a rule, is eaten everywhere on the islands (in the Aeolians, as well as in Ischia and in Lampedusa), where in the absence of roads and cars, donkeys are the only means of transportation, especially in mountainous areas. When the animal is worn out and its performance significantly diminished, the time has come to turn the old friend into a meal. And the donkey must necessarily be stewed for not less than seven hours, because its stringy meat cannot compare to buttery Angus fillets.

Donkey meat is eaten not only in the islands but also on the mainland, where it is prepared differently. In Castelvetro, in Piedmont, the *sagra* of donkey salamis is held every autumn. And in the very heart of the Italian plain lies a city whose inhabitants have elevated donkey *ragù* to the pearl of their cuisine: the refined, sumptuous, glorious city of the Gonzagas, Mantua.

Sardinian lobsters are prized, but perhaps no less esteemed is Sardinian octopus. The octopus is considered a kind of Aristotle of the animal world because of its intelligence. Despite having a high regard for its intellect, however, the inhabitants of the Apennine Peninsula and of the Italian islands eat it quite often. When buying octopus, experts observe a number of rules. First, they count the suction cups on the tentacles, which must be in two rows: if the suction cups are arranged in a single row, it means that the animal comes from the North Atlantic and is better left alone. Its flavor can never compete with that of octopuses found along the Italian coast.

The end of the Mediterranean octopus's life is humiliating and sad. It is banged against the rocks until it loses consciousness and its poor body goes completely limp. The ancient Greeks recommended slamming the octopus against the rocks no less than a hundred times. The only chance the creature has to avenge itself is to bite, as long as it has the strength to do so, and an octopus's bite is rather painful. But compassionate (or prudent) fishermen can use their teeth as well, and before striking the animal, they sever the nerve center located in its neck with a quick, precise chomp.

The most glorious fishermen, surrounded by a romantic aura and aggrandized in films, live on the other coast of Sardinia, on San Pietro Island. The only village on this island, which in itself is not very populous, is the sleepy town of Carloforte, which has become a fashionable vacation spot for northern Italian executives. The town comes alive from May–June until the end of August, when the *tonnara*, the system of tuna traps, is lowered into the sea. For a thousand years now *ala azzurra*, bluefin tuna, have migrated to these shores each year in May, to then continue on to Tokyo aboard a cargo plane: there they serve to replenish the supply of ingredients for sashimi in the refrigerators of high-class restaurants.

William Black recounts how, as a journalist and photographer, he managed to obtain permission to participate in the *mattanza* (tuna slaying), a restricted, inaccessible ritual.[4] Other civilians on the motorboat were the owner of the fishing company, in a jacket and tie, and the expert assigned to inspect the tuna meat, who had come expressly from Japan. In the presence of the Japanese inspector-supplier, no hunter would harpoon the tuna in the side. The Japanese believe that this type of killing compromises the quality of the meat. Tuna can only be killed by slitting the throat.

The *mattanza*, the battle with the tuna amid fountains of spurting blood, against a background of ocean waves, is described as an exhilarating spectacle. Leading the team is the head harpooner, called the *rais* (as in Puglia), a sign of the ritual's Arab origin. Despite the undisputed barbarity of the *mattanza*, experts believe that it is a type of fishing that is acceptable from both an ecological and an ethical point of view. It is a battle between equals, and the number of prey caught with so much effort does not ultimately disturb the natural balance in a given area of the sea. It is an entirely different matter when the hunt takes place, perhaps in a more sanitized and less picturesque way, with the use of electronic equipment. In the wake of this type of "merciful fishing," practically not a single live specimen remains in a radius of many kilometers.

The *mattanza* is a kind of Spanish bullfight, except that the deadly ballet takes place on the water. A tuna may weigh as much as three quintals (over six hundred pounds). In ancient, legendary times, specimens of four or even five quintals ended up in the traps. The tuna are caught when they are ready to reproduce (the males are then called "racing tuna"), at the peak of their sex hormone production.

Just as the killing of the pig brings all the farmers in the village together in the north and the south (some stuff the sausage, some boil the blood, others bring the new wine), so the entire community participates in the tuna butchering in Carloforte, just as in Calabria and Sicily. Before cans for preserving came into use, the meat was placed in wooden barrels. It was kept raw for a few days and was exquisite, but unscrupulous wholesalers sometimes extended the process on purpose, just to lower the prices with the threat that the meat might go bad. Like it or not, the fishermen of

Carloforte armed themselves with preservatives, albeit weak ones of short duration; this gave them the chance to fittingly place Sardinian tuna meat in wholesale fish markets all over the world.

The Sardinians have their sheep to thank for another illustrious typical product, Sardinian pecorino cheese, which appears on the table of every inhabitant of the island and of every Italian, as well as on the shelves of all the supermarkets on the planet. Sheep have always contributed to the survival and well-being of the people here. The animal, as we know, has a meek, gentle nature, and is sympathetic to its shepherds— even to the point that it ceases to require care just at the time when unbearable heat descends on all of Italy and the country closes down for the *ferie* (vacation period), namely, the month of August. At that time sheep stop giving milk; since there is no need to milk them, the shepherds can enjoy a well-deserved respite. It is no coincidence that Italy, mindful of these patriarchal rhythms, chooses August to rest. The culmination of the vacation period coincides with the Feast of the Assumption of the Virgin on August 15, when all Italians celebrate: signs posted on the rolled-down shutters of shop windows unconditionally proclaim CLOSED FOR FERRAGOSTO (from *feriae augusti*, August holidays). In patriarchal society, this same period was considered ideal for making new acquaintances and engaging in courtships. It was then that farmers and shepherds could leave their villages for a few days, visit with friends and relations in neighboring towns, find a *fidanzata* (girlfriend) and get to know her. During this period feasts and drinking, (see "The *Sagra*"), contests among popular poets and ballad singers, sack racing, and displays of physical strength were organized, and are still held today. Even the religious processions of the Assumption are occasions to show off one's physical vigor. It is the moment of glory for the region's brawny specimens, who in many towns and villages parade through the streets carrying statues weighing hundreds of pounds along with wooden crucifixes three meters high. And all thanks to the noble behavior of the inhabitants of the sheepfold.

It is the sheep that influence the rural calendar. In each season a particular cheese is produced. There are dozens of varieties of Sardinian pecorino known, in fact. The most famous of all is the Fiore (flower) or Fioretto (little flower). It is so named because at one time a flower was carved in the bottom of the chestnut wood molds (*pischeddas*) in which it was produced, and the imprint was then left on the ripe cheese. Now stainless-steel molds are used instead, but pecorino still retains this trade name. Sardinian Fiore, in the past, ripened in special storehouses in maritime pine-woods, and the cheese acquired the fragrance of resin. Fiore is made with lamb rennet, its flavor is very intense, and even after a long ripening period it melts in the mouth.

As we have seen, the Ligurians use Sardinian cheese exclusively for their pesto. This is a legacy of the trading between Arborea, the ancient Sardinian capital, and Genoa, its ally on the continent. A taste for Sardinian pecorino is particularly endur-ing. Italians in America, who by and large have lost the fundamental concepts of a traditional cuisine, continue to demand their Sardinian pecorino in the supermarkets of the New World.

Antipasti *Agliata*; garlic sauce is known in many different regions of Italy. In Piedmont *agliata* is intended not as a gravy for meat, but as a sauce for tagliatelle, and it is made with walnuts, salt pork, and soft crustless bread, or with garlic, egg yolks, chopped parsley, and extra-virgin olive oil; there is also green *agliata*, with parsley, basil, celery leaves, garlic, olive oil, and lemon. The Ligurians make their *ajada* with vinegar and spread it on ship's biscuits. In Sardinia, on the other hand, particularly in its Catalan area, *agliata* acquires a bright red color because tomato is a major ingredient. It goes well with fish, especially served cold, as an appetizer, and is wonderful with octopus.

Burrida (the same dish that in Liguria is called *buridda*): dogfish boiled with pine nuts, walnut kernels, vinegar, capers, bread crumbs, garlic, and flour. This dish is also known in other Italian regions, such as Liguria: Sardinian and Ligurian cuisine have many things in common. For the *burrida* the fish is boiled, then marinated (with myrtle in Sardinia) for one or two days. The same is done with chickens and piglets, according to Sardinian tradition.

First Courses *Culingionis* or *culurgiones*: large "bundles" of pasta filled with a mixture of potatoes and mint. *Fratau*, sometimes a dry dish, at other times a bread soup that is made with "music paper" (*carasau* bread), softened with water or broth, topped with grated pecorino, tomato sauce, and a raw or soft-boiled egg. Couscous. *Fregola* or *fregula*: semolina balls just slightly larger than those of couscous, made by adding saffron and eggs. They are served with tomato sauce and cured meats.

Second Courses Lobster, octopus. Meat and fish cooked on the fire. *Leputrida*, a clear distortion of the Spanish *olla podrida*, made of pig feet, mutton, and salt pork with vegetables.

Desserts The variety of desserts and sweets here is extraordinary: the ingredients include semolina wheat, *sapa* or *saba* (cooked must), honey, almonds, candied fruits, and orange peel. To mention a few; *sebadas*, pasta *ravioloni* filled with fresh cheese, then fried and served warm sprinkled with honey; *pàrdulas*, small dough "baskets" filled with ricotta or fresh cheese and saffron, baked in the oven; *pabassinas*, a kind of tiny *panforte* made of flour, *sapa*, almonds, raisins, orange peel, etc.; *pistoccheddus* and *pirrichittus*, flour-and-egg dough with sugar and lemon icing; *suspirus*, balls of almond paste, sugar, and lemon, wrapped up like candy; *torrone* (nougat) with almonds, honey, and egg white; Sardinian amaretti (macaroons); cookies with strange shapes; and *gattò*, dry cakes made with caramelized sugar and Sardinian almonds, with a semi-French name (from *gâteau*).

TYPICAL PRODUCTS OF SARDINIA

According to widespread conviction, all the island's vegetables and fruits can be defined as typical products, since all the plants grown here are a genetically pure, insular form. Sardinian lands are fertile: wherever you go there is an abundance of herbs, artichokes, tomatoes, and vegetables, grown in soil fertilized by seaweed, and consequently very rich and appetizing. Large fields are planted with wheat, which is exported from Porto Torres (this city, founded by the Phoenicians and fortified by the Carthaginians, was called Turris Libisonis in Roman times and was the Roman Empire's chief port for wheat trading).

Cheeses Sardinian pecorino. This cheese has a more delicate flavor than pecorino romano, because it is made not with mutton rennet, but with that of veal. It is also much more delicate than Sardinian Fiore, the slightly smoky cheese whose forms are stamped with stylized flowers. Casu Marzu cheese (with worms) from the provinces of Sassari and Nuoro. Casizolu, a cheese of stretched-curd (*pasta filata*), little known until recent times, that had almost disappeared from use and was recovered by activists in the Slow Food movement.

Sardinian artichokes, the Camone variety of tomatoes. Mullet *bottarga*. Sardinian honey. Myrtle. Saffron. *Carasau*, or "music paper" bread.

TYPICAL BEVERAGE

Myrtle (a liqueur obtained by crushing the berries of the shrub of the same name, a plant sacred to Venus).

JOY

Anyone who has read this book will no longer wonder why Italians love to talk about food. Indeed Petrarch, in *De remediis utriusque fortunae* (Remedies for fortune fair and foul), noted that his compatriots preferred talking about food to discussing literature: "These are the just deserts of our rotten age, which neglects the needs of learning in favor of the kitchen and scrutinizes cooks but not the scribes."[1]

But even when writers are actually discussed, or when literary or artistic movements are created, if you look closely you'll find that the Italian mind inevitably returns to matters of cuisine, the table, and food. Take the Futurists, for example, with their cultural revolution, and read the proclamations they launched from the very beginning: "While recognizing that badly or crudely nourished men have achieved great things in the past, we affirm this truth: men think, dream and act according to what they eat and drink."[2]

Since it is necessary and even indispensable for Italians to talk about food, there's all the more reason to talk about it at the table. Indeed, these are the best moments! Among the other pleasures of the table, Brillat-Savarin, the illustrious metaphysician and philosopher of cuisine, particularly appreciated the joy of convivial conversation. Food, he wrote, is life's greatest pleasure:

> Aphorisms of the Professor. Aphorism V. The Creator, when he obliges man to eat, invites him to do so by appetite, and rewards him by pleasure . . . Aphorism VII. The pleasure of the

table belongs to all ages, to all conditions, to all countries, and to all eras; it mingles with all other pleasures, and remains at last to console us for their departure . . . Aphorism IX. The discovery of a new dish confers more happiness on humanity, than the discovery of a new star . . . At the first course every one eats and pays no attention to conversation; all ranks and grades are forgotten together in the great manufacture of life. When, however, hunger begins to be satisfied, reflection begins, and conversation commences. The person who, hitherto, had been a mere consumer, becomes an amiable guest.[3]

It is true that not all philosophers saw things the way he did. The hypochondriac poet Giacomo Leopardi was very skeptical with regard to convivial conversations at meal-times:

Now, I cannot comprehend why the one time of day when the mouth is occupied, when the external organs of speech are otherwise employed (a most interesting employment, whose proficient execution matters greatly, since man's well-being, sturdy physical condition, and therefore sound moral and mental states as well depend largely on good digestion, and digestion cannot be good if it is not begun well in the mouth, according to the well-known proverb and medical aphorism), must be precisely a time when we are obliged to talk more than ever, given that there are many who, devoting the rest of the day to study or seclusion for whatever reason, only converse at the table.[4]

But despite the views of taciturn men such as he, the majority of Italians, as well as true lovers of Italy, would only give up chatting about food at the table if their tongues were to wither. In this school of thought, communicating one's culinary tastes to the world is a declaration of belonging—to a certain city or town, as well as to a macroregion of the country, east or west, north or south. Moreover, it's a demonstration of one's involvement in the grand Italian culinary tradition, popular and beloved by all. It should be evident from reading through the chapters of this book that the culinary code common to Italians reflects both a variety of small hometowns and a general sense of the entire history of Italian culture, which is really a collage of cultures.

The *Fischietto* of January 13, 1849, published a "Scena storica al Caffè del Cambio" (Historic scene at the Café del Cambio), where a democrat hurls a stool at an aristocrat's head:

(The room is filled with people eating, among them many deputies of Parliament.)

BARON N.: Waiter, bring me some bread.

WAITER: Would you like some *grissini*?

BARON: I don't eat *grissini*; I don't wish to support Piedmont.

A PIEDMONTESE: Waiter.

WAITER: Yes, sir?

THE PIEDMONTESE: Bring me a plate of antipasto.

WAITER: Would you like some salami?

THE PIEDMONTESE: No, I don't want any salami. I don't wish to support the barons who have been granted amnesty.[5]

In this succinct example we see how an alimentary metaphor can convey political and idealistic meanings, in place of a lengthy, positivistic-rationalistic exposition. Moreover, the food metaphor has the merit of containing a certain amount of good-natured humor, which is the principal glue that holds Italian culture together, as well as its essential engine.

Literature, painting, and history also speak to us in the language of the culinary code. It's a code that includes amusing metonymies, gags of all kinds, and cheerful burlesque parodies, thanks to which everyone enjoys themselves more.

In speaking about small Italian hometowns, we are not always aware of the extent to which Italians identify the different regions with specific products or dishes, whose names have become synonymous with the culture and history of a certain region. The entire geography of Italy and its conquerors, the entire history of invasions and incursions, political dealings and wars, is contained in these names.

The Neapolitan writer Gabriele Fasano (second half of the seventeenth century), in his *Lo Tasso napoletano, Gerusalemme liberata votata a llengua nostra* (*Neapolitan Tasso: Jerusalem Delivered in our language*), lists the playful nicknames of the inhabitants of various places in Italy: the Lombards are *mangiarape*, or turnip eaters; the Venetians *magnapolenta*, or polenta eaters; the people of Vicenza *magnagatti*, or cat eaters; the Tuscan and Emilian mountain folk *mangiamarroni*, or chestnut eaters; those of Cremona *mangiafagioli*, or bean eaters; the Abruzzese *mangiatori di panunto*, who eat *panunto* or oiled bread; the Florentines *cacapiselli*, who shit peas; and the Neapolitans *cacafoglie*, who shit leaves: "That's what we Neapolitans are antonomastically called." Naples is referred to as the "city of broccoli" by Antonio Abbondanti in the *Gazzette menippee di Parnaso* (Menippean journals of Parnassus):

. . . what matters most, a lot of broccoli . . .

Whereby the location is so fair and pleasant
that nature seems to reign
in that most fertile land,
since it seems that April there is always verdant
amid turnip, cabbages, and chard
and among those great lords of the seven *seggi* . . . *

---

*The Seggi were the aristocratic body of Naples's city government.

The same Antonio Abbondanti, in the book *Viaggio di Colonia* (Cologne journey), writes about the prince of Bisignano (whose feudal estate is located in Calabria), who was of Neapolitan origin:

> . . . with that the prince of Bisignano had betaken himself
> through those bitter seas,
> toward his native broccoli and clear waters . . .

In the heroicomic poem *L'Agnano zeffonato* (the poem is in Neapolitan dialect, and the Agnano of the title refers to a volcanic crater found northwest of Naples in the Campi Flegrei) by Andrea Perruccio, broccoli is depicted as a blazon on the flag of Naples:

> This the Neapolitans carried,
> who make a big fuss over leaves . . .
>
> On their banner was a bunch
> of broccoli, and the words: In my belly
> I have hope of victory!

This association of the flag of Naples with the image of broccoli triggered the idea of describing the regional dishes and typical products as "gastronomic emblems." In a novella by Giambattista Basile we read: "Farewell, parsnips and beetroots, farewell fritters [*zéppole*, fritters with honey] and cakes; farewell cauliflowers and pickled tunny fish; . . . Farewell Naples, the *nec plus ultra* . . . I leave you and shall be deprived of your cabbage soups; driven out of this dear village [Naples was called *il casalone*, the big village], oh, my broccoli, I must leave you behind!"[6]

Awareness of the origin of all products served at the table was typical of the population of the Italian peninsula, Sicily, and Sardinia since the days of antiquity. Gourmands in imperial Rome were distinguished by unusual discernment and competence in this area. Juvenal recalls a certain Montano: "None in my day had greater gastronomic skill: whether oysters were natives of Circeii or the Lucrine rocks or bred in the beds of Richborough he had the knowledge to discern at the first bite, and could tell at a glance the habitat of a shell-fish."[7]

This art of identification bordered on a mania among the ancients. Enormous importance was attributed not only to the place of origin but also to the time of the animal's capture or the harvesting of fruits intended for the table. Jean-François Revel writes about the chef Archestratus of Syracuse:

> But what is most striking about Archestratus' advice is the extraordinary attention paid to places and origins. This is a constant preoccupation of the cuisine of antiquity: the place where an animal is caught, the region where a fruit or vegetable is cultivated are the object of observations that are as meticulous, as lengthy as the description as to the ways in which these products are cooked or prepared for the table, and often even more so. It would thus seem that the ancient Greeks and Romans had *a more acute sensibility than ours when it came to the native tang of things and the characteristics of different regions* [italics mine]. Sturgeon (galeos), for instance, was to be eaten principally at Rhodes. And if one chances to see one in the market of this city, it is necessary, if need be, according to Archestratus, "to carry it off by force, even at the price of later having to bear the legal consequences of this kidnapping."[8]

The French scholar, referring to a less acute perception of typical local products in contemporaries as compared with the ancients, is perhaps not referring to Italians. As far as Italy is concerned, in fact, we can say that everything has remained as it was in Archestratus's day. For centuries, a strong awareness of belonging to small hometowns—the places of their origin, or their permanent residence—has remained deeply rooted in the psychology of Italians. This attachment becomes *campanilismo*, local pride, and often manifests itself through a code of social identification based on purely culinary criteria: "I am one of those who eat this, and I am against those who eat that."

"The least breath of published criticism against his local poet or sculptor will set any Italian in a towering rage—a fury whose expression outstrips the most elementary bounds of decency," wrote Stendhal on January 1, 1817.[9] "I, who had grown firmly convinced of the high intelligence of the Bolognese, now find myself in imminent peril of having to eat my own words. For ninety unrelenting minutes I have been subjected to an eruption of backstairs patriotism of the most imbecile variety—and in the best of company at that! This is indeed the besetting sin of Italy."[10]

Indeed, everyone fights with all his might against "the others" to defend what is his, uniquely so. Life in the medieval village, where isolated neighbors in cantons, districts, or quarters were divided by centuries-old rivalries (once described by Shakespeare), was subject to this law. Yet even today, during the Palio held in Piazza del Campo in Siena, in

July and August, the jockeys of the Contrada dell'Onda compete with those of the district of Tortuca in a breakneck race, putting their reputation and destiny on the line.

> You do not need telling that these different peoples are very far from forming a homogeneous nation. Bergamo detests Milan, which is likewise execrated by Novara and Pavia; whereas your Milanese himself, being fully preoccupied with keeping a good table and acquiring a warm pastran (overcoat) against the winter, hates nobody; for hatred would merely disturb the unruffled serenity of his pleasures. Florence, which in days gone by so bitterly abhorred Siena, now is so reduced to impotence that she has no strength for loathing left; yet, allowing for these two exceptions, I search in vain to discover a third; each city detests its neighbours, and is mortally detested in return.[11]

And yet, despite the flaring of passions, the diversity of attachments, the desire to fight for one's own bell tower, this world of contrasts is actually coherent. Sidestepping the provincial narcissism, everything is bound together, especially at the table, by the common culinary language. Unity under the gastronomic emblems extends to the entire nation. As variegated as the peninsula is, some gastronomic topics fill the souls of both southerners and northerners with equal pride.

To begin with, pride in the insuperable quality of the espresso, authentic Italian espresso, prepared the way God intended.

The next object of Italians' pride is gelato. Enthusiasm for the national ice cream exists more in theory than in actual consumption, since many adult Italians, albeit with regret, give up gelato so as not to get fat. But, in general, Italy has reason to boast of its cold desserts industry. The legendary (from a technological standpoint) art of chilling anything—water, sorbets,[12] gelato[13]—has been linked to Italian know-how since the Middle Ages.

It is ironic that Italians, pioneers of the freezing industry, suffer simultaneously from an amusing phobia: a wild hatred of anything that is frozen. Frozen foods in supermarkets are purchased reluctantly, mostly out of necessity (to have supplies in the freezer in case of emergencies). As soon as the tiny image of the snowflake is spotted on the menu of a restaurant (indicating that the dish was prepared with frozen fish or meat), the immediate tendency is not to order that dish; indeed, some customers actually lose their enthusiasm for the restaurant itself. Proud of the wonderful taste of his own fruit ("In America the fruit looks beautiful, but has no taste"), the Italian buyer eyes with distrust exotic fruits imported both in summer and winter ("They must have frozen them") and is attracted instead to seasonal products, all the better if grown right there in Italy.

This mistrust rivals the hatred for genetically modified foods (which no one in Italy has actually ever seen, since their importation is prohibited by law). Conversations on these topics provide material for newspaper articles, and the discussion of newspaper articles is a pretext for new conversations. Thus, the *Corriere della Sera*'s shocked correspondent in Japan lists the prohibitive prices of fruit in a Tokyo supermarket: cherries are counted one by one and a basket costs $100 or more; a single shiny, red apple or four strawberries cost $60; the same for a banana or fifteen grapes "so identical that they appear to be made of marzipan." Until the classic conclusion: " and of course they have no taste."[14] The epithets "shiny and red" or "identical" (in reference to the grapes) are intended to shift reader's horror at the exorbitant prices of the products to their unnatural aspect, to their presumed "artificiality." In this way, the reader is subtly encouraged to rejoice: in Italy, thank heavens, a kilo of cherries, in season, costs four euros, and those cherries may even be worm-eaten—hurray!

That's the way the culinary code works: it transmits messages. Messages of self-respect, pride, contentment, and sharing. It enables significant social differences to be leveled out and even makes it possible to sidestep disgrace. The prince of Savoy, Vittorio Emanuele, having returned to Italy after a political exile that lasted almost a lifetime, was imprisoned in Potenza for corruption a few years later (in June 2006). When asked by journalists how he would endure prison and the shame, he replied: "In Italy we eat well anywhere, I have always said so."

Ippolito Nievo, in *Le Confessioni di un italiano* (Confessions of an Italian), wrote:

One eats more in Bologna in a year than in Venice in two, in Rome in three, in Turin in five, and in Genoa in twenty. Though in Venice one eats less because of the sirocco, and in Milan more thanks to the cooks. As for Florence, Naples, and Palermo, the first is too fussy to inspire its guests to gorge, and in the other two, the contemplative life fills the stomach through the pores, without troubling the jaws. One lives on air, infused with the volatile oil of cedar and the fecund pollen of fig trees. How does this relate to the rest of the matter of eating? Perfectly, because digestion works by virtue of activity and good humor. A quick-witted, varied conversation which skims over all the sentiments of your heart, like a hand on a keyboard, which trains your mind and tongue to run, to leap here and there wherever they are summoned, and which excites and overexcites your intellectual life, prepares you for a meal better than all the absinthes and vermouths on earth. They did well to invent vermouth in Turin, where they talk and laugh little.[15]

This important feature of the language of culinary allusions could not have been better described. In the perception of Italians, good humor, integrity, and intelligence are to be found wherever one eats with appetite and where digestion functions well. Many judge the quality of the merchandise by the happy, satisfied look of the vendor. Gourmets use very precise rules that help them find high-quality ingredients. Take, for instance, the ingenious rule invented in the sixteenth century by Castore Durante: to compare the quality of vegetables and fruit, he suggests observing the outer appearance of keepers of vineyards, orchards, and fields. Durante affirms that the more satisfied and fat the custodian is, the better the orchards and vineyards will be, since caretakers predominantly eat what is entrusted to their care.

All the literature suggests that the Italian who eats with gusto and is an expert in gastronomy cannot be a scoundrel, a swindler, or a liar. Even the police judge people according to this principle! Andrea Camilleri's Commissioner Montalbano changes his opinion about a witness, from suspicious to totally reliable, the moment he discovers her attitude toward food:

"Well, signora, thank you so much . . . ," the inspector began, standing up.

"Why don't you stay and eat with me?"

Montalbano felt his stomach blanch. Signora Clementina was sweet and nice, but she probably lived on semolina and boiled potatoes.

"Actually, I have so much to . . ."

"Pina, the housekeeper, is an excellent cook, believe me. For today she's made pasta alla Norma, you know, with fried eggplant and ricotta salata."

"Jesus!" said Montalbano, sitting back down.

"And braised beef for the second course."

"Jesus!" repeated Montalbano.

"Why are you so surprised?"

"Aren't those dishes a little heavy for you?"

"Why? I've got a stronger stomach than any of these twenty-year-old girls who can happily go a whole day on half an apple and some carrot juice. Or perhaps you're of the same opinion as my son Giulio?"

"I don't have the pleasure of knowing what that is."

"He says it's undignified to eat such things at my age. He considers me a bit shameless. He thinks I should live on porridges. So what will it be? Are you staying?"

"I'm staying," the inspector replied decisively.[16]

It was precisely while talking about food that Goethe revealed the Italians' astonishing nobility of spirit, unlike the incivility and arrogance that were more widespread in other populations:

The sun was shining brightly when I arrived in Bolzano. I was glad to see the faces of so many merchants at once. They had an air about them of purpose and well-being. Women sat in the square, displaying their fruit in round, flat-bottomed baskets more than four feet in diameter. The peaches and pears were placed side by side to avoid bruising. I suddenly remembered a quatrain I had seen inscribed on the window of the inn at Regensburg:

> Comme les pêches et les melons
> Sont pour la bouche d'un baron,
> Ainsi les verges et les bâtons
> Sont pour les fous, dit Salomon.

Evidently this was written by a northern baron, but one can be equally sure that, if he had visited these parts, he would have changed his mind.[17]

Indeed, since the time of the ancient Romans the subject of food in this fruitful land has assumed joyous tints for the most part—excluding, of course, the periods of wars, epidemics, and natural disasters. The relationship between man and food, even when humble, was often characterized by serene dignity:

. . . I saw an old Corycian, under Tarentum's towers,
where the dark Galaesus waters the yellow fields,
who owned a few acres of abandoned soil,
not fertile enough for bullocks to plough,
not suited to flocks, or fit for the grape harvest:
yet as he planted herbs here and there among the bushes,
and white lilies round them, and vervain, and slender poppies,
it equalled in his opinion the riches of kings,
and returning home late at night
it loaded his table with un-bought supplies.[18]

Imbued with the attitude of the ancient poets toward the land and daily life, following in the footsteps of illustrious predecessors who had formerly described Italy, such as Ferdinand Gregorovius, Jacob Burckhardt, Vernon Lee, Stendhal, and Goethe, and of course observing with his own eyes, Pavel Muratov also idealized the Italian peasant:

> [One is] filled with a profound benevolence toward the Italian populace. Such a fantastic, diverse crowd is to be found in the narrow city streets! Such warmth and kindness toward foreigners, such dignity and self-awareness, such ability to to be among people yet remain oneself, to be part of the crowd and not lose one's human face! In such a crowd panic is unthinkable, it bears no resemblance to a blind, bestial flock, everyone knows his place and recognizes that of others, no one drives or pushes anyone, and even in moments of heightened excitement, a vulgar word is never heard.[19]

To make sense of this earthiness, which also contains great spirituality, a lengthy study was needed. A substantial part of the facts and information contained in this book was perceived from "inside." Living in Italy for twenty years, the author has by this time absorbed Italian concepts and, to some extent, has learned to distinguish the subtle nuances. Still, whatever people may say, some things are more evident from the "outside" looking in. In this sense, the author of this book has benefited from a privileged position: in effect, she has both an insider's vision and the gaze of an outsider. Goethe understood this mechanism, and on November 7, 1786, confessed: "When I was a young man, I sometimes indulged in a daydream of being accompanied to Italy by an educated Englishman, well versed in general history and the history of art."[20]

It is precisely the culinary code, I believe, that is the universal key to understanding Italy and its "authenticity." Some years ago a curious passage by the brilliant Russian philologist Michail Gasparov drew me to the idea of taking up the theme of food:

> O. Sedakova said: "Umberto Eco in his paper tried very hard and passionately to demonstrate that there is no authenticity in the world, nor can there be. Yet when we went to lunch, he studied the menu so carefully, I thought: No, something authentic does exist for him."[21]

In my quest to find the key that would unlock the authenticity and mystery of Italy— to discover the secret of its combination lock, as it were—I traveled the country from north to south. And most of the time the doors of the temples of gastronomy opened for me. At other times I was able to peer through the window. The window that looks into kitchen. There inside is Beatrice.

Cooking Methods for Meat, Fish,
Eggs, and Vegetables

A beccafico. Fish preparation: small fish, split open and without the heads, are sprinkled with bread crumbs and cheese and baked in the oven.

Affogato. Immersed in boiling liquid.

Al cireghet. Piedmontese name for egg with butter.

Alla cacciatora. Browned in oil with rosemary, garlic, and red pepper, then braised in wine.

Alla canevera. Enclosed in an ox bladder, then boiled in hot water with a special hollow cane stuck in to act as a vent and let air out of the bladder.

Alla diavola. Stewed in vinegar with black pepper, hot red pepper, and tomato sauce.

Alla giudia. Fried in boiling oil.

All'agro. In sour sauce.

Alla livornese. Stewed in tomato sauce with olive oil, garlic, onion, bay leaf, and parsley.

All'americana. In shrimp sauce.

Alla piastra. Cooked on a red-hot slab.

Alla romagnola. With peas and tomato sauce.

Alla tartara. Raw, minced, with spicy sauce.

Alla toscana. Marinated for twenty-four hours with lemon rind, olive oil, bay leaf, tarragon, and chervil, then stewed with potatoes and mushrooms.

Alla vaccinara. Cooked over low heat in a tomato sauce with celery, chopped pancetta, white wine, onion, and carrot.

All'uccelletto. Cut into small pieces and fried in oil, garlic, and rosemary.

Arracanato. Cooked in a pan on the burner with olive oil, tomatoes, white wine, oregano, garlic, and parsley (such as mussels and anchovies *arracanate*).

A scapece (from the Spanish for "marinated"). Fish preparation: fried, then sprinkled with bread crumbs, and seasoned with olive oil, vinegar, garlic, and mint. Eaten cold.

Bagnomaria. Cooked in a bain-marie, a small pot placed in a larger pot of boiling water. It is not the same as steam cooking, when the product is placed in a basket or sieve.

Brasato. Braised over low heat (braised beforehand and then kept a long time in a hot oven).

Escabeche. The same as *a scapece*, q.v.

Gratinato. Baked in the oven with a golden crust, usually of grated Parmesan, more rarely in a béchamel-and-cream sauce.

Grigliato. Roasted on the grill.

In cagnone. Seasoned with a sauce of butter melted in a pan with garlic and sage (boiled rice).

In carpione. Roasted, then marinated in vinegar.

In cereghin. Milanese name for egg with butter.

In civet. Boiled in red wine with onion, and seasoned with a marinade of the blood in which the meat was left to rest before cooking.

In salmì. Marinated for two days, in pieces, then braised in wine with spices.

Sauces and Gravies for Pasta

Aglio-olio-peperoncino. Boiling olive oil, garlic, hot red pepper, salt.

Alla brava. Onion, shrimp, cream, thyme, marjoram.

Alla caprese. Cherry tomatoes, *mozzarella di bufala*, capers.

Alla carbonara. Pancetta, egg, grated Parmesan.

Alla ciociara. Anchovies, *mozzarella di bufala*, garlic, tomatoes, whole black pepper-corns, sugar.

Alla contadina. Tomatoes, olive oil, oregano, cheese.

Alla Gaeta. Meat sauce of wild boar piglets.

Alla marinara. Tomato purée, olive oil, garlic.

All'amatriciana. Smoked *guanciale* (pork cheek) cut into cubes, tomatoes, onion, pecorino.

Alla napoletana. Ricotta, mozzarella, egg, prosciutto.

Alla Norma. Eggplant, tomatoes, ricotta, garlic.

Alla papalina. Egg, *prosciutto crudo*, Parmesan, onion, cream.

Alla pizzaiola. Tomatoes, oil, oregano, garlic.

Alla potentina. White wine, egg, Scamorza, olive oil, all sprinkled with bread crumbs.

Alla puttanesca. Anchovies, black olives, capers, tomatoes, garlic, hot red pepper, oil.

Alla romana. Smoked *guanciale* (pork cheek) cut into cubes, peas, onion, egg, pepper, pecorino.

All'arrabbiata. Tomatoes, pancetta or salt pork, garlic, onion, raisins, olives, red pepper, white wine, pecorino.

Alla sarda. Oil, sage, myrtle, white wine, broth, olives, basil.

Alla siracusana. Broccoli, soaked raisins, garlic, two types of Caciocavallo cheese, fresh and aged.

Alla trasteverina. Salted anchovies, tuna, porcini mushrooms, tomato.

Alle vongole. Heated oil, garlic, parsley, fresh tomatoes, clams.

All'ortolana. Onion, garlic, peppers, eggplant, tomatoes, parsley.

Al pepe e cacio. Grated red pepper, sometimes Parmesan.

Al pomodoro e basilico. Fresh tomatoes, warm oil, basil, salt.

Con le sarde. Sardines, raisins, almonds, onion, saffron, pine nuts.

Del buongustaio. Minced meat, *prosciutto cotto*, tomatoes, garlic, parsley, olive oil, basil, grated cheese.

Pesto genovese. Basil, garlic, pine nuts, Sardinian pecorino, olive oil.

Pesto siciliano. Tomatoes, basil, sharp Ragusan cheese, red pepper, garlic, olive oil.

Pesto trapanese. Basil, garlic, tomatoes, almonds, olive oil (this recipe does not call for cheese).

Pairings of Pasta Shapes and Sauces*

Agnolotti (ø 50 mm, round or rectangular ravioli with bread crumbs, meat, vegetables, cheese). With potatoes (Friuli); with three meats—pork, rabbit, and salami paste—and cabbage (Trentino and Alto Adige); with truffle sauce (Piedmont); with meat sauce and Parmesan (Emilia Romagna); with spinach, ricotta, Parmesan, egg, nutmeg, and sage (Marches).

Amorini (ø 5 mm, length 50 mm, hollow spirals). With walnuts, marjoram, cream, and grated cheese (Abruzzo).

Anelli (ø 8 mm). With walnut sauce (Liguria).

Anolini (ø 4 mm, round ravioli). In broth or braised beef sauce in the regions of Parma and Piacenza (Emilia Romagna).

Avemarie (ø 20 mm, length 20 mm, cylinders). In broth (everywhere); in saffron sauce (Sicily and Lombardy).

Ballerine (twisted into cornets). With anchovy sauce (everywhere).

Bavette (width 1.8 mm, long and flat). With fish (Livorno, Tuscan coast); with mushrooms (Puglia); *alla trasteverina*: with salted anchovies, tuna, porcini mushrooms, and tomatoes (Lazio); Lipari-style: with tuna, olives, capers, and oregano (Aeolian Islands, Sicily).

---

*The symbol ø refers to the pasta's diameter.

Bigoli (ø 3 mm, long, round and filled). With duck (Veneto); with puree of sardines (Veneto).

Bombolotti (ø 20–30 mm). *Allo sparaceddo*: with broccoli, sausage, garlic, Parmesan, milk, and nutmeg (Naples, Campania).

Bucati (ø 4–5 mm, long, round and hollow). *All'amatriciana*: smoked *guanciale* (pork cheek) cut into cubes, tomatoes, onion, and pecorino (Lazio).

Bucatini (ø 2.9 mm, length 300 mm or more, long, round and hollow). *Garganello*: with wild duck (Trentino); with mushrooms (Emilia Romagna); *all'amatriciana* (Lazio); *alla romana*: smoked *guanciale* (pork cheek) cut into cubes, peas, onion, eggs, pepper, and pecorino (Lazio); *alla Gaeta*: with meat sauce of wild boar piglets (Campania); *alla Norma*: with eggplant, tomatoes, ricotta, and garlic (Sicily); with sardines (Palermo, Sicily); *alla brava*: with onion, shrimp, cream, thyme, and marjoram (everywhere).

Busa or *busiati* (flat pasta made by hand, rolled on a knitting needle, the *busa* (20 x 100 mm). With porcini mushroom sauce (Tuscany); with pork *ragù* (Sicily).

Canederli (from the German *Knödeln*, gnocchi, ø 40 mm). Dumplings of bread, *speck* (ham), milk, flour, and egg, served in a concentrated broth (Trentino and Alto Adige).

Cannelloni (ø 30 mm, length 100–150 mm). *Agliata*: with garlic (Piedmont); filled with egg, chicken livers, and gizzards with garlic, prosciutto, and parsley, with a sauce of chicken giblets, onion, broth, grated Parmesan, nutmeg, and white wine (Rome, Lazio); *alla partenopea* (Parthenopean-style): ricotta, mozzarella, egg, and *prosciutto cotto* (Naples, Campania); with broccoli (Sicily); with pine nuts, raisins, ricotta, and peppers (Sicily).

Capelli d'angelo (angel hair pasta, ø 1.5–2 mm). With light sauces, broths, or simply mixed with olive oil and boiled vegetables (everywhere).

Capellini (ø 1.2–1.4 mm, length 300 mm or more). With capers and olives (everywhere).

Cappellacci (ø 40 mm). A type of pumpkin ravioli (Emilia Romagna).

Cappelletti (ø 30 mm). Ravioli with cheese, prosciutto, and three kinds of meat: veal, beef, and pork; they are served in broth and sprinkled with Parmesan cheese (Emilia Romagna); with *ragù* sauce and dried mushrooms (Emilia Romagna).

Capunti (fresh egg pasta, 20–25 mm in length). Fresh pasta dumplings with shrimp and *bottarga* (roe) (Sardinia).

Casarecce (strips folded in two and curled like a scroll, 40 mm long). Ricotta sauce (Basilicata).

Casoncelli (ø 50–70 mm). Ravioli with pancetta, parsley, bread crumbs, and salami paste (Brescia, Lombardy).

Cavatelli (fresh egg pasta, 20 mm long, shaped like orange segments with a deep cleft). With tuna and tomato (everywhere); with mushrooms (Molise); with beans and mussels (Puglia).

Cavatellucci (smaller than *cavatelli*, shaped like orange segments with a deep cleft, ø 15 mm). With broccoli, cooked in fish broth and served with pieces of skate (Lazio).

Cavatieddi (round gnocchi with a cleft). With pork sauce (Basilicata, Puglia, and Sicily, especially the province of Caltanissetta).

Chifferi lisci, smooth (from the German *Kiefer*, jaws, ø 20 mm). Egg sauce with green pepper (everywhere).

Chifferi rigati, ribbed (ø 25–30 mm). With olives and anchovies (everywhere).

Cialzons (square ravioli with an upturned corner, ø 50 mm). Filled with spinach, topped with melted butter, ricotta, and grated cheese (Friuli Venezia Giulia).

Conchiglie (shells, length 35 mm). Sauce of Brussels sprouts (Friuli Venezia Giulia).

Conchiglie rigate (ribbed shells, 35–40 mm in length). With celery, potatoes, and zucchini (Molise).

Corzetti (from *croce*, cross {see *croxette*}; fresh pasta in sheets 40 mm long, twisted into the shape of a figure eight). With fresh salmon, onion, and walnuts (Ligurian Riviera and in particular Val Polcevera).

Creoli (ø 3 mm, length 300 mm or more, in square sections, passed through a bronze wire mesh). With pancetta, pepper, and cheese (Molise).

Crespelle (large and square, sometimes folded into a pocket). With mozzarella (Sicily).

Creste di gallo (cock's combs, hollow semicircles with crimped edges). With pork, fatback, and onion (Emilia Romagna).

Croxette (from *croce*, cross {see *corzetti*}; printed in wooden molds, in the shape of coins with escutcheons or crosses; legend dates them back to the Crusades). With walnut sauce (Liguria).

Culurzones (rye flour dumplings with egg). With cheese, saffron, and spinach (Sardinia).

Ditalini (ø 4 mm, hollow). In soups or pasta salads, with beef for example (everywhere).

Eliche (propellers, ø 4 mm, corkscrew-shaped). With red pepper (Calabria).

Elicoidali (helixes, ø 6 mm, straight, hollow little tubes, with curved ribs on the surface). *Alla creola* (Creole-style): with mayonnaise, corn, spinach, pancetta, and olive oil (everywhere).

Farfalle (butterflies, length 35 mm). With smoked salmon (Lombardy); with *prosciutto cotto*, béchamel, whipped cream, and red radicchio of Treviso (Veneto); with peas, *prosciutto cotto*, butter, chives, and Parmesan (everywhere); with chicken and shrimp, onion, white wine, and cream (everywhere).

Fenescecchie (ø 6 mm, length 40 mm, rolled around a knitting needle). With meat sauce and tomato or fish and tomato (Puglia).

Fettuccelle (fresh egg pasta, ø 6–7.3 mm, length 300 mm or more). With truffles (Piedmont).

Fettuccine (fresh egg pasta, ø 8–10 mm, length 300 mm or more; long, flat noodles, wider than linguini, but can substitute for them in all recipes). With thick sauces: especially good with a sauce of cream and walnuts (Piedmont); with Bolognese *ragù*: chopped meat, dried mushrooms, flour, carrots, pancetta, parsley, butter or lard, white wine, sugar, nutmeg, and pepper (Emilia Romagna); sautéed with bread crumbs and basil (Umbria); with pan drippings from a roast (Molise); *alla papalina*: with *prosciutto crudo*, egg, Parmesan, onion, and cream (Lazio).

Fresine (ø 6–7 mm). *Del buongustaio*: with *prosciutto cotto*, chopped beef, tomatoes, garlic, parsley, olive oil, basil, and grated cheese (everywhere).

Fusilli (ø 5 mm; the classic length is 40 mm; there are different types depending on the manufacturer: short and fat, short and thin, long and thin). With fontina cheese, cream, and *lardo d'Arnad* (Valle d'Aosta); with asparagus, milk, cream, and nutmeg (Lombardy), *alla beneventana* (Benevento-style): with olive oil, onion, garlic, beef, white wine, mint, parsley, celery, tomatoes, and Parmesan (Campania); with salami paste, garlic, and vegetables (Campania); *alla partenopea*: with ricotta (Campania); *alla vesuviana* (Vesuvian-style): with clams, mussels, squid, and shrimp (Campania); *alla sorrentina* (Sorrento-style): with eggplant and basil (Campania); cold with shrimp and lemon (Calabria); with lemon, olive oil, tomato, basil, and parsley (Calabria); with hot red pepper (Basilicata).

Garganelli (disks ø 40 mm, rolled into a tube). With white sauce: raisins, pine nuts, carrots, celery, and onion (Emilia Romagna); with porcini mushrooms (Tuscany).

Gemelli (twins; rolled double ropes). With endive, porcini mushrooms, pine nuts, garlic, and cheese (Valle d'Aosta); with ricotta and Gorgonzola cheese (Piedmont); with Sicilian pesto (Sicily).

Gnocchetti (length 20 mm). With fava beans, pancetta, garlic, and parsley (Veneto).

Gnocchetti sardi (little Sardinian gnocchi, also called *malloreddus*, which in Sardinian means "young bulls"; fresh pasta 10–20 mm in length, often with saffron). With peas, garlic, and parsley (Sardinia); with lamb sauce (Sardinia).

Gnocchi (length 30 mm). *Alla veronese* (Verona-style): with chicken gizzards, dried mushrooms, and cheese (Veneto); *all'ortolana* (areas of Bergamo and Sondrio, Lombardy).

Gnocchi alla romana (of semolina, Parmesan cheese, butter, milk, egg). With melted butter (Rome, Lazio).

Gobbetti (short, hollow "hunchbacks"). *Alla caprese*: with *mozzarella di bufala*, cherry tomatoes, capers (Campania); *al limone*: with lemon, a kosher dish of Jewish cuisine (Tuscany).

Gomiti rigati (ribbed elbows). *Ai tre formaggi* (with three cheeses): fontina, mozzarella, Parmesan (Valle d'Aosta).

Lagane (wide lasagna noodles). With lentils (Puglia); with milk (Calabria).

Lancette (little spears: flat, folded into cornets 45–60 mm long). In broth and with cheese sauce (Valle d'Aosta).

Lasagne (long and very wide; their edges may be smooth or rippled). Baked in the oven with Bolognese *ragù* sauce (Emilia Romagna); with veal, *prosciutto crudo*, celery, and butter (Emilia Romagna); with nettle (Liguria); with pesto Genovese (Liguria); *incassettate*, that is, barely scalded, then baked in a mold in the oven (Marches).

Lasagne festonate (festooned lasagna; 35 x 300 mm or more). With frittata, cheese, and prosciutto (Piedmont).

Lasagnette (small *lasagne*, 20 x 100 mm). With snails (Trentino Alto Adige).

Linguine. With thick sauces, for example, marinara or *alla Gaeta*: with anchovies and garlic, capers, and olives (Campania).

Lumache rigate grandi (large ribbed snails, ø 35 mm). Fried in lard (Sicily).

Lumaconi (snails). *Ai quattro formaggi* (with four cheeses: Parmesan, Sbrinz, Emmenthal, fontina), with nutmeg and egg yolk (Lombardy).

Maccheroncelli (long macaroni, broken up, length 20 mm). *Alla ciociara*: with *mozzarella di bufala*, anchovies, garlic, tomatoes, black peppercorns, and sugar (Lazio); with sardines (Calabria); *alla potentina*: with white wine, egg, Scamorza, and olive oil, sprinkled with bread crumbs and baked in the oven (Basilicata); with sardines, raisins, pine nuts, and anise (Sicily).

Maccheroni (ø 4 mm, length 300 mm or more). With *ragù* and tomato sauces (Bobbio, Emilia Romagna); *alla pesarese* (Pesaro-style): with *prosciutto cotto*, turkey breast, chicken livers, veal, cheese, butter, black truffle, onion, broth, and cream, baked in the oven (Marches); with peas (Lazio); *alla siciliana* (Sicilian-style): with onion, peppers, black olives, anchovies, garlic, tomatoes, oregano, and eggplant (Sicily); with octopus (Puglia); baked in the oven with eggplant and garlic (Campania); with lamb *ragù* and rosemary (Molise); with cauliflower, raisins, pine nuts, Pecorino cheese, onion, anchovies, and saffron (Sicily).

Maccheroni alla chitarra (guitar-style). With veal *ragù* and tomato, egg, onion, and Pecorino (Abruzzo).

Mafalde (long noodles with rippled edges). Tomatoes, onion, dried mushrooms, pancetta, and parsley (Rome, Lazio).

Malloreddus (see *Gnocchetti sardi*; with saffron, length 10–20 mm). With tomato sauce and browned salami paste (Sardinia); with carrots, peas, celery, and onion (Sardinia); with lamb *ragù* (Sardinia).

Maltagliati. Alla rustichella: with fresh peas, *prosciutto cotto*, Gruyère, Parmesan, and pepper (everywhere); *alla sangiovaniello*: with pumpkin or zucchini flowers, San Giovanni Rotondo–style (Puglia).

Maniche (sleeves). With tuna and artichokes in white wine (everywhere).

Mezze maniche (half sleeves). With pork rind and red beans (Veneto).

Mezze maniche rigate (ribbed half sleeves). With rosemary and pecorino (Sardinia).

Mezze penne (half penne, quills). *Dell'orto e del mare* (land and sea): with artichokes and shrimp (Friuli Venezia Giulia); with basil, garlic, and olive oil (Liguria, Tuscany).

Mezze zite (half ziti, "bridegrooms"). *Alla livornese*: with smoked pork shoulder, onion, olive oil, garlic, basil, pepper, red pepper, and thyme (Tuscany).

Minuicchi (fresh egg pasta balls made by hand). *Alla potentina*: with smoked pancetta, pork, white wine, and grated sheep and goat cheese (Basilicata).

Ofelle (ravioli with veal, spinach, and potatoes). With cheese (Friuli Venezia Giulia and Veneto).

Orecchiette ("little ears"; fresh egg pasta, ø 20–25 mm). With lobster, carrots, red onion, butter and oil, champagne, and fish broth (Emilia Romagna); with turnip tops, tomato sauce, basil, and garlic (Puglia); *alla lucana*: made with rye flour, seasoned with onion and tomato sauce (Basilicata).

Pansoti (ravioli, ø 50 mm). With walnut sauce (Liguria).

Panzerotti di magro (meatless panzerotti, ø 50 mm). Fried in olive oil (Lazio).

Pappardelle (long, flat noodles, wound up into a ball, width 11–15 mm). With hare *ragù* (Arezzo, Tuscany); *alla cacciatora*: with mushrooms; *alla boscaiola*: with fresh peas and meat sauce (Piedmont); *ai cinque formaggi*: with five cheeses (ricotta, Parmesan, pecorino, Emmenthal, and Gruyère), cream, spinach, oil, and garlic (Emilia Romagna); with fish and vegetables (Puglia).

Pasta trita (various shapes, crushed). With fresh porcini mushrooms (Lombardy).

Penne lisce (smooth "quills," ø 8 mm, length 40 mm). *Alla contadina*: with tomatoes, olive oil, oregano, and cheese (everywhere); *all'arrabbiata*: with tomatoes, pancetta or fatback, garlic, onion, raisins, walnuts, hot red pepper, white wine, and Pecorino (Basilicata); *alla pescatora*: with crayfish and tomato sauce (on the coasts); with raw zucchini and garlic (everywhere); with woodcock (Veneto); with pumpkin, ricotta, onion, milk, and grated Parmesan (Emilia Romagna); *alla calabrese*: with anchovies, black olives, green olives, capers, and tuna (Calabria).

Penne mezzane (ø 4 mm, length 25 mm). With *musciame*, sun-dried fillet of tuna or dolphin (Sardinia); *penne con la 'nduja*: with the typical soft Calabrian salami (Calabria).

Penne mezzi ziti (ø 5 mm, length 20 mm). With sardines (Sicily).

Penne rigate (ribbed penne). With cabbage and provolone (Piedmont); with grated truffle (Umbria); with Trapani pesto (almonds, basil, garlic) (Sicily).

Pennette (ø 5 mm, length 25 mm). *Ncasciata*: with veal, chicken, salami paste, peas, pecorino, and Caciocavallo cheese (Sicily); with broccoli, raisins, anchovies, saffron, pine nuts, and pecorino (Sicily).

Pennette rigate (ribbed pennette). With mascarpone, cream, and spinach (Lombardy).

Perciatelli (ø 4 mm, length 300 mm or more, long, round, and hollow). *Alla napoletana*: with chopped meat, tomato paste, milk, mozzarella, egg, and peas (Campania); with snails (Calabria).

Perline (little pearls). Small pasta for soups and broths (everywhere).

Pipe rigate (ribbed pipes, 6 x 30 mm). *Alla sarda*, Sardinian-style: with olive oil, sage, myrtle, white wine, broth, olives, and basil (Sardinia).

Pizzicotti (ø 20 mm). Gnocchi with spinach, ricotta, and nutmeg; served with salt and pepper (Rome, Lazio).

Pizzoccheri (wheat flour and buckwheat noodles, 10 x 40 mm). With cheese and vegetables or with pigeon sauce (Valtellina, Lombardy); with a sauce of cabbage, potatoes, sage, and cheese (Lombardy).

Quadrucci (squares, 12–15 mm per side). With swordfish sauce (Messina, Sicily).

Ravioli (with herbs and ricotta, ø 40 mm). Of rye flour, with spinach and nutmeg (Alto Adige); *alla mantovana* (Mantua-style): with *ragù* and Parmesan (Lombardy).

Ravioli alle noci (walnut ravioli, ø 40 mm). With pesto (Liguria).

Reginette ("little queens," long, wide noodles with curled edges). With melted cheese, walnuts, and shaved black truffle (Piedmont).

Riccia (long, narrow noodles with curved edges). With *ragù* (Abruzzo).

Riccioli ("curls," length 250 mm; long, narrow noodles with rippled edges). With purée of lentils (Abruzzo).

Rigatoncini (slightly curved tubular pasta that is larger than *penne rigate* but smaller than rigatoni. It has a ridged surface and straight-cut ends). With purée of fava beans (Ragusa, Sicily).

Rigatoni (13 x 60 mm). With zucchini (Veneto); *all'uccelletto*: with larks, buntings, and figpeckers; with bird's breast in a *ragù* of chopped meat with onion, garlic, white wine, sage, and tomato paste (Bergamo, Lombardy); *alla romana*: with *prosciutto crudo*, pork, offal, peas, oil, and pecorino (Lazio); with fava beans (Lazio); *alla pajata* (Lazio); with eggplant, mozzarella, tomatoes, egg, bread crumbs, onion, and basil (Puglia); *alla napoletana*: baked with chopped meat, tomatoes, onion, mozzarella, and egg (Campania); with eggplant, tomatoes, garlic, and olives (Sicily).

Rotini. With very thick sauces or in pasta salads (everywhere).

Schiaffoni or *schiaffettoni* ("slaps" or "cuffs," ø 10 mm, length 55 mm). With broccoli; with sea urchins (Calabria).

Sedani rigati ("ribbed celery," ø 8–10 mm, ø 50–60 mm in length). With capers, basil, and mozzarella (everywhere); with chicory, fava beans, and ricotta (everywhere).

Spaghetti (ø 1.8–2 mm, length 300 mm or more). With tomato sauces or timbale (everywhere); *all'amatriciana*: with diced smoked veal cheek, tomatoes, onion, and pecorino (Lazio); *spaghetti alle vongole veraci*: with clams (Marches); *alla norcina*: with truffles (Umbria); *ai quattro gusti*, with four tastes: tongue, chicken breast, Gruyère, black truffles, grated Parmesan, and peppercorns (Marches); *alla toscana*: with tomatoes, garlic, pepper, basil, pancetta, and capers (Tuscany); *macco*: with beans, celery, onions, and fresh tomatoes (Tuscany); *alla carbonara*: with pancetta, egg, and grated Parmesan (Lazio); *all'arrabbiata*: with pork tripe or pancetta, garlic, onion, hot red pepper, walnuts, and white wine (Lazio); *alla carrettera*: with pancetta or salt pork, tuna, porcini mushrooms, garlic, olive oil, and grated cheese (Lazio); *alla caprese*: with tomato, mozzarella, basil, and oregano (Campania); with clams, white wine, olive oil, parsley, and garlic (Campania); *alla puveriello*: with fried egg and cheese (Campania); *alla puttanesca*: with anchovies, black olives, capers, tomatoes, garlic, hot red pepper, and olive oil (Campania); *alla barese*: with turnip tops, tomatoes, and basil (Puglia); with black cuttlefish ink and tomatoes (Sicily); *alla Norma*: with eggplant, tomatoes, ricotta, and garlic (Sicily); *alla bottarga*, with roe (Sardinia); *all'algherese*: with olive oil, garlic, oregano, clams, and capers (Sardinia).

Spaghettoni (ø 18.5 mm). *Carbonada*: with meat, red wine, rosemary, and butter (Valle d'Aosta).

Stellette (little stars). Pastina to be added to chicken broth (everywhere).

Strangolapreti ("priest-stranglers," 15 x 40 mm). Rolled-up pasta made of soaked white bread, flour, egg, herbs, and cheese, served with cheese, butter, and sage (Trentino Alto Adige).

Strozzapreti ("priest-chokers," short rolled *bucatini*). *Al burro nero* ("dark" butter): browned with parsley (Basilicata).

Tagliatelle (fresh pasta, length 300 mm). *Smalzade, smacafam*: cut strips of pasta coiled up into a "nest" and seasoned with melted lard (Trentino); with mountain goat meat and clover sprouts (Alto Adige); *alla veneta*: with veal, spicy salami paste, nutmeg, red wine, onion, and cream (Veneto); with lobster (Adriatic coast, Emilia Romagna); with salmon, milk, red onion, and tomato purée (Emilia Romagna); with mascarpone, egg yolk, and black pepper (Umbria); with mussels (Calabria).

Tagliatelle all'uovo (egg noodles, 4.3–5.8 x 300 mm or more). With garlic butter (Emilia Romagna); with mascarpone (Emilia Romagna); with shrimp (Emilia Romagna).

Taglierini (3 x 300 mm or more). With roast drippings (Piedmont).

Tagliolini (flat, long, wound up in a ball, width of 2 mm). With herbs (sage, marjoram, rosemary, basil, parsley, and chives) and butter, egg yolk, and cream (Emilia Romagna).

Timau (ravioli in a shape characteristic of the village of the same name). With poppy seeds (Friuli Venezia Giulia).

Tortelli (ø 50 mm, with meat filling). With cream (Crema, Lombardy).

Tortellini (ø 15–20 mm, with meat and cheese filling). With pumpkin and Cremona *mostarda* (Lombardy); with pork, egg, and three types of meat (Emilia Romagna).

Tortelloni (ø 50–70 mm). With asparagus and mushrooms (Piedmont); with cuttlefish ink (Abruzzo).

Trenette (ø 3.5 mm, length 300 mm or more). With pesto Genovese (Liguria); *alla marinara*: with tomatoes, parsley, seafood, and white wine (Liguria).

Trofie (fresh pasta of wheat and chestnut flour, length 40 mm). With pesto Genovese (Liguria); with walnut sauce (Recco, Liguria).

Vermicelli (ø 2.5 mm, length 20 mm). With light sauces. Eaten cold, mixed with vegetable salads (Campania); *alla partenopea*: with pecorino, tomatoes, and basil (Campania); with feta cheese and olives (Puglia); *alla pizzaiola*: with tomatoes, olive oil, oregano, and garlic (Campania); with grape snails (*carrozze*, carriages) (Calabria); *alla calabra*: with herring, bread crumbs, red pepper, and olive oil (Calabria), *mille cosedde* (a thousand little things): with fava beans, lentils, peas, white beans, cabbage, onion, carrot, celery, pancetta, and Pecorino (Calabria); *alla siracusana*: with ripe tomatoes, peppers, eggplant, black olives, capers, salted anchovies, garlic, basil, and grated Pecorino (Sicily).

Vincisgrassi (broad, flat lasagna noodles, 100 mm wide). With brains and white truffle; baked in the oven with egg, onion, Marsala, and chicken giblets (Marches).

Ziti or *zite* (ø 10–12 mm, 20–60 mm in length, hollow). *All'amalfitana*: with veal, carrots, white wine, pancetta, Caciocavallo cheese, and tomato purée (Campania); in tomato sauce (Sicily).

Notes

Unless otherwise noted, works cited by their English titles can be found in the translator's bibliography. All other works can be found in the author's biobliography.

PREFACE
1. XÁOS. *Giornale di confine* 4, no. 1 (March–June 2005–2006).
2. In a letter to his friend Pletnev, November 2, 1837.
3. *Pis'ma iz Francii i Italii*, letter VII, February 25, 1848.
4. Montanari, ed., *Il mondo in cucina. Storia, identità, scambi* (C. Petrini's note). Petrini, *Buono, pulito e giusto*. Einaudi, Turin, 2005, p. 75.

FRIULI VENEZIA GIULIA
1. *Italian Journey*, September 14, 1786, pp. 33–34.

THE *SAGRA*
1. Utilized here and further on in this chapter are abundant materials drawn from Ceccarelli, *Lo stomaco della Repubblica*, pp. 90–91, 95.
2. Martini, "D'Alema: noi e l'Ulivo per governare," in *La Stampa*.
3. "Era buon governo efficiente," in *Il Foglio*.
4. Montanelli, "La cosa due e i tortellini."
5. "D'Alema e Montanelli, tortellini di lotta o di governo?," in *Corriere della Sera*.
6. "La prevalenza del tortellino, Guazzaloca si annette il simbolo dell'identità bolognese," in *La Stampa*.
7. Rodotà, "La strategia delle brigate tortellino."
8. "Italiani mangiatori di rane alle feste del partito," in *L'Unità*, January 21, 1991.

VENETO AND THE CITY OF VENICE
1. Cuttlefish are rounder and shorter than calamari (squid), whose name not by accident derives from *calamarion*, which means "depository of black humor."

2. From Artusi, *La scienza in cucina e l'arte di mangiar bene*, p. xii, since Camporesi's introduction is not included in the English edition. Subsequent citations are from the English translation, *Science in the Kitchen and the Art of Eating Well* (see translator's bibliography).

3. Artusi, *Science in the Kitchen*, p. 357.

4. Fochesato and Pronzati, *Stoccafisso & Baccalà*; Ferrari, *Merluzzo, baccalà o stoccafisso?*

5. *Italian Journey*, September 14 and 19, 1786, pp. 32, 46.

6. Celebrated in the unforgettable epitaph of a fisherman: *"Oui zaze Bernardin de Ca' Donao, che morì in tel pescar cape de deo, co la camisa curta e l'cul bagnao del millecinquecento. Ora pro eo."* ("Here lies Bernardin de Ca' Donao of 1500, who died fishing for the *Capa de deo*, with a short shirt and a wet behind. Pray for him.")

7. *Revue culturelle de Droit de l'Art*, April 25, 2005.

8. Benedetto Varchi, *L'Ercolano. Dialogo di M. Benedetto 'Varchi nel quale si ragiona delle lingue*, pp. 82–83.

OLIVE OIL

1. "Oration for Sextus Roscius of Ameria," XVII, XVIII.

2. *The Georgics*, Book II, 513–15.

TRENTINO ALTO ADIGE

1. *Italian Journey*, September 11, 1786, p. 21.

2. Ibid., October 3, 1786, p. 69.

3. Ibid., March 12, 1787, p. 194.

LOMBARDY

1. Bertolino, *Milanesi. Lavoro, guadagno, spendo, pretendo*, pp. 65–70.

2. *Rome, Naples and Florence*, December 5, 1816, pp. 120–21.

3. Ibid., December 28, 1816, pp. 164–65.

4. Cattaneo, "Notizie sulla Lombardia," p. 472.

5. *Rome, Naples and Florence*, December 16, 1816, p. 149.

6. In Marchi, *Quando siamo a tavola*, p. 17.

7. *Inferno*, XXXIII:80.

8. *Canzoniere*, CXLVI.

9. *Lettere a Milano* (Letters to Milan), p. 69 (cited in Ceccarelli, *Lo stomaco della Repubblica*, p. 94).

10. Caprara, *Togliatti, il comintern e il gatto selvatico*, pp. 13–14.

11. Stendhal, *Rome, Naples and Florence*, January 4, 1817, pp. 208–209.

VALLE D'AOSTA

1. *Viaggi e assaggi*, vol. 1, p. 8.

2. *The Praise of Folly*, pp. 1–2.

JEWS

1. *I discorsi di Pietro Andrea Mattioli su De materia medica di Dioscoride*, chapter 78.

2. *Pratica, e scalcaria*, p. 245.

3. *L'economia del cittadino in villa*, p. 244.

4. *Science in the Kitchen*, p. 295ff.; recipe 399, *petonciani*.

5. *Il Novellino*, 35.

6. *L'Ameto*, p. 66.

7. Deuteronomy 14:4–23; New International Version.

PIEDMONT

1. *Baudolino*, pp. 27–28.
2. *Physiology of Taste*, p. 126.
3. Ibid., p. 127.
4. Ceccarelli, *Opusculum de tuberibus, Alphonso Ciccarello physico de Maeuania auctore. Adiecimus etiam opusculum de Clitumno flumine, eodem auctore. Cum duplici indice, capitum scilicet, & auctorum*, 1564.
5. Summary by Annamaria Sigalotti in *E-Art*, January 2005.

LIGURIA

1. *Del conseruare la sanità, et del viuere de' genouesi*, p. 418.
2. Gueglio, *Mario! Storia vera tragica e avventurosa del polpo Mario*, pp. 23–24.

THE EARLY GIFTS FROM THE AMERICAS

1. Airaldi (ed.), *I viaggi dopo la scoperta*. Cited in Di Wine taste, *Cultura e informazione enologica*, Feb. 2007, no. 49.
2. "The *molandaie*, the women who grind it, take a quantity of this grain and soak it in cold water the night before; in the morning they pulverize it little by little with two stones; some stand, and some kneel on the ground; nor do they watch whether hair or lice fall in. When the dough, which they have sprinkled with water and little by little kneaded with their hands, is ready, they make certain long or round loaves; wrapping them in cane leaves, they let them cook with as little water as possible. This is the bread of the common folk; it lasts three days, then it gets moldy. The upper class makes it like this: they soak the grain, the *molandaie* pound it with the stones, and after washing it with hot water and removing the husk, they are left with the kernel; they grind it as much as possible and, forming the dough, make small flatbreads and cook them on a round disk, over a very low flame." Benzoni, *La historia del mondo nuovo di M. Girolamo Benzoni milanese*.
3. "One may reasonably count among the types of grain the one that is wrongly [named] since it should be called Indian and not Turkish given that it was brought from the West Indies and not from from Turkish Asia." Mattioli, *I discorsi di Pietro Andrea Mattioli su De materia medica di Dioscoride*, chap. 21, vol. 3, p. 281.
4. "I do not believe that maize grain is inferior to wheat; it is larger and richer and generates blood, the reason why those who consume it for the first time in large quantities suffer from swelling and itching." De Acosta, *Historia naturale e morale delle Indie*.
5. "Maize is one of the grains that should be more appreciated in the world . . . It is ground on a stone and the bread that is made, without using salt or leavening or anything other than some cold water, is quickly toasted or cooked in a casserole or on an earthenware disk." De Cardenas, *Problemas y secretos maravillosos de las Indias*.
6. "They [the Indians] eat it in place of bread, grilled or boiled in water . . . From maize flour the Spaniards make biscuits, fritters, and other delicate dishes both for the sound of health and for the sick." Garcilaso de la Vega, *Commentari reali sul Perù degli Incas*.
7. *Lettera al Cardinale Ascanio Sforza Visconti*. In the second edition of 1516 the word "maize" appears for the first time.
8. *La Pratica agricola* (1778). Cited in Montanari, *Il pentolino magico*, p. 95.
9. This is mentioned in Crosby, *The Columbian Exchange*. (See author's bibliography.)
10. Clini, *L'alimentazione nella storia*.
11. *Scritti naturalistici*.
12. The history of the dominant scarlet color scheme found in Italian cuisine is the theme of a curious illustrated volume by Alberto Capatti, with texts by the famous chef Gianfranco Vissani: *Pomi d'oro: immagini del pomodoro nella storia del gusto* (Golden apples: images of the tomato in the history of flavor).

EMILIA ROMAGNA

1. Naturally, this is not a prerogative of only Italian cities. Paris is the City of Light, Istanbul the City of the Golden Horn, Damascus the Desert Pearl, Aberdeen the City of Granite. And finally Baghdad (who would believe it today?) has been known as the City of Peace since the dawn of time.
2. *Obrazy Italii*, vol. 1, p. 121.
3. In the Middle Ages all parts of the animal were consumed: heads, in particular, had an important symbolic value as a sign of power and authority.
4. The story is contained in the chronicle of Cherubino Ghirardacci, *Storia di Bologna* (History of Bologna), cited in Montanari, *Il pentolino magico*, pp. 81–83. The precious descriptions of similar celebrations are contained in Maioli and Roversi, *Civiltà della tavola a Bologna*.
5. *Nuovi poemetti*, pp. 60–70.
6. Here and in subsequent passages we summarize the notable descriptions of the life of these marsh dwellers contained in Black, *Al Dente: The Adventures of a Gastronome in Italy*, pp. 141–51. See translator's bibliography.
7. *Al Dente*, p. 150.
8. *Banchetti compositioni di vivande*, 1529.
9. *Le donne, i cavalier, l'armi, gli amori*, translated by William Stewart Rose, vol. 1, p. xvii.

CALENDAR

1. *The Ash Wednesday Supper*, p. 67.
2. Ibid., pp. 67–68.
3. Ibid., p. 68.
4. *"Chi la squallida cervogia / alle labbra sue congiugne, / presto muore, o rado giugne / all'età vecchia e barbogia."* (He who puts to his lips a distasteful beer will die young, or rarely reach an old, decrepit age), a pseudomedical observation by ultra-Tuscan Francesco Redi (1626–98), a poet, surgeon, and member of the Accademia della Crusca.
5. *The Satires*, Book II, Satire VI, "The Delights of the Country."
6. *The Natural History of Pliny*, XVIII, 118.

TUSCANY

1. *The Voyage of Italy, or A Compleat Journey Through Italy*.
2. *Pictures from Italy*, p. 156.
3. *Italian Journey*, October 25, 1786, pp. 103–104.
4. *Rome, Naples and Florence*, October 4, 1816, p. 23.
5. *Nicolo Machiavelli, the Florentine*, p. 103.
6. *Rome, Naples and Florence*, December 6, 1816, p. 123.
7. Prezzolini, *Nicolo Machiavelli, the Florentine*.
8. *The Natural History of Pliny*, p. 246.
9. *Paradiso*, XVII: 58–60.
10. *Purgatorio*, XXIV: 28–29.
11. Prezzolini, *Nicolo Macchiavelli, the Florentine*, pp. 180–82.
12. Ceccarelli, *Lo stomaco della Repubblica*, p. 67.
13. Mocci, "Il partito della bistecca."
14. *Italian Journey*, October 25, 1786, p. 104.
15. Cited in Black, *Al Dente*, p. 49.
16. *Science in the Kitchen*, p. 63.
17. *Al Dente*, p. 45
18. *Decameron*, VI: 10.

PASTA

1. *The Pentamerone of Giambattista Basile*, IV, 3, p. 254.
2. *The Memoirs of Herr von Schnabelewopski*, pp. 138–39.
3. *Maccheroni & C.*, p. 15.
4. *Quando siamo a tavola*, p. 24.
5. Ligabue, *Storia delle forniture navali e dell'alimentazione di bordo.*
6. Tonelli, *La pittura a Genova come fonte per la storia dell'alimentazione.*
7. Agnesi, *È tempo di pasta*, pp. 38–39, 56.
8. Letter to V. N. Repnina from Rome, June 14, 1838.
9. *Underworld*, pp. 698–99.

UMBRIA

1. Muratov, *Obrazy Italii*, vol. 3, p. 223.

THE MARCHES

1. Codex Atlanticus, overleaf of sheet 5.
2. *Purgatorio*, XXIV: 21–24.

THE LATER GIFTS FROM AMERICA

1. From a collection of fragments, aphorisms, and epigrams by Leo Longanesi, *Parliamo dell'elefante* (Let's talk about the elephant). Longanesi, Milano, 2005, p. 161. Note dated January 14, 1944.
2. Mureddu, *Il Quirinale dei presidenti*, p. 27.
3. Here and elsewhere in this chapter, some materials and citations are drawn from Ceccarelli, *Lo stomaco della Repubblica*, pp. 22–23, 30ff.
4. Catti De Gasperi, *De Gasperi uomo solo*, p. 193.
5. Zatterin, "La nave dell'amicizia sbarca i suoi doni a Napoli."
6. "La 500esima nave americana" (The 500th American ship), *La Stampa*, April 4, 1948. The article is signed with the initials V.G.; according to Filippo Ceccarelli (*Lo stomaco della Repubblica*, p. 34), they are the initials of Vittorio Gorresio.
7. "Il cardine della lotta elettorale: i rifornimenti americani e le relazioni con la Russia," in *La Stampa*, February 23, 1948.
8. Ginsborg, *A History of Contemporary Italy*, p. 117.
9. As proof of the philosoviet and philorussian sympathies on the part of the vast majority of the Italian Left, a monstrosity like *pastasciutta alla vodka* (pasta with vodka sauce) appeared on restaurant menus. The creation involved sprinkling the rigatoni with vodka. To this day, ordering this dish may be considered an elegant gesture in the spirit of the "radical-chic" intelligentsia.
10. "Sogno americano e mito sovietico nell'Italia contemporanea," in *Nemici per la pelle*, p. 31.
11. "Coca-cola dal Viet Nam a Silvio" (Coca-Cola from Vietnam to Silvio), in *Corriere della Sera*, February 9, 2000. See also "Quando le bevande irrompono in politica" (When beverages erupt into politics), in *Il Tempo*, February 9, 2000.
12. Elena Babaytseva, "Bodalsya Turin s Koka-koloi."
13. Ariès, *I figli di McDonald's.*

LAZIO AND THE CITY OF ROME

1. Platina (real name: Bartolomeo Sacchi, 1421–1481) was prefect at the Vatican Library, the Church's first lay historian, a well-known humanist, and, among other things, a friend of Master Martino, that is, Martino De Rossi, the celebrated cook originally from Canton Ticino, and author of Italy's first

cookbook, *De arte coquinaria* (1457). Starting from the second half of the fifteenth century, everyone stole recipes from Martino's book, including his friend Platina. Platina's own treatise, *De honesta voluptate et valetudine* (1468), based on the book his teacher wrote, had a much wider circulation. Sacchi even admits that his book is a revised version of Master Martino's recipes ("What cook, oh immortal gods, can compete with my Martino di Como, from whom I have taken the greater part of what I record here?"). Platina's work is the first cookbook to be printed (it came out in Latin in 1474, in Rome). The Italian translation was published quite soon, in 1487, in Venice, followed by the German, French, and English versions. With regard to style, Platina created a comical macaronic Latin, since this parodied the language of Apicius (see further on in the present chapter), imitating the style of classical literature, in the manner of the humanists, and creating calques from the Italian in a hybrid of macaronic Latin and Greek (for example, he calls blancmange *leucophagium*, leukophagy).

2. *Platynae historici Liber de vita Christi ac omnium pontificum*, pp. 20–23.
3. *Nicolo Machiavelli, the Florentine*, pp. 50–51.
4. Stendhal, *A Roman Journal*, pp. 201–202.
5. Petronius, *Satyricon*, p. 28.
6. Ibid., p. 40.
7. Ibid., p. 26.
8. *Thirteen Satires of Juvenal*, Satire 11, p. 76.
9. *The Travel Diary of Peter A. Tolstoi: A Muscovite in Modern Europe*, p. 225.
10. The facts about artichokes are combined with information taken from the magazine *Grand Gourmet*, 2004, no. 6, pp. 64ff.
11. He may well comment behind their backs, though. Notable is the recollection of Galina Muravieva, a well-known Moscow Italianist and professor: "In an Italian bar two Russians are enjoying a slice of pizza with a cappuccino. Behind their backs the waiter is heard saying in a not very low voice: 'Imbeciles, pizza and cappuccino!' " Muravieva, "O ede," p. 215.
12. Herzen, *Pis'ma iz Franzii i Italii*, letter V, December 6, 1847, p. 145.
13. *Italian Journey*, March 23, 1787, p. 209.
14. Muratov, *Obrazy Italii*, vol. 2, p. 100.

THE MEDITERRANEAN DIET

1. *The Futurist Cookbook*, p. 23.
2. *Nicolo Machiavelli, the Florentine*, p. 182.
3. *Journey Through Germany and Italy*, p. 601.
4. *Breve racconto di tutte le radici di tutte l'erbe e di tutti i frutti che crudi o cotti in Italia si mangiano*, p. 143.
5. *Opera dell'arte del cucinare.*
6. Malandra and Renon, *Le principali frodi dei prodotti della pesca*, p. 13.
7. This type of harpoon fishing is described in the chapters devoted to Calabria, Sicily, and Sardinia.
8. *Il mestiere del gastronauta*, p. 56.
9. *Journey Through Germany and Italy*, p. 585.
10. *Scritti naturalistici.* Vegetable food is also the subject of a treatise by Salvatore Massonio of Aquila (1627): *Archidipno, ovvero Dell'insalata e dell'uso di essa* (The best banquet, or about salad and its use).
11. Available at www.pomonaitaliana.it.
12. *Italian Journey*, March 2, 1787, p. 180.
13. *The Art of Living Long*, p. 87.
14. Ibid., p. 87.
15. *Cognizione del dolore*, Part I, p. 88.
16. "Essay on Orthorexia: Unhealthy Obsession with Healthy Foods." See author's bibliography.

ABRUZZO AND MOLISE

1. De Nino, *Usi e costumi abruzzesi*, vol. 3, p. 51.
2. Falconi, *Amico castello.*
3. *Italian Journey*, May 2, 1787, p. 273.
4. *Grande dizionario di cucina*, p. 1152. (The page number refers to the Italian edition.)

DEMOCRACY

1. *Pis'ma iz Franzii i Italii*, Letter V, December 6, 1847.
2. *La sua signora*, January 7, 1957.
3. "A true life experience. In Rome, a reception is held at the home of a translator and specialist in Russian culture, in honor of a writer who has come from Moscow. It is one o'clock, lunch is served. After lunch the writer asks when they will drink tea. 'I was dumbstruck, but I did not lose heart!' the hostess laughs enthusiastically. 'I decided to amuse everyone. Guess what I devised! I said, now we'll all have tea! And no one batted an eye! I brought the cups, and everyone started drinking! That's how I managed to get out of it!' Think about it: if an expert in Russian culture, a person who lived in Moscow for ten years, considers it so barbarous and uncivilized to request tea at the wrong time, what can we expect from other Italians? Russians, on the other hand, will not understand what there was to be dumbstruck about, not knowing that Italians drink only coffee after lunch, and only afterwards have dessert. 'Much good may it do them,' the Russian will say. 'But if there was tea in the house and it could easily be made, what harm was there in serving the guest tea with dessert?' In Russia there would be nothing wrong with it, but in Italy such a thing is inconceivable." Muravieva, "O ede," p. 215.
4. Marchi, *Quando siamo a tavola*, p. 114.
5. *La dolce vita*, chapter entitled "Kolobok," p. 103.
6. Parkinson, *Mrs Parkinson's Law and Other Studies in Domestic Science*, p. 53.
7. "'Another slice of prosciutto?' the hostess asks the Russian guest. 'Thank you, I'll have it later,' the guest replies distractedly, continuing the interesting conversation with his neighbor. All the Italians around the table stiffen. The hostess is confused. What does later mean, how long will they have to wait? In fact, as long as the antipasti are still on the table, the first course cannot be served." Muravieva, "O ede," p. 217.
8. Paolo Conti, in *Corriere della sera*, April 13, 2006.
9. Some materials referred to on this page are taken from Ceccarelli, *Lo stomaco della Repubblica*, pp. 60–66.
10. *La Stampa*, May 16, 1953.
11. *La Stampa*, June 5, 1953.
12. Gorresio, *I carissimi nemici*, pp. 236–37.
13. A great deal of interesting information on the subject can be found in the books of Tonino Tosto: *Le ricette democratiche* and *La cucina dell'Ulivo*.

CAMPANIA AND THE CITY OF NAPLES

1. *Italian Journey*, May 29, 1787, pp. 319–20.
2. *Italy: Rome and Naples*, p. 89
3. *Rome, Naples and Florence*, December 6, 1816, p. 123, and February 20, 1817, p. 358.
4. *Il cibo e l'impegno*, p. 62.
5. This is how Aldo Buzzi describes them in his amusing and ironic book *The Perfect Egg and Other Secrets* (p. 86). And he adds: "Alas, the moment you get away from Naples you're bound to run into stringy string beans. This world is full of mysteries. Here is one of them: why do nurserymen continue to plant beans with strings in them?"
6. Catullus, Ode XXVII.

INGREDIENTS

1. Horace, *The Satires*, Book II, Satire IV.
2. Brillat-Savarin, *The Physiology of Taste*, p. 71.
3. Marchi, *Quando siamo a tavola*, p. 16.
4. Petrini, *Buono, pulito e giusto*, p. 73.

PUGLIA

1. The term is used elsewhere in the south as well to designate the leader of a team of fishermen. The man who harpoons the tuna during the *mattanza* in Sardinia, for example, is called *rais*.
2. *The Satires*, Book I, Satire V, "Onward to Supper at Cocceius' Villa."
3. Ibid., "And So by Stages to Journey's End."

EROS

1. *Physiology of Taste*, pp. 184–185.
2. *Italy: Rome and Naples*, pp. 321–22.
3. Ibid., p. 321.
4. Ibid.
5. Prezzolini, *Nicolo Machiavelli, the Florentine*, p. 100.
6. Buzzi, *L'uovo alla kok*, p. 53.
7. Camilleri, *The Snack Thief*, p. 225.
8. Ibid., pp. 266–68, 277.

BASILICATA

1. *Franceide*, VI, 18.

RESTAURANTS

1. "Che bontà dietro il banco . . ." (What delicacies behind the counter . . .), *Il Sole—24 Ore*, May 14, 2006, Sunday insert.
2. "Breakfast. The Italian woman downs her coffee with a thin cookie and offers her guest bread, butter, and jam, as if to say: Help yourself. But her imagination does not go beyond this. She should see the breakfast menu in a Russian boarding house, little changed since Soviet times: wheat kasha, chicken cutlet, ricotta pudding with jam, cheese, butter, chocolate!" Muravieva, "O ede," p. 217.
3. Black, *Al Dente*, p. 149.
4. *Pictures from Italy*, p. 49.
5. Heine's notes, cited in Marchi, *Quando siamo a tavola*, p. 237.
6. "O ede," p. 220.

CALABRIA

1. Homer, *The Odyssey*, XII, 92–101, pp. 290–91.

PIZZA

1. *Italian Journey*, May 29, 1787, pp. 320–21.
2. *Pictures from Italy*, p. 55.

SICILY

1. Cited in Daniel B. Levine, *Tuna in Ancient Greece*.
2. *Il cibo e l'impegno*, p. 73.

3. Ibid.

4. Cited in Revel, *Culture and Cuisine*, p. 32.

5. Chiaramonte and Paolini, "Tra i banchi del mercato con il Cuciniere." Carmelo Chiaramonte is the chef at the restaurant Katane of Catania.

TOTALITARIANISM

1. Marinetti, *The Futurist Cookbook*.

2. Ibid.

3. Sigalotti, "La cucina futurista tra manifesti, banchetti e ricette 'antipassatiste.' "

4. "Il libro dei cibi buoni e sani sovietici."

5. *Al Dente*, pp. 210ff.

6. Ibid., p. 210.

7. *Menu e dossier*, pp. 60–61.

8. Corbi and Zanetti, "Non lasciamoci distrarre dall'olio."

9. "No, lo sterco no . . ." in *L'Espresso*, December 20, 1959.

SARDINIA

1. Bevilacqua and Mantovano, *Laboratori del gusto*, p. 21.

2. *Al Dente*, p. 187.

3. For the description of the life of Sardinian fisherman, much is owed to the oft cited work of William Black.

4. *Al Dente*, pp. 171ff.

JOY

1. *Petrarch's Remedies for Fortune Fair and Foul*, vol. 1, p. 140.

2. Marinetti, *The Futurist Cookbook*.

3. *Physiology of Taste*, pp. 25–26, 203.

4. *Zibaldone di pensieri*, July 6, 1826, p. 4183.

5. Marchi, *Quando siamo a tavola*, p. 86.

6. *The Pentamerone (Lo cunto de li cunti)* of Giambattista Basile, vol. 1, pp. 67–68.

7. *Thirteen Satires of Juvenal*, Satire 4, p. 27.

8. *Culture and Cuisine*, p. 36.

9. *Rome, Naples and Florence*, January 1, 1817, p. 189.

10. Ibid., January 1, 1817, p. 187.

11. Ibid., December 6, 1816, p. 122.

12. The history of sorbets is older, but the fundamental discourse on this subject was written in 1775 by Baldini in *De'Sorbetti*.

13. The situation was such as early as the sixteenth century. In 1583 the physician Baldassarre Pisanelli affirms: "Now every poor drudge wants bread, wine and snow."

14. Polato, "Si inaugura '2001 Italia' in Giapone," p. 138.

15. *Le confessioni di un italiano*, chapter 18, p. 306.

16. *The Snack Thief*, pp. 64–65.

17. *Italian Journey*, September 11, 1786, p. 20.

18. Virgil, *The Georgics*, IV, 127–49.

19. *Obrazy Italii*, vol. 3, p. 294.

20. *Italian Journey*, November 7, 1786, p. 122.

21. *Zapisi i vypiski*, p. 49.

Author's Bibliography

Abbondanti, Antonio. *Gazzette menippee di Parnaso capitoli piacevoli d'Antonio Abbondanti da Imola, coll'aggiunta d'alcune rime giocose del medesimo autore.* Francesco Baba, Venice, 1629.

———. *Viaggio di Colonia, capitoli piaceuoli d'Antonio Abbondanti da Imola . . . Con un'aggiunta del medesimo autore. Opera piena di bellissimi pensieri, e di leggiadrissimi concetti intessuta, nouamente mandata in luce, & aggiunta alle Rime del Berni.* Francesco Baba, Venice, 1627.

Acosta, José de. *Historia naturale e morale delle Indie.* With articles by Gabriella Airaldi and Francesco Barbarani. Cassa di Risparmio di Verona, Vicenza, Belluno and Ancona, Verona, 1992 (first edition, in Latin, 1596). The following edition was also used: *The Natural and Moral History of the Indies by Father Joseph de Acosta.* Translated by Edward Grimston (1604); edited by Clements R. Markham (1880). Franklin, New York, 1970.

Agnello Hornby, Simonetta. *La mennulara.* Feltrinelli, Milan, 2003.

Agnesi, Vincenzo. *È tempo di pasta, scritti 1960–1976.* Gangemi, Rome, 1992.

Airaldi, Gabriella, ed. *I viaggi dopo la scoperta.* Cassa di Risparmio di Verona, Vicenza, Belluno, Verona, 1985.

Alberici, Annalisa. *La cucina del giorno della festa: al disna dal di la festa.* Torchio De' Ricci, Pavia, 1986.

Alberini, Massimo. *4000 anni a tavola. Dalla bistecca preistorica al picnic sulla Luna.* Fabbri, Milan, 1972.

———. *Storia del pranzo all'italiana: dal triclinio allo snack.* Rizzoli, Milan, 1966.

Alessio, Giovanni. "Storia linguistica di un antico cibo rituale: i maccheroni," *Atti dell'Accademia Pontaniana,* n.s., 7 (1958), pp. 261–80.

Alighieri, Dante. *La Divina Commedia.* Edizioni Paoline, Rome, 1976.

Alliata Duca di Salaparuta, Enrico. *Cucina vegetariana e crudismo vegetale: manuale di gastrosofia naturista con raccolta di 1030 formule scelte d'ogni paese.* Hoepli, Milan, 1932.

Anau, Roberta, and Elena Loewenthal. *Cucina ebraica.* Fabbri, Milan, 2000.

André, Jacques. *L'alimentation et la cuisine à Rome.* Les Belles Lettres, Paris, 1981.

Angelita Roco, Giovanni Francesca, *I pomi d'oro di Gio. Francisco Angelita Roco Academico Disuguale doue si contengono sue lettioni de' fichi l'una, e de' melloni l'altra . . . Aggiuntaui una lettione della lumaca doue si proua, ch'ella sia maestra della vita humana*. Introduction and notes by Franco Foschi. Micheloni Edizioni, Recanati, 1978 (facsimile reproduction of the first edition by Antonio Braida, Recanati, 1607).

Anghiera, Pietro Martire d'. *Lettera al Cardinale Ascanio Sforza Visconti, inviata dalla corte di Spagna il 13 novembre 1493, pubblicata nella Prima Decade, Libro primo, nel 1511 a Siviglia.*

Anthimus. *De observatione ciborum (On the Observance of Foods)*. Edited by Mark Grant. Prospect Books, Blackawton, United Kingdom, 1996.

Antropologia e storia dell'alimentazione: il pane. Edited by Cristina Papa. Electa, Perugia, 1992.

Apicius. *De re coquinaria (L'art culinaire)*. Edited by Jacques André. Les Belles Lettres, Paris, 1974.

Archestratus. *Gastronomia*. Translated by Domenico Scinà. Antonelli, Venice, 1842.

Ariès, Paul. *I figli di McDonald's: la globalizzazione dell'hamburger*. Translated by Maria Chiara Giovannini. Dedalo, Bari, 2000.

Arte della cucina: libri di ricette, testi sopra lo scalco, il trinciante e i vini dal XIV al XIX secolo. Edited by Emilio Faccioli. Edizioni Il Polifilo, Milan, 1966.

Artusi, Pellegrino. *La scienza in cucina e l'arte di mangiar bene. Manuale pratico per le famiglie*. Edited by Piero Camporesi. Einaudi, Turin, 1995 (first Italian edition: 1891).

Babaytseva, Elena. "Bodalsya Turin s Koka-koloi." *Nezavisimaya Gazeta*, November 28, 2005.

Bacchelli, Riccardo. *Il mulino del Po*. Introduction by Indro Montanelli. Mondadori, Milan, 1986.

Bacci, Andrea. *De conviviis antiquorum* (first edition, in Latin: 1597). In Gronovius, *Thesaurus graecarum antiquitatum*, Lyons, 1701.

———. *De naturali vinorum historia*. Anastatic reprint by the Ordine dei Cavalieri del Tartufo. Edited by Mariano Corino. Toso, Turin, 1990 (first edition, in Latin: Mutii, Rome, 1596).

Baldini, Filippo. *De' Sorbetti*. Arnaldo Forni, Sala Bolognese, 1979 (facsimile reproduction of the edition of Stamperia Raimondiana, Naples, 1784; first edition, 1775).

Balducci Pegolotti, Francesco. *La pratica della mercatura*. Edited by Allan Evans. Kraus Reprint Co., New York, 1970.

Balzani, Francesco. *La tiorba a taccone de Felippo Sgruttendio de Scafato*. Magma, Naples, 2000.

Barth, Hans. *Osteria: Kulturgeschichtlicher Führer durch Italiens Schenken von Verona bis Capri*. J. Hoffmann, Stuttgart, 1908 (Italian edition: *Osteria: guida spirituale delle osterie italiane*, preface by Gabriele D'Annunzio, introduction by Marco Guarnaschielli Gotti, F. Muzzio, Padua, 1998; first Italian edition: *Osteria: guida spirituale delle osterie italiane da Verona a Capri*, translated by Giovanni Bistolfi, preface by Gabriele D'Annunzio, E. Voghera, Rome, 1909).

Barthes, Roland. "Lecture de Brillat-Savarin." In *Le bruissement de la langue. Essais critiques*, vol. 4. Éditions du Seuil, Paris, 1984, pp. 303–56.

Basile, Giambattista. *Lo cunto del li cunti*. Edited by Ezio Raimondi. Einaudi, Turin, 1976.

Basini, Gian Luigi. *L'uomo e il pane: risorse, consumi e carenze alimentari della popolazione modenese nel Cinque e Seicento*. A. Giuffrè, Milan, 1970.

Battarra, Giovanni. *La pratica agricola* (1778). In Massimo Montanari, *Il pentolino magico*, Laterza, Rome and Bari, 1995, p. 95.

Bay, Allan. *Cuochi si diventa: le ricette e i trucchi della buona cucina italiana di oggi*. Feltrinelli, Milan, 2003.

———. *Cuochi si diventa 2: le ricette e i trucchi della buona cucina italiana di oggi*. Feltrinelli, Milan, 2004.

———. *Le parole dei menu: dalla A alla Z guida ai piatti e alle specialità di tutto il mondo*. Idealibri, Milan, 1988.

Beauvert, Thierry. *Musica per il palato: a tavola con Rossini*. Edited by Piero Meldini. Mondadori, Milan, 1997.

Bell, Rudolph M. *How to Do It: Guides to Good Living for Renaissance Italians*. University of Chicago Press, Chicago, 1999.

Belli, Giuseppe Gioacchino. *Sonetti.* Edited by Giorgio Vigolo with the collaboration of Pietro Gibellini. Mondadori, Milan, 1984.

Benincasa, Gabriele. *La pizza napoletana. Mito, storia e poesia.* Guida, Milan, 1992.

Benporat, Claudio. *Storia della gastronomia italiana.* Mursia, Milan, 1990.

Benzi, Ugo. *Regole della sanità et natura de' cibi di Ugo Benzo senese. Arricchite di vaghe annotazioni & di copiosi discorsi, naturali e morali dal sig. Lodovico Bertaldi medico delle serenissime altezze di Savoia. Et nuouamente in questa seconda impressione aggiontoui alle medeme materie i trattati di Baldasar Pisanelli e sue Historie naturali & annotationi del medico Galina.* By the heirs of Gio. Domenico Tarino, Turin, 1620.

Benzoni, Gerolamo. *La historia del mondo nuovo di M. Girolamo Benzoni milanese. La qual tratta delle isole, & mari nuouamente ritrouati, et delle nuoue città da lui proprio vedute, per acqua, et per terra in quattordici anni.* Edited by Alfredo Vig. Giordano, Milan, 1964 (first edition, in Italian: 1572).

Berchoux, Joseph. *La gastronomie, ou l'homme des champs à table, poème didactique en quatre chants.* Giguet, Paris, 1801.

Berni, Francesco. *Rime.* Edited by Danilo Romei. Mursia, Milan, 2002.

Bertolino, Enrico. *Milanesi. Lavoro, guadagno, spendo, pretendo.* From the series *Le guide xenofobe. Un ritratto irriverente dei migliori difetti dei popoli d'Italia,* edited by Federico Tibone. Edizioni Sonda, Turin, 1997.

Bevilacqua, Osvaldo, and Giuseppe Mantovano. *Laboratori del gusto. Storia dell'evoluzione gastronomica.* SugarCo, Milan, 1982.

Bezzola, Guido. *La vita quotidiana a Milano ai tempi di Stendhal.* Rizzoli, Milan, 1991.

Bianchi, Augusto Guido. *Giovanni Pascoli nei ricordi di un amico.* Modernissima, Milan, 1922.

Biasin, Gian Paolo. *I sapori della modernità. Cibo e romanzo.* Il Mulino, Bologna 1991.

Black, William. *I bucatini di Garibaldi. Avventure storico-gastronomiche di un inglese innamorato dell'Italia.* Translated by Annalisa Carena. Piemme, Casale Monferrato, 2004 (first edition, in English: 2003; original title: *Al Dente*).

Boneschi, Marta. *Poveri ma belli.* Mondadori, Milan, 1995.

Bonetta, Gaetano. *Corpo e nazione: l'educazione ginnastica, igienica e sessuale nell'Italia liberale.* F. Angeli, Milan, 1990.

Bracalini, Romano. "L'alimentazione: usi e costumi a tavola." In *L'Italia prima dell'unità.* Rizzoli, Milan, 2001, pp. 186–94.

———. *La regina Margherita.* Rizzoli, Milan, 1983.

Bracciolini, Francesco. *Lo scherno degli Dei.* Ferrando, Genoa, 1838.

Bratman, Steven. "Essay on Orthorexia: Unhealthy Obsession with Healthy Foods." *Yoga Journal,* October 1997.

Brighenti, Nerio. *Il gastruario: manuale del buongustaio.* Edited by Gino Pesavento; drawings by Egidio Demelli. Campironi, Milan, 1973.

Brillat-Savarin, Jean-Anthelme. *Physiologie du goût, ou méditations de gastronomie trascendante* (includes: Joseph Berchoux, *La gastronomie;* Colnet, *L'art de dîner en ville*). Flammarion, Paris, 1982 (first edition, in French: 1825). The Italian edition was also used: *Fisiologia del gusto,* translated by Roberta Ferrara, edited by Michel Guibert, Sellerio, Palermo, 1975.

Bruno, Giordano. *Dialoghi italiani.* Edited by G. Gentile; new edition edited by G. Aquilecchia. Sansoni, Florence, 1958.

Buonassisi, Rory. *La cucina mediterranea: ricette di terra e di mare.* Giunti, Florence, 1993.

———. *La pizza: il piatto, la leggenda.* Mondadori, Milan, 1997.

———. *Ricette mondiali di zuppe & minestre: dalla preistoria al 3. millenio: gratificanti & salutari.* Mondadori, Milan, 1999.

Buonassisi, Vincenzo. *La cucina di Falstaff.* Milano Nuova, Milan, 1964.

———. *Il libro della pizza.* Fabbri, Milan, 1982.

————. *Il nuovo codice della pasta.* Rizzoli BUR, Milan, 1999.

————. *Piccolo codice della pasta: ricette per preparare spaghetti, maccheroni, tagliatelle, gnocchi, tortellini.* Rizzoli BUR, Milan, 1977.

————. *Storia del pane e del forno.* SIDALM, Milan, 1981.

Buzzi, Aldo. *L'uovo alla kok.* Adelphi, Milan, 2002 (first edition: 1979).

Camilleri, Andrea. *Il ladro di merendine.* Sellerio, Palermo, 1996.

————. *La prima indagine di Montalbano.* Mondadori, Milan, 2004.

Campolieti, Giuseppe. *Il re lazzarone. Ferdinando IV di Borbone, amato dal popolo e condannato dalla storia.* Mondadori, Milan, 1999.

Camporesi, Piero. *Il brodo indiano. Edonismo ed esotismo nel Settecento.* Garzanti, Milan, 1990.

————. "Il formaggio maledetto." In *Le officine dei sensi.* Garzanti, Milan, 1985, pp. 47–77.

————. *La maschera di Bertoldo. G.C. Croce e la letteratura carnevalesca.* Einaudi, Turin, 1976.

————. *La terra e la luna. Alimentazione, folclore e società.* Il Saggiatore, Milan, 1989.

Cancellieri, Francesco. *Lettera di F. Cancellieri al Ch. Sig. Dottore Koreff professore di medicina nell'Università di Berlino sopra il tarantismo, l'aria di Roma e della sua Campagna, etc. . . . .* Francesco Bourlié, Rome, 1817.

Cannas, Marilena. *La cucina dei sardi.* EDES, Cagliari, 1975.

Capasso, Niccolò. *De curiositatibus Romae.* Published posthumously in *Poesie varie.* Simoniana, Naples, 1761.

Capatti, Alberto. *Pomi d'oro: immagini del pomodoro nella storia del gusto.* Preface by Gianfranco Vissani. Arti Grafiche Torri, Cologno Monzese, 1999.

Capatti, Alberto, and Massimo Montanari. *La cucina italiana. Storia di una cultura.* Laterza, Rome and Bari, 1999.

Caprara, Massimo. *Togliatti, il Comintern e il gatto selvatico.* Bietti, Milan, 1999.

Cardenas, Juan de. *Problemas y secretos maravillosos de las Indias.* Edited by Angeles Duran. Alianza, Madrid, 1988 (first edition: Mexico, 1591).

Carnacina, Luigi. *La grande cucina.* Edited by Luigi Veronelli. Garzanti, Milan, 1960.

————. *Mangiare e bere all'italiana.* Edited by Luigi Veronelli. Garzanti, Milan, 1967.

————. *Roma in cucina.* Martello, Milan, 1975.

Carnacina, Luigi, and Vincenzo Buonassisi. *Il libro della polenta.* Giunti Martello, Florence, 1974.

Castelvetro, Giacomo. *Breve racconto di tutte le radici di tutte l'erbe e di tutti i frutti che crudi o cotti in Italia si mangiano. Con molti giovevoli segreti (non senza proposito per dentro sono scritti) tanto intorno alla salute de' corpi umani quanto ad utile de' buoni agricoltori necessari.* Edited by Emilio Faccioli. Arcari, Mantua, 1988 (first edition: 1614).

Cattaneo, Carlo. "Notizie sulla Lombardia" from *La città* (1844). In *Opere scelte,* edited by Delia Castelnuovo Frigessi, vol. 2. Einaudi, Turin, 1972.

Catti De Gasperi, Maria Romana. *De Gasperi uomo solo.* Mondadori, Milan, 1964.

Cavalcanti duca di Buonvicino, Ippolito. *Cucina casareccia in dialetto napolitano ossia cucina casarinola co la lengua napoletana.* Edited by Emilio Faccioli. Il Polifilo, Milan, 1965.

————. *Cucina teorico-practica comulativamente col suo corrispondente riposto piccola parte approssimativa della spesa con la pratica di scalcare, e come servirsi dei pranzi e cene che vengono coadjuvati da diversi disegni in litografia finalmente quattro settimane secondo le stagioni della vera cucina casareccia in dialetto napolitano. 7. ed. migliorata del tutto, per quanto più possibile, dalle altre precedenti.* Printing Works of Domenico Capasso, Naples, 1852 (first edition: 1837).

Cavazzana, Giuseppe. *Itinerario gastronomico ed enologico d'Italia a cura di Banco Ambrosiano.* Oras-Ospitalita Romana Assistenza Stranieri, Milan, 1950.

Ceccarelli, Alfonso. *Opusculum de tuberibus, Alphonso Ciccarello physico de Maeuania auctore . . .* Toso, n.p., 1976 (reproduction of the edition of L. Bozetti, Padua, 1564).

Ceccarelli, Filippo. *Lo stomaco della Repubblica: cibo e potere in Italia dal 1945 al 2000.* Longanesi, Milan, 2000.

Cenne della Chitarra. *Le rime di Folgore da San Gemignano e di Cene da la Chitarra d'Arezzo.* Giulio Navone, Bologna 1968.

Cervio, Vincenzo. *Il trinciante.* Arnaldo Forni, Sala Bolognese, 1980 (facsimile reproduction of the edition printed by Gabbia, Rome, 1593; first edition: 1581).

Chapusot, Francesco. *La cucina sana, economica ed elegante.* Edited by Milo Julini. Arnaldo Forni, Sala Bolognese, 1990 (facsimile reproduction of the edition of Tip. Favale, Turin, 1846).

Chendi, Vincenzo. *Il vero campagnol ferrarese.* Ferrara, 1761.

Chiaramonte, Carmelo, and Davide Paolini. "Tra i banchi del mercato con il Cuciniere." *Il Sole-24 Ore,* January 9, 2005.

Il cibo e l'impegno. Supplement of *MicroMega,* no. 4. Gruppo Editoriale L'Espresso, Rome, 2004.

Il cibo e l'impegno/2. Supplement of *MicroMega,* no. 5. Gruppo Editoriale L'Espresso, Rome, 2004.

Cipolla, Carlo Maria. *Storia economica dell'Europa preindustriale.* Il Mulino, Bologna, 1974.

———. *Uomini, tecniche, economie.* Feltrinelli, Milan, 1966.

Cipolla, Joe. *La cucina di Cosa nostra.* Preface by Aldo Busi. Sperling & Kupfer, Milan, 1993 (original edition: *The Mafia Cookbook,* Ballantine Books, New York, 1970).

Clementi, Federico. *L'allevamento della gallina da uova in città.* Arte e storia, Rome, 1940.

Clini, Claudio. *L'alimentazione nella storia: uomo, alimentazione, malattie.* Regione Emilia Romagna, Bologna, 1987 (first edition: Francisci, Abano Terme, 1985).

"Coca-cola dal Viet Nam a Silvio." *Corriere della Sera,* February 9, 2000.

Cocchi, Antonio. *Del vitto pitagorico per uso della medicina: discorso di Antonio Cocchi preceduto da un discorso su' progressi del vegetarianismo . . . per Nicola Parisio.* Vincenzo Onofrio Mese, Naples, 1882 (first edition: 1743).

Collier Galletti di Cadilhac, Margareth. *La nostra casa sull'Adriatico: diario di una scrittrice inglese in Italia, 1873–1885.* Translated by Gladys Salvadori Muzzarelli; preface by Joyce Lussu. Il Lavoro Editoriale, Ancona, 1981.

Collodi, Carlo. *Il viaggio per l'Italia di Giannettino. Parte terza. L'Italia meridionale.* Paggi, Florence, 1886.

Colnet. *L'art de dîner en ville à l'usage des gens de lettres: poème en 4. chants: suivi de la biographie des auteurs morts de faim.* Bureau de la Bibliothèque Choisie, Paris, 1853.

Colombus, Christopher. *Il giornale di bordo: libro della prima navigazione e scoperta delle Indie (1492–1498).* Edited by Paolo Emilio Taviani and Consuelo Varala. Istituto Poligrafico e Zecca dello Stato, Rome, 1988.

Colorsi, Giacomo. *Breuità di scalcaria di Giacomo Colorsi da Pelestrina per li giouani virtuosi. All'ill.mo & reu.mo . . . card. Degli Albizi.* Angelo Bernabo dal Verme, Rome, 1658.

Concini, Wolftraud de. *Le minoranze in pentola: storia e gastronomia delle 10 minoranze linguistiche delle Alpi italiane.* Banca di Trento e Bolzano, Trent, 1997.

Consiglio, Alberto. *Sentimento del gusto, ovvero della cucina napoletana.* Parenti, Naples, 1957.

———. *La storia dei maccheroni con cento ricette e con Pulcinella mangiamaccheroni.* Edizioni Moderne, Naples, 1959.

———. *Storia dei maccheroni: origini, curiosità e leggende della più celebre creazione della cucina napoletana.* Tascabili Economici Newton, Rome, 1996.

Contrasto curioso tra una giovine pisana e una livornese. Tipografia Valenti, Pisa, 1882.

Contrasto curioso tra Venezia e Napoli. Florence, 1879 (written in 1663).

Corbi, Gianni, and Livio Zanetti. "Non lasciamoci distrarre dall'olio." *L'Espresso,* December 20, 1959.

Corbier, Mireille. "Le statut ambigu de la viande à Rome." In *Dialogues d'Histoire ancienne.* Annales Littéraires de l'Université, vol. 15, no. 2, Besançon, 1989, pp. 107–58.

Cornaro, Alvise. *Discorsi di Luigi Cornaro intorno alla vita sobria; L'arte di godere sanita perfetta di Leonardo Lessio e Discorso di Antonio Cocchi sul vitto pitagorico.* G. Silvestri, Milan, 1841 (the first academic edition was also used: *Scritti sulla vita sobria; Elogio; and Lettere,* edited by Marisa Dilani, Corbo e Fiore, Venice, 1983).

Corrado, Vincenzo. *Del cibo pitagorico ovvero erbaceo per uso de' nobili e de' letterati, opera meccanica dell'oritano*. Raimondi, Naples, 1781 (also used was the edition *Del cibo pitagorico ovvero erbaceo seguito dal Trattato delle patate per uso di cibo*, edited by Tullio Gregory, Donzelli, Rome, 2001).

———. *Il credenziere di buon gusto; La manovra della cioccolata e del caffè*. Edited by Claudio Benporat. Arnaldo Forni, Sala Bolognese, 1991 (facsimile reproduction of the edition of Stamperia Raimondiana, Naples, 1778).

———. *Il cuoco galante*. Arnaldo Forni, Sala Bolognese, 1990 (facsimile reproduction of the edition of Stamperia Raimondiana, Naples, 1786).

Crainz, Guido. *Storia del miracolo italiano: culture, identità, trasformazioni fra anni Cinquanta e Sessanta*. Donzelli, Rome, 1996.

Crisci, Giovanni Battista. *Luce de prencipi nella quale si tratta del modo di bene operare pubblicamente, e di essi, e di ciascuna persona con autorità di graui autori . . . Composta da Gio. Battista Crisci nap.no*. Lazarum Scorigium, Naples, 1638.

Cristoforo Colombo nella Genova del suo tempo. Edited by Piero Sanavio, Adriana Martinelli, and Caterina Porcu Sanna. ERI-Edizioni RAI, Turin, 1985.

Cristoforo da Messisbugo. *Libro novo nel qual s'insegna a far d'ogni sorte di vivanda secondo la diversità de i tempi cosi di carne come di pesce*. Arnaldo Forni, Sala Bolognese, 1982 (new edition edited by F. Bandini, Neri Pozza, Vicenza, 1992) (facsimile reproduction of the edition *Libro novo nel qual s'insegna a far d'ogni sorte di vivanda secondo la diversità de i tempi cosi di carne come di pesce*, fourth edition, Eredi Giovanni Padovano, Venice, 1557; first edition, in Italian: *Banchetti compositioni di vivande*, Giovanni de Buglhat and Antonio Hucher, Ferrara, 1529).

Croce, Giulio Cesare. *Le sottilissime astuzie di Bertoldo le piacevoli e ridicolose semplicità di Bertoldino Con il dialogus Salomonis et Marcolphi e il suo primo volgarizzamento a stampa*. Edited by Piero Camporesi. Einaudi, Turin, 1978.

Crosby, Alfred W. *Imperialismo ecologico. L'espansione biologica dell'Europa (900–1900)*. Laterza, Rome and Bari, 1988.

———. *The Columbian Exchange: Biological and Cultural Consequences of 1492*. Greenwood, Westport (Conn.), 1972.

La cucina del '500: in occasione delle celebrazioni per il 5. centenario della nascita di Giovanni Antonio de' Sacchis detto il Pordenone: agosto–novembre 1984. Introduction by Amedeo Giacomini. Azienda Autonoma del Turismo, Pordenone, 1984.

La cucina dell'Itaglietta. Edited by Piero Meldini. *La cucina della famiglia fascista; la cucina del tempo di guerra; la cucina dell'età giolittiana; la cucina degli anni ruggenti*. Guaraldi, Rimini-Florence, 1977.

La cucina italiana d'oggi nell'immagine e nella realtà: 8. Convegno internazionale. Venezia, 10–11 novembre 1984. Accademia Italiana della Cucina. A. Pizzi, Cinisello Balsamo, 1985.

Cucina mantovana di principi e di popolo: testi antichi e ricette tradizionali. Edited by Gino Brunetti (contains *L'arte di ben cucinare del cuoco ducale Bartolomeo Stefani; Lista di vivande per banchetti di cavalieri e altre persone di qualità; Ricette della tradizione popolare mantovana; Uve e vini del Mantovano*). Istituto Carlo D'Arco per la Storia di Mantova, Mantua, 1963.

La Cucina rinascimentale di corte: nel triangolo padano, Parma, Ferrara, Mantova. Edited by the Accademia Italiana della Cucina (contains the proceedings of the congresses "I Farnese," Parma, April 30, 1994; "Gli Estensi," Ferrara, May 14, 1994; and "I Gonzaga," Mantua, June 22, 1994). Accademia Italiana della Cucina, Milan, 1995.

Le Cucine della memoria: testimonianze bibliografiche e iconografiche dei cibi tradizionali italiani nelle biblioteche pubbliche statali. De Luca, Rome, 1995.

Il cuoco milanese e la cuciniera piemontese, lombardo-veneta, spagnuola, inglese, francese, viennese, italiana. Pagnoni, Milan, 1862.

Il cuoco piemontese perfezionato a Parigi. Edited by Silvano Serventi, in collaboration with the Società Studi Storici di Cuneo and the Società Storica Vercellese. Slow Food, Bra, 2000 (first edition: Turin, 1766).

Curioso contrasto fra una romana ed una fiorentina. A. Salani, Florence, 1917.

D'Amato, Federico Umberto. *Menu e dossier*. Rizzoli, Milan, 1984.

De Bourcard, Francesco. *Usi e costumi a Napoli (1857–1866)*. Longanesi, Milan, 1977.

De Leo, Carmine. *Il pane dei santi: le pietanze nella religiosità popolare*. Edizioni Incontro alla Luce, Foggia, 1998.

DeLillo, Don. *Underworld*. Turin, Einaudi, 1999.

Della Verde, Maria Vittoria. *Gola e preghiera nella clausura dell'ultimo '500*. Edited by Giovanna Casagrande, translated and notes by Giovanni Moretti. Edizioni dell'Arquata, Foligno, 1988.

Delli Colli, Laura. *The Taste of Italian Cinema in 100 Recipes*. Elleu Multimedia, Rome, 2003.

De Nino, Antonio. *Usi e costumi abruzzesi*. G. Barbera, Florence, 1887.

De Nolhac, Pier, and Angelo Solerti. *Il viaggio in Italia di Enrico III re de Francia*. DeRoux, Rome, Turin, and Naples, 1890.

Denti di Pirajno, Alberto. *Il gastronomo educato*. Neri Pozza, Venice, 1950.

Diamond, Jared. *Armi, acciaio e malattie: breve storia del mondo negli ultimi tredicimila anni*. Translated by Luigi Civalleri; edited by Luca and Francesco Cavalli-Sforza. Einaudi, Turin, 2005 (first edition, in English: 1997; original title *Guns, Germs and Steel: The Fates of Human Society*).

Dickens, Charles. *Impressioni italiane*. Translated by Claudio Messina. Robin Edizioni (by permission of Biblioteca del Vascello), Rome, 2005 (first Italian edition: 1989; first edition, in English: 1846; original title: *Pictures of Italy*).

D'Ideville, Henry. *Il re, il conte e la Rosina*. Longanesi, Milan, 1981.

Disegni del convito fatto dall'illustrissimo signor senatore Francesco Ratta all'illustrissimo publico, eccelsi signori anziani, & altra nobilta. Terminando il suo confalonierato li 28 febraro 1693. Edited by Claudio Benporat. Arnaldo Forni, Sala Bolognese, 1991 (facsimile reproduction of the edition of Peri, Bologna, 1693).

Donizone. *Matilde e Canossa: il poema di Donizone*. Edited by Ugo Bellocchi and Giovanni Marzi. Aedes Muratoriana, Modena, 1970.

Dubini, Angelo. *La cucina degli stomachi deboli, ossia, Pochi piatti non comuni, semplici, economici e di facile digestione: con alcune norme relative al buon governo delle vie dirigenti*. Tipografia Bernardoni, Milan, 1882 (first edition: 1842).

Ducceschi, Virgilio. *Gli olii ed i grassi nella storia dell'alimentazione*. Consorzio nazionale fra produttori olii di semi, Milan, no date.

Dumas, Alexandre (père). *Il grande dizionario di cucina*. Edited by Carlo Carlino. Sellerio, Palermo, 2004.

———. *Napoli borbonica*. La Biblioteca del TCI, Milan, 1997.

Durante, Castore. *Herbario nuovo di Castore Durante medico, & cittadino romano con figure che rappresentano le viue piante, che nascono in tutta Europa, & nell'Indie orientali & occidentali . . . Con discorsi, che dimostrano i nomi, le spetie, la forma, il loco, il tempo, le qualità, & le virtu mirabili dell'herbe . . . Con due tauole copiosissime, l'vna dell'herbe, et l'altra dell'infermità, et di tutto quello che nell'opera si contiene*. By Bartholomeo Bonfadino, & Tito Diani (In Rome: by Iacomo Bericchia, & Iacomo Tornierij, 1585, at the printing works of Bartholomeo Bonfadino, & Tito Diani, 1585).

L'eccellenza e il trionfo del porco: immagini, uso e consumo del maiale dal XIII secolo ai giorni nostri. Edited by Emilio Faccioli. Reggio Emilia: Comune, Assessorato alla Cultura, Mazzotta, Milan, 1982.

Eco, Umberto. *Baudolino*. Bompiani, Milan, 2002.

"Era buon governo efficiente." *Il Foglio*, June 29, 1999.

Erasmus of Rotterdam. *Elogio della follia*. With an essay by Ronald H. Bainton; translated by Luca D'Ascia. Rizzoli, Milan, 1993.

Ercolani, Gian Luca. *La dieta ermetica: l'alimentazione nel Rinascimento*. Edited by Donato Lo Scalzo. Todaro, Lugano, 1999.

European Food History: A Research Review. Edited by Hans J. Teuteberg. Leicester University, Leicester, U.K., 1992.

Evangelista, Anna, and Giovanni Del Turco. *Epulario e segreti vari. Trattati di cucina toscana nella Firenze Seicentesca (1602–1623)*. Arnaldo Forni, Sala Bolognese, 1992.

Evitascandalo, Cesare. *Libro dello scalco di Cesare Evitascandalo. Quale insegna quest'honorato seruitio*. Carlo Vullietti, Rome, 1609.

Faccioli, Emilio. *Libri di ricette e trattati sulla civiltà della tavola dal XIV al XIX secolo*. Einaudi, Turin, 1987.

Falconi, Rodolfo. *Amico castello: origini, storia, turismo e immagini di Castelsantangelo sul Nera*. Pieraldo, Rome, 1986.

Fantoni, Giovanni. *Contrasto curioso fra il Padrone e il Contadino che vuol mangiare a tutti i costi*. A. Salani, Florence, 1888.

Fasano, Gabriele. *Lo Tasso Napoletano. Gerusalemme liberata votata a llengua nostra*. Edited by Aniello Fratta. Benincasa, Rome, 1983 (facsimile reproduction of the edition of Raillardo, Naples, 1689).

Felici, Costanzo. *Scritti naturalistici, I, Del'insalata e piante che in qualunque modo vengono per cibo del'homo*. Edited by G. Arbizzoni. Quattro Venti, Urbino, 1986 (first edition: 1569).

Ferrari, Miriam. *Merluzzo, baccalà o stoccafisso? Leggende, miti, ricette di un grande pesce dei mari del Nord*. Bibliotheca Culinaria, Lodi, 1998.

Ferrario, Guido. *Al sangue o ben cotto*. Meltemi, Rome, 1998.

Ferraris Tamburini, Giulia. *Come posso mangiar bene?* Hoepli, Milan, 1900.

Fioravanti, Leonardo. *Capricci medicinali dell'eccellente medico, & cirugico M. Leonardo Fiorauanti Bolognese, libri tre . . . Di nouo corretti, & in molti luoghi ampliati, & ristampati. Aggiontoui il quarto libro non più stampato, nel quale altre bellissime materie si contengono*. Lodouico Auanzo, Venice, 1565.

———. *Dello specchio di scientia universale*. Heirs of Melchior Sessa, Venice, 1572.

———. *Del tesoro della vita humana*. Heirs of Melchoir Sessa, Venice, 1582.

Fiordelli, Aldo. *Il buon tartufo. Usi e costumi del "diamante" della tavola*. Polistampa, Florence, 2005.

Fischler, Claude. *L'onnivoro. Il piacere di mangiare nella storia e nella scienza*. Mondadori, Milan, 1992.

Flandrin, Jean-Louis. "Internationalisme, nationalisme et régionalisme dans la cuisine des XIVe et XVe siècles: le témoignage des livres de cuisine." In *Manger et boire au Moyen Age 2: Cuisine, manières de table, regimes alimentaires. Actes du Colloque de Nice, 15–17 octobre 1982, Centre d'études médievales de Nice*. Les belles lettres, Paris, 1984, pp. 75–91.

———. "Le goût et la nécessité: reflexions sur l'usage des graisses dans les cuisines de l'Europe occidentale (XIVe–XVIIIe siècles)." *Annales ESC* 38 (1983), pp. 369–401.

———. *L'ordre des mets*. Odile Jacob, Paris, 2002.

Foa, Anna. "La cucina del marrano." *Il Mondo* 3/2, no. 2–3 (August–December 1995).

Fochesato, Walter, and Virgilio Pronzati. *L'acciuga: donne, donne, pesci freschi, pesci vivi: tutto sull'acciuga: dalla padella alla brace e 54 ricette*. Feguagiskia' Studios Edizioni, Genoa, 1997.

———. *Stoccafisso & Baccalà. Storie, usi e tradizioni popolari dal Baltico al Mediterraneo*. Feguagiskia' Studios Edizioni, Genoa, 1999.

Folengo, Teofilo. *Baldus*. Edited by Mario Chiesa. UTET, Turin, 1997.

Folgore da San Gimignano. *Collana dei mesi*. Mondadori, Milan, 1953.

———. *Sonetti de la semana*. G. Ferrari, Milan, 1966.

Forcella, Enzo. *Celebrazione di un trentennio*. Mondadori, Milan, 1974.

———. "Pastasciutta calda con contorno nuova arma 'segreta' di Lauro." *La Stampa*, May 16, 1953.

Frejaville, Mario. *Il libro d'oro della cucina familiare italiana*. Mursia, Milan, 1977.

Frizzi, Antonio. *La salameide, poemetto giocoso con le note*. Zerletti, Venice, 1772.

Frugoli, Antonio. *Pratica, e scalcaria d'Antonio Frugoli lucchese, intitolata pianta di delicati frutti da seruirsi a qualsiuoglia mensa di prencipi . . . con molti auuertimenti circa all'honorato officio di scalco, con le liste di tutti i mesi dell'anno, compartite nelle quattro stagioni. Con un trattato dell'inuentori delle viuande, e beuande, cosi antiche, come moderne, nouamente ritrouato, e tradotto di lingua armenia in italiana. Con le qualità, e stagioni di tutti li cibi da grasso, e da magro, e lor cucina di viuande diuerse. Ristampato di nuouo con la giunta del Discorso del trinciante . . . Diuisa in otto libri.* Francesco Cavalli, Rome, 1638.

Gadda, Carlo Emilio. *Le meraviglie d'Italia.* Einaudi, Turin, 1964.

———. *La cognizione del dolore.* With an essay by Gianfranco Contini. Einaudi, Turin, 1973.

Gaggiotti, Gino. *I grandi piatti della cucina regionale italiana: origini, notizie, curiosità, segreti, ricette e abbinamento ai vini.* ECIG, Genoa, 1990.

Garcilaso de la Vega, known as El Inca. *Commentari reali sul Perù degli Incas.* Translated by René L.F. Durand. Paris, 1982 (first edition: Lisbon, 1609).

Garzoni, Tommaso. *La piazza universale di tutte le professioni del mondo.* Edited by Paolo Cherchi and Beatrice Collina. Einaudi, Turin, 1996 (first edition: 1585).

Gasparov, Michail. *Zapisi i vypiski.* NLO, Moscow, 2000.

Gastronomia del Rinascimento. Edited by Luigi Firpo. UTET, Turin, 1974.

Gaudentio, Francesco. *Il panunto toscano.* Restored and annotated by Gianni Guido; glossary by Adele Zito. Trevi Editore, Rome, 1974.

Genis, Aleksandr. *Sladkaya Zhizn.* Vagrius, Moscow, 2004.

Gerard, John. *The Herball.* First edition, in English: 1597.

Gessi, Leone. *Soste del buongustaio: itinerari utili e dilettevoli.* Preface by Antonio Baldini. Società Editrice Internazionale, Turin, 1957.

Ginsborg, Paul. *Storia d'Italia dal dopoguerra a oggi: società e politica 1943–1988.* Einaudi, Turin, 1989.

Giovenale, Decimo Giunio. *Satire.* Introduction, translation, and notes by Mario Ramous. Garzanti, Milan, 1996.

Giusti, Giuseppe. *Poesie e prose.* Edited by Ferdinando Giannessi. Fabbri, Milan, 2001.

Giustiniani, Vincenzo. "Dialogo fra Renzo e Aniello napolitano sugli usi di Roma e di Napoli" (1600–1610). In *Discorsi sulle arti e sui mestieri*, edited by Anna Banti. Sansoni, Florence, 1981, pp. 135–58.

Goethe, Johann Wolfgang von. *Viaggio in Italia.* Translated by Emilio Castellani. Mondadori, Milan, 1983 (original title: *Italienische Reise*, 1786–88).

Gorresio, Vittorio. *I carissimi nemici.* Bompiani, Milan, 1977.

Gran banchetto (Cucina italiana del Rinascimento). Edited by Carla Della Beffa and Africo Paolucci. Cencograf-Rotografica, Milan, 1986.

Grande Bagna Caòda Annuale degli Acciugai e dei Buongustai del Piemonte. Edited by the Accademia Italiana della Cucina e degli Acciugai d'Italia associated with the AVALMA (Associazione Venditori Acciughe della Val Maira), n.p., 1989.

Grandi, Laura, and Stefano Tettamanti. *Atlante goloso: luoghi e delizie d'Italia.* Garzanti, Milan, 2002.

Gregorovius, Ferdinand. *Wanderjahre in Italien*, bd. 2. Leipzig, 1870. The Italian translation was also used: *Passeggiate romane.* F. Spinosi, Rome, 1965.

Greimas, Algirdas Julien. "La soupe au pistou ou la programmation d'un objet de valeur." In *Du Sens II*, Seuil, Paris, 1983, pp. 168–69.

Grieco, Allen J. *Dalla vite al vino.* Edited by Jean-Louis Gaulin and Allen J. Grieco. Clueb, Bologna, 1994.

Gueglio, Vincenzo. *Mario! Storia vera tragica e avventurosa del polpo Mario, del pescatore Gnussa e di Cesare Ziona, principe dei fiocinatori e re della famosa baia di Portobello.* F.lli Frilli, Genoa, 2004.

Guerri, Giordano Bruno. *Gli Italiani sotto la Chiesa.* Mondadori, Milan, 1992.

Harris, Marvin. *Buono da mangiare.* Einaudi, Turin, 1990.

Hašek, Jaroslav. *Il buon soldato Sc'vèik* (1923). Translated by Renato Poggioli. Feltrinelli, Milan, 2003.

Heers, Jacques. *Fêtes, jeux et joutes dans les sociétés d'Occident à la fin du Moyen Age: Conférence Albert Le Grand, 1971.* Montreal/Paris: Publications de l'Institut d'études medievales, 1977.

———. *Genova nel '400: civiltà mediterranea, grande capitalismo e capitalismo popolare*: "L'attività marittima nel XV secolo." Translated by Jaka Book. Milan, 1991 (original edition: *Gênes au XV siecle: Activité économique et problèmes sociaux*. SEVPEN, Paris, 1961).

———. *La Roma dei papi ai tempi dei Borgia e dei Medici (1420–1520)*. Translated by Franca Caffa. Rizzoli BUR, Milan, 2001 (original edition: *La vie quotidienne à la cour pontificale au temps des Borgia et des Medicis, 1420–1520*. Hachette, Paris, 1986).

———. *Le travail au Moyen Age*. Presses Universitaires de France, Paris, 1965.

Heine, Heinrich. *Aus den Memoiren des Herren von Schnabelewopski*. Reclam, Stuttgart, 1981 (first edition: 1836).

———. *Impressioni di viaggio, Italia*. Translated by Bruno Maffi; introduction by Alberto Destro. Rizzoli BUR, Milan, 2002 (original title: *Reisebilder*).

Henrico da S. Bartolomeo del Gaudio. *Scalco spirituale per le mense dei religiosi e de gl'altri deuoti opera nuoua . . . composta dal P.F. Henrico da S. Bartolomeo del Gaudio dell'ordine dei Predicatori. Diuisa in tre trattati*. Secondino Roncagliolo, Naples, 1644.

Herzen, Aleksandr. *Pis'ma iz Francii i Italii (1847–1852)*. Sobr. soč. v 30 tomach, t. 5, Moscow, 1955.

In forma a tavola: guida all'alimentazione consapevole. Edited by Eugenio Del Toma. 7 vols. Gruppo Editoriale l'Espresso, Rome, 2002.

Iovino, Roberto. *Musica & gastronomia: un viaggio nel tempo*. Sagep, Genoa, 1997.

L'Italia della cultura: festival del cinema, del teatro, della musica e premi letterari di 25 città italiane e 50 ricette per scoprire la tradizione gastronomica. Part 4. Coptip, Modena, 1985.

L'Italia del Medioevo: 25 città, cittadine, borghi e villaggi di clima medioevale e 50 ricette per scoprire la tradizione gastronomica. Part 3. Coptip, Modena, 1985.

Jannattoni, Livio. *Osterie e feste romane*. Newton Compton, Rome, 1977.

Kurlansky, Mark. *Il merluzzo*. Mondadori, Milan, 2003 (first edition, in English: *Cod*, 1997).

La Cecla, Franco. *La pasta e la pizza*. Il Mulino, Bologna, 1998.

La Lande, Joseph Jerome. *Voyage d'un françois en Italie, fait dans les années 1765 & 1766. Contenant l'histoire & les anecdotes les plus singulieres de l'Italie, & sa description; les moeurs, les usages, le gouvernement . . .* Paris, Desaint, 1769.

Lalli, Giovanni Battista. *La Moscheide e La Franceide*. Introduction and notes by Giuseppe Rua. UTET, Turin, 1927.

Lando, Ortensio. *Commentario delle più notabili e mostruose cose d'Italia e altri luoghi di lingua aramea in italiana tradotto. Con un breve Catalogo de gli inventori delle cose che si mangiano e bevono, novamente ritrovato*. Edited by G. and S. Salvatori. Pendragon, Bologna, 1994 (first edition: 1553).

Lassels, Richard. *The Voyage of Italy, or A Compleat Journey through Italy: in Two Parts*. V. Du Moutier, Paris, 1670.

Lastri, Marco. *Calendario del seminatore*. Graziosi, Venice, 1793.

———. *Calendario del vangatore*. Graziosi, Venice, 1793.

———. *Corso di agricoltura di un accademico georgofilo autore della Biblioteca georgica*. 5 vols. Stamperia del Giglio, Florence, 1801–1803.

———. *Regole per i padroni dei poderi verso i contadini, per proprio vantaggio e di loro. Aggiuntavi una raccolta di avvisi ai contadini sulla loro salute*. Graziosi, Venice, 1793.

Latini, Antonio. *Autobiografia. La vita di uno scalco*. Furio Luccichenti, Rome, 1992.

———. *Scalco alla moderna overo l'arte di ben disporre i conviti*. Vols. 1–2. Parrino e Mutii, Naples, 1692–94.

Laurioux, Bruno. "Cuisiner à l'antique. Apicius au Moyen Age." *Médiévales* 26 (1994), pp. 17–38.

Lechi Morelli, Patrizia. *La tavola di Piero: colori e sapori della cucina al tempo di Piero della Francesca*. La Versiliana, Florence, 1992.

Le Goff, Jacques. "L'Italia fuori d'Italia. L'Italia nello specchio del Medioevo." In *Storia d'Italia*, vol. 2, section 2, *Dalla caduta dell'Impero romano al secolo XVIII*. Einaudi, Turin, 1974, pp. 1933–2088.

Lemene, Francesco. *Poesie diverse del signor Francesco de Lemene raccolte, e dedicate all'illustriss. e rev.mo signore il sig. conte abbate Maurizio Santi.* Monti, Milan, 1711.

Leopardi, Giacomo. *Zibaldone di pensieri.* Selected and edited by Anna Maria Moroni. Oscar Mondadori, Milan, 2001.

Lessius, Leonardus. *Hygiasticon seu Vera ratio valetudinis bonae et vitae vna cum sensuum, iudicii, & memoriae integritate ad extremam senectutem conseruandaei.* Officina Plantiniana, Moreti, Anversa, 1614.

Levi, Carlo. *Cristo siè fermato a Eboli.* Einaudi, Turin, 1945.

Levintov, Aleksandr. *Zhratva. Zhizn po-sovetski.* Jauza, Eksmo, Moscow, 2005.

Il libro della cucina del sec. XIV: testo di lingua non mai fin qui stampato. Edited by Francesco Zambrini. Gaetano Romagnoli, Bologna, 1863 (modern edition: Commissione per i Testi di Lingua, Bologna, 1968 [printed 1969]).

Il libro del pesce azzurro. Texts by Giovanni Bombace, Emanuele Djalma Vitali, and Vincenzo Buonassisi. Ministero della Marina, Rome, 1980.

Ligabue, Giancarlo. *Storia delle forniture navali e dell'alimentazione di bordo.* Alfieri, Venice, 1968.

Lombardi, Mario. *Italia in controluce: Storia illustrata di genti e cucine.* In collaboration with Pietro Mercatini. S.I.L.A., Cesena, 1985.

Longanesi, Leo. *La sua signora, taccuino di Leo Longanesi.* Introduction by Indro Montanelli. Rizzoli, Milan, 1975.

Longhi, Giuseppe. *Le donne, i cavalier, l'armi, gli amori, e . . . la Cucina Ferrarese: più storia che leggenda.* Calderini, Bologna, 1984.

Lopez, Roberto Sabatino. *Byzantium and the World Around It: Economic and Institutional Relations.* Variorum Reprints, London, 1978.

———. *Il predominio economico dei genovesi nella monarchia spagnola.* Tipografia L. Cappelli, Rocca S. Casciano, 1936.

———. *La rivoluzione commerciale del Medioevo.* Translated by Aldo Serafini. Einaudi, Turin, 1989 (original edition: *The Commercial Revolution of the Middle Ages, 950–1350,* 1971).

———. *Storia delle colonie genovesi nel Mediterraneo.* Zanichelli, Bologna, 1938.

Loren, Sophia. *In cucina con amore.* Rizzoli BUR, Milan, 1985.

Luraschi, Giovanni Felice. *Nuovo cuoco milanese economico quale contiene la cucina grassa, magra e d'olio e serve pranzi all'uso inglese, russo, francese ed italiano utile ai cuochi, ai principianti ed ai particolari esperimentato e compilato dal cuoco milanese Gio. Felice Luraschi.* Arnaldo Forni, Sala Bolognese 1980 (facsimile reproduction of the edition of Carrara, Milan, 1853; first edition: 1829).

I Maccheroni. Poemetto giocoso. In M. Zampieri and A. Camarda, *Sotto il segno dei maccheroni. Rito e poesia nel Carnevale veronese.* Cierre, Verona, 1990.

Maestro Martino de Rossi (Martino da Como). *Libro de arte coquinaria.* Edited by Emilio Montorfano; preface by Ernesto Travi. Terziaria, Milan, 1990 (original edition: 1450). The following edition was also used: *Libro de arte coquinaria.* Edited by Luigi Ballerini and Jeremy Parzen. G. Tommasi, Milan, 2001.

Maioli, Giorgio, and Giancarlo Roversi. *Civiltà della tavola a Bologna.* Annibali, Bologna, 1981.

Malandra, Renato, and Pietro Renon. *Le principali frodi dei prodotti della pesca.* Libreria Universitaria Multimediale, Milan, 1998.

Mantovano, Giuseppe. *L'avventura del cibo. Origini, misteri, storie e simboli del nostro mangiare quotidiano.* Gremese, Rome, 1989.

Marchesi, Gualtiero, and Luca Vercelloni. *La tavola imbandita: storia estetica della cucina.* Laterza, Rome and Bari, 2001.

Marchi, Cesare. *Quando siamo a tavola. Viaggio sentimentale con l'acquolina in bocca da Omero al fast-food.* Rizzoli, Milan, 1990.

Marchi, Ezio, and Carlo Pucci. *Il maiale.* Hoepli, Milan, 1914.

Marinetti, Filippo Tommaso, and Fillia (Luigi Colombo). *La cucina futurista (Contro gli spegnitori di Milan)*. Longanesi, Milan, 1986 (first edition: 1932).

———. *Il manifesto della cucina futurista*. Spes/Salimbeni, Florence, 1980 (facsimile reproduction of the edition *La cucina futurista*, Sonzogno, Milan, 1932).

Marino, Giovanbattista. *La galleria*. Edited by Guido Battelli. G. Carabba, Lanciano, 1926 (first edition: 1620).

Martini, Fabio. "D'Alema: noi e l'Ulivo per governare." *La Stampa*, February 15, 1998.

Massonio, Salvatore. *Archidipno, ovvero Dell'insalata e dell'uso di essa*. Introduction by Sergio Ferrero; new annotated and revised edition edited by Maria Paleari Henssler and Carlo Scipione. Artes, Milan, 1990 (first edition: 1627).

Mattioli, Pietro Andrea. *I discorsi di Pietro Andrea Mattioli su De materia medica di Dioscoride*. Edited by Roberto Peliti. Tipografia Julia, Rome, 1977 (first edition: 1557).

Mazzucotelli, Mauro. *Cultura scientifica e tecnica del monachesimo in Italia*. 2 vols. Abbazia San Benedetto, Seregno, 1999.

McNair, James. *Pizza*. Chronicle Books, San Francisco, 1987.

Mediterranea, la cucina del vivere sano. Bonechi, Florence, 2004.

Meldini, Piero. "La tavola pitagorica." *La Gola*, April 1986, p. 6.

Messedaglia, Luigi. *Il mais e la vita rurale italiana: saggio di storia agraria*. Federazione Italiana dei Consorzi Agrari, Piacenza, 1927.

———. *Vita e costume della Rinascenza in Merlin Cocai*. Edizione Antenore, Padua, 1974.

Metz, Vittorio. *La cucina del Belli: settanta ricette della Roma papalina, condite con i piccanti sonetti di G. Gioachino Belli*. SugarCo, Milan, 1984.

Milano, Serena, Raffaella Ponzio, and Piero Sardo, eds. *L'Italia dei presidi. Guida ai prodotti da salvare*. Slow Food, Bra, 2004.

Mintz, Sidney W. *Tasting Food, Tasting Freedom: Excursions into Eating, Culture and the Past*. Beacon Press, Boston, 1996.

Mintz, Sidney W., and R. Just. "Sugar, Spice and How Coca-Cola Conquered the World and Other Social Histories of Food." *The Times Literary Supplement*, May 23, 1997.

Missieri, Bruno. *La tavola dei Farnese*. Associazione di Arte, Cultura e Turismo, Piacenza, 1998.

Mocci, Paolo. "Il partito della bistecca." *Il Tempo*, April 11, 1953.

Molinari Pradelli, Alessandro. *Il grande libro della cucina italiana in oltre 5000 ricette regionali*. Newton & Compton, Rome, 2000.

Monelli, Paolo. *Il ghiottone errante: viaggio gastronomico attraverso l'Italia*. With 94 drawings by Novello. Second revised edition. F.lli Treves, Milan, 1935.

Mongitore, Antonino. *Bibliotheca sicula, sive de scriptoribus siculis qui tum vetera, tum recentiora saecula illustrarunt, notitiae locupletissimae*. Forni, Bologna, 1971 (facsimile reproduction of the edition of Panormi, Felicella, 1708–1714).

Montaigne, Michel Eyquem de. *L'Italia alla fine del secolo 16: giornale del viaggio di Michele De Montaigne in Italia nel 1580 e 1581*. Edited by Alessandro D'Ancona. S. Lapi, Città di Castello, 1895.

Montanari, Massimo. *Alimentazione e cultura nel Medioevo*. Laterza, Rome and Bari, 1988.

———. *Convivio*. Laterza, Rome and Bari, 1989.

———. *Convivio oggi: storia e cultura dei piaceri della tavola nell'età contemporanea*. Laterza, Rome and Bari, 1992.

———. *La fame e l'abbondanza. Storia dell'alimentazione in Europa*. Laterza, Rome and Bari, 1996.

———. "Maometto, Carlo Magno e lo storico dell'alimentazione." *Quaderni medievali* 40 (1995), pp. 64–71.

———. *Nuovo Convivio. Storia e cultura dei piaceri della tavola nell'Età moderna*. Laterza, Rome and Bari, 1991.

————. *Il pentolino magico*. Laterza, Rome and Bari, 1995.

Montanelli, Indro. "La cosa due e i tortellini." *Corriere della Sera*, February 18, 1998.

Morlacchi, Lorenzo. *Tutta pasta*. Fratelli Melita, La Spezia, 1988.

Muffatti Masselli, Giliana. "Per una storia dell'alimentazione povera in epoca romana: la puls nelle fonti letterarie archeologiche paleobotaniche." *Rivista Archeologica dell'Antica Provincia e Diocesi di Como* 170 (1988), pp. 270–90.

Muratov, Pavel. *Obrazy Italii*. Vols. 1–2 (comprising original three volumes). Galart, Moscow, 1994.

Muravieva, Galina. "O ede." In *Dialog und Divergenz: Interkulturelle Studien zu Selbst- und Fremdbildern in Europa*. Peter Lang, Frankfurt, Berlin, Berne, New York, Paris, and Vienna, 1997.

Mureddu, Matteo. *Il Quirinale dei presidenti*. Feltrinelli, Milan, 1982.

Nada Patrone, Anna Maria. *Il cibo del ricco ed il cibo del povero: contributo alla storia qualitativa dell'alimentazione*. Centro Studi Piemontesi, Turin, 1989.

Nardelli, Giuseppe Maria. *Alla tavola del monaco: il quotidiano e l'eccezionale nella cucina del monastero tra XVII e XVIII secolo: con 100 ricette dell'epoca*. Quattroemme, Ponte San Giovanni 1998.

Nascia, Carlo. *Li quatro banchetti destinati per le quatro stagioni dell'anno*. Edited by Massimo Alberini. Arnaldo Forni, Sala Bolognese, 1981 (facsimile reproduction of the manuscript preserved in Soragna, 1685).

Nell'800 si mangiava così. Nicolini, Gavirate, 1995.

Nemici per la pelle. Edited by Pier Paolo D'Attorre. Franco Angeli, Milan, 1991.

Niceforo, Alfredo. "Per la storia numerica dell'alimentazione italiana: pagine riassuntive." *Difesa sociale* (monthly journal of the INFPS) 15, nos. 8–9.

Nievo, Ippolito. *Le confessioni di un italiano*. Garzanti, Milan, 1973.

Notari, Umberto. *Il giro d'Italia . . . a tavola*. Edizioni d'Italia, Perledo, no date.

Olio ed olivi del Garda veronese. Le vie dell'olio gardesano dal medioevo ai primi del Novecento. Edited by Gian Maria Varanini; texts by Andrea Brugnoli, Paolo Rigoli, and Gian Maria Varanini. Turi, Caivon, 1994.

Origo, Iris. *Il mercante di Prato: Francesco di Marco Datini*. Bompiani, Milan, 1958.

Pane, Rita, and Mariano Pane. *I sapori del Sud: alla riscoperta della cucina mediterranea*. Rizzoli BUR, Milan, 1993.

Panorama gastronomico d'Italia. Introduction by Angelo Manaresi; texts by Amedeo Pettini et al. Sponsored by the Municipio di Bologna, Bologna, 1935.

Pantaleone da Confienza. *Trattato dei Latticini (1477, tit. or. Pillularium omnibus medicis quam necessarium clarissimi doctoris magistri Panthaleonis. Summa lacticiniorum completa omnibus idonea eiusdem doctoris. Cautele medicorum non inutiles clarissimi doctoris magistri Gabrielis Zerbi veronensis)*. Edited by Emilio Faccioli; introduction by Carlo Scipione Ferrero. Consorzio per la Tutela del Formaggio Grana Padano, Milan, 1990.

Paolini, Davide. "Che bontà dietro al banco . . . ," *Il sole—24 ore*, May 14, 2006.

————. *Cibovagando: gli itinerari per scoprire i tesori golosi italiani: dove comprare, dove gustare, i luoghi da visitare, le curiosità*, Il Sole-24 Ore, Milan, 2003.

————. *Dal riso ai risotti: cultura e creatività del made in Italy in cucina*. Mondadori, Milan, 1999.

————. *I luoghi del gusto: cibo e territorio come risorsa di marketing*. Baldini & Castoldi, Milan, 2002.

————. *Il mestiere del gastronauta*. Sperling & Kupfer, Milan, 2005.

————. *Il pane dalla A alla Z*. Rizzoli, Milan, 2003.

————. *La pasta dalla A alla Z*. Rizzoli, Milan, 2003.

————. *Viaggio nei giacimenti golosi: prodotti e itinerari*. Mondadori, Milan, 2000.

Paolini Davide, Tullio Seppilli, and Alberto Sorbini. *Migrazioni e culture alimentari*. Editoriale Umbra, Foligno, 2002.

Parisella, Agata. *Oli e aceti d'Italia*. Gremese, Rome, 2000.

Parkinson, Cyril Northcote. *Mrs Parkinson's Law and Other Studies in Domestic Science*. Penguin Books, Harmondsworth, U.K., 1971.

Parmentier, Antoine Agostin. *Dei pomi di terra ossia patate articolo del Sig. Parmentier traduzione dal francese.* Simon Tissi e Figlio, Belluno, 1802.

———. *Della pentola americana del Sig. Parmentier. Mém. d'agric. de la soc. R. de Paris, 1786.* Translated from the French. Marelli, Milano, 1787.

———. *Instruzione a i panattieri sul modo il più facile e vantaggioso di far pane con le regole di scegliere, conservare, e macinare il grano, mantener la farina, apparecchiare e usare il lievito, manipolare la pasta, costruir forni, e altre necessarie cognizioni.* Translated from the French. Giacomo Marsoner, Rimini, 1794.

———. *Le mais ou blé de Turquie apprecié sous tous ses rapports; memoire couronne, le 25 août 1784, par l'Académie royale des sciences, belles-lettres et arts de Bordeaux.* New expanded edition. De l'Imprimerie Imperiale Paris, 1812.

Paschetti, Bartolomeo. *Del conseruare la sanità, et del viuere de' genouesi di Bartolomeo Paschetti . . . libri tre. Ne' quali si tratta di tutte le cose appartenenti alla conseruatione della sanità di ciascuno in generale, & in particolare de gli huomini, & donne genovesi.* Giuseppe Pauoni, Genoa, 1602.

Pasta & Pizza. Mondadori, Milan, 1974.

Pastario, ovvero Atlante delle paste alimentari italiane: primo tentativo di catalogazione delle paste alimentari italiane (Pastario, or Atlas of Italian Pastas: A First Attempt to Catalogue Italian pastas). Second edition. Alessi, Crusinallo-Omegna, 1989.

Perrucci, Andrea. *Le opere napoletane. L'Agnano zeffonato. La Malatia d'Apollo.* Edited by Laura Facecchia. Benincasa, Rome, 1986.

Pestelli, G. *Contrasto fra un Fiorentino ed un Contadino.* A. Salani, Florence, 1888.

Petrarca, Francesco. *Petrarch's Remedies for Fortune Fair and Foul: A Modern English Translation of De Remediis utriusque Fortune, with a commentary by Conrad H. Rawski.* Indiana University Press, Bloomington and Indianapolis, 1991.

Petrini, Carlo. *Buono, pulito e giusto: principi di nuova gastronomia.* Einaudi, Turin, 2005.

———. *Slow food revolution: da Arcigola a Terra madre: una nuova cultura del cibo e della vita.* Conversation with Gigi Padovani; preface by Vandana Shiva. Rizzoli, Milan, 2005.

Petrocchi, Massimo. *Roma nel Seicento.* Cappelli, Bologna, 1975.

Petronio, Alessandro Traiano. *Del viver delli romani e del conservar la sanità . . . Libri cinque dove si tratta del sito di Roma, dell'aria, de' venti, delle stagioni, delle acque, de vini, delle carni, de pesci, de frutti, delle herbe.* Domenico Basa, Rome, 1592.

Petronius Arbiter. *Satyricon.* Translated by Guido Reverdito. Garzanti, Milan, 2005.

Pierce, Guglielmo. "A pranzo con la Furtseva." In *I magnifici anni '50.* Edizioni del Borghese, Milan, 1979.

Piovene, Guido. *Viaggio in Italia.* Mondadori, Milan, 1957.

Piretto, Gian Piero. "Il libro dei cibi buoni e sani sovietici." Paper presented at the conference "Happiness Soviet Style," May 5–6, 2006. University of Nottingham, School of Modern Languages and Cultures, Department of Russian and Slavonic Studies.

Pisanelli, Baldassarre. *Trattato della natura de' cibi et del bere.* Arnaldo Forni, Sala Bolognese, 1972 (facsimile reproduction of the edition of Imberti, Venice, 1611; first edition: Bonfaldino e Diani, Rome, 1583).

La pittura in cucina: pittori e chef a confronto. Edited by Luca Mariani, Agata Parisella, and Giovanna Trapani. Sellerio, Palermo, 2003.

La Pizza napoletana: storia, aneddoti, ricette. Il benessere dell'uomo e della donna sta tutto in un pizzico di farina, pomodoro e basilico. Edited by Ettore Bernabo Silurata. Marotta, Naples, 1992.

Placucci, Michele. *Usi e pregiudizi de' contadini della Romagna.* Barbiani, Forlì, 1818.

Platina, known as Sacchi Bartolomeo. *Il piacere onesto e la buona salute (De honesta voluptate et valetudine).* Edited by Emilio Faccioli. Einaudi, Turin, 1985 (original edition: 1468).

———. *Platynae historici Liber de vita Christi ac omnium pontificum: aa. 1–1474.* Edited by Giacinto Gaida. S. Lapi, Citta di Castello; later Zanichelli, Bologna, 1913–1932.

Plautus, Titus Maccius. *Pseudolus*. Translated by Mario Scandola. Rizzoli BUR, Milan, 2003.

Plebani, Tiziana. *Sapori del Veneto: note per una storia dell'alimentazione*. De Luca, Rome, 1995.

Pliny the Elder. *Storia naturale*. Preface by Italo Calvino. Einaudi, Turin, 1982.

Polato, Raffaella. "Si inaugura '2001-Italia' in Giappone." *Sette*, supplement of *Corriere della Sera*, July 26, 2001.

Il potere delle immagini: la metafora politica in prospettiva storica. Edited by Walter Euchner, Francesca Rigotti, and Pierangelo Schiera. Il Mulino, Bologna, Duncker & Humblot, Berlin, 1993.

Pozzetto, Graziano. *La salama da sugo ferrarese*. Panozzo, Rimini, 2002.

Prezzolini, Giuseppe. *Maccheroni & C.* Rusconi, Milan, 1988 (first edition, in English: *Spaghetti Dinner*, Abelard-Shuman, New York, 1955).

———. *Vita di Nicolò Machiavelli fiorentino*. Arnoldo Mondadori, Milan, 1960.

Pucci, Antonio. *The Oxford Text of the Noie of Antonio Pucci*. Edited by K. MacKenzie. Ginn & Co., Boston, 1913.

Pujati, Giuseppe Antonio. *Riflessioni sul vitto pitagorico*. Odoardo Foglietta, Stamperia del Seminario, Feltre, 1751.

Quaini, Massimo. *Mediterraneo: cibo e cultura*. Edited by Maurizio Sentieri: photos by Anna Maria Guglielmino. Sagep, Milan, 1998.

———. *Per la storia del paesaggio agrario in Liguria: note di geografia storica sulle strutture agrarie della Liguria medievale e moderna*. Camera di Commercio Industria Artigianato e Agricoltura di Savona, Savona, 1973.

Quaranta, Gennaro. *Maccheronata. Sonetti in difesa dei maccheroni*. Arti Grafiche La Nuovissima, Naples, 1943.

Rajberti, Giovanni. *L'arte di convitare spiegata al popolo*. In *Tutte le opere*, Gastaldi, Milan, 1964 (first edition: Bernardoni, 1850–51).

Il rancio di bordo: storia dell'alimentazione sul mare dall'antichità ai giorni nostri. Il Geroglifico, Gaeta, 1992.

Raspelli, Edoardo. *Italia golosa: cronache di un viaggiatore esigente*. Mondadori, Milan, 2004.

Rauch, Andrea. *Leggere a tavola: il tesoro della cucina toscana nelle pagine della grande letteratura*. Mandragora, Florence, 1999.

Rebora, Giovanni. *La civiltà della forchetta: storie di cibi e di cucina*. Laterza, Rome and Bari, 1998.

———. "La cucina medievale italiana tra Oriente e Occidente." In *Miscellanea storica ligure* 19 (1987), nos. 1–2, pp. 1431–1579.

Redon, Odile, and Bruno Larioux. "L'apparition et la diffusion des pâtes sèches en Italie (XIIIe–XVIe siècles)." In *Techniques et économie antiques et médievales: le temps de l'innovation*. Errance, Aix-en-Provence, 1997, pp. 101–108.

Redon, Odile, François Sabban, and Silvano Serventi. *A tavola nel Medioevo: con 150 ricette dalla Francia e dall'Italia*. Translated by M. Salemi Cardini; edited by Georges Duby. Laterza, Rome and Bari, 1994 (original edition: *La gastronomie au Moyen Age: 150 recettes de France et d'Italie*, Stock, Paris, 1991).

Regimen sanitatis salernitanum. La Scola Salernitana per acquistare, e custodire la sanità, tradotta fedelmente dal verso latino in terza rima piaceuole volgare dall'Incognito academico Viuo morto. Con li discorsi della vita sobria del sig. Luigi Cornaro. Gio. Pietro Brigonci, Venice, 1662 (first edition, in Latin: 1474 or 1480). The following edition was used: *La regola sanitaria salernitana*, Canesi, Rome, 1963. Also noted is the edition *La regola sanitaria salernitana*, translated by Fulvio Gherli, edited by Cecilia Gatto and Roberto Michele Sozzi. Tascabili economici Newton, Rome, 1993.

Reichl, Ruth. *Comfort Me with Apples: More Adventures at the Table*. Random House, New York, 2001.

———. *Garlic and Sapphires: The Secret Life of a Critic in Disguise*. Penguin, New York, 2005.

———, ed. *Remembrance of Things Paris: Sixty Years of Writing from* Gourmet. Random House, New York, 2004.

Revel, Jean-François. *3000 anni a tavola*. Translated by Giovanni Bugliolo. Rizzoli, Milan, 1979 (original edition: *Un festin en paroles. Histoire litteraire de la sensibilité gastronomique de l'antiquité a nos jours*, Suger, Paris, 1985; new edition, Plon, Paris, 1995).

Revue culturelle de Droit de l'Art-Rivista culturale di Diritto dell'Arte. April 25, 2005.

Ricettario italiano: la cucina dei poveri e dei re. Edited by Chiara Scudelotti. Demetra, Colognola ai Colli, 2002.

Rigotti, Francesca. *La filosofia in cucina: piccola critica della ragion culinaria*. Il Mulino, Bologna, 2004.

Rodotà, Maria Laura. "La strategia delle brigate tortellino." *La Stampa*, June 14, 2000.

Romano, Ruggiero. *Paese Italia. Venti secoli di identità*. Donzelli, Rome, 1994.

Romoli, Domenico (known as Il Panonto, Il Panunto). *La singolare dottrina di M. Domenico Romoli . . . nel qual si tratta dell'officio dello scalco, de i condimenti di tutte le viuande, le stagioni che si convengono a tutti*. The following edition was used: *Il libro del Panonto Domenico Romoli; con un'appendice di Carlo Nascia relativa alla maniera di ammannire ogni sorta di carne e pesce*. Novedit, Milan, 1962 (original edition: 1560).

Rosenberger, Bernard, et al. "La cucina araba e il suo apporto alla cucina europea." In *Storia dell'alimentazione*, edited by Jean-Louis Flandrin and Massimo Montanari, Laterza, Rome and Bari, 1997, pp. 266–81.

Rosselli, Giovanni de. *Opera nova chiamata Epulario la quale tratta il modo di cucinare ogni carne, uccelli, pesci di qualsiasi sorte. E per fare sapori, torte, pasticci al modo di tutte le province e molte altre gentilezze, composta da Maestro Giovanni de' Rosselli, francese*. A. Riccio, Rome, 1973 (original edition: 1516).

Rossetti, Giovan Battista. *Dello scalco del sig. Gio. Battista Rossetti, scalco della serenissima madama Lucretia da Este duchessa d'Vrbino, nel quale si contengono le qualità di vno scalco perfetto, & tutti i carichi suoi, con diuersi vfficiali a lui sottoposti: . . . Con gran numero di banchetti alla italiana, & alla alemana, di varie, e belissime inuentioni, e desinari*. With annotation by Claudio Benporat. Arnaldo Forni, Sala Bolognese, 1991 (anastatic reprint of the edition of Domenico Mammarello, Ferrara, 1584; first edition: 1584).

Rossini, Gioacchino. *Lettere*. Edited by Enrico Castiglione. Edizioni Logos, Rome, 1992.

Rumford, Count of (Benjamin Thompson). *Estratto delle opere del conte di Rumphort sulla maniera di comporre minestre sostanziose ed economiche colle esperienze fatte dalla Società agraria, ad istruzione e vantaggio del popolo piemontese*. From the printing works of Pane e Barberis Stampatori Della Società Agraria, Turin, 1800.

Sabban, Françoise, and Silvano Serventi. *La pasta. Storia e cultura di un cibo universale*. Laterza, Rome and Bari, 2000.

———. *A tavola nel Rinascimento*. Laterza, Rome and Bari, 1996.

Sacerdoti, Mira. *Cucina ebraica in Italia*. Edited by Rita Erlich. Piemme, Casale Monferrato, 1994.

Sada, Luigi. *Liber de coquina: libro della cucina del XIII secolo: il capostipite meridionale della cucina italiana*. Puglia Grafica Sud, Bari, 1995.

Salani, Massimo. *A tavola con le religioni*. Edizioni Dehoniane, Bologna, 2000.

Salaris, Claudia. *Cibo futurista: dalla cucina nell'arte all'arte in cucina*. Stampa Alternativa, Rome, 2000.

Salvadori, Roberta. *La dieta mediterranea*. In collaboration with Margherita and Laura Landra. Idealibri, Milan, 1983.

Saperi e sapori: a cena nel convento: presentazione della cucina tradizionale regionale rivisitata in chiave moderna. Edited by Igles Corelli and Dolores Veschi. Edit Faenza, Faenza, 1991.

Sapersi nutrire. Edited by Cesare Alimenti. By the propaganda office of the Partito Nazionale Fascista: Ufficio di Propaganda, Editoriale Arte e Storia, Rome, no date.

Sapori, Armando. *La mercatura medioevale*. Sansoni, Florence, 1972.

Savioli, Arminio. "Ricompaiono pasta e olio nella campagna elettorale Dc." *L'Unità*, April 30, 1953.

Savonarola, Michele. *Libreto di tutte le cose che se magnano. Un'opera di dietetica del sec. XV*. Edited by J. Nystedt. Almqvist & Wiksell, Stockholm, 1988 (text reproduced in accordance with the manuscript version of Codice Casanatense 406).

Scaglioni, Clara. *Stoccafisso e baccalà nel piatto. Interpretazioni della tradizione veneta.* Terra Ferma, Regione del Veneto, 2001.

Scappi, Bartolomeo. *Opera dell'arte del cucinare.* Edited by Giancarlo Roversi. Arnaldo Forni, Sala Bolognese, 1981 (facsimile reproduction of the edition of Michele Tramezino, Venice, 1570: *Opera di M. Bartolomeo Scappi, cuoco secreto di papa Pio 5. diuisa in sei libr. . . Con il discorso funerale che fu fatto nelle esequie di papa Paulo 3. Con le figure che fanno bisogno nella cucina & alli reuerendissimi nel Conclave*).

Scarpi, Paolo. "La rivoluzione dei cereali e del vino. Demeter, Dionysos, Athena." In *Homo edens. Regimi, miti e pratiche dell'alimentazione nella civiltà del Mediterraneo,* texts presented at the conference "Homo edens," held by the Fiera di Verona on April 13, 14, 15, 1987, edited by Oddone Longo and Paolo Scarpi, Diapress, Milan, 1989.

Schiavone, Aldo. *Italiani senza Italia. Storia e identità.* Einaudi, Turin, 1998.

Schipperges, Heinrich. *Il giardino della salute, la medicina nel Medioevo.* Garzanti, Milan, 1988.

Schlosser, Eric. *Fast Food Nation: The Dark Side of the All-American Meal.* Houghton Mifflin, Boston and New York, 2001.

Scopoli, Giovanni Antonio. *De diaeta litteratorum.* Wagner, Innsbruck, 1743. The following edition was used: *Dissertatio de diaeta litteratorum,* translated by Domenico Magnino, edited by Gianguido Rindi and Carlo Violani, Cisalpino, Milan, 1991.

Scully, Terence. *The Art of Cookery in the Middle Ages.* Boydell Press, Woodbridge, U.K., 1995.

Sentieri, Maurizio. *Cibo e ambrosia: storia dell'alimentazione mediterranea tra caso, necessità e cultura. In appendice: ricette, curiosità e osservazioni dietetiche.* Dedalo, Bari, 1993.

———. *L'orto ritrovato. Qualità, vizi e virtù delle piante mediterranee.* Sagep, Genoa, 1994.

Sentieri, Maurizio, Paolo Boero, Claudio Bertieri, et al. *Il cibo raccontato: nel mondo dell'alimentazione tra fantasia e realta.* Coop, Carlini, Genoa, after 1992.

Sentieri, Maurizio, and Guido Nathan Zazzu. *I semi dell'Eldorado: l'alimentazione in Europa dopo la scoperta dell'America.* Dedalo, Bari, 1993.

Serao, Matilde. *Il paese di cuccagna: romanzo napoletano.* F.lli Treves, Milan, 1891.

Sereni, Emilio. *Note di storia dell'alimentazione nel Mezzogiorno: i Napoletani da "mangiafoglia" a "mangiamaccheroni."* Argo, Lecce, 1998 (first published in *Cronache meridionali,* 1958).

Sigalotti, Annamaria. "La cucina futurista tra manifesti, banchetti e ricette 'antipassatiste.'" *E-Art,* January 16, 2005.

Soldati, Mario. *Sua maestà il Po.* Photos by Mauro Galligani. Mondadori, Milan, 1984.

Solitro, Antonio, and Pasquale Troia. *A tavola con i santi: un anno per l'Italia tra la buona cucina delle feste patronali.* With the collaboration of the AICS committees (Associazione Italiana Cultura e Sport) of Agrigento, Campania, Grosseto, Ravenna, Sardegna, Trapani, Trieste, etc. Essegi, Ravenna, 1991.

Somogyj, Stefano. "L'alimentazione nell'Italia unita." In *Storia d'Italia,* vol. 5; *I documenti.* UTET, Turin, 1973, pp. 839–87.

Sorcinelli, Paolo. *Gli italiani e il cibo. Appetiti, digiuni e rinunce dalla realtà contadina alla società del benessere.* Clueb, Bologna, 1999 (first edition: 1992).

Sotis, Lina. "Sapore di mare. L'arte di gustare il pesce fresco." *Corriere della Sera,* April 8, 2006.

Spagnol, Elena. *L'apriscatole della felicita.* Mondadori, Milan, 1987.

———. *La gioia della cucina.* R.L. Libri, Milan, 1999.

———. *In cucina: come mangiare d'ora in poi.* Salani, Milan, 2002.

Spagnol, Luigi. *La pasta, corso di cucina.* Magazzini Salani, Milan, 2005.

———. *Il pesce, corso di cucina.* Magazzini Salani, Milan, 2005.

Specialità d'Italia. Le regioni in cucina. Edited by Eugenio Medagliani and Claudia Piras. Könemann Verlag, Cologne, 2000.

Stefani, Bartolomeo. *L'arte di ben cucinare.* Arnaldo Forni, Sala Bolognese, 1983 (facsimile reproduction of the edition in Mantua: Osanna Stampatori Ducali, 1662).

Stendhal. *Passeggiate romane.* Translated by Marco Cesarini Sforza. Laterza, Rome and Bari, 1973.

———. *Roma, Napoli e Firenze. Viaggio in Italia da Milano a Reggio Calabria.* Preface by Carlo Levi; translated by Bruno Schlacherl. Laterza, Rome and Bari, 1974 (first edition, in French: 1817).

Lo stivale allo spiedo: viaggio attraverso la cucina italiana. Edited by Piero Accolti and Gian Antonio Cibotto. Canesi, Rome, 1965.

Stopani, Renato. *La via Francigena.* Le Lettere, Florence, 1997.

Stoppani, Antonio. *Il bel Paese. Conversazioni sulle bellezze naturali: la geologia e la geografia fisica d'Italia. Con aggiunta delle Marmitte dei giganti di Spirola e delle lettere sulla Cascata della Troggia; sulle valli di Non, di Sole e di Rabbi; e sul Tonale e l'Aprica / Antonio Stoppani; e note di eminenti scienziati italiani per cura del prof. Alessandro Malladra; trentacinque disegni di Orlando Sora.* E. Bartolozzi, Lecco, 1983 (original edition: Agnelli, Milan, 1878).

Storchi, Mario R. "L'alimentazione nel Regno di Napoli." In *Studi sul Regno di Napoli nel Decennio francese,* edited by A. Lepre, Liguori, Naples, 1985.

———. *Il poco e il tanto: condizioni e modi di vita degli italiani dall'unificazione a oggi.* Liguori, Naples, 1999.

———. *Prezzi, crisi agrarie e mercato del grano nel Mezzogiorno d'Italia: 1806–1854.* Liguori, Naples, 1991.

———. *La vita quotidiana delle popolazioni meridionali dal 1800 alla grande guerra.* Liguori, Naples, 1995.

Taine, Hippolyte Adolphe. *Viaggio in Italia.* Edited and translated by Vito Corbello. Nino Aragno, Turin, 2003 (original edition: *Voyage en Italie,* 1866).

Tanara, Vincenzo. *L'economia del cittadino in villa.* Li Causi, Bologna, 1983 (facsimile reproduction of the edition of Monti, Bologna, 1644).

Targioni Tozzetti, Giovanni. *Relazioni d'alcuni viaggi fatti in diverse parti della Toscana per osservare le produzioni naturali e gli antichi monumenti di essa.* Vol. 5, Arnaldo Forni, Sala Bolognese, 1971–1972 (facsimile reproduction of the edition of Gaetano Cambiagi, Stamperia Granducale, Florence, 1768–1779).

Tasca Lanza, Anna. *The Heart of Sicily: Recipes and Reminiscences of Regaleali, a Country Estate.* Cassel, London, 1993.

Tedeschi, Edda. *Le regioni italiane in tavola.* Sperling & Kupfer, Milan, 1994.

Tivaroni, Carlo. *L'Italia degli italiani.* Vols. 1–2. Roux, Turin, 1895.

Toaff, Ariel. *Mangiare alla giudia: la cucina ebraica in Italia dal Rinascimento all'età moderna.* Il Mulino, Bologna, 2000.

Tomasi di Lampedusa, Giuseppe. *Il Gattopardo.* Feltrinelli, Milan, 1958.

Tonelli, Laura. *La pittura a Genova come fonte per la storia dell'alimentazione (1559–1699).* Dissertation, University of Genoa, Faculty of Humanities and Philosophy, academic year 1997/1998.

Torre, Silvio. *Colombo. Il nuovo mondo a tavola.* Edited by Mariarosa Schiaffino. Idealibri, Milan, 1991.

Tosto, Tonino. *La cucina dell'ulivo. Le ricette gastronomiche del centro-sinistra e degli altri ingredienti.* EDUP, Rome, 1998.

———. *Le ricette democratiche. Gusti e sapori e sperimentazioni gastronomiche per una nuova cucina di governo.* EDUP, Rome, 1995.

Toussaint-Samat, Maguelonne. *Storia naturale & morale dell'alimentazione.* Translated by Valeria Trifari. Sansoni, Florence, 1991 (original title: *Histoire naturelle et morale de la nourriture,* Bordas, Paris, 1987; first edition, in French: 1957).

Traglia, Gustavo. *Le ghiottornie di Gabriele D'Annunzio,* Veronelli, Milan, 1957.

———. *Il lunario della pastasciutta.* Ceschina, Milan, 1956.

Varchi, Benedetto. *L'Ercolano. Dialogo di M. Benedetto Varchi nel quale si ragiona delle lingue ed in particolare della toscana e della fiorentina.* Tartini e Franchi, Florence, 1730.

Varrone, Marco Terenzio. *Varrone menippeo {Le satire menippee}.* Edited by Ettore Bolisani. Messaggero, Padua, 1936.

Vasselli, Giovanni Francesco. *L'Apicio: overo il maestro de' conviti.* Introduction by Livia Orlandi Frattarolo. Arnaldo Forni, Sala Bolognese, 1998 (facsimile reproduction of the edition of HH. del Dozza, Bologna, 1647).

Vené, Gian Franco. *Mille lire al mese: la vita quotidiana della famiglia nell'Italia fascista.* Mondadori, Milan, 1988.

Veronelli, Luigi. *Alla ricerca dei cibi perduti: guida di gusto e di lettere all'arte di saper mangiare.* DeriveApprodi, Rome, 2004.

———. *Vietato vietare. Tredici ricette per vari disgusti.* Eleuthera, Milan, 1991.

Veronelli, Luigi, and Pablo Echaurren. *Le parole della terra. Manuale per enodissidenti e gastroribelli.* Stampa Alternativa, Rome, 2003.

La via Francigena: cammino medioevale di pellegrinaggio quale proposta per un itinerario religioso, culturale e turistico del 2000. Edited by the Centro Regionale per la Documentazione dei Beni Culturali e Ambientali del Lazio. De Luca, Rome, 1995.

La via Francigena: The Paths of the Pilgrims. Texts by Paola Foschi, Italo Moretti, and Pier Giorgio Oliveti. Touring Club Italiano, Milan, 1995.

I viaggi dopo la scoperta / Cristoforo Colombo. Edited by Gabriella Araldi; introduction by Gino Barbieri. Cassa di risparmio di Verona, Vicenza e Belluno, Verona, 1985.

Viaggi e Assaggi. Guida ai percorsi enogastronomici d'Italia. 3 vols.: *Nord Italia, Centro Italia, Sud Italia.* Touring Club Italiano, Milan, 2000.

Il viaggio dello scalco Pëtr A. Tolstoj in Europa—Puteshestvie stol'nika P.A. Tolstogo po Evrope. Edited by L. Olshevskaya and S. N. Travnikov. Nauka, Moscow, 1992.

Vialardi, Giovanni. *Trattato di cucina, pasticceria moderna, credenza e relativa confettureria basato sopra un metodo economico, semplice, signorile e borghese . . . il tutto scritto e disegnato dall'autore.* Arnaldo Forni, Sala Bolognese, 1986 (facsimile reproduction of the edition of Tipografia G. Favale, Turin, 1854).

Vilardo, Francesco Maria. *Dialoghi della Compania della Lesina.* Baglioni, Venice, 1647.

Vittorelli, Jacopo. *I maccheroni. Poemetto giocoso di Jacopo Vittorelli. Aggiuntovi un'inno cantabile sul medesimo argomento del sig. De' Rogatis.* Graziosi, Venice, 1803.

Viviani, Antonio. *Li maccheroni di Napoli.* Stamperia della Società Filomatica, Naples, 1824.

Vogel, Cyrille. "Symboles culturels chrétiens. Les aliments sacrés: poisson et refrigeria." In *Simboli e simbologia nell'alto Medioevo: Settimane di Studi del Centro Italiano di Studi sull'Alto Medioevo,* 23, I (1976), pp. 197–252.

Voltaire. *Les anciens et les modernes ou la toilette de Madame Pompadour.* Gallimard, Paris, 1961.

Warman Gryj, Arturo. *La historia de un bastardo: maiz y capitalismo.* UNAM, Instituto de Investigaciones Sociales, Mexico City, 1988.

Zacchia, Paolo. *Il vitto quaresimale di Paulo Zacchia medico romano. Oue insegnasi come senza offender la sanità si possa viuer nella quaresima. Si discorre de' cibi in essa vsati, de gli errori, che si commettono nell'vsargli, dell'indispositioni, ch'il lor'vso impone, In Roma: per Pietro Antonio Facciotti. Ad istanza di Gio. Dini libraro in Nauona all'insegna della Gatta.* 1637 (first edition: 1636).

Zannoni, Mario. *A tavola con Maria Luigia: il servizio di bocca della duchessa di Parma dal 1815 al 1847.* Artegrafica Silva, Parma, 1991.

Zatterin, Ugo. "La nave dell'amicizia sbarca i suoi doni a Napoli." *La Stampa,* December 30, 1947.

Zingali, Gaetano. "Il rifornimento dei viveri dell'esercito italiano." In Riccardo Bachi, *L'alimentazione e la politica annonaria in Italia,* Laterza, Rome and Bari, 1926.

Zucchi, Linda. *I menù delle feste. Tutti insieme a tavola. Natale, San Silvestro, capodanno, carnevale, Pasqua e altre feste. Le tradizioni regionali e la cucina dei nostri giorni.* Edizioni del Riccio, Florence, 1996.

Translator's Bibliography

Works cited by the translator in the original English or in English translation.

Alighieri, Dante. *The Divine Comedy: The Inferno, Purgatorio, and Paradiso*. Translated by Allen Mandelbaum. Everyman's Library, Knopf Publishing Group, New York, 1995.

Archestratus of Syracuse. From Athenaeus of Naucratis, *Deipnosophistai* (The Dinner of Savants), 7.278a–d. Cited in Daniel B. Levine, *Tuna in Ancient Greece*, American Institute of Wine and Food, New York, 2006.

Ariosto, Ludovico. *The Orlando Furioso*. Translated into English verse, from the Italian of Ludovico Ariosto, with notes by William Stewart Rose. 2 vols. Henry G. Bohn, London, 1858.

Artusi, Pellegrino. *Science in the Kitchen and the Art of Eating Well*. The Lorenzo Da Ponte Italian Library. Edited by Luigi Ballerini and Massimo Ciavolella. University of Toronto Press, Toronto, 2003, 2004. (Original title: *La scienza in cucina e l'arte di mangiar bene*). This English edition (first published by Marsilio Publishers in 1997) features an introduction by Luigi Ballerini and is translated by Murtha Baca.

Basile, Giambattista. *The Pentamerone of Giambattista Basile*. 2 vols. Translated from the Italian by Benedetto Croce; edited by Norman Mosley Penzer. John Lane the Bodley Head Ltd. and E. P. Dutton and Co., London and New York, 1932 (original title: *Pentamerone. Lo cunto de li cunti*). The following edition was also used: Basile, Giambattista. *The Pentamerone, or, The Story of Stories*. Translated by J. E. Taylor. David Bogue, London, 1848.

Black, William. *Al Dente: The Adventures of a Gastronome in Italy*. Bantam, London, 2003.

Boccaccio, Giovanni. *L'Ameto*. Translated by Judith Powers Serafini-Sauli. Garland, New York, 1985.

———. *The Decameron of Giovanni Boccaccio*. Translated by J. M. Rigg. London, 1921 (first printed 1903).

Brillat-Savarin, Jean-Anthelme. *Physiology of Taste*. Translated by Fayette Robinson from the last Paris edition. Lindsay & Blakiston, Philadelphia, 1854.

Bruno, Giordano. *The Ash Wednesday Supper*. Edited and translated by Lawrence S. Lerner and Edward A.

Gosselin. RSART: Renaissance Society of America Reprint Text Series. University of Toronto Press, Toronto, 1995.

Buzzi, Aldo. *The Perfect Egg and Other Secrets*. Translated by Guido Waldman. Bloomsbury Publishing, London, 2005 (original title: *L'uovo alla kok*).

Camilleri, Andrea. *The Snack Thief*. Translated by Stephen Sartarelli. Viking, New York, 2003 (original title: *Il ladro di merendine*).

Capatti, Alberto, and Massimo Montanari. *Italian Cuisine: A Cultural History*. Translated by Aine O'Healy. Columbia University Press, New York, 2003.

Cicero, M. Tullius. "Oration for Sextus Roscius of Ameria." In *The Orations of M. Tullius Cicero*, translated by C. D. Yonge. London: George Bell & Sons, 1903.

Cornaro, Luigi. *The Art of Living Long*. Joseph Addison, Francis Bacon, William Temple, contributors. William F. Butler, Milwaukee, 1903.

DeLillo, Don. *Underworld*. Simon & Schuster, New York, 1997.

Dickens, Charles. *Pictures from Italy*. Bradbury & Evans, Whitefriars, London, 1846.

Eco, Umberto. *Baudolino*. Translated by William Weaver. Harcourt, New York, 2002.

Erasmus. *The Praise of Folly*. Written by Erasmus 1509 and translated by John Wilson in 1668. Edited by P. S. Allen. Clarendon Press, Oxford, 1913.

Frederick II of Hohenstaufen. *The Art of Falconry*. Translated by Casey Wood and F. Fyfe. Stanford University Press, Stanford, California, 1943 (original title: *De arte venandi cum avibus*).

Ginsborg, Paul. *A History of Contemporary Italy: Society and Politics, 1943–1988*. Palgrave Macmillan, New York, 2003.

Goethe, Johann Wolfgang von. *Italian Journey 1786–1788*. Translated by W. H. Auden and Elizabeth Mayer. Pantheon Books, New York, 1962 (original title: *Italienische Reise*).

Hašek, Jaroslav. *The Good Soldier Svejk: and His Fortunes in the World War*. Translated by Cecil Parrott. Penguin Classics, New York, 2005.

Heine, Heinrich. *Pictures of Travel*. Translated by Charles Godfrey Leland. D. Appleton and Co., New York, 1904.

———. *The Works of Heinrich Heine*. Vol. 1: *Florentine Nights: The Memoirs of Herr Von Schnabelewopski . . .* Translated by Charles Godfrey Leland. William Heinemann, London, 1906.

Homer. *The Odyssey of Homer*. Books 1–12. Translated into English verse by the Earl of Carnarvon. Macmillan and Co., London and New York, 1886.

Horace. *The Satires*. Translated by A. S. Kline. 2005. Online at: http://www.tonykline.co.uk/PITBR/Latin/HoraceSatiresBkISatI.htm.

Juvenal. *Thirteen Satires of Juvenal*. Translated by S. G. Owen. Methuen, London, 1903.

Levine, Daniel B. *Tuna in Ancient Greece*. American Institute of Wine and Food, New York, 2006.

Marinetti, Filippo Tommaso. From *The Futurist Cookbook* by Filippo Tommaso Marinetti. Translated by Suzanne Brill. Trefoil Publications, Ltd., London, 1989.

Montaigne, Michel de. *The Works of Michael de Montaigne: Comprising His Essays, Letters, Journey Through Germany and Italy*. Edited and translated by W. Hazlitt. C. Templemon, London, 1845.

Il Novellino. Online bilingual edition. Edited by Steven M. Wight. Online at: http://scrineum.unipv.it/wight/novellino.htm#100.

Parkinson, Cyril Northcote. *Mrs. Parkinson's Law: And Other Studies in Domestic Science*. Houghton Mifflin, Boston, 1968.

Petrarch. *Petrarch's Remedies for Fortune Fair and Foul*. A Modern English Translation of *De remediis utriusque Fortune*, with a Commentary by Conrad H. Rawski, in five volumes. Indiana University Press, Bloomington and Indianapolis, 1991.

Petronius Arbiter. *Satyricon*. Translated by Sarah Ruden. Hackert Publishing Company, Indianapolis, 2000.

Pliny. *The Natural History of Pliny*. Translated by John Bostock and H. T. Riley. Henry G. Bohn, London, 1856.

Plutarch. "Alcibiades." In *Lives*. Edited by Bernadotte Perrin. Online at: http://www.perseus.tufts.edu/cgi-bin/ptext?doc=Perseus%3Atext%3A1999.01.0182;query=chapter%3D%2315;layout=;loc=Alc.%2014.1

Prezzolini, Giuseppe. *Nicolo Machiavelli, the Florentine*. Translated by Ralph Roeder. Brentano's, New York 1928 (original title: *Vita di Nicolò Machiavelli*).

Redon, Odile, Françoise Sabban, and Silvano Serventi. *The Medieval Kitchen: Recipes from France and Italy*. Translated by Edward Schneider. University of Chicago Press, Chicago, 1998.

Revel, Jean François. *Culture and Cuisine: a Journey Through the History of Food*. Translated by Helen R. Lane. Doubleday, Garden City, New York, 1982 (original title: *Festin en paroles*).

Stendhal. *A Roman Journal*. Edited and translated by Haakon Chevalier. Orion Press, New York, 1957. Based on Henri Martineau's critical edition of *Promenades dans Rome*.

———. *Rome, Naples and Florence*. Translated by Richard N. Coe. George Braziller, New York, 1959.

Taine, Hippolyte Adolphe. *Italy: Rome and Naples, Florence and Venice*. Translated by J. Durand. Third edition. Leypoldt & Holt, New York, 1871 (original title: *Voyage en Italie*).

Virgil. *The Georgics*. Book 4. Translated by A. S. Kline. 2002. Online at: http://www.tonykline.co.uk/PITBR/Latin/VirgilGeorgicsIV.htm.

Acknowledgments

In addition to many personal observations gathered in the field and specific reading materials, systematic descriptions of regional dishes written by other authors before me were used for this book: *Specialità d'Italia. Le regioni in cucina* (Specialties of Italy: the regions in cuisine), edited by Eugene Medagliani and Claudia Piras; the encyclopedic guide *Viaggi & Assaggi* (Travels and tastings) in three volumes; and the special supplements to the *Corriere della Sera* (Fall 2005) dedicated to *la grande cucina regionale* (great regional cuisine).

I found ideas, facts, and very valuable descriptions in William Black's book *Al Dente: The Adventures of a Gastronome in Italy*. The Englishman William Black, a fish merchant by profession, is familiar with all the fishing markets and ports in the country and has observed and described many vivid details of the culinary panorama in his book, without which a study of Italian gastronomy simply would not be complete. I also reproduced with pleasure many unique materials relating to the role of cuisine in the development of Italian politics and state life, collected by Filippo Ceccarelli in the monograph *Lo stomaco della Repubblica: cibo e potere in Italia dal 1945 al 2000* (The stomach of the Republic: food and power in Italy from 1945 to 2000).

Also taken into consideration were ancient recipe collections, the first compendia of Italian gastronomy: the seventeenth-century book by Giovanni Battista Crisci, *Luce de prencipi nella quale si tratta del modo di bene operare pubblicamente, e di essi, e di ciascuna persona con autorità di graui autori* . . . (The courtiers' lamp . . .), and many other learned works written in the seventeenth, eighteenth, and nineteenth centuries. They are written in a delightfully antiquated language (for this reason citing them is a true pleasure), and are striking for their depth and soundness, together with their affinity to our way of dealing with cuisine *sub species philosophiae.*

We followed the glorious historical-gastronomic itineraries of illustrious connoisseurs of Italy and its culinary treasures, such as the German journalist Hans Barth, author of *Osteria: Kulturgeschichtlicher Führer durch Italiens Schenken von Verona bis Capri* (*Osteria*: a historical guide to Italy's inns, from Verona to Capri). Paolo Monelli, whose 1935 foray was described and published with the title *Il ghiottone errante* (The roving gourmand); and the writer Mario Soldati, who immortalized northern Italy in his *Sua maestà il Po* (His majesty the Po), with photographs by Mauro Galligani (1984). We were intrigued by the impressions of one of the fattest men in Italy, Edoardo Raspelli, author of the compendium *Italia golosa: cronache di un viaggiatore esigente* (Mouthwatering Italy: reports of a demanding traveler). Accompanying us were the encyclopedic works of Luigi Veronelli, the great connoisseur of cuisine and wines who died in 2004, author of the study *Alla ricerca dei cibi perduti: guida di gusto e di lettere all'arte di saper mangiare* (In search of lost foods: a guide to taste and literature on the art of eating well). And naturally we reflected on the ideas and thoughts that abound in the volumes and articles of Davide Paolini, which for many years now have appeared in the Sunday section of the *Sole-24 Ore*, along with the more recent restaurant pieces by Camilla Baresani. Following the lastest trends of alimentary ideology, I used for my work the lists and descriptions of products under the specific protection of the Slow Food Association: *L'Italia dei presidi. Guida ai prodotti da salvare* (In defense of Italy: a guide to products to be saved).

As for my folkloristic-culinary expeditions, I have had the good fortune, over the course of many years, to gather precious materials on the history of daily life and nutrition at the Cerreto farm, in Liguria, whose knowledgeable, hardworking manager, Gio Batta Bruzzone, supplied me with detailed information on the cultivation of forest trees and of olives, as well as on the culinary methods and typical dishes of various Italian locales. I take this opportunity to express my infinite gratitude to him.

Additional thanks to Ludmila Ulitskaya, also at the Cerreto farm, for sharing culinary and ethnographic joys with me, reading the first version of this book, and advising me to transform it from a treatise to a cultural itinerary.

The manager of the wholesale fish market of Milan, Professor Renato Malandra, also pointed out and explained many things to me. My thanks to the well-known cookbook writer and recipe collector Elena Spagnol for her valuable opinions and clarifications. Margherita, Leo, and Andrei Bourtsev not only did not despise me while I was busy writing this book but at times proposed extremely useful changes and furnished suitable photographic material.

Many thanks to Mrs. Carol Field for her generous, insightful, and engaging preface.

In Anne Milano Appel, I found not only a translator, but an adviser and an ideal collaborator as well.

I am deeply grateful to Jonathan Galassi, who believed in this book's unique value and allowed me to collaborate with his wonderful publishing house, Farrar, Straus and Giroux. I'm also grateful to all of the individuals I had the honor and pleasure of meeting at FSG in the two years of our work together: Gena Hamshaw, Susan Goldfarb, Jeff Seroy, and other talented and gracious members of the staff. With his versatile and elegant design, Jonathan D. Lippincott contributed to a book that delights the eye.

Warm thanks to the literary agent Linda Michaels (United States), who with touching interest and enthusiasm followed the creation of this book, from its initial planning to the final typescript, and helped me transform it into an international publishing project.

I am grateful to Umberto Eco not only because he agreed to write a foreword to my book but for everything: having translated and annotated his work for twenty-five years, I find in him a guide who is indispensable to me as to everyone, an example of brilliant erudition, lofty integrity, and dedication to his profession. Which helps.

Index

Image Credits